War and Peace in Modern India

War and Peace in Modern India

Srinath Raghavan

Lecturer, Defence Studies Department, King's College London, UK

Orginating Publisher PERMANENT BLACK
'Himalayana', Mall Road, Ranikhet Cantt
Ranikhet 263645
perblack@gmail.com

Copublished 2010 by

PALGRAVE MACMILLAN for sale outside South Asia

Palgrave Macmillan in the UK is an imprint of Macmillan Publishers Limited,
registered in England, company number 785998, Houndmills, Basingstoke,
Hampshire RG21 6XS.

Palgrave Macmillan in the US is a division of St Martin's Press LLC, 175
Fifth Avenue, New York, NY 10010.

Palgrave Macmillan is the global academic imprint of the above companies
and has companies and representatives throughout the world.

Palgrave® and Macmillan® are registered trademarks in the United States,
the United Kingdom, Europe and other countries.

ISBN: 978–0–230–24215–9 hardback

This book is printed on paper suitable for recycling and made from fully
managed and sustained forest sources. Logging, pulping and manufacturing
processes are expected to conform to the environmental regulations of the
country of origin.

A catalogue record for this book is available from the British Library.

A catalog record for this book is available from the Library of Congress.

10 9 8 7 6 5 4 3 2 1
19 18 17 16 15 14 13 12 11 10

Printed and bound in Great Britain by
CPI Antony Rowe, Chippenham and Eastbourne

To Pritha

Contents

Maps

Acknowledgements

This book is the outcome of a decade spent in two different worlds and two outstanding institutions. As a junior infantry officer in the Indian army I had a worm's eye view of India's long-standing disputes with China and Pakistan, including the India–Pakistan crises of 1999 and 2001–2. As a novice historian in the War Studies Group at King's College London, I researched and reflected on India's handling of similar crises and conflicts in the past. Along the way I have incurred many debts of gratitude, and it is a pleasure to thank all those who assisted in the creation of this book.

I should like to thank the Inlaks Foundation for a scholarship that facilitated my transition from the military to the academe. The Defence Studies Department, King's College London, supported this book from the outset. Dean Matt Uttley offered me a doctoral fellowship, subsequently a lectureship, and finally leave of absence to complete the book. His unfailing kindness and generosity quickened my steps in this journey. The research was also supported by an overseas research student award and by travel grants from King's College London. In researching this book I have benefited from the expertise of archivists in fourteen institutions across four continents. But for their professionalism this book would never have got off the ground. It may seem invidious to single out an individual, but I am particularly grateful to Dr N. Balakrishnan, Deputy Director, Nehru Memorial Museum and Library.

On successive research trips to Delhi I enjoyed the hospitality of Lalitha and S.C. Sekhar. They are such wonderful hosts that it seems almost absurd to thank them: a bit like thanking Yehudi Menuhin for music.

My foremost intellectual debt is to Sir Lawrence Freedman. This book began as a doctoral thesis inspired by his work and written under his watch. He read and commented on numerous draft chapters, demanding at all times that I strive for accuracy and clarity in argument and presentation. His cheerful encouragement spurred me to write the thesis and the book more quickly than I might otherwise have done. For all of these and more, I am profoundly grateful.

Judith Brown and Odd Arne Westad examined the thesis on which this book is based. Their observations and suggestions on both detail and structure made a significant difference to the shape of the book.

Ramachandra Guha and Sunil Khilnani have nurtured the book almost from its inception and right up to its publication. The penultimate draft of this manuscript benefited immensely from their attention to detail and their knowledge of the history of the Nehru years. I am deeply indebted to them for the time that they invested in this book and for their advice and encouragement over the years.

Special thanks are also due to Mahesh Rangarajan, ever a wise and generous mentor. His support has been crucial at every stage of the writing of this book.

Geraint Hughes read an early version of the manuscript and offered sage advice. Andrew Kennedy provided extremely helpful comments on the chapters on Kashmir and China. Bill Reid allowed me to share the fruits of his considerable labours on the Australian archives pertaining to Kashmir. His ongoing work on Owen Dixon's attempt at mediation promises to be a major contribution to the history of Kashmir. My approach and treatment in this study have been shaped by discussions with Mats Berdal, Peter Busch, Rudra Chaudhuri, Christopher Dandeker, John Darwin, Mervyn Frost, Jan Willem Honig, Sir Michael Howard, S. Kalyanaraman, Bhashyam Kasturi, Sergey Radchenko, and Rajesh Rajagopalan.

Working with my editor, Rukun Advani, on the final version of this book was very like attending a master class in literary craftsmanship. His insightful and detailed comments on practically every page of the manuscript showed me how to write a more lucid and engaging historical narrative. With all this help, the remaining errors and deficiencies must surely be mine alone.

Some debts, unfortunately, cannot be acknowledged in person. But I was kept going by the memory of three remarkable individuals. Captain Sylvester Rajesh Ratnam, companion in arms and a close friend, died in action on 2 August 2002. His sunny optimism and irrepressible zest for life continue to inspire me. And whenever I begin to take myself too seriously, I think of his talent for puncturing pretension and pomposity with exquisite charm and politeness. The artiste and educationist Kumudha Padmanabhan provided an outstanding model of intellectual independence and integrity. Her guidance and support were crucial at various points. As an impressionable teenager I was fortunate to be mentored by the lawyer, activist, and scholar N.T. Vanamamalai. N.T.V. taught me how to think about politics and kindled an abiding interest in political history. It is a matter of lasting regret that I never had the chance to discuss this book with him. I can only hope that he would have approved of it.

Without the support of my family, work on this book would never have begun, let alone been completed. My parents, Geetha and K.S. Raghavan, followed the vagaries of my career with admirable equanimity. My mother-in-law, Sukanya Venkatachalam, reposed more faith in my abilities than was justified by performance or promise. To my wife, Pritha, I owe more than I can say. She gave me more solace and encouragement than I could have asked; and put up with more annoyance and irritation than I care to remember. Above all, she has sustained me with her affection, her wisdom, and her labour. With love and gratitude I dedicate this book to her.

Abbreviations

AHC	Australian High Commission
APAC	Asia, Pacific, and Africa Collection
BL	Bodleian Library
CGS	Chief of General Staff
C-in-C	Commander-in-Chief
CPI	Communist Party of India
CPSU	Communist Party of the Soviet Union
CRO	Commonwealth Relations Office
CWIHP	Cold War International History Project
DEA	Department of External Affairs
DMO	Director of Military Operations
FO	Foreign Office
FRUS	*Foreign Relations of the United States*
IB	Intelligence Bureau
JIC	Joint Intelligence Committee
JFKL	John F. Kennedy Presidential Library
LHCMA	Liddell Hart Centre for Military Archives
MEA	Ministry of External Affairs
MP	Member of Parliament
NAA	National Archives of Australia
NAM	National Army Museum
NEFA	North Eastern Frontier Agency
NMML	Nehru Memorial Museum and Library

NWFP	North-West Frontier Province
OHT	Oral History Transcript
PLA	People's Liberation Army
PMSIR	*Prime Minister on Sino-Indian Relations*
PRC	People's Republic of China
RG	Record Group
SPC	*Sardar Patel's Correspondence*
SS	Secretary of State
SSCR	Secretary of State for Commonwealth Relations
SWGBP	*Selected Works of Govind Ballabh Pant*
SWJN	*Selected Works of Jawaharlal Nehru*
TNA	The National Archives
UK	United Kingdom
UKHC	United Kingdom High Commission
UN	United Nations Organization
UP	Uttar Pradesh
US	United States of America
USNA	United States National Archives and Research Administration
USSR	Union of Soviet Socialist Republics

Dramatis Personae

Abbas, Ghulam. Leader of Muslim Conference.

Abdullah, Sheikh Mohammed. Prime minister of Kashmir from 1948 to 1953, when he was dismissed and arrested; served long terms in prison thereafter.

Acheson, Dean. US secretary of state, 1949–53.

Ali, Laik. Prime minister of Hyderabad, November 1947–September 1948.

Ali, Mohammed. Secretary general of the Pakistan cabinet, 1947–51; finance minister of Pakistan, 1951–55; prime minister, 1955–6.

Attlee, Clement R. Prime minister of the United Kingdom, 1945–51.

Auchinleck, Field Marshal Sir Claude. Supreme commander in India and Pakistan, 1947.

Ayyangar, N. Gopalaswami. Union minister without portfolio, 1947–50; minister for states, 1950–2; minister for defence, 1952–3.

Azad, Maulana A.K. Union minister of education, 1947–58.

Bajpai, Sir Girja Shankar. Secretary general in the ministry of external affairs, 1947–52; governor of Bombay, 1952–4.

Banerjee, P.K. Charge d'affaires, Indian embassy in Beijing, 1962–3.

Bhutto, Shah Nawaz. Dewan (chief minister) of Junagadh, May–November 1947.

Bogra, Mohammed Ali. Prime minister of Pakistan, 1953–5.

Bucher, General Sir Roy. Chief of staff, Indian army headquarters, August–December 1947; commander-in-chief, Indian army, 1948–9.

Cariappa, General K.M. Army commander, Delhi and East Punjab (later Western) Command, January 1948–January 1949; commander-in-chief, Indian army, 1949–53.

Chhatari, Nawab. President of Hyderabad executive council, 1941–6; June–November 1947.

Chaudhuri, General J.N. Deputy chief of general staff, Indian army headquarters, 1948; commander of military operation against Hyderabad, 1948; chief of army staff, 1962–6.

Chen Yi. Vice-premier, People's Republic of China, 1954–72; foreign minister, 1958–72.

Cunningham, Sir George. Governor, North West Frontier Province of Pakistan, 1947–8.

Dalai Lama. Temporal and spiritual leader of Tibet. Fled Lhasa and sought refuge in India, March 1959.

Deng Xiaoping. General secretary, Communist Party of China, 1956–66.

Desai, M.J. Foreign secretary, 1961–3; secretary general, ministry of external affairs, 1963–4.

Desai, Morarji. Minister in Bombay government, 1946–52; chief minister of Bombay, 1952–6; union minister of commerce, 1956–8; minister of finance, 1958–63.

Dhebar, U.N. Leading member of Congress Party; chief minister of Saurashtra, 1948–54; president of the Congress Party, 1957–9.

Dixon, Sir Owen. United Nations mediator in Kashmir dispute, 1950.

Dutt, Subimal. Foreign secretary, 1954–61.

Gandhi, M.K. Barrister who led the Indian nationalist movement in non-violent passive resistance against British rule; assassinated by a Hindu fanatic in January 1948.

Gandhi, Samaldas. Nephew of M.K. Gandhi; leader of the "Provisional Government of Junagadh," September–November 1947.

Gracey, General Sir Douglas. Chief of staff, Pakistan army, 1947–8; commander-in-chief, Pakistan army, 1948–51.

Graham, Frank. United Nations mediator in Kashmir dispute, 1951.

Grafftey-Smith, Sir Laurence. British high commissioner to Pakistan, 1947–51.

Henderson, Loy. US ambassador to India, 1948–51.

Ismay, General (Lord) Hastings Lionel. Chief of staff to Mountbatten, March–November 1947.

Jiang Jieshi. Generalissimo, president of the Republic of China, 1950–75.

Jinnah, M.A. Governor general of Pakistan, 1947–8.

Kaul, Lieutenant General B.M. Chief of general staff, Indian army, 1961–2; corps commander in North East Frontier Agency, 1962.

Kaul, T.N. Joint secretary, ministry of external affairs, 1953–4; ambassador to the Soviet Union, 1962–6.

Kaur, Rajkumari Amrit. Union minister for health, 1947–57.

Kennedy. John F. President of the United States, January 1961– November 1963.

Khan, General Ayub. Commander-in-chief, Pakistan army, 1951–4; minister for defence, 1954–5; president of Pakistan, 1958–69.

Khan, Liaquat Ali. Prime minister of Pakistan, 1947–51.

Khan, Muhammad Mahabat. Nawab of Junagadh, 1911–47; thereafter lived in exile in Karachi until his death in 1959.

Khan, Sir Osman Ali. Nizam of Hyderabad, 1911–56.

Khan, Sir Muhammad Zafrullah. Foreign minister of Pakistan, 1947–54.

Khan, Sirdar M. Ibrahim. President of Azad Kashmir, 1948–50.

Khrushchev, Nikita. First secretary of the central committee of the Communist Party of the Soviet Union, 1953–64; chairman, council of ministers of the Soviet Union, 1958–64.

Korbel, Josef. Member and chairman of the United Nations Commission on India and Pakistan, 1948–9.

Krishnamachari, T.T. Union minister for commerce and industry 1952–6; for finance, 1956–8; without portfolio, 1962; for economic and defence coordination, 1962–3.

Liu Shaoqi. President of the People's Republic of China, 1959–66.

Lockhart, General Sir Rob. Commander-in-chief, Indian army, August–December 1947.

Macdonald, Malcolm. British high commissioner in India, 1955–60.

Mao Zedong. Chairman of the central committee of the Chinese communist party, 1935–76; chairman of the People's Republic of China, 1949–59.

Macmillan, Harold. Prime minister of the United Kingdom, 1957–63.

Menon, K.P.S. Ambassador to China, 1947; foreign secretary 1948– 52; ambassador to the Soviet Union, 1952–61.

Menon, V.K. Krishna. High commissioner in London, 1947–52; minister without portfolio, 1956–7; minister for defence, 1957–62.

Menzies, Sir Robert. Prime minister of Australia, 1949–66.

Mohammad, Bakshi Ghulam. Deputy prime minister of Kashmir, 1948–53; prime minister of Kashmir, 1953–63.

Mohammed, Ghulam. Finance minister of Pakistan, 1947–51; governor general of Pakistan, 1951–5.

Monckton, Walter. Constitutional adviser to the Nizam of Hyderabad and the Sheikh of Mangrol, 1946–8.

Mookerjee, Syama Prasad. Union minister for industry and supply, 1947–50; founded Jan Sangh in 1952; died in prison in 1953.

Mountbatten, Lord Louis. Viceroy of India, March–August 1947; governor general of India, August 1947–June 1948.

Mullik, B.N. Director of the Intelligence Bureau, 1950–64.

Munshi, K.M. Agent general to Hyderabad, 1948; Union minister of food and agriculture, 1950–2.

Narayan, Jayaprakash. One of the founders of the Congress Socialist Party in 1934; after 1947 was for some time a leading member of the Socialist Party.

Nehru, R.K. Foreign secretary, 1952–5; ambassador to China, 1955–8; secretary general, ministry of external affairs, 1960–3.

Nehru, Jawaharlal. Prime minister and foreign minister of India, 1947–64.

Noel-Baker, Philip. British secretary of state for commonwealth relations, 1947–50.

Nu, U. Prime minister of Burma, 1947–58 and 1960–2.

Nye, Lieutenant General Sir Archibald. Governor of Madras, 1946–8; British high commissioner in India, 1948–52.

Palit, Brigadier D.K. Director of military operations, Indian army headquarters, 1961–3.

Pandit, Vijayalakshmi. Sister of Jawaharlal Nehru; ambassador to the Soviet Union, 1947–9; to the United States, 1949–51; high commissioner in London, 1954–61; governor of Maharashtra, 1962–4.

Panikkar, K.M. Ambassador to China, 1948–52; to Egypt, 1952–3; to France, 1956–9.

Pant, G.B. Chief minister of UP, 1946–55; Union home minister, 1955–61.

Patel, Vallabhbhai. Deputy prime minister, and minister for home, states, and information and broadcasting, 1947–50.

Pillai, Sir N. Raghavan, Secretary general, ministry of external affairs, 1952–60.

Prasad, Major General Niranjan. General officer commanding, 4 Division, North East Frontier Agency, 1962.

Radhakrishnan, Sarvepalli. Ambassador to the Soviet Union, 1949–52; vice-president of India, 1952–62; president of India, 1962–7.

Raghavan, N. Ambassador to China, 1952–5.

Rajagopalachari, C. Governor general of India, 1948–50; Union minister without portfolio and then for home affairs, 1950–1; chief minister of Madras, 1952–4; founder of the Swatantra Party.

Razvi, Kasim. President of the Ittehad-i-Muslimeen of Hyderabad, 1946–8.

Sen, Lieutenant General L.P. Chief of general staff, Indian army, 1958–61; eastern army commander, 1961–3.

Singh, Baldev. Minister for defence, 1947–52.

Singh, Hari. Maharaja of Jammu and Kashmir; succeeded as ruler in 1925 and withdrew in favour of his son in 1949.

Singh, Karan. Son of Maharaja Hari Singh; regent of Kashmir, 1949–52; elected head of state of Kashmir, 1952–65.

Singh, Lieutenant General Umrao. General officer commanding 33 Corps in 1962.

Thapar, General P.N. Chief of army staff, 1961–2.

Thimayya, General K.S. Chief of army staff, 1957–61.

Thorat, Lieutenant General S.P.P. Chief of general staff, 1950–3; eastern army commander, 1959–61.

Truman, Harry S. President of the United States, 1945–53.

Zhou Enlai. Prime minister of the People's Republic of China, 1949–76.

Introduction

At the time of his death in 1964 Jawaharlal Nehru, the first prime minister of India, had held the reins of state for seventeen years. Nehru's commanding presence in this crucial period left a deep impress on every facet of independent India. Among his most striking contributions was the attempt to fashion a distinctive international personality for the country. From the outset he declared that India would resist the seductions of both sides in the Cold War; that it would steer its own course unfettered by the views of the great powers; that it would stand for a world order based on reason and persuasion rather than bigotry and violence. Nehru's reputation, in his lifetime and after, was largely built on the claim that he had substantially succeeded in this endeavour. India's prominent role in creating the "non-aligned bloc," in pushing for a ban on nuclear tests, in mediating conflicts within Korea and Indo-China: all seemed to attest this success. Writing two decades after Nehru's death his biographer, Sarvepalli Gopal, could assert that "these are no mean achievements and place Nehru among the leading statesmen of the twentieth century."[1]

Yet this verdict has been contested in much of the subsequent scholarship on Nehru. Such works have fallen into two categories. The majority claim that Nehru's foreign policy was little more than an expression of an ingenuous idealism. Shashi Tharoor, to take but one example, argues that Nehru immolated India's interests at the altar of his ideals: "never once was there a mention of India's

---

[1] Sarvepalli Gopal, *Jawaharlal Nehru: A Biography*, vol. 3 (London: Jonathan Cape, 1984), 274.

national interests, or an understanding of how they would be served by this messianic utopianism."[2] In these accounts Nehru is usually admonished for flaccid and inept policies on Kashmir and China. Then there are the revisionists, who argue that Nehru's policies were starkly at variance with his ostentatious advice to others on the peaceful resolution of disputes. In this reading the Indian prime minister had been self-righteous and intransigent in dealing with neighbours, and had had no qualms about the use of force.[3] As one historian trenchantly puts it, Nehru was "a mindless and arrogant hardliner."[4] Interestingly, the revisionists tend to chide Nehru for obdurate and aggressive policies on Kashmir and China.

The chronic character of the disputes with China and Pakistan helps to explain the continued polarization of opinion. Indeed, most of the literature is suffused with a sense that Nehru, who was at the helm for so long, should (and could) have tackled these problems. The perceived miscalculations and excessive caution, or missed opportunities and recklessness, continue to draw scholars to the Nehru years. And yet, it is their preoccupation with the current dimensions of these disputes that very often obstructs a disinterested view of Nehru's own historical role.

Books about Nehru flow off the presses, the bulk of them relying on the same set of sources: Nehru's books and speeches, newspaper reports and secondary accounts, memoirs and interviews. The shelves groan under this hefty literature; yet there have been few well-researched historical studies of Indian foreign policy in the Nehru years.[5] Even the more serious biographies tend to eschew close

---

[2] Shashi Tharoor, *Reasons of State: Political Development and India's Foreign Policy under Indira Gandhi, 1966–1977* (New Delhi: Vikas Publishing House, 1982), 26. Also see idem, *Nehru: The Invention of India* (New Delhi: Penguin, 2003).

[3] Most prominently, Neville Maxwell, "Jawaharlal Nehru: Of Pride and Principle," *Foreign Affairs* 52, no. 3 (April 1974): 633–43. Also see idem, *India's China War* (London: Jonathan Cape, 1970); Benjamin Zachariah, *Nehru* (London: Routledge, 2004).

[4] A.G. Noorani, "Our Secrets in Others Trunks," *Frontline* 22, no. 14 (2 July 2005).

[5] These include Gopal, *Nehru*, vols 2 & 3; C. Dasgupta, *War and Diplomacy in Kashmir 1947–48* (New Delhi: Sage, 2002); Steven Hoffmann, *India*

examination of international affairs. This is partly because diplomacy and strategy have been relegated to the margins in nationalist and Marxist, as well as postcolonial, historiographies.[6] Furthermore, with few exceptions, historians have ignored research on independent India, preferring to toil on the British and earlier periods.[7]

This book is a historical study of Nehru's foreign policy, concentrating on matters most related to the fundamental questions of war and peace. This ambition is lent focus by an inquiry into Nehru's handling of a string of foreign policy crises, events that unfolded in the twilight zone between peace and war. These include the disputes over the fate of Junagadh, Hyderabad, and Kashmir in 1947–8; the refugee crisis in East and West Bengal in 1950; the Kashmir crisis of 1951; and the boundary dispute with China from 1949 to 1962.

In examining each of these, my study seeks to show how they would have appeared to Nehru at that time; how policy options and strategies came to be defined; how these were couched in terms of the prevalent beliefs about the nature of the underlying conflict and the risks attached to various courses of action; and how and why these policies and strategies succeeded or failed. By so doing, the book aims at once to delineate Nehru's approach to strategy and shed light on his core beliefs about international politics. Though these episodes are explored individually, the book also tries to demonstrate the interconnections between them—especially in terms of revealing a continuity and consistency of approach. Some of these—Junagadh, Hyderabad, and Kashmir—were inherently interlinked. All of these, moreover, served a pedagogic function, setting the background assumptions and expectations for the next round. To understand why these crises took the course they did, it is essential to grasp these linkages.

---

and the China Crisis (Berkeley: University of California Press, 1990); Ramachandra Guha, India After Gandhi: The History of the World's Largest Democracy (London: Macmillan, 2007).

[6] See Douglas Peers, "Stocktaking the New Military History of India," 1–2. Paper presented at the Workshop on New Military History of South Asia, Wolfson College, Cambridge, April 1997.

[7] Cf. Ramachandra Guha, "The Challenge of Contemporary History," Economic & Political Weekly (28 June 2008), 192–200.

In adopting this method, I am more interested in explanation than judgement. "All *post-mortems*," writes the historian Mukul Kesavan, "simplify historical choices and thus exaggerate the stupidity or insensitivity or wickedness of actors who, in retrospect, seem to make the wrong ones."[8] Hindsight is an essential part of the historian's quiver, but it should be used with humility; for decisions of life and death are made by leaders in real time, not by scholars in retrospect. Equally important to the task of explanation is a willingness to enter into and to empathize with the worldviews of the past. For instance, looking back from the blasted heath of contemporary Indian secularism, many writers find it difficult to take seriously Nehru's arguments on the importance of Kashmir to a pluralist India. It is tempting to assume that the claims that now seem blatantly cynical were always deemed as such and were scarcely believed by those who articulated them. Part of the challenge for a historian of foreign policy is to get back to the ideas and beliefs held by the decision-makers. I have attempted, therefore, to set the intellectual as well as political context to the events under study.

This book presents the first full-length comparative treatment of these crises. To be sure, the Kashmir crisis of 1947–8 and the conflict with China have been scrutinized on numerous occasions. Yet the recent expansion of the documentary record—especially the unlocking of private papers and foreign archives—makes it possible to understand and interpret them anew. By contrast, the other crises have seldom been studied. Insofar as they are considered, Junagadh and Hyderabad tend to be treated as side shows to Kashmir. I have found it useful, however, to address them in their own terms. The crises of 1950 and 1951—when India and Pakistan teetered at the brink of war—almost never feature in the literature. I have sought to provide a detailed account of these crises, both because they are intrinsically important and because they bring into focus Nehru's attitudes on the deciding issues of foreign policy: war and peace. Owing to these considerations, I have had to overlook other episodes that involved the

---

[8] Mukul Kesavan, "A New History of Indian Nationalism," *Contemporary Perspectives: History and Sociology of South Asia* 1, no. 1 (January–June 2007), 129.

threat or use of force—Goa and Congo, for instance. This is not to suggest that these latter historical events were trivial; merely that they are marginal to the analytical concerns of this study.

Whilst the principal aim of this book is to illuminate the past, it is written with an eye to the present. These crises are not only of historical concern and significance, but also of contemporary interest and relevance. An integral part of the international history of India, they need to be introduced into strategic debates. What's past may not be prologue. But history could be an important resource, enabling us better to understand the present even as we prepare for the future. The historian Arthur Schlesinger Jr. puts it well: "History, by putting crisis in perspective, supplies the antidote to every generation's illusion that its own problems are uniquely oppressive."[9] As India impatiently awaits an invitation to the high table of international politics, a historical perspective is more important than ever. Too often today, we are presented with stark choices: unless we jettison the Nehruvian legacy, we are told, India cannot measure up to the responsibilities of a great power.[10] Such assertions, of course, rest on the bleary-eyed assessment purveyed by much of the existing body of work. Through this study I hope to underscore the continuing validity and force of the intellectual and political logic that underpinned Nehru's approach to international politics; and in so doing to help enlarge and diversify our repertoire of policy options and approaches.

On Strategy

Undergirding this study is a conceptual framework about how actors make strategic choices.[11] Strategy is the creative element in the

---

[9] Arthur M. Schlesinger Jr., *War and the American Presidency* (New York: W.W. Norton & Company, 2004), 130.

[10] See, for instance, Jaswant Singh, *Defending India* (London: Macmillan, 1999), *passim.*

[11] From an enormous literature on modern strategy, I have found the following particularly useful. Thomas Schelling, *Arms and Influence* (New Haven: Yale University Press, 1966); idem, *The Strategy of Conflict*, new edn (Cambridge, Mass.: Harvard University Press, 1980); Lawrence Freedman, *Deterrence* (Cambridge: Polity, 2004); Patrick Morgan, *Deterrence Now* (Cambridge: Cambridge University Press, 2003).

exercise of power. It is the use of available military means to achieve desired political ends. The essence of strategy is interdependent decision-taking between adversaries. This implies that actors will rarely be able to achieve all their objectives. Striking a bargain will usually entail adjusting one's ends to one's means; for the efficacy of the latter will depend on the means at the opponent's disposal.

Strategies can broadly be categorized as consensual, controlling, and coercive. The key difference lies in the degree of choice available to the adversary. A consensual strategy involves the adjustment of one's objectives with an opponent without the threat or use of force. A controlling strategy implies the use of overwhelming force to deprive the adversary of all choice in the matter, so imposing one's will. A coercive strategy involves the use of threats of force, or the limited use of force, to influence the opponent's choices. But the latter retains the capacity to make critical choices throughout the conflict. Thus defined, coercive strategies can further be divided into two types: deterrence and compellence. The former is used to dissuade an adversary from initiating an undesirable act; the latter to make an adversary do something or stop doing something. Coercive strategies need not rely solely on threats; they could also use inducements. These are especially important when the cost of implementing the threat is disproportionate to the benefit arising out of the target's compliance.

In the first instance, all strategic choices will have to be defined with reference to the capability possessed by the adversary. But decision-makers are often responsive to other considerations too. Political leaders, especially in democracies, are sensitive to domestic concerns and constituencies, bureaucracies and special interest groups. In making strategic choices, leaders will also take into account international factors. At one level, they may be concerned with the likely stance of powerful external actors. At another, they will have to reckon with the normative standards of international behaviour. Furthermore, decision-makers are apt to be anxious about the issue of "reputation." For their actions in one encounter might create expectations regarding future performance. If the opponent is convinced that they are soft, he may be emboldened. A concern with reputation, as Thomas Schelling observes, is a concern about "the inter-dependence of a country's commitments."[12] All these might explain why leaders sometimes adopt courses of action that depart from a "rational" standard. Unless we assume that the decision-makers were victims of ill-informed theory, the explanatory task requires us to attend to the political considerations at work.

I hope, in what follows, to overlay this conceptual framework with historical context and content, and to show how it affords an insight into Nehru's policies and practice.

Sources and Contents

Despite an ostensible thirty-year rule in relation to declassification, most of the documents pertaining to these crises have not in fact been declassified by the Government of India. The official papers of Jawaharlal Nehru are also closed to most researchers. This book, therefore, relies upon a diverse array of published and unpublished sources. Amongst the former, the *Selected Works of Jawaharlal Nehru* has been especially useful; though, being a work in progress, it so far only covers the period up to 1957. I draw extensively on Lord Mountbatten's papers—available at the British Library and at Southampton University—as governor general of independent India. These contain important official documents, including minutes of cabinet and defence committee meetings. They also include a number of records of conversation prepared by Mountbatten's staff and often dictated by Mountbatten himself. These, however, have to be used carefully, for they present an exaggerated account of Mountbatten's role.

I have also made substantial use of documents in the British National Archives. This rich vein of untapped sources has been particularly valuable for two reasons. Until the mid-1950s both India and Pakistan had British officers as military chiefs. Unsurprisingly, Whitehall was rather well informed of day-to-day developments during crises. Moreover, British officials in the subcontinent still maintained close relations with a number of Indian and Pakistani officials, many of whom were from the former Indian Civil Service.

---

[12] Schelling, *Arms and Influence*, 194.

I have drawn also upon official material in the Asia, Pacific, and Africa Collections (formerly the India Office Library) at the British Library, the US National Archives, and the National Archives of Australia. In addition, I have used several collections of private papers in India, Britain, and the United States. These sources cast fascinating light not just on India's foreign policy but also the policies of its adversaries. Two collections, hitherto neglected by Indian historians, have been particularly useful. The Walter Monckton papers at the Bodleian Library, Oxford University, are indispensable for a thorough understanding of Hyderabad's approach to its relations with India. So are the Jinnah papers—available in the British Library and yet more conveniently as a documentary series—for the early Pakistan–India crises.

Archival material has been supplemented by oral history transcripts and by open sources such as the main newspapers and periodicals reporting these events. The documentary record on the China crisis is thinner than the rest. Fortunately, there is a rich set of memoirs pertaining to this episode. But these have to be approached with care: the authors invariably sought to defend their own turf. The Indian official history of the conflict is also available in the public domain. I have conducted some interviews on this episode but have used them sparingly. My analysis of the Chinese and Soviet perspectives draws on fine works by Roderick MacFarquhar, John Garver, and Sergey Radchenko, among others. I have also consulted the records of the Central Committee (Plenum) of the Communist Party of the Soviet Union— the apex decision-making body in the erstwhile USSR. These are available both in a microfiche collection at the Lamont Library, Harvard University, and in a published documentary collection.

The chapters of the book are broadly chronological and thematic. Chapter 1 traces the intellectual background to Nehru's strategic outlook, his views on the role of force in international politics, and on the nature of political leadership. It argues that an admixture of liberal values and realist outlook predisposed Nehru to favour coercive rather than controlling strategies. Furthermore, Nehru's innate circumspection in the exercise of power led him towards an incremental approach to managing crises. The chapter also looks at the structures of decision-making and the key personalities who helped Nehru shape and implement foreign policy.

The next three chapters deal with Nehru's handling of the disputes over the so-called princely states in the immediate aftermath of Independence. Chapter 2 examines the case of Junagadh, a state in western India comprising mostly Hindus but ruled by a Muslim prince who decided to join Pakistan. India responded by deploying its forces around the state; but Nehru was keen to avoid an armed confrontation with Pakistan. Ultimately, the beleaguered government of Junagadh invited India to take over the administration and the crisis was settled short of war.

The next chapter looks at events surrounding the accession of Hyderabad. The problem here was akin to that in Junagadh: a Muslim prince (the nizam) ruling over a predominantly Hindu population. The nizam, however, wanted to remain entirely independent. Diplomatic negotiations with him dragged on for nearly a year. As sectarian violence increased in the state, India deployed its forces to coerce Hyderabad to come to terms. Owing to the nizam's recalcitrance, Nehru reluctantly resorted to force and annexed the state.

Chapter 4 considers the first stage of the confrontation with Pakistan over Jammu and Kashmir. The Hindu maharaja of Kashmir, whose population was largely Muslim and whose state was of importance to both Pakistan and India, dithered in the matter of accession. Forced by a Pakistan-abetted tribal invasion of his state, in October 1947 the maharaja joined India, so locking Pakistan and India in a bitter and violent dispute that endures even now. Nehru's actions during the course of this crisis have been of abiding interest. Why did he agree to a plebiscite? Why did he choose to take the dispute to the United Nations? Why did he fail to evict the invaders from the entire state? What was his stance on the plebiscite? Questions such as these are not new, but I attempt to provide some new answers.

The next two chapters examine the forgotten crises with Pakistan in 1950 and 1951. The India–Pakistan crisis of 1950 turned on the movement of refugees between East and West Bengal. These were triggered by attacks against Hindus in the former and against Muslims in the latter. India urged Pakistan to initiate a series of steps aimed at restoring the confidence of the minority communities in both countries. Pakistan, however, blamed India for the developments and asked Delhi to put its house in order. Owing to the scale of the refugee influx, Nehru mobilized India's forces to coerce Pakistan into accepting his proposals. Hectic diplomacy ensued. At length, Pakistan's prime minister, Liaquat Ali Khan, accepted an invitation to meet Nehru. The Nehru–Liaquat pact of April 1950 arrested the slide to war.

A little over a year later, India and Pakistan were embroiled in another crisis in Kashmir. Faced with the possibility of an attack, Nehru again decided to mobilize the Indian forces. The aim was to deter Pakistani action in Kashmir by threatening to retaliate in Punjab. Pakistan responded by concentrating its troops on the Punjab border. Simultaneously, the prime ministers exchanged a series of missives; but the correspondence proved futile. Just when the possibility of war seemed to peak, Liaquat Ali Khan was assassinated in October 1951. Liaquat's tragic death enabled the situation to be defused. Although the Kashmir dispute remained deadlocked, the 1951 crisis was the last armed confrontation during Nehru's tenure. Chapter 6 also examines the subsequent turning points in the course of the dispute.

Chapters 7 and 8 focus on Nehru's policy towards China. The first deals with the course of the boundary dispute up to 1960. It revises the claims that Nehru had decided in the early 1950s not to negotiate the boundary, and that he rejected reasonable offers by the Chinese in 1960 because he had set his mind against compromise. I suggest that such claims provide a misleading simplicity and fixity to what was in fact a nuanced and shifting policy.

Chapter 8 examines the run-up to the Sino-Indian war of October–November 1962. From the summer of 1960 Delhi was concerned about efforts by the Chinese to move forward in certain areas and occupy more Indian-claimed territory. Towards the end of 1961 the Indian government adopted a "forward policy" of planting military posts to deter further Chinese incursions. Ultimately, this strategy proved disastrous in the face of a determined Chinese attack. India's abject defeat throws up intriguing questions. Why did Nehru adopt the "forward policy?" Why did he believe that a much more powerful China could be deterred? How open was he to a negotiated settlement? The chapter tries to answer these and other questions that continue to haunt the history of Indian foreign policy.

A brief conclusion considers the larger interpretive questions about Nehru's performance in foreign affairs. The Nehru that emerges from this study is more fallible and flawed than the clear-sighted and visionary statesman of posthumous adulation. But he is also far more adroit and pragmatic than the naïf and idealist of retrospective detraction. And, in contrast to the revisionist portrayal, he is also more cautious, genuinely desirous of diplomatic settlements, and, above all, eager to avoid war.

1

Ideas, Strategy, and Structures

Born in 1889 to a family of Kashmiri Brahmins, Jawaharlal Nehru was the eldest of three children. His father Motilal Nehru was an immensely successful and ambitious lawyer in the city of Allahabad. Like many of his contemporaries, Motilal was active in the Indian National Congress in its early avatar as a loyalist organization. Socially, he was more venturesome and sought to recast his family in Western mores. At the age of 15 Jawaharlal was sent to England for an education at Harrow followed by Trinity College, Cambridge; his subsequent intellectual development owed more to yet another British institution—His Majesty's Prisons, where he virtually inhaled books during long periods of enforced leisure.

Jawaharlal returned to India in 1912 and, somewhat lackadaisically, began a legal practice in Allahabad. Four years later he was married. After his wife Kamala's death in 1936 he did not marry again. By 1919 he was pulled into the ruck of nationalist politics under the inspiration of Mohandas Karamchand Gandhi. From the age of about 30, Nehru's life was consumed by politics. Well before India attained independence, Gandhi had anointed him his chosen successor. In August 1947 Nehru took over as independent India's prime minister. Re-elected thrice, he remained in office for the next seventeen years until he succumbed to a stroke in May 1964.

Over his lifetime Nehru sought to sequester his public and private lives. But the links between them have engendered much interest. On the one hand there has been ceaseless speculation about his relationship with Edwina Mountbatten and its influence on his political choices. Stanley Wolpert in his frequently speculative biography claims, for instance, that at the height of the Bengal crisis in 1950 Nehru contemplated eloping with Edwina.[1] Little evidence has emerged to substantiate such assertions. On the other hand, a straight line is often drawn from Nehru's Kashmiri origins to his apparently intransigent handling of the dispute with Pakistan. Nehru, we are told, was obsessed with his ancestral homeland.[2] These contentions, too, are difficult to evaluate. Nehru himself agreed that he was "attached to Kashmir for a large variety of reasons. It may be that many of them are sentimental." But he was equally clear that he was "not moved by sentiment" and that his policy was actuated by strategic and domestic political concerns.[3]

Indeed, the one aspect of Nehru's character that is germane to a political assessment is his conscious sense of restraint: a tendency to avoid plunging headlong into a situation or succumbing to the emotions it aroused.[4] As he explained to his daughter, Indira Priyadarshini, it was "impossible for me to lay bare my heart before anybody," a trait that afforded "self-protection against a fear I always had of being swept away by too much emotion." This facet of his personality was shaped in important ways by Motilal. Jawaharlal's sisters were much younger, and in consequence he was the prime object of paternal hopes and ambitions. His inclination to shy away from full-blown confrontations owed something to a powerful father. During the years in England he acquired a further integument of reserve and a pronounced aversion to intimacy. As Sunil Khilnani perceptively observes, there was "a connection between this self-restraint and his judgements about the use of power in the public realm."

[1] Stanley Wolpert, *Nehru: A Tryst with Destiny* (New York: Oxford University Press, 1996).

[2] For example Alastair Lamb, *Incomplete Partition: The Genesis of the Kashmir Dispute, 1947–48* (Hertingfordbury: Roxford Books, 1997).

[3] Nehru to Roy Bucher, 7 August 1949, 7901-87-30, Bucher Papers, National Army Museum (NAM), London.

[4] This paragraph draws on Sunil Khilnani, "Nehru's Judgement," in Raymond Geuss and Richard Bourke, eds, *Political Judgement* (forthcoming, 2009).

Nehru and Liberal Realism

As independent India's first foreign minister as well as prime minister, Nehru had no experience in the conduct of foreign policy, let alone that of handling crises. But he brought to the task a long-standing interest in international affairs dating back to the 1920s. His travels in Europe and Asia, and his wide reading in world history and politics, had given him a perspective on international relations and on India's place in historical developments. Throughout these years, Nehru had been the Congress Party's principal spokesman on international affairs and future foreign policy.

In his understanding of the role of force in international relations, Nehru stood at the juncture of the liberal and realist traditions. Like many liberals he abhorred war for its inherently illiberal effects and consequences, and yet maintained that "in this imperfect world a national State [sic] will have to use force to defend itself against unprovoked attack from outside."[5] But unlike the liberals Nehru also held that conflict was an endemic feature of politics; for all national and social groups were inevitably moved by self-interest.

In the early years Nehru had been influenced by the idealism of liberal thinkers like Bertrand Russell. Subsequently, his immersion in anti-colonial politics, his reflection on contemporary international affairs, and his exposure to Marxist ideas deepened his appreciation of the role of interests and power. The realist turn in Nehru's thinking also owed much to the early works of the theologian Reinhold Niebuhr, who later became the most influential philosopher of American realism.[6] By the early 1930s Nehru's liberal idealism had morphed into liberal realism. In this he was very much a product of the intellectual currents of his age. Influenced by the ideas of Marx and Niebuhr,

---

[5] Jawaharlal Nehru, *An Autobiography* (London: John Lane, 1936; reprint, New Delhi: Penguin, 2004), 560–1. The classic study of liberal attitudes to war is Michael Howard, *War and the Liberal Conscience* (London: Temple Smith, 1978).

[6] Nehru to John Gunther, 16 March 1938, *Selected Works of Jawaharlal Nehru*, 1st series, ed. Sarvepalli Gopal (New Delhi: Orient Longman, 1972–82) (hereafter *SWJN-FS*), 8: 867–71. On Niebuhr, see H.W. Brands, *What America Owes the World: The Struggle for the Soul of Foreign Policy* (New York: Cambridge University Press, 1998), ch. 7.

contemporary international relations scholars like E.H. Carr were also moving away from the idealist tradition.[7]

In his classic *Moral Man and Immoral Society*, Niebuhr criticized both religious moralists and liberal rationalists for failing to grasp "the brutal character of the behaviour of all human collectivities, and the power of self-interest and collective egoism in all inter-group relations." Collective power whether in the form of imperialism or class domination, he argued, could never be dislodged without countervailing power.[8] "All life is full of conflict and violence," wrote Nehru in his *Autobiography*, following Niebuhr. "Neither the growth of reason nor of the religious outlook nor morality have checked in any way this tendency to violence."[9]

But these years were also the period of Nehru's apprenticeship under Gandhi. Nehru's debates with the Mahatma on the question of non-violence moulded his views on the role of force in subtle but important ways. In contrast to Gandhi, Nehru believed that non-violence was not "a religion or an unchallengeable creed or dogma": "It could only be a policy and a method promising certain results, and by those results it would have to be finally judged."[10] "After much discussion and argument," Nehru was convinced "that if we use violence against the British it would not lead to our ultimate good."[11] Given this instrumental understanding of non-violence, it is not surprising that Nehru considered it inapplicable to a free India. There was, he observed, "no question of the doctrine of non-violence coming in the way of armed conflict for defence or against aggression."[12] This position led to a serious rift with Gandhi in the summer of 1940, when the Mahatma wanted the Congress Party to declare that independent India would adhere to the norm of non-violence in confronting external aggression

[7] E.H. Carr, *The Twenty Years' Crisis, 1919–1939: An Introduction to the Study of International Relations* (London: Macmillan, 1939).

[8] Reinhold Niebuhr, *Moral Man and Immoral Society: A Study in Ethics and Politics* (New York: Charles Scribner's Sons, 1932).

[9] Nehru, *Autobiography*, 558–60.

[10] Ibid., 90.

[11] Gopalkrishna Gandhi (ed.), *Gandhi is Gone. Who Will Guide us Now?: Sevagram, March 1948* (New Delhi: Permanent Black, 2007), 70.

[12] Jawaharlal Nehru, *The Discovery of India* (n.p., 1946; reprint, New Delhi: Penguin, 2004), 467.

and internal disorder.[13] Be that as it may, Gandhi's influence was perceptible in Nehru's thought, albeit at one remove.

Nehru held that force was an ineluctable element in relations between states: "The necessity for this will only disappear when there is only a single World-State [*sic*]."[14] But this was not tantamount to accepting that the use of force was par for the course. Nehru concurred with Gandhi that the choice of means, too, was important: "violence is undoubtedly bad and brings an unending trail of evil consequences." The resort to violence, then, could only be the lesser of two evils. As Nehru summed up his ruminations, "the best we can do is to limit this compulsion and use it in such a manner that its evil is lessened."[15] The awareness of the dilemmas inherent in any exercise of power, the "diabolic forces lurking in all violence,"[16] deepened with the passage of time. In particular, the experience of the partition of India had a significant impact. As Khilnani argues, "It showed him the destructive potentialities of politics, and therefore the need to use power with great circumspection."[17]

This blend of liberalism and realism shaped Nehru's stand on the international crises of the 1930s. He staunchly opposed European fascism and Japanese militarism, and advocated a tough stance over a range of issues including Manchuria, Abyssinia, Spain, and Czechoslovakia. On the whole, he favoured a policy akin to containment, involving effective sanctions and a united front of Britain, France, Soviet Union, and Czechoslovakia. These measures, he argued, would deter Nazi and fascist aggression.[18] Interestingly, the positions adopted by Nehru had a certain affinity with those advocated by the British military commentator Basil Liddell Hart—who is now regarded as the pioneering and archetypal liberal strategic thinker. Indeed, Nehru admired Liddell Hart's thinking and met him to discuss strategic issues during

[13] Ibid., 489–95.

[14] Nehru, *Autobiography*, 561.

[15] Ibid., 570–1.

[16] Max Weber, "Politics as a Vocation," in H.H. Gerth and C. Wright Mills (eds), *From Max Weber: Essays in Sociology*, new edn (London: Routledge, 1991), 125–6.

[17] Khilnani, "Nehru's Judgement," 25.

[18] See Nehru's numerous articles on these issues in *SWJN-FS*, vols 8 and 9.

visits to England in 1938 and 1949.[19] Looking back at the events of the 1930s Nehru explained British and French appeasement and American isolationism in realist terms. "In a contest between nationalism and internationalism," he wrote in his prison cell in 1944, "nationalism was bound to win." The Western democracies had adopted their policies "for what they considered, wrongly as events proved, their national interests."[20]

This realist outlook invariably framed Nehru's understanding of international affairs during his years in office. Like many latter-day "Realist" international relations scholars, he held that nationalism was more potent than any ideology in influencing the behaviour of states. Thus, he interpreted the Cold War not as a clash of ideologies but as a conflict of the national interests of great powers. "Both China and the U.S.S.R.," Nehru told the American ambassador, "were great and powerful Nations. Communism came in the way of our understanding the situation, which was the development of two great and vital Nations tending to expand."[21] Visiting the Soviet Union in the summer of 1955, Nehru thought that despite all the revolutionary changes communism had not supplanted nationalism. "The Russians might be communists but they were more Russian than communists."[22]

Politics, Strategy, and Crisis Management

Long before assuming office Nehru understood that leadership, particularly in a democratic polity, required sensitivity to popular opinion

[19] See, LH 1/540: Correspondence with Jawaharlal Nehru, Liddell Hart Centre for Military Archives (hereafter LHCMA), King's College London. On Liddell Hart, see Azar Gat, *A History of Military Thought: From the Enlightenment to the Cold War* (Oxford: Oxford University Press, 2001), 645–783.

[20] Nehru, *The Discovery of India*, 462.

[21] Nehru's note on conversation with US ambassador, Loy Henderson, 15 September 1951, subject file 56, Vijayalakshmi Pandit Papers, Nehru Memorial Museum and Library (hereafter NMML).

[22] Note, 1 August 1955, *Selected Works of Jawaharlal Nehru*, 2nd series, ed. Sarvepalli Gopal, Ravinder Kumar, H. Y. Sharada Prasad, A. K. Damodaran, Mushirul Hasan (New Delhi: Jawaharlal Nehru Memorial Fund, 1984–) (hereafter *SWJN-SS*), 29: 297.

and an ability to persuade others about one's views and ideas.[23] This also implied that, at times, compromises might have to be accepted. In *The Discovery of India* he quoted at length Liddell Hart on the distinction between prophets and leaders: "The prophets must be stoned; that is their lot, and the test of their self-fulfilment. But a leader who is stoned may merely prove that he has failed in his function through a deficiency of wisdom, or through confusing his function with that of a prophet." The underlying argument was that while a prophet could hold on to what he regarded as the truth irrespective of consequences, the statesman might have to recognize his limitations and strike a balance.[24] Years later, discussing the question of leadership with Field Marshal Bernard Montgomery, Nehru "emphasized the point constantly that a leader cannot act to a degree beyond what the people will take; he must, of course, have courage, but if the people will not follow his decisions, he will inevitably fail. He must therefore be a persuader."[25] Nehru considered this not just a practical problem but as another aspect of the morally corrosive effect of wielding power.

As prime minister he was forced to confront these twin dilemmas several times in a career littered with crises. When asked why he, a follower of Gandhi, had used force to annex Hyderabad, Nehru responded by invoking both these aspects. Unlike prophets, he observed, democratic leaders had to work through others and therefore accept compromises. The important thing was to avoid sliding down the slippery slope of compromise and opportunism. "But if he [the statesman] remembers the truth all the time then he might keep himself from slipping too far." As for the use of force: "Violence is bad and yet something is [*sic*] worse than violence and sometimes you have to choose . . . between the greater and lesser evil."[26] Over a decade later Nehru explained India's action against Goa in a similar vein. He

[23] A.K. Damodaran, *Jawaharlal Nehru: A Communicator and Democratic Leader* (New Delhi: Radiant Publishers, 1997).

[24] Nehru, *The Discovery of India*, 496–7.

[25] TS chapter on Nehru in "The Path to Leadership," 1960, Montgomery Papers (Part II), Imperial War Museum, London.

[26] Press Conference at Rangoon, 22 June 1950, *SWJN-SS*, 14, pt. II: 417–18.

wrote to the British prime minister that sometimes leaders had to choose the lesser of two evils. Moreover, there were limits to a democratic leader's freedom of manoeuvre in the face of widespread and resentful public opinion.[27]

This admixture of liberal values and realist outlook predisposed Nehru to favour coercive rather than controlling strategies. As seen, even in the 1930s he had advocated measures aimed at deterring and containing Nazi and fascist aggression in Europe. Nehru understood the function of coercion with clarity: "the bringing about of circumstances which make it more worth while for the vested interests to accept change than to suffer greater loss in an attempt to avoid it."[28] In practice, he constantly recoiled at the prospect of war and sought to minimize the possibility of escalation to full-scale hostilities.

Nehru's style of strategy and crisis management mirrored his own description of his approach to foreign policy. As he told President Nasser of Egypt: "always take the first step . . . then take the second step . . . then take the third step."[29] Even metaphorically this step-by-step approach was opposed to the idea of escalation—a term that conjured up the image of a moving staircase that could not be stopped: if you got aboard an escalator you could only step out at the top.[30] By contrast, Nehru's method implied a preference for measures that demonstrated resolve without recklessness, for coupling military moves to pressurize the adversary with diplomatic ones to explore opportunities for a settlement. It was an approach that fitted well with Nehru's innate

[27] Nehru to Macmillan, 15 December 1961, cited in Judith Brown, *Nehru: A Political Life* (New Delhi: Oxford University Press, 2004), 296. The notion of "the lesser of two evils" and the concomitant "ethic of responsibility" was central to the political thought and practice of another protégé of Gandhi and colleague of Nehru, C. Rajagopalachari. See Vasanthi Srinivasan, *Gandhi's Conscience Keeper: C. Rajagopalachari and Indian Politics* (Ranikhet: Permanent Black, 2009), *passim*. On the ethic of responsibility, see Weber, "Politics as a Vocation."

[28] "The Way to Peace," 1936, *SWJN-FS*, 7: 124.

[29] Cited in Gopal, *Nehru*, 3: 276.

[30] On the escalator metaphor in strategic vocabulary, see Lawrence Freedman, "On the Tiger's Back: Development of the Concept of Escalation," in Roman Kolkowicz, ed., *The Logic of Nuclear Terror* (Boston: Allen and Unwin, 1987), 109–52.

wariness towards the exercise of power. And it was buttressed by his conviction that it was the best way to avoid war without forsaking India's interests.

Foreign Policy Framework: Non-Alignment as Pragmatism

The contours of independent India's foreign policy were adumbrated even before the British Raj had wound up. As vice president of the Interim Government, Nehru stated in September 1946: "We propose, so far as possible, to keep away from the power politics of groups aligned against one another, which have led in the past to world wars and which may again lead to disasters on an even vaster scale." The speech heralded a distinctive framework for the conduct of foreign policy, which came to be known as non-alignment.

From the outset Nehru stressed that non-alignment embodied pragmatism as much as principle. It was, he observed, "not a wise policy to put all our eggs in one basket . . . purely from the point of view of opportunism . . . an independent policy is the best."[31] The pursuit of interests lay at the core of the idea. As he told the constituent assembly of India: "Whatever policy you may lay down, the main feature of the foreign policy of any country has to be to find out what is most advantageous to her." But non-alignment itself could neither define these interests nor positively suggest how they might best be promoted. At most it could provide a supple framework for building India's foreign policies from the ground up.

Later, Nehru increasingly began to couch the idea of non-alignment in the language of morality and principles. By so doing he deservedly laid himself open to criticism for a mismatch between his rhetoric and his actions. The extent of this gap will be explored subsequently. For now it bears emphasizing that the doctrine of non-alignment stemmed from Nehru's desire to craft a distinguishing persona for India on the international stage, by means of which India might pursue its interests with legitimacy. But this was also an undertaking that he deemed integral to the smelting of a new identity for the dizzyingly variegated

---

[31] On Nehru's early statements, see Jawaharlal Nehru, *India's Foreign Policy: Selected Speeches* (New Delhi: Government of India, 1961).

country.[32] Nehru's references to the ethical bases of non-alignment were as much for the consumption of domestic audiences as for any external ones. After all, a core task of political leaders is to demonstrate the links between policies, interests, and values.

People and Structures: Fashioning a New Foreign Policy

Fashioning a new foreign policy entailed not just articulating ideas but also creating structures and roping in people. British India had had no dedicated foreign service. As foreign minister in the Interim Government, Nehru had started planning for a professional diplomatic corps. Officers were drawn from a variety of sources: the civil services and the armed forces provided the largest pools. In the initial years after Independence, diplomatic representation was restricted to countries that were considered central to India's interests.[33] The choice of the top-level officials was a critical decision. After some deliberation Nehru appointed Sir Girja Shankar Bajpai as the secretary general of the ministry of external affairs (MEA) and K.P.S. Menon as the foreign secretary.

A near contemporary of Nehru, Bajpai had been to Oxford before joining the Indian Civil Service in 1914. A gifted wordsmith and administrator, he rose steadily up the chain and was a member of the Viceroy's Council by 1940. Thereafter he spent six years in Washington as India's Agent-General. The appointment surprised many of Nehru's colleagues, for Bajpai had had to push Britain's anti-Congress line during the war. But Bajpai quickly rose in Nehru's esteem for his forthrightness as much as his competence. Soon, Nehru was referring to Bajpai as his "tower of strength." Politically, Bajpai was a self-professed conservative and an old school realist (he began one of his few published writings by quoting Thucydides). Even after Bajpai left the foreign office in 1952, Nehru continued to use his expertise for negotiations on Kashmir. No subsequent secretary general played a comparable role in policy formulation as well as execution.

[32] Sunil Khilnani, *The Idea of India* (London: Hamish Hamilton, 1997; rpnt Harmondsworth: Penguin, 2003).

[33] Brown, *Nehru*, 247.

K.P.S. Menon was a few years younger. He too had been at Oxford, taking a First in History at Christ Church. After a few years in the Indian Civil Service he had been seconded to the Political Service. Before returning to New Delhi he had served as ambassador to China. Endowed with a pragmatic mind and a strong literary sensibility, Menon tended to state his views with concision and occasional acerbity. Owing to his experience he took the lead on issues relating to China and Tibet. Menon too left his post in 1952, and was ambassador to Moscow till 1961.

He was succeeded by Ratan Kumar Nehru, a cousin of Jawaharlal. Ratan Nehru had a long association with China policy, first as foreign secretary, then as ambassador to Beijing, and finally as secretary general in 1961–2. His performance did not equal his vanity: in later years he would claim that he could have restored relations with China to an even keel. The next two foreign secretaries—Subimal Dutt and M.J. Desai—were closely involved with policies on Tibet and China. Austere, laconic, and sedulous, Dutt enjoyed Nehru's confidence; but he habitually tended to defer to the prime minister. Desai was more active in shaping policy, in part because an aged Nehru could no longer stay close to the detail.

Officials apart, Nehru relied on select ambassadors for advice on foreign affairs. V.K. Krishna Menon was undoubtedly the most important. Before being appointed as high commissioner, he had spent nearly two decades in London as secretary of the India League. Menon's mind was keen and agile, incisive in argument even when defending untenable positions. He had the ability quickly to pare down issues to their essentials, and had a talent for evolving compromises. These, coupled with seemingly boundless energy, made him a strong negotiator. But his judgement did not match his intelligence, and consequently he was not very reliable. With a tongue as sharp as his mind, Krishna Menon easily made enemies. His proclivity to darken his surroundings like a cuttlefish did not endear him to his associates either. Nehru was aware that he was "a frightfully sensitive and rather emotional person" and sought to treat him gently.[34] But his unwillingness to curb Menon's excesses did neither of them any favours.

[34] Nehru to Vijayalakshmi Pandit, 3 August 1948, *SWJN-SS*, 7: 685.

As defence minister from 1957 Menon played an important part in fashioning policy towards China. His political views tended to accord with those of the prime minister. But he had little political standing of his own and had to rely heavily on Nehru's patronage. In consequence Krishna Menon often served as a lightning rod for the prime minister.

Another envoy whose inputs informed policy was K.M. Panikkar. An academic historian, Panikkar had worked in the princely states before being appointed to Beijing. In Nehru's judgement he was "a man of extraordinarily acute intelligence and powers of observation. In fact, his mind is so keen that it over-shoots the mark and goes much further than facts warrant."[35] And, Nehru might have added, willing to defend any stance, however far removed from those he had previously espoused. This enabled him to establish his intellectual and political credentials with Nehru. Even after standing down as ambassador in 1952, Panikkar continued to advise on China policy from his perch in Cairo.

Other influential ambassadors in the early years were Nehru's sister Vijayalakshmi Pandit, initially in Moscow and then in Washington, and the philosopher Sarvepalli Radhakrishnan in Moscow.[36] All four envoys had good access to the leadership in their countries and tended to launch independent initiatives. The officials in Delhi resented their over-reaching. Thus, when Vijayalakshmi visited, K.P.S. Menon noted in his diary: "Most agreeable. Most ingratiating. Butter will not melt in her mouth. But . . . she is utterly unreliable."[37] All of this made for a less than harmonious foreign policy team.

Even more problematic, at the time of Independence, was the absence of inter-departmental structures for decision-making. The Defence Committee of the Cabinet was created only after a crisis broke over Junagadh. The Chiefs of Staff Committee was placed under the Defence Committee, and subsequently a Joint Intelligence Sub-Committee was also established. A Foreign Affairs Committee was

[35] Nehru to Vijayalakshmi Pandit, 30 August 1950, subject file 60, Vijayalakshmi Pandit Papers, NMML.

[36] On the latter, see Sarvepalli Gopal, *Radhakrishnan: A Biography* (New Delhi: Oxford University Press, 1989), 213–56.

[37] Entry of 20 August 1951, Diary 32, K.P.S. Menon Papers, NMML.

set up to provide a forum for discussion of foreign policy issues that did not require a military input.

A curious feature of the Defence Committee mechanism was the presence of British officers as service chiefs until the mid-1950s. The Raj had blocked large-scale introduction of Indians in the officer cadre until the late 1930s.[38] During the transfer of power the seniormost Indian officer in the army was a two-star general. Hence, British officers had to be taken on secondment. The first Indian chief of the army staff was appointed in early 1949—the other two services had to wait a few more years. The role of British officers has naturally attracted much attention. It has been contended that during the Kashmir conflict of 1947–8 the British officers thwarted Nehru from taking stronger measures against Pakistan.[39] Such claims, we shall see, are much exaggerated. In fact the British chiefs were at their most influential when their views were in consort with those of the prime minister. A second, and overlooked, consequence of delayed "Indianization" was that after Independence a set of officers rose rapidly from one-star to three- and four-star positions. Their record as tactical commanders was usually excellent; but their preparation for the higher direction of war was less than adequate. This would tell with considerable effect on the quality of military advice tendered to the government during the China crisis.

The Joint Intelligence Sub-Committee subsequently branched out into a full-fledged committee. It comprised civilian and military intelligence agencies, presided by an official from the foreign office. But over time the Joint Intelligence Committee (JIC) atrophied, and the market was largely cornered by the civilian Intelligence Bureau (IB). During the Raj intelligence agencies were mostly focused on internal concerns. Moreover, at the time of Partition the seniormost Indian intelligence officer opted for Pakistan. Consequently, in the initial months after Independence Delhi's intelligence apparatus was rather deficient both in gathering and analysing external intelligence. A major overhaul of the system did not occur until early in the next

---

[38] Anirudh Deshpande, *British Military Policy in India, 1900–1945: Colonial Constraints and Declining Power* (New Delhi: Manohar, 2005), 87–122.

[39] Dasgupta, *War and Diplomacy*.

decade. Among directors of the IB, B.N. Mullik was the most influential. Although he was politically much to the right of the prime
minister, Mullik was taken seriously. Over the years Nehru came to
regard him as "able, conscientious and thoroughly straightforward."[40]

The committee system worked reasonably well in the first decade
after Independence. It provided a suitable forum for senior ministers
to express their views and ideas, and to mould policies and choices.
Later, when most of Nehru's trusted political colleagues had passed on,
he preferred to operate in smaller, looser, and more intense groups,
reserving final decisions for the cabinet. This less orderly structure had
its pitfalls as well as payoffs, especially during a crisis. Important questions of interests and options tended to be addressed and assessed without sufficient evidence and time for deliberation.

In either format Nehru's dominance on issues of foreign policy was
seldom unchallenged. As we shall see, both within the cabinet and
the party, Nehru was mostly on the liberal side of the spectrum of
opinions. He often found himself moderating the views of his associates and managing the politics that drove the policy. The prime
minister never avoided consulting his colleagues; he seldom laid
down the law. But nor did he ever let them forget that he was first
among equals.

[40] Nehru to Krishnamachari, 2 November 1962, Correspondence with
Nehru, 1962, T.T. Krishnamachari Papers, NMML.

2

Junagadh 1947

The edifice of the Raj in India rested on two pillars: the provinces directly ruled by the British and the indirectly ruled princely states. The political relationship between the British and the states can be traced back to the mid-eighteenth century when the East India Company began establishing diplomatic relations with Indian kingdoms. By the 1850s most of the major kingdoms were linked to the Company by treaty but were not subsumed within the colonial bloc. More important, by this time the central elements of what came to be known as "paramountcy" were in place. A vague and ill-defined term, paramountcy included among other things a system of British "Residents" in princely states, control over the states' foreign affairs, and the regulation of succession within such states. In 1947 there were around 600 states of varying importance, ranging from Kashmir and Hyderabad, which rivalled France in area and population, to princi- palities of just a few villages. Between them the states accounted for two-fifths of the area and a third of the population of the empire in India. The fate of the princely states thus held momentous consequences for the subcontinent once the British decided to quit.[1]

[1] The best overall study is Ian Copland, *The Princes of India in the End- game of Empire* (Cambridge: Cambridge University Press, 1999). For an earlier assessment, see R. Jeffrey, ed., *People, Princes and Paramount Power: Society and Politics in the Indian Princely States* (New Delhi: Oxford University Press, 1978). V.P. Menon, *The Story of the Integration of Indian States* (London: Longmans Green, 1956) remains the most detailed account of the period immediately preceding and following the transfer of power. Also useful is

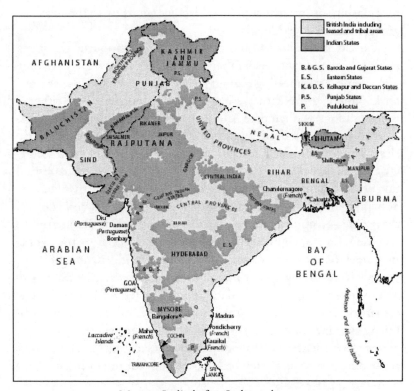

Map 1. India before Independence

The Partition of India was spelt out in the plan of 3 June 1947. This tersely stated that the British government's policy towards the states remained as expounded in the Cabinet Mission's memorandum of 12 May 1946. The memorandum had declared that when British India became independent, paramountcy would cease to operate: all rights surrendered by the states to the paramount power would revert to them. The states would have to fill this void by entering into a "federal relationship" or "particular political arrangements" with the successor government or governments.

The Congress and Muslim League's interpretation of the states' rights was at odds with each other's, and their leaders expressed sharp disagreement at a meeting chaired by the viceroy, Lord Mountbatten, on 13 June 1947.[2] Nehru averred that the states had to join either of the dominions; Mohammed Ali Jinnah claimed they could also opt to stay independent. Indeed, by this time Travancore and Hyderabad had already announced their decision to remain independent and sovereign entities. Congress leaders feared that this foreshadowed a balkanization of India. They passed a stern resolution emphasizing that the lapse of paramountcy did not mean independence for the states, and that the people—as opposed to the princes—should decide the question of accession. Jinnah, for his part, issued statements espousing the right of the rulers to decide on accession and to remain independent.

Jinnah's reasoning is not difficult to fathom. Given a Pakistan with a partitioned Bengal and Punjab, Jinnah was left with what he had earlier contemptuously described as "a maimed, mutilated and moth-eaten Pakistan."[3] Not surprisingly, he sought to redress the balance by enticing some states, such as Jodhpur, to join Pakistan, and by encouraging others, such as Hyderabad, to hold out for independence. In a

---

H.V. Hodson, *The Great Divide: Britain–India–Pakistan* (London: Hutchinson, 1969).

[2] Minutes of Viceroy's Meeting, 13 June 1947, *Constitutional Relations between Britain and India: The Transfer of Power 1942–7*, ed. Nicholas Mansergh and Penderel Moon (London: Her Majesty's Stationery Office, 1970–83) (hereafter *Transfer of Power*), 11: 320–3.

[3] Ayesha Jalal, *The Sole Spokesman: Jinnah, the Muslim League and the Demand for Pakistan* (Cambridge: Cambridge University Press, 1985), *passim*.

deeper sense the manoeuvres over the states were a continuation of the long and bitter rivalry between the leadership of the Congress and the League, a rivalry that would cast a baleful shadow on the relationship between India and Pakistan.

Among those pondering the question of the states was the secretary of the ministry of states, V.P. Menon. Of humble origins, Menon began his career not as an officer in the Indian Civil Service but as a lowly clerk in the Madras Presidency. His outstanding administrative abilities enabled him to transcend this handicap and rise steadily up the ladder, rung by rung. In 1924 he was appointed assistant secretary in the newly created Reforms Office; eighteen years later he was heading the office as Reforms Commissioner. In 1947 few officials had comparable knowledge and experience of the administrative and legal framework of the Raj. This made Menon an indispensable adviser to the viceroy, Lord Mountbatten, and subsequently to the deputy prime minister and states minister Sardar Vallabhbhai Patel. As secretary of the ministry of states V.P. Menon would play a significant role in the consolidation of independent India. After his death an obituary in *The Times* cattily remarked that Menon found this task congenial: "He, the ex-secretariat clerk, was in a position to enforce upon the proudest dynasties of ancient India the settlements, which in his judgment, the interests of the new India required."[4]

To get the states on board prior to the transfer of power, Menon contrived a simple yet ingenious idea of proffering accession on three subjects alone: defence, foreign affairs, and communications. More important, Menon along with Patel managed to enlist Mountbatten to the cause. In the following weeks, deploying a potent mix of charm, bullying, and cajoling, Mountbatten, Patel, and Menon managed to get most of the states to accede. By 15 August 1947 the Indian leaders had managed to secure the accession of most states, barring Hyderabad, Kashmir, and Junagadh.

In Hyderabad a Muslim prince (the nizam) ruled over a predominantly Hindu population. The nizam claimed independence and sought dominion status, a quest in which he was encouraged by Jinnah. After preliminary discussions the viceroy realized it was impossible

[4] *The Times* (London), 4 January 1966.

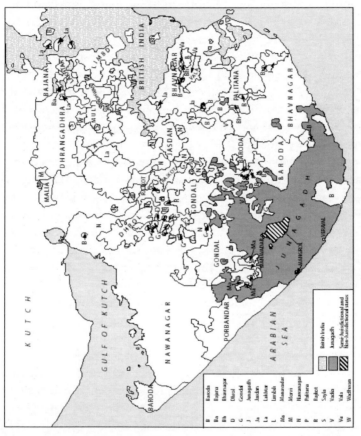

Map 2. Kathiawar before 15 August 1947

to secure Hyderabad's accession by 15 August and asked the Indian government to grant the state two more months. The cabinet assented and asked Mountbatten, who was staying on as governor general, to continue the negotiations.

Kashmir's position was the obverse of Hyderabad's: its ruler, Maharaja Hari Singh, was a Hindu whereas the majority of the state's population was Muslim. For both India and Pakistan, Kashmir was of great importance, not least because of its strategic location. The maharaja, however, vacillated on the issue of accession. By the end of August 1947 the Pakistanis feared Kashmir might join India. To pre-empt this possibility they decided to wrest Kashmir—by force if required.

The most immediate problem confronting the Indian government was, however, Junagadh. The premier state of Kathiawar, Junagadh was ruled by a Muslim nawab, with over 80 per cent of his nearly 700,000 subjects being Hindu. No part of the state's land bordered Pakistan and its main port, Veraval, was about 300 miles from Karachi. Furthermore, the political geography of Kathiawar was an intricate tessellation, with parts of Junagadh embedded in other states of the region and vice versa. The nawab of Junagadh, Muhammad Mahabat Khan, had one consuming passion: animals, especially dogs. His menagerie included 2000 pedigree canines on whose upkeep he expended lavish sums. On one occasion, when two of his favourite hounds mated, the nawab spent Rs 300,000 in celebrations and declared a state holiday as well. The nawab's interest in animals extended to wildlife too. Indeed, his interventions were critical in preserving the Asiatic lion, which was on the verge of extinction. His laudable solicitude for animals apart, the nawab seemed to evince little interest in matters connected with human beings, such as the prospects of those in his state. In the summer of 1947, when the future of his domains hung in the balance, Mahabat Khan was on holiday in Europe.[5]

Junagadh's Accession to Pakistan

At a meeting on 25 July 1947 Junagadh's constitutional adviser told Mountbatten that "he had every intention that it [Junagadh] should

[5] Guha, *India After Gandhi*, 49.

accede to India." He conveyed a similar message to Vallabhbhai Patel.[6] But earlier that year the dewan (chief minister) of Junagadh had invited a Muslim League politician from Karachi, Sir Shah Nawaz Bhutto (father of Pakistan's future prime minister Zulfikar Ali Bhutto), to join the Junagadh State Council. When the dewan went abroad for treatment in May 1947 Bhutto assumed the appointment. Thereafter, links between Junagadh and the leaders of Pakistan were quickly forged. On 16 July Bhutto met Jinnah, who advised him and the nawab "to keep out [of India] under any circumstances until August 15. If per chance we allow our neck to be put under the guillotine, we shall be cut and finished." Jinnah assured Bhutto that he would not allow Junagadh to be "starved out or tyrannized and that Veraval was not far from Karachi."[7] Junagadh in turn managed to mislead Delhi and other neighbouring states by issuing proclamations of Kathiawar unity. On 11 August the nawab, having returned from his European sojourn, informed Jinnah of his decision to join Pakistan and sent a representative for negotiations.[8] When Delhi sent an instrument of accession to Junagadh, Bhutto temporized and replied that the matter was under discussion. On 15 August 1947 Junagadh issued a communiqué announcing accession to Pakistan.

The decision to accede to Pakistan was not conveyed to the Indian government, which only learnt of it from the newspapers. V.P. Menon cabled Bhutto, who confirmed that Junagadh had cast its lot with Pakistan. Junagadh's move startled Delhi for it ran counter to India's interests on several counts. Given the complex political geography of Kathiawar, Junagadh would not merely be an isolated outpost of Pakistan on Indian territory: it could additionally jeopardize the economic and administrative unity of the region. At a time when Punjab was

[6] Aide Memoire on Junagadh and Kashmir, 25 February 1948, enclosed in Mountbatten to the King, 26 February 1948, F200/90D, Mountbatten Papers, Asia, Pacific, and Africa Collection (hereafter APAC), British Library, London.

[7] Bhutto to Jinnah, 11 August 1947, *Jinnah Papers*, ed. Z.H. Zaidi (Islamabad: Quaid-i-Azam Papers Project, Culture Division, Government of Pakistan, 1993–), 4: 324–6.

[8] Nawab to Jinnah, 11 August 1947; Jinnah's reply, 12 August 1947, ibid., 330–1, 341.

riven by communal violence, Menon also worried that Junagadh's decision could stir the cauldron of sectarian tensions. Furthermore, Delhi was concerned that Junagadh's temerity would bolster Hyderabad's obduracy.[9] From the outset, then, the Indians perceived Junagadh's actions as not only impinging upon the security of Kathiawar but also affecting their stance towards Hyderabad. Consequently, concerns over reputation played an important role in India's response to the crisis.

The Indian government wrote to Pakistan's high commissioner on 21 August, drawing attention to considerations of geographical contiguity and the composition of Junagadh's population. The letter also stressed the need for finding out the views of the people on the question of accession. As the accession had not yet been accepted, India asked Pakistan to enunciate its policy. A fortnight later a reminder was sent; but this, too, elicited no response. Even as Pakistan maintained a studied silence, India initiated measures to pressurize Junagadh to withdraw its as yet unaccepted offer of accession. Initially this assumed the form of an embargo on supply into the state of essential items including coal, petroleum, and sugar.[10]

Soon Bhutto was impelled to send Jinnah "a personal appeal for assistance to Junagadh." Junagadh, he wrote, was humming with fantastic rumours put about by Congress sympathizers regarding the consequences of accession to Pakistan. India had stopped the supply of essential items such as coal in order "to paralyze our railway communication." Bhutto thought that Pakistan should "lodge a strong protest" with India and extend its "powerful protection" to Junagadh. Reminding Jinnah of his earlier assurances, Bhutto entreated him to "not abandon Junagadh and its people to be devoured by the wolves."[11]

On 9 September the Pakistan government announced that they had signed a standstill agreement with Junagadh. Nehru now wrote to Prime Minister Liaquat Ali Khan of Pakistan. The states, wrote Nehru,

[9] Menon, *Integration of Indian States*, 127.

[10] Report on Junagadh by V.P. Menon, n.d. (*c.* 21 September 1947), paragraph 21; Note on Junagadh State, n.d. (*c.* 20 October 1947), paragraph 13, in *Sardar Patel's Correspondence 1945–50*, ed. Durga Das (Ahmedabad: Navjivan, 1971–4) (hereafter *SPC*), 7: 694, 700.

[11] Bhutto to Jinnah, 4 September 1947, *Jinnah Papers*, 8: 264–6.

were admittedly free to accede to either dominion; but the choice must "necessarily be made with due regard to its geographical contiguity." Further, 80 per cent of Junagadh's population were Hindus who did not want the state to join Pakistan. India, Nehru stated, "would be prepared to accept any democratic test in respect of the accession . . . ascertained under the joint supervision of Dominion of India and Junagadh." If the nawab would not consent to a referendum, and if Pakistan, "in utter disregard of the wishes of the people" accepted the accession, "the Government of India cannot be expected to acquiesce in such an arrangement."[12] Nehru, in effect, was demanding that the principles governing the Partition of India be applied to Junagadh. The Partition plan had catered for "democratic tests" in provinces whose desire to join Pakistan or India was dubious: votes in the elected assemblies of Bengal and Punjab; referenda in the North West Frontier Province and the Sylhet district of Assam. The proposition that *India* should oversee a referendum in Junagadh was evidently advanced as a bargaining point: Delhi could later claim to make a concession on this aspect.

Pakistan replied the following day to say they had accepted Junagadh's accession. Liaquat later revealed that they had reached the decision after much deliberation. The offer was taken up because the ruler was Muslim and because the port of Veraval was not far from Karachi.[13] For the leaders of Pakistan, who had been forced to settle for a smaller country than they had demanded, the prospect of additional territory was naturally attractive. It is also possible, as claimed by some scholars,[14] that Jinnah had calculated that Junagadh would come in handy in case the ruler of Kashmir decided to join India: a referendum would then have to be applied to both states. But we cannot conclude that Junagadh was solely a bargaining counter for Pakistan. For one thing, by this time Pakistan was already preparing to use force to forestall the possibility of Kashmir's accession to India. For another, Jinnah's stances, both before Independence and after the

[12] Nehru to Liaquat, 12 September 1947, ibid., 269–70.

[13] Note of discussions with PM India and PM Pakistan, 1 October 1947, F200/90B, Mountbatten Papers, APAC.

[14] See, for example, Hodson, *The Great Divide*, 430; Gopal, *Nehru*, 2: 18–19.

Kashmir dispute erupted, suggest that he had no interest in referenda or plebiscites. Pakistan clearly had an intrinsic territorial interest in Junagadh, albeit less than in Kashmir.

Jinnah had, however, miscalculated Pakistan's capability to secure Junagadh's accession militarily in the face of Indian opposition. Prior to the transfer of power the Pakistan army's commander-in-chief (C-in-C) designate, General Frank Messervy, had submitted what Mountbatten described as "a most disturbing paper" on Pakistan's military potential after Partition. Messervy had argued that Pakistan's military capability would be emasculated by a drastic reduction in the number of battalions from sixty-seven to thirty-five. The remainder, too, would be pruned by the departure of Hindu and Sikh companies.[15] To acquaint Jinnah with the position without alarming him Mountbatten had sent him "a bowdlerised version" of the paper. Jinnah would fully be put in the picture only after India deployed its troops around Junagadh. This miscalculation was compounded by Karachi's misapprehension to the effect that Delhi would not respond forcefully to Junagadh's accession to Pakistan. As we shall see, Pakistan's actions in the early stages of the crisis were influenced by this belief.

Once it became obvious that Junagadh would join Pakistan, parts of its territory that had been feudatories grew restive. A portion of the state comprising some fifty villages collectively known as Babariawad was held by a group of "guaranteed landowners." These local grandees proclaimed independence on the grounds that they had been attached to Junagadh by the erstwhile political department: with the dissolution of paramountcy that arrangement no longer held. They then sought the Indian government's permission to accede. After a "rough and ready" assessment of the wishes of the villagers concerned, Delhi accepted Babariawad's accession.[16]

The other states of Kathiawar also raised a chorus of protest at Junagadh's accession to Pakistan. The ruler of Nawanagar came to Delhi and informed the government that the rulers and people of Kathiawar were incensed. It was difficult to restrain their Hindu population from retaliating against the Muslims. Nawanagar made it clear that "unless the Government of India had the will and the capacity to

[15] Viceroy's Personal Report, 8 August 1947, *Transfer of Power*, 12: 599–600.
[16] Note on Junagadh State, n.d. (*c.* 20 October 1947), *SPC*, 7: 697.

prevent Junagadh from going over to Pakistan, the confidence of the Princes as a whole in the value of their own Accession Instruments would be shattered; and the position of Kathiawar states would be particularly seriously jeopardised."[17] He further informed Menon that Kathiawar was aswirl with rumours that Pakistan was offering financial and military assistance to Junagadh.[18]

Pressure from this quarter heightened Delhi's sense of urgency. As a fledgling government trying to brand its authority on a turbulent country, it could hardly afford to lose the confidence of the newly acceded states, and so encourage fissiparous tendencies. Delhi responded by redeploying local troops, particularly to protect Babariawad from punitive action by Junagadh.[19] V.P. Menon, considering this insufficient, sought to persuade Mountbatten of the desirability of making a "military and naval demonstration,"[20] an opinion he is unlikely to have refrained from expressing to Patel as well. Consequently, at a meeting on 17 September the cabinet decided to deploy additional forces around Junagadh. The cabinet also directed Menon to visit Junagadh and explain to the nawab and Bhutto the implications of accession to Pakistan.[21]

Meantime, the local redeployment of Indian troops had touched off the tocsin in Junagadh. Bhutto wrote to Liaquat that these portended an imminent attack and requested Pakistan to protest strongly. "The disputed rights, if any, may be decided by the two Dominions constitutionally on merits." Further, he requested Pakistan to dispatch "a fighter or a bomber" to raise Junagadh's morale. He also asked for a fully equipped battalion and for arrangements to protect Junagadh's sea lines of communication. Bhutto ended his letter on a bleak note: "If Pakistan is unable to come to our rescue at this critical moment, we shall be finished."[22]

---

[17] Aide Memoire on Junagadh and Kashmir, 25 February 1948, F200/90D, Mountbatten Papers, APAC.

[18] Menon, *Integration of Indian States*, 129–30.

[19] Note on Junagadh State, n.d. (*c.* 20 October 1947), *SPC*, 7: 697–9.

[20] Alan Campbell-Johnson, *Mission with Mountbatten* (London: Robert Hale, 1951), 192.

[21] Minutes of Cabinet Meeting, 17 September 1947, MB1/D201, Mountbatten Papers, Southampton University.

[22] Bhutto to Liaquat, 16 September 1947, *Jinnah Papers*, 8: 270–3.

Jinnah cabled a terse message to Mountbatten, warning that any encroachment on Junagadh would amount to a "hostile act."[23] Pakistan also sent a naval sloop with supplies of coal to Junagadh, but did not send any troops.[24] Jinnah evidently thought that Delhi would be chary of making robust moves on the ground. His assessment at this stage was accurate. Mountbatten wrote back that Junagadh's accession to Pakistan had generated "serious concern and apprehensions." Hence, they had deployed "a small force of troops as a very natural precautionary counter-measure." Pakistan's acceptance of Junagadh's accession was "an encroachment on Indian sovereignty and territory... a clear attempt to cause disruption in the integrity of India by extending the influence and boundaries of the Dominion of Pakistan in utter violation of principles on which partition was agreed upon and effected." Mountbatten asked Jinnah to reconsider the accession; else Pakistan would be responsible for the ensuing consequences. He reiterated that Delhi stood for a plebiscite jointly conducted by Junagadh and India.[25]

V.P. Menon Does the Rounds

V.P. Menon, meanwhile, had flown out to confer with the Junagadh authorities.[26] Since the nawab claimed he was indisposed, Menon had a long discussion with Bhutto and argued that Junagadh was so situated that accession to Pakistan created "a pocket of foreign territory" inside Kathiawar. Moreover, the overwhelming Hindu majority was desirous of joining India. Menon made it clear that "this situation could not be tolerated." Bhutto conceded that the majority of the population favoured joining India, although they were heavily influenced by propaganda. He suggested tripartite discussions between India, Pakistan, and Junagadh, and said though he personally favoured

[23] Jinnah to Mountbatten, 19 September 1947, F200/90A, Mountbatten Papers, APAC.

[24] Report on Junagadh by V.P. Menon, n.d. (c. 21 September 1947), SPC, 7: 694.

[25] Mountbatten to Jinnah, 21 September 1947, F200/90A, Mountbatten Papers, APAC.

[26] The next four paragraphs draw upon Report on Junagadh by V.P. Menon, n.d. (c. 21 September 1947), SPC, 7: 688–95. Also see Menon, *Integration of Indian States*, 131–5.

a referendum he could not commit his government to it. Soon after the meeting, Menon learnt that Junagadh's forces had entered Babariawad.

While in Kathiawar, Menon also dealt with the accession of two tiny states: Manavadar and Mangrol. With an area of about a hundred square miles and a large majority of Hindus, Manavadar was surrounded on three sides by Junagadh and on the north by a state that had joined India. The dewan of Manavadar informed Menon that he had decided to join Pakistan. Menon retorted that it was "intolerable that pockets of foreign territory should be created on Indian soil." The dewan seemed nonplussed. He promised to mull over the issue and get back to Menon the next day. He never did.

The situation in Mangrol was somewhat different. This state consisted of forty-two villages, over half of which Junagadh exercised civil and criminal jurisdiction. The arrangement had received the imprimatur of the Raj on the understanding that Junagadh would not misuse its powers. With the lapse of paramountcy, the sheikh of Mangrol had proclaimed independence. Junagadh had refused to countenance this claim. The sheikh now expressed his willingness to join India and promptly signed the instrument of accession. Two days later, however, he wrote that he had signed the instrument hastily and had, upon reconsideration, decided against it.[27] By the time this news of the sheikh's volte face reached Delhi his accession had already been accepted. Besides, the Indian government believed that the sheikh had been forced to revoke his accession by Junagadh, and so in any case chose to ignore his change of mind.

Menon's next stop was Bombay, where he met the home minister of the province, Morarji Desai. Desai informed him that the government and people of Bombay were anxious that Delhi should take a firm line. "The position of the Bombay Government will also to a great extent depend on our attitude in the Junagadh affair. He [Desai] asked me to mention this to the Cabinet with as much emphasis as I could." The pressure on the Indian government was also palpable at Menon's meeting with representatives of the Congress Party and the Indian states peoples' organizations of Kathiawar. They were emphatic that

[27] Regional Commissioner Rajkot to Ministry of States, 21 September 1947, F200/90A, Mountbatten Papers, APAC.

the government had not done enough to secure Babariawad, and that if Delhi gave in on Junagadh "the whole prestige of the Government would suffer badly."

In his memoirs Menon claimed that the Kathiawar leaders were determined to set up a parallel government and organize intense agitation against the nawab: "All I could do . . . was to counsel restraint."[28] In fact, the injudicious idea of a parallel government was suggested by Menon. As he wrote in a report: "I also outlined to them the course of action which they would be well advised to take. They went away quite satisfied."[29] U.N. Dhebar, secretary of the Kathiawar Political Conference, wrote to Patel that the decision had been taken "after fullest discussion with Menon." The people of Junagadh in the "largest possible gathering" would issue a proclamation disavowing accession to Pakistan and establishing a provisional government comprising "the true representatives of the people." The headquarters of the government would be on Indian soil. "As we acquire Junagadh territories, Government will shift there." Menon had assured them that they would receive "moral and material support."[30]

On returning to Delhi, Menon presented a detailed account of his trip to Patel. He argued that the cabinet's decision not to violate Junagadh territory needed to be reconsidered. Junagadh forces were already inside Babariawad; Junagadh was pressurizing Mangrol and would soon occupy it. Both of these would be hostile acts and India should counter them. Menon was clearly reacting to the demands for a tougher stance on Junagadh. He recommended dispatching additional forces to the region and urged the cabinet to review the situation.[31]

The deputy prime minister, however, was not pleased with the decision to form a parallel government. Patel hailed from the same

---

[28] Menon, *Integration of Indian States*, 135.

[29] Report on Junagadh by V.P. Menon, n.d. (*c.* 21 September 1947), *SPC*, 7: 693.

[30] Dhebar to Patel, 21 September 1947, *Sardar's Letters—Mostly Unknown*, ed. Manibehn Patel and G.M. Nandurkar (Ahmedabad: Sardar Vallabhbhai Patel Smarak Bhavan, 1978), 2: 75–6.

[31] Report on Junagadh by V.P. Menon, n.d. (*c.* 21 September 1947), *SPC*, 7: 694–5.

region and spoke the same language as the people of Junagadh. The state's accession to Pakistan, an official observed, touched him "in a particularly 'tender spot.'"[32] But he felt that Junagadh was "a difficult task," for the nawab was merely a marionette in Pakistan's hands. The situation demanded careful handling. He wrote to an advocate of the provisional government: "A hasty step might invite disaster. Some people of Kathiawad [sic] have become impatient, but they are not aware of the entire situation. Only prudence will help us act in the right manner."[33] Nonetheless, at a massive rally in Bombay on 25 September, the provisional government was proclaimed.[34]

It has been claimed that "the 'Provisional Government' [of Juna-gadh] was New Delhi's creation."[35] The available evidence, however, suggests otherwise. Soon after the proclamation, the president of the provisional government, Samaldas Gandhi (a nephew of the Mahatma), wrote to the ministry of states seeking "recognition and assistance from the Government of India." Dhebar wrote to Mountbatten asking for a favourable consideration of the request.[36] But Delhi turned it down. The cabinet felt that the provisional government could not be recogniz-ed unless "India was at war with Junagadh or Pakistan." Recognition "would in itself be tantamount to an act of war" by India. Indeed, "Pakistan had already addressed [the matter] to us saying that the anti-Junagadh agitation had been encouraged by India."[37] Given V.P. Menon's role in the genesis of the provisional government, it is possible that he kept open some channels of communication with Samaldas Gandhi. But it is far from clear that the Indian government was in

[32] Guha, *India After Gandhi*, 50.

[33] Patel to K.M. Munshi, 22 September 1947, *Sardar's Letters—Mostly Unknown*, 2: 76.

[34] The text of the declaration is available in F200/90B, Mountbatten Pap-ers, APAC.

[35] A.G. Noorani, "History as Prison," *Frontline* 22, no. 19 (10 September 2005).

[36] Dhebar to Private Secretary to Governor General, 28 September 1947, F200/90B, Mountbatten Papers, APAC.

[37] Meeting of Cabinet, 1 October 1947, MB1/D202, Mountbatten Papers, Southampton University.

cahoots with the provisional government. A final verdict, however, will have to await the opening of Government of India records pertaining to this episode.

The Options over Junagadh in
Late 1947

On 22 September Mountbatten met Nehru and Patel with the army and navy chiefs to discuss the situation.[38] Mountbatten said he had spoken to Pakistan's prime minister about Junagadh and that Liaquat had struck a defiant note: "All right, go ahead and commit an act of war and see what happens." Mountbatten was convinced that the whole affair was a trap designed to lure India into aggressive action. The governor general's views echoed those of his chief of staff, General Hastings Ismay, who believed that Jinnah "hopes by luring India into a militant reaction to secure a verdict on legal points and to create a valuable precedent . . . For, Junagadh is in some respects a Hyderabad in miniature."[39] V.P. Menon reported on his visit to Junagadh and on the latest developments, including the arrival of a Pakistani sloop and Junagadh's forces in Babariawad. He asserted that India's entry position on Babariawad and Mangrol was "unassailable," indicating that India could use force with impunity.

But the prime minister refused to be hustled, preferring a deliberate and graduated approach. Nehru insisted that "before any military action was taken the constitutional position of Babariawad and Mangrol had to be absolutely straightened out . . . The next step should be to point out the legal position to Junagadh. Only if no action was taken to withdraw their troops should military action start." Force requirements were considered next. Not only did the balance of military capability clearly favour India, the Indian general staff was also well aware of Pakistan's infirmities: the armies were still in the process of being partitioned. The army C-in-C, General Rob Lockhart, thought that "Pakistan would be in no position to take any military

[38] Record of Interview, 22 September 1947, F200/90A, Mountbatten Papers, APAC.

[39] Campbell-Johnson, *Mission with Mountbatten*, 193.

action in Junagadh." Menon chimed in, saying the neighbouring states' forces would also be available to India. The navy chief, Rear Admiral Hall, added that three sloops and two sweepers were at hand. It was decided that the military should prepare plans to occupy Babariawad and assist Mangrol, and that it should be ready, if Junagadh took further aggressive action, to occupy Junagadh itself. Menon was directed to draft a telegram to the Junagadh administration and a statement to the press.[40]

Since there was a possibility of military action, Nehru was keen to forestall adverse international reaction, especially from Britain. If the latter threw its weight behind Pakistan, India's position would be impaired. Nehru wrote to Patel that the situation was "developing rapidly and may lead to all manner of consequences." He suggested that a message be sent to the British government explaining the situation.[41] Patel, however, was "not quite sure whether we need to say anything to the British government at this stage."[42]

The situation was considered at another meeting on 24 September. Mountbatten said he had discussed Mangrol with Sir Walter Monckton, the constitutional adviser to the sheikh of Mangrol. Monckton was certain that Junagadh could no longer claim jurisdiction over parts of Mangrol and that there could be no objection to Indian troops being sent to Mangrol. Monckton also held that the sheikh could not claim to have acceded under duress: if anything, his attempt to resile from it could be challenged on those grounds. The meeting then considered the question of making India's stance clear to the international community. It was agreed that a copy of Nehru's letter to Liaquat, articulating India's position, should be sent to His Majesty's Government.[43]

The following day Delhi issued a press communiqué stating that Junagadh had acceded to Pakistan without any warning. India's representations to Karachi had not evoked any response. Although

[40] Record of Interview, 22 September 1947, F200/90A, Mountbatten Papers, APAC.

[41] Nehru to Patel, 23 September 1947, *SPC*, 7: 384–5.

[42] Patel to Nehru, 24 September 1947, ibid., 385.

[43] Record of Interview, 24 September 1947, F200/90A, Mountbatten Papers, APAC.

Bhutto had suggested discussing the issue at a conference, neither Pakistan nor Junagadh had followed it up. The accession of Junagadh, the communiqué claimed, would be "a source of constant friction." India was "determined to find a solution": a referendum to establish the people's wishes. Whilst India was willing to solve the problem by "friendly discussion," it had an obligation to protect the interests of states within and around Junagadh that had acceded to India. "This responsibility they will fully and faithfully discharge."[44] The statement was aimed at several audiences and intended to convey different messages: to clarify India's interest in the issue to Pakistan and Junagadh but also reassure them that force would not be used if they agreed to a referendum; to assure domestic constituencies that the government was seized of the problem; to demonstrate resolve to the states, especially Hyderabad; and to convince the international community of India's peaceful intentions.

Meantime, Pakistan accelerated its efforts on the diplomatic front. On 22 September Karachi sent a cable challenging Mangrol's accession to India on the grounds that it was not a sovereign entity. Menon had the constitutional position examined and was convinced that the accession was legal. Delhi accordingly responded to Pakistan's representation.[45] Jinnah then wrote to Mountbatten taking the legal high ground: the states were free to join either India or Pakistan; by insisting on geography and religious composition India was "trying to import fresh criteria." Jinnah brusquely turned down the suggestion of a referendum: it was "a matter between Ruler constituted authority and the people of Junagadh." He went on to state that India's "policy and action are infringing the sovereignty of Pakistan."[46]

Junagadh, too, wrote to Delhi, asserting that the accession of Babariawad and Mangrol to India was illegal and unacceptable. The nawab also refused India's demand to remove his troops from Babariawad. Patel took a grim view of Junagadh's stance.[47] These developments

---

[44] Communiqué, 25 September 1947, ibid.

[45] Menon to Brockman, 24 September 1947; New Delhi to Karachi, 24 September 1947, ibid.

[46] Jinnah to Mountbatten, 25 September 1947, ibid.

[47] Menon, *Integration of Indian States*, 137–8.

were discussed at a meeting on 27 September.[48] N.G. Ayyangar (minister without portfolio) remarked that "it was strictly and legally correct" for any state to have joined either dominion. Patel, however, argued that the decision lay with the people and not with the ruler. Furthermore, the larger, reputational, implications of the problem had to be considered: "if India did not now support the popular demand of the people of Junagadh, there was a danger that Hyderabad would decide to accede to Pakistan." For, at this point, the nizam of Hyderabad was staunchly opposed to the idea of accession to India, offering instead to conclude a "Treaty of Association" with Delhi. When Mountbatten interjected, arguing that the nizam had assured him on this count, Patel sardonically remarked that Junagadh had given two such assurances before joining Pakistan. Junagadh, he argued, had already committed "an act of war" in sending troops to Babariawad. Ayyangar concurred with Patel that India had the right to send troops to Babariawad and Mangrol.

Mountbatten suggested that Junagadh's aggression be referred to the United Nations. Patel demurred. "There was a grave disadvantage in being a plaintiff in such cases. Possession was nine cases of the law." Nehru and Ayyangar also opposed this course. Anxious to head off military action against Babariawad, Mountbatten underscored the danger that the ongoing preparations might culminate in fighting in Babariawad. This would create "an enormous sensation in the world." In the end it was agreed that confirmatory legal advice would be sought; that Nehru would fully explain the legal position in a telegram to Liaquat and demand the withdrawal of Junagadh's troops from Babariawad; and that Nehru would discuss the issue at his next meeting with Liaquat. But military preparations would not be delayed.[49]

The chiefs of staff now threw a spanner in the works. In a joint paper they expressed their concerns over the possible outcome of the measures being initiated on Mangrol and Babariawad. Whatever the plan, there was "a very real danger of a clash" with Junagadh forces. Moreover, Pakistan might extend support to the latter. Thus, "military

[48] Note of meeting, 27 September 1947, F200/90A, Mountbatten Papers, APAC.
[49] Ibid.

action in Kathiawar may lead to a war between the two dominions and with the bulk of the army involved in Internal Security the army is in no position to wage war." This assessment, of course, ran contrary to the army chief's earlier assertion that Pakistan was incapable of assisting Junagadh. The actual reason for the chiefs' stance was stated in the penultimate paragraph: the position of British officers including the chiefs themselves. "These officers belong to the British Fighting services and it would be impossible for any of them to take part in a war." The paper concluded by urging that the movement of troops be stopped and that the Junagadh dispute be settled by negotiations.[50]

The chiefs' paper did not dilate on their real concern for the position of British officers: the "stand down" instructions issued to British personnel serving with Indian and Pakistani armed forces. These instructions required all British officers to step aside in the event of war between the two dominions; for British officers serving on the same list and owing allegiance to their king could not fight each other. Be that as it may, the concluding paragraphs of the paper suggested that British officers in the Indian armed forces would not carry out the government's directions. In any event, the military chiefs were obviously exceeding their bounds in offering political advice.

The cabinet met late next evening to review the situation. Nehru wrote to Mountbatten saying there was "considerable feeling over this matter." Patel appears to have pressed for moving troops into Babariawad. But it was the chiefs' paper which roused the ministers' ire. "In effect," Nehru observed, "it was an announcement that they could not carry out the Government's policy in case they didn't agree with it." Another cabinet meeting was scheduled for the following evening to which the chiefs of staff were invited.[51] To avert the possibility of a showdown between his ministers and the chiefs, the governor general summoned Lockhart and got him to retract from the position stated in the letter. Mountbatten's chief of staff, Ismay, drafted a letter from Lockhart to Nehru which stated that the chiefs had only desired to put forward military considerations as discussed with the defence minister. The letter also clarified that all British officers in India and Pakistan

[50] Projected Operations in Kathiawar, 27 September 1947, ibid.
[51] Nehru to Mountbatten, 28 September 1947, ibid.

were currently on a single service list: all of them continued to serve the British monarch and hence could not wage war against each other.[52]

On the evening of 29 September, Mountbatten met Nehru and Patel and handed them Lockhart's letter. Mountbatten suggested that to ensure coordination between the civilian and military leaders, and to preclude the possibility of such misunderstandings, a defence committee of the cabinet be formed. They then discussed the situation in Junagadh. In a note composed later, Mountbatten claimed that he had saved the government from collapsing. "Patel had told Nehru that he intended to resign unless the Cabinet backed his aggressive policy against Junagadh."[53]

Despite being self-serving,[54] parts of the account are plausible. First, Mountbatten and Nehru convinced Patel to put off action against Babariawad. Second, Mountbatten urged Nehru to inform Pakistan about the impending movement of troops. Third, he suggested that the prime minister make a statement that, in the case of states whose accession was disputed by the people or which had not yet acceded, India would go by the will of the people. In particular, this would apply to states where the ruler and the majority of the population belonged to different communities.

Mountbatten's suggestion to form a defence committee of the cabinet was accepted by the Indian government. Owing to Mountbatten's military background and Ismay's familiarity with the functioning of

---

[52] Lockhart to Nehru, 29 September 1947, ibid.

[53] Notes on 29 September—The Junagadh Crisis, 30 September 1947, ibid. Mountbatten was clearly exaggerating the differences between Nehru and Patel. For instance, he claimed to have prevented a split "with the assistance of Nehru who no longer insisted on taking the case to UNO." In fact, Nehru had already expressed his opposition to doing so in the previous meeting. Similarly, Mountbatten asserted that he had worked out a *via media* by getting them to divert the force being sent to Veraval to Porbandar instead. Veraval was Junagadh's main port and there were no plans to send troops there.

[54] Menon had apparently told him that "unless I was able to pull off another miracle . . . the Government of India would split within 24 hours and disaster would take over the country;" "The Prime Minister had said that if the Cabinet at any time over-rode my advice, he himself would resign;" "The Deputy Prime Minister had said that he had eaten out of my hand from the day I had arrived;" and so on.

the committee system in Britain during the Second World War, the governor general was asked to act as chairman of the committee. This has led some scholars to conclude that Mountbatten exercised great influence on matters of foreign policy and strategy. Chandrashekar Dasgupta writes, for instance, that "A vitally important Cabinet committee was headed not by the Prime Minister but by the Governor-General, who thereby acquired a major role in the executive branch of the state."[55] Mountbatten's biographer asserts that "he [Mountbatten] was virtually acting as Prime Minister" on strategic issues.[56] These arguments, however, rest on a less than critical reading of the notes and memoranda dictated by Mountbatten, almost invariably with an eye on posterity. The chairmanship certainly offered Mountbatten an opportunity to vent his views, volubly and persistently; but he seldom carried the day against the wishes of his ministers.

Nehru's Junagadh Strategy

In a policy note which he prepared on the night of 29 September 1947, Nehru spliced together the various strands of his thinking about the crisis.[57] This crucial document has for some reason been excluded from Nehru's own *Selected Works* and is available only in the Mountbatten papers. But it deserves much wider attention for it provides a close insight into Nehru's approach to strategy and crisis management.

The nub of the matter, wrote Nehru, was that the crisis was a conflict between India and Pakistan. The Pakistan government claimed that both Mangrol and Babariawad were parts of Junagadh, and, following the last's accession, were part of Pakistan. While the claim had "little basis in law," it meant that any action by India might be characterized by Pakistan as aggression against its territory. Still, Junagadh's move against Babariawad had to be countered. Interestingly, domestic and reputational considerations played an important role in

[55] Dasgupta, *War and Diplomacy*, 26. Also see, Narendra Singh Sarila, *The Shadow of the Great Game: The Untold Story of India's Partition* (London: Constable, 2006), 357.

[56] Philip Zeigler, *Mountbatten: The Official Biography* (Glasgow: William Collins, 1985), 445.

[57] The following five paragraphs draw upon Note on Junagadh by Nehru, 29 September 1947, F200/246, Mountbatten Papers, APAC.

Nehru's reasoning: "[if] Junagadh's aggression is tolerated, then the prestige of the Government of India suffers greatly with disastrous results in Kathiawar and in other states. This is likely to affect the position of Hyderabad also. It may be followed by other acts of aggression by Pakistan authorities. Each particular act may be relatively small. But it will help in breaking up the states acceding to the Union." Pakistan and Junagadh had refused to withdraw forces from Babariawad. Militarily, it would be easy to dislodge them. But Nehru was worried about the chances of escalation: "The only difficulty that arises is the possibility of conflict with Pakistan leading to some incident which might provoke war."

The prospect of war seemed to Nehru highly undesirable. "War at any time is to be avoided;" there were additional reasons for avoiding it now. For one thing, the government was new and had had no time to settle down. For another, the army was being reorganized and a war at this juncture might do "grave injury" to it. For a third, given the turmoil in Punjab, a war would be disastrous for the minority communities in both countries, potentially imperilling the lives of up to two million people forced into migrating across the newly drawn border in Punjab. A far greater number of Muslims in India would be endangered and "it might be impossible for Government of India to protect Muslims all over India." Finally, a war would dent India's international standing and might place it in an unfavourable position at the UN.

What, then, could India do? Nehru outlined a strategy of compellence. Indian forces, including tanks, should be deployed round Junagadh and at the borders of Mangrol and Babariawad. Naval sloops and some aircraft should also be stationed hard by. "The forces we gather in Kathiawar should be enough to deal with the whole Junagadh problem if necessary." This would present a serious threat: "It will shake up the security of Junagadh and be a continuous danger to Pakistan in Kathiawar . . . The policy outlined above will keep the initiative in our hands, will exercise a strangling pressure on Junagadh State." The costs of complying with India's demands would then seem acceptable. There would be ancillary pay-offs, too: "Public opinion in India will be satisfied that something at last has been done. Public opinion in Kathiawar will be reassured." More important, India would "avoid an armed conflict leading to war."

To obviate the possibility of escalation Nehru suggested that Indian troops should not pass through Junagadh. Nor should any forces enter Babariawad or Mangrol until "definite orders" were given. The establishment of a provisional government by the people would impose additional pressure: "How this government will function is not known. But there can be little doubt that it will make the position of the Ruler of Junagadh difficult in the extreme."

This course of action would at once "indicate to all concerned that we mean business" and "avoid any act which may be described as aggressive and leading possibly to armed conflict." Of course, "if any further aggressive step is taken by Pakistan authorities in Kathiawar we must immediately counter it." It was conceivable that Pakistan would appeal to the UN and the latter would issue some directions: "If so, we shall naturally abide by these directions." For the present, Karachi should be informed that India did not accept Junagadh's accession to Pakistan; that India disagreed with Pakistan's contentions regarding Mangrol and Babariawad; and that Junagadh's forces must be withdrawn from Babariawad. Nehru also wanted to reassure Pakistan of India's intentions and of the limited nature of its demands. He suggested that Karachi be told about the troop movements made by India. Delhi should also clarify that it wanted an amicable solution and so it proposed that "wherever there is a dispute in regard to any territory, the matter should be decided by a referendum or plebiscite of the people concerned. We shall accept the result of this referendum whatever it may be." In short, Nehru was prepared for a referendum in Kashmir and Hyderabad, as well as in Junagadh.

The following day, 30 September, Nehru expounded this policy at a meeting of the Provisional Defence Committee. During the discussion it was suggested that Junagadh should be denied permission to move troops across Indian territory to reach its outlying enclaves. A reciprocal ban on the movement of Indian troops across Junagadh territory was likely and would be accepted. The committee directed the military chiefs to outline plans accordingly.[58] The cabinet, too,

---

[58] Provisional Defence Committee Meeting, 30 September 1947, ibid; Nehru's note for cabinet ministers, 30 September 1947, F200/90A, Mountbatten Papers, APAC.

approved of the measures recommended by the prime minister, agreeing that if Junagadh forces in Babariawad were withdrawn "the urgency of the present situation would be removed."[59]

The Prime Ministers Meet in Delhi

On 1 October Nehru, Liaquat, and Mountbatten met and discussed Junagadh. The Pakistani prime minister had come to Delhi for a meeting of the Joint Defence Council. Chaired by Mountbatten, the council supervised the division of armed forces between India and Pakistan. Mountbatten used this opportunity to bring together the two prime ministers for a discussion.[60] At the meeting Mountbatten informed Liaquat that, according to Walter Monckton, Mangrol could claim independence from Junagadh and join India. The Pakistani prime minister retorted that the sheikh had renounced his accession. Mountbatten objected, saying there was a good case to be made for the sheikh having acted under duress. Liaquat said that, in the light of Monckton's opinion, he would re-examine the matter. Nehru observed that the position of Babariawad was analogous and asked Liaquat to remove Junagadh's troops from there. As if on cue, a telegram was received stating that Junagadh's forces had entered Mangrol. Nehru requested that these, too, be withdrawn. Liaquat agreed to consider the matter. Interestingly, he added that Karachi had no intention of sending troops to Junagadh.[61]

Liaquat's statement reflected Pakistan's belated realization that it was militarily incapable of securing Junagadh's accession. Jinnah was now fully aware of Pakistan's military position and the scales had dropped from his eyes.[62] Indeed, at a meeting of Pakistani civil and military officials Liaquat frankly acknowledged "the weakness of the

---

[59] Meeting of Cabinet, 1 October 1947, F200/90B, Mountbatten Papers, APAC.

[60] Campbell-Johnson, *Mission with Mountbatten*, 214–15.

[61] Discussion with PM India and PM Pakistan, 1 October 1947, F200/90B, Mountbatten Papers, APAC. Also see, Note of talk with Nehru by Ismay, 3 October 1947, 3/7/68, Ismay Papers, Liddell Hart Centre for Military Archives (LHCMA), London.

[62] Ayesha Jalal, *The State of Martial Rule: The Origins of Pakistan's Political Economy of Defence* (Cambridge: Cambridge University Press, 1990), 44.

Pakistan army, particularly in the matter of equipment and stores, and the necessity therefore of preventing any clash between Pakistan and India."[63]

Nehru was relieved that the possibility of war had receded. He expressed satisfaction and assured Liaquat that Indian troops would not enter Junagadh territory, nor would they be sent to Mangrol and Babariawad until the legal position was clarified. Mountbatten informed Liaquat of the move of troops to Kathiawar. When Liaquat remonstrated, Nehru tried to reassure him, claiming that "we are protecting all the peoples of this State [sic] whom Junagadh's action had frightened so much." Although he disavowed aggressive intent, Nehru insisted that "the whole Junagadh question must be reviewed." In such cases, the will of the people should be ascertained; India would abide by their decision. Mountbatten hastened to add that this applied to *any* state. The implications for Kashmir were obvious.[64] Nehru wrote to Liaquat the next day, reiterating his request to have Junagadh's forces in Babariawad and Mangrol "withdrawn immediately." This would ease the tension and help arrive at a peaceable solution consonant with the people's wishes. He would await Liaquat's response before issuing a press communiqué.[65]

Meanwhile, the so-called provisional government had arrived at Rajkot amidst fanfare and forcibly taken possession of Junagadh House in the town. Shortly thereafter the Indian government took over the estates of Sardargadh and Bantwa. These had been attached to Junagadh under the Attachment Scheme of 1943, which had terminated with the lapse of paramountcy. After a request from the officials and people of these estates, Delhi had assumed the residuary jurisdiction exercised by the Raj in the pre-attachment period. This had been announced in the Government of India's communiqué of 13 August 1947 and had been intimated to Junagadh on 25 August. The administration was taken over on 1 October.[66]

[63] Entry of 2 October 1947, Diary 1947–8, Mss Eur D670/6, Cunningham Papers, APAC.

[64] Discussion with PM India and PM Pakistan, 1 October 1947, F200/90B, Mountbatten Papers, APAC.

[65] Nehru to Liaquat, 2 October 1947, ibid.

[66] Menon, *Integration of Indian States*, 139.

Penned in by Indian troops and confronted with the spectre of a local uprising, Bhutto frantically asked Pakistan for assistance. "It is essential," he implored, "that we should have aeroplanes at our disposal and also an armed force." An attack on Babariawad seemed imminent. He hoped that by the time Karachi acted Junagadh would not be "overwhelmed by superior forces hanging over us."[67] Despite its military weakness and its desire to avoid a clash with India, Pakistan could hardly afford to ignore these requests. The onerous task of asserting its hold on the provinces would be greatly hindered if the Pakistan government was seen as backing out of a commitment to Junagadh. Pakistan, therefore, responded by offering a few companies of armed police. But Bhutto wanted more and declined the offer.

Once it became evident that Pakistan could not respond robustly, there was increased pressure on the Indian prime minister to act decisively. The military chiefs expected that, as the pressure progressively built up, Junagadh would request Pakistan for assistance. But Pakistan could only reinforce Junagadh to "a limited degree," a view seconded by Liaquat having already said that Pakistan would not send in troops. Nonetheless, the chiefs recommended that "if Pakistan shows any sign of acceding to a request from Junagadh for reinforcements it will be desirable to set in motion any direct military action which Government of India may have in mind (e.g. placing Indian troops in Babariawad) as early as possible."[68] The deputy prime minister, too, was raring to send troops into Babariawad and Mangrol. Patel was sure that Pakistan was merely posturing: "They will either have to go to war which I personally think they are in no position to do, or they will be exposed for the weak and blustering State that they are."[69]

The Defence Committee met again on 4 October. It approved the chiefs of staffs' appreciation with minor amendments. Nehru then gave an account of his discussion with Liaquat. He had received no reply to his message sent the following day. But Pakistan had since sent

[67] Bhutto to Ikramullah (copy to Jinnah), 3 October 1947, *Jinnah Papers*, 8: 327.

[68] Joint Appreciation of Situation in Kathiawar, 2 October 1947, F200/90B, Mountbatten Papers, APAC.

[69] Note of interview with Patel and Menon, 3 October 1947, F200/195B, Mountbatten Papers, APAC.

a telegram describing the creation of a provisional government as an unfriendly act and demanding removal of the economic blockade. The committee decided to inform Pakistan that they were not interfering with the provisional government, nor should Karachi: the issue should be decided by the people of Junagadh. India should insist again on the withdrawal of Junagadh's forces from Babariawad and Mangrol. "If this demand was finally refused, it would have to be decided what action India would take." [70]

V.P. Menon observed that the accession of Babariawad and Mangrol to India was legally sound. Patel favoured escalation. He argued that "if the Government of India supported Babariawad and Mangrol, the question of Junagadh would itself be speedily settled." At length, the committee agreed that the chiefs should direct the commander of the "Kathiawar Defence Force" to formulate a plan to occupy Babariawad and Mangrol "with the object of avoiding an exchange of shots, as far as possible."

The Indian prime minister cabled his Pakistani counterpart, denying that the provisional government had been "set up or encouraged by Government of India or any authority subordinate to them." It was an outcome of popular resentment against Junagadh's accession; the best way to deal with it was to hold a referendum. Nehru claimed that the entry of Junagadh forces into Mangrol was "a unilateral act of aggression," off-kilter with Pakistan's calls for friendly negotiations. He then laid out a sharp choice for Pakistan to make: "The only basis on which friendly negotiations can start and be fruitful is reversion, in Junagadh, Babariawad and Mangrol to the status quo preceding the accession of Junagadh to Pakistan. The alternative to negotiation is a referendum or plebiscite by the people of Junagadh."[71] The Indians knew they held all the aces.

Pakistan in turn played for time. Liaquat replied that he was prepared to ask Junagadh to withdraw its troops if India promised not to send troops into Junagadh, Mangrol, and Babariawad. The Indian

[70] Defence Committee of the Cabinet (hereafter DCC) Meeting, 4 October 1947, F200/246, Mountbatten Papers, APAC.

[71] Nehru to Liaquat, 5 October 1947, F200/90B, Mountbatten Papers, APAC.

troops in Sardargadh and Bantwa should be withdrawn simultaneously with the removal of Junagadh's forces. Furthermore, Mangrol
and Babariawad's status should be referred for arbitration. If these
conditions were acceptable, Pakistan would issue instructions to Junagadh. Liaquat wrote saying he hoped these measures would pave
the way for discussion of the "conditions and circumstances in
which Plebiscite should be taken by any State or states."[72] Liaquat was
obviously suggesting that Pakistan would demand a plebiscite in Kashmir as well as in Junagadh. In retrospect, it is evident that this was a
tactical stance; for preparations to invade Kashmir were proceeding
apace in Pakistan.[73]

The Indian prime minister responded by presenting his case on
Sardargadh and Bantwa. He drew Liaquat's attention to a press communiqué stating that Indian troops would not enter Junagadh or
Babariawad or Mangrol. Nehru noted that whilst Liaquat had advanced suggestions on Babariawad and Mangrol, he had elided the central
issue of Junagadh. "In our opinion it is essential to reach a settlement
on this fundamental issue first." Once a referendum was agreed upon for Junagadh, the subsidiary issues of Babariawad and Mangrol
could easily be settled.[74] Clearly, Delhi was determined to press home
its advantages.

On 7 October 1947 Pakistan issued a press note detailing its case.
The note sought to confute India's claims about the accession of
Junagadh, Babariawad, and Mangrol. Pakistan was ready both to refer
Mangrol for legal opinion if India withdrew from Sardargadh and
Bantwa, and to discuss the conditions for plebiscite in any state or
states.[75] But Liaquat did not respond to Nehru's message.

A week later Delhi was informed that Junagadh troops had crossed the territory of another state that had acceded to India in order to
enter a pocket of Junagadh territory. The prime minister was peeved
at this seemingly "deliberate flouting of our proposals." "All this," he
wrote to Mountbatten, "is rather difficult to swallow and we can

---

[72] Liaquat to Nehru, 5 October 1947, ibid.

[73] For a full discussion with the evidence, see chapter 4.

[74] Nehru to Liaquat, 6 October 1947, F200/90B, Mountbatten Papers,
APAC.

[75] Press Note, 7 October 1947, *Jinnah Papers*, 8: 346–8.

hardly sit by watching these developments." As earlier, domestic and reputational concerns weighed heavily in his thinking. The smaller states of Kathiawar, he noted, were nervous and frightened, and were appealing to Delhi for assistance and protection.[76] At a cabinet meeting Nehru stated that Pakistan had neither replied to his last message nor withdrawn Junagadh's troops. The latest moves by Junagadh had coincided with a visit by a senior Pakistani minister to the state. "This state of affairs was unsatisfactory."[77]

Spurred by these occurrences, Nehru cabled Liaquat. India had waited long for a reply to its urgent request. Meanwhile, further incursions had taken place. All this "does not encourage the conclusion that you desire an amicable settlement." Nehru asked for an immediate reply on whether Junagadh's troops would be withdrawn from Babariawad and Mangrol, and whether they would refrain from entering Indian soil. The alternative was obvious: "The undertaking we gave not to enter Junagadh territory was based on reciprocal action on the other side."[78]

The Military Options in Junagadh

Mountbatten was in Lahore the next day and spoke to the Pakistani prime minister. Liaquat, he could see, was persisting with his dilatory tactics: "he was prepared to ask Junagadh to withdraw their troops from Babariawad and Mangrol on the condition that we disband our concentration of troops." When Mountbatten retorted that India was entitled to station troops on its own territory, Liaquat bristled, "How would you like if I sent a lot of Pakistan troops into Junagadh by air or sea?" Mountbatten changed tack and urged him to agree to a plebiscite in Junagadh. Liaquat said that "he might consider that if the same general principle was to apply to other cases." He was ready to discuss the issue with Nehru but, being unwell, could not fly out to Delhi.[79] Liaquat sent a telegram to Nehru on 19 October expressing

---

[76] Nehru to Mountbatten, 15 October 1947, F200/90C, Mountbatten Papers, APAC.

[77] Meeting of Cabinet, 15 October 1947, ibid.

[78] Nehru to Liaquat, 16 October 1947, ibid.

[79] Mountbatten to Nehru, 18 October 1947, ibid.

hope that the question of plebiscites in states could soon be discussed
by them; he said he had directed Junagadh to withdraw troops from
Babariawad and Mangrol; he asked India to pull out forces from Sardargadh and Bantwa.

Delhi took umbrage at Junagadh's seeming refusal to remove its
troops despite Liaquat's assurance. Moreover, Junagadh officials had
started collecting rent and imposing fines in these areas. Babariawad
had already threatened to retract its accession if India refused armed
support. Patel threw his weight behind military action in Babariawad
and Mangrol and asked for a meeting of the Defence Committee.[80]

On 21 October the Defence Committee considered the latest communication from Pakistan.[81] Liaquat, Mountbatten remarked, had
indicated that he would be prepared to consider a plebiscite. Nehru
rejoined that the principle had come up several times. He had no doubt
that Pakistan's stance was based on its hopes for Kashmir—"Pakistan's
main objective at the present time." The committee decided that since
Liaquat was unwell, Menon could fly to Lahore to discuss the matter with him. Patel complained that by procrastinating on Babariawad and Mangrol the government was facing serious domestic
difficulties. He argued that the aim of sending Indian troops was to
enable a plebiscite; he was suggesting no action that might hinder a
final decision. Menon pointed out that Junagadh officials were
gathering the harvest in Babariawad and unless action was taken by
10 November the entire harvest would be removed.

The prime minister now agreed that further delay on Babariawad
and Mangrol would be to Pakistan's advantage. He emphasized that by
sending troops into these places India could dismantle Junagadh's administrative machinery. Nehru evidently felt that if Junagadh continued to administer these places India's claim might be diluted. As
Patel had observed, possession was nine-tenths of the law. Moreover,
these moves would signal Delhi's resolve, and so enhance the credi-
bility of the threat to Junagadh. The committee agreed that action in
Babariawad was more urgent than in Mangrol and should be taken

[80] Crum to Lockhart, 20 October 1947, ibid.
[81] The next three paragraphs are based on DCC Meeting, 21 October 1947,
F200/246, Mountbatten Papers, APAC.

at the earliest. The people's wishes regarding accession would there-after be ascertained. Mountbatten suggested that troops should enter Babariawad with a flag of truce and with overwhelming superiority to preclude resistance. Simultaneously, a press statement amplify-ing India's case should be issued. Mountbatten subsequently wrote to the British king: "I came to the conclusion that I could not, short of threatening to resign myself, stay the hands of my Ministers any longer, and would have to accept with good grace their unanimous decisions."[82]

Nehru cabled Liaquat that Junagadh had not responded to Pakis-tan's directives. Its authorities were taking oppressive action against the people of Babariawad. The chieftains and the people had sought India's protection, and Delhi was "honour bound to give this protec-tion by such action as may be considered necessary." The position of Sardargadh and Bantwa, as explained earlier, was entirely different. Nehru further suggested that if Liaquat was unable to travel to Delhi to discuss the details of plebiscite, Menon could meet him at Lahore.[83]

Meantime the question of Manavadar came to the fore. This tiny state, we may recall, had been asked by Menon to reconsider its decision to accede to Pakistan but had evaded him. Delhi now received reports that the khan of Manavadar was arresting local leaders and harassing the people; unless swift action was taken there was danger of a flare up which could spread to the neighbouring states. Patel discussed the situation with Nehru and they decided to send a small police force to occupy Manavadar.[84]

The Defence Committee met on 23 October to consider the ins-tructions for the impending operation—"Exercise Peace" as the chiefs named it.[85] Menon recalled that the committee had previously decid-ed that action should be taken in Babariawad before Mangrol. He now advocated simultaneous action. If troops entered Babariawad first, Pakistan and Junagadh might anticipate the move against Mangrol

[82] Cited in Hodson, *The Great Divide*, 437.

[83] Nehru to Liaquat, 21 October 1947, F200/90C, Mountbatten Papers, APAC.

[84] Menon, *Integration of Indian States*, 141.

[85] See Draft Army Headquarters India "Exercise Peace" Instruction no. 2, F200/90C, Mountbatten Papers, APAC.

by stationing a sloop outside that territory. It was agreed, at length, that the operations should be concurrent. To ensure this the operation in Babariawad might be delayed by a couple of days. The committee chose 1 November as the last possible date to launch the operations. It emphasized that orders must be issued to prevent any communal incident: Muslims had to be afforded complete protection.[86]

Since no reply had been received from Pakistan regarding Menon's proposed visit, the prime minister's private secretary was told to speak to his counterpart. The latter informed him that Liaquat had asked the Pakistan cabinet to consider the matter and was awaiting their response.[87] A message from Liaquat to Nehru was telegraphed the next morning. It underlined that Pakistan was prepared to discuss a plebiscite or referendum in "Any State or states . . . You must have no doubt realised that Junagadh is not the only State regarding which this question arises." Menon should, therefore, come to Karachi for preliminary discussions with the ministry of foreign affairs.[88] Delhi now realized that Karachi was marking time.

Junagadh and Kashmir

Even as these exchanges occurred, a Pakistan-abetted tribal invasion of Kashmir was under way. On 22 October 1947 nearly 5000 tribesmen seized the towns of Muzaffarabad and Domel; Uri fell soon after; and the raiders surged towards Srinagar. A beleaguered and panicky maharaja asked Delhi for military assistance. On 26 October the Defence Committee decided to airlift troops to Srinagar. It was also agreed that Kashmir's accession would be accepted subject to the proviso that a plebiscite would be held in Kashmir when the situation permitted. The same day Nehru cabled Liaquat, reiterating India's desire for a plebiscite in Junagadh: "It is and always has been our view that where there is a dispute plebiscite or referendum should be held

[86] DCC Meeting, 23 October 1947, F200/246, Mountbatten Papers, APAC.

[87] Iengar to Brockman, 23 October 1947, F200/90C, Mountbatten Papers, APAC.

[88] Liaquat to Nehru, 24 October 1947, ibid.

in any State or states." Holding one in Junagadh was a "matter of practical urgency;" hence India's suggestion that Menon meet Liaquat at Lahore. Nehru thought that preliminary discussions at Karachi would not help for the question could only be settled at the ministerial level.[89]

By this time the provisional government of Junagadh had set in train an insurrection against the nawab. As one of its champions recalled it, "Young men from all over Saurashtra [Kathiawar] flocked to its banner of freedom. Large sums of money flowed in, volunteers were armed and trained . . . [on] October 24, 1947 the volunteers of the Provisional Government began their operations. People rose against the Nawab's rule in several parts of Junagadh."[90] The economic and military blockade imposed by India had by now begun to cripple Junagadh: the state's sources of revenue had plummeted and the food situation was desperate. Whilst the military threat from India remained, Pakistan had offered nothing beyond a few companies of armed police. Consequently the nawab, leaving Shah Nawaz Bhutto in charge, decamped to Karachi towards the end of October 1947.[91]

The Junagadh State Council sent its senior member, Harvey Jones, to inform the Pakistan government of its dire straits. In a letter to Jinnah on 27 October, Bhutto painted a dismal picture. The Muslims of Junagadh, he claimed, had despaired of Pakistan. He sarcastically observed that he had refused Pakistan's offer of seven companies of police because it would have been "sheer wastage of human material and equipment." The situation had so deteriorated that responsible Muslims were pressing him to break the impasse. Bhutto concluded his plaintive missive by urging Jinnah to arrange a meeting of Indian and Pakistani representatives forthwith.[92]

Meanwhile, Mountbatten made a final attempt to persuade the Indian government to stay its hand in Kathiawar. At a Defence

[89] Nehru to Liaquat, 26 October 1947, *Jinnah Papers*, 8: 368.

[90] K.M. Munshi, *Somanatha: The Shrine Eternal* (Bombay: Bharatiya Vidya Bhavan, 1965), 65.

[91] On the nawab's hasty departure, see Oral History Transcript (hereafter OHT), H.C. Sarin, 198–9, NMML. Sarin was private secretary to the then defence minister, Sardar Baldev Singh.

[92] Bhutto to Jinnah, 27 October 1947, cited in Menon, *Integration of Indian States*, 142–3.

Committee meeting on 28 October he said that they must review the situation in light of the developments in Kashmir.[93] India had declared its readiness to hold a plebiscite in Kashmir following the restoration of law and order; Pakistan would accept one in Junagadh. India was therefore "in a very strong position." Plans to enter Babariawad and Mangrol under a flag of truce could miscarry and result in bloodshed, weakening India's case. Nehru agreed that the risks of military action in Kathiawar had to be re-evaluated. If there was any chance that it would affect the military effort in Kashmir, it might be better to deal with "the major problem—Kashmir—first." Besides, other implications, such as world opinion and the legal position, would have to be weighed.

Patel sharply differed and argued against any change in plans. So far as international opinion was concerned, he felt that the longer the Junagadh issue persisted the more intractable it would become. He was certain that not a shot would have to be fired in Babariawad or Mangrol. After further discussion, Patel relented. The committee decided that if Pakistan accepted an immediate plebiscite in Junagadh, the military action scheduled to take place on 1 November would be cancelled.

When no response was received from Pakistan by 30 October, the Defence Committee met in Nehru's absence (caused by illness) to authorize military action in both places. Mountbatten made a final attempt to postpone action by suggesting that the police would be more suitable for the operation. Patel testily replied that he saw no objection to using the armed forces. Besides, "he was much opposed to any further delay taking place." Patel added that Mountbatten should inform Jinnah about these steps when they met in Lahore. The committee further decided that Mountbatten would ask the Pakistani leaders to agree to the general principle of ascertaining the people's wishes and that a draft joint statement should be prepared.[94]

Mountbatten and Ismay went to Lahore on 1 November 1947 and met Pakistan's governor general. When Mountbatten suggested

---

[93] DCC Meeting, 28 October 1947, F200/246, Mountbatten Papers, APAC.

[94] DCC Meeting, 30 October 1947, ibid.

plebiscites, Jinnah argued that a plebiscite was "redundant and undesirable." If India would hand him Kashmir, he would let go of Junagadh. Mountbatten made it clear that this would be unacceptable to his government. The discussion failed to make headway.[95] The reasoning behind Jinnah's stance will be explored subsequently; suffice it to note here that it was animated by calculations over Kashmir and Hyderabad.

Junagadh Capitulates

Even as Mountbatten and Jinnah met, Indian troops took over Babariawad and Mangrol. The director of military operations informed the Defence Committee that Babariawad had been peacefully occupied. Most of the Junagadh armed police in the state had withdrawn hours before the entry of Indian troops; the remainder had surrendered. In Mangrol, too, there had been no incident. The defence minister told the committee that he was issuing orders for the withdrawal of superfluous forces from the area.[96]

By now the provisional government had begun to occupy patches of Junagadh territory that lay outside the state. The Junagadh administration viewed these with mounting concern. The nawab cabled Bhutto, asking him to use his "judicious discrimination as the situation demands to avoid bloodshed."[97] On 2 November the provisional government took over the town of Nawagadh, and then Kutyana. In the latter, the rebels met some resistance and in turn indulged in arson and looting. Soon it was obvious that the Junagadh government could not hold out much longer. Menon thought that it would "crumble in 15–20 days time."[98] It happened sooner. The Junagadh State Council decided on 5 November that owing to the profusion of

[95] Note of a discussion, 1 November 1947, F200/90C, Mountbatten Papers, APAC.

[96] DCC Meeting, 3 November 1947, F200/245, Mountbatten Papers, APAC.

[97] *Pakistan Times* (Karachi), 11 November 1947.

[98] Report of conversation with V.P. Menon, UK High Commission (hereafter UKHC) Pakistan to Commonwealth Relations Office (hereafter CRO), IOR L/PS/13/1845b, APAC.

pressures it was "necessary to have a complete reorientation of the State policy. . . even if it involves a reversal of the earlier decision to accede to Pakistan."[99]

Bhutto initially negotiated with the leader of the provisional government, Samaldas Gandhi. When influential Muslims in Junagadh opposed this course, Bhutto wrote to the regional commissioner at Rajkot and sent copies to the Indian and Pakistani governments. He requested the Indian government to take over the administration of Junagadh, and restore law and order pending a final settlement.[100] Delhi accepted this suggestion with alacrity and instructed its forces to enter Junagadh. To avoid being wrongfooted by international opinion Nehru sent a telegram to Liaquat informing him of India's moves.[101] Delhi also issued a press communiqué giving details of the entry into Junagadh.[102] The army was enjoined to withdraw at the earliest.[103]

The following day Nehru sent another cable to Liaquat reiterating India's desire for a final settlement by plebiscite in consultation with Pakistan.[104] An emergency meeting of the Indian cabinet was held on 10 November to consider the situation. The cabinet decided that India could not agree to a joint India–Pakistan plebiscite in Junagadh, but it could agree to a plebiscite under "an independent body like the United Nations." In any event, the plebiscite should be held soon.[105]

Liaquat replied saying neither the dewan nor the nawab could negotiate any settlement, temporary or permanent, with India. Pakistan's government had delegated no such authority to Bhutto. India's

---

[99] Cited in Menon, *Integration of Indian States*, 143.

[100] Bhutto to Regional Commissioner Rajkot, 8 November 1947, cited in ibid, 143–4.

[101] Note on situation in India, 11 November 1947, 3/7/66, Ismay Papers, LHCMA.

[102] *The Statesman* (Calcutta), 10 November 1947.

[103] Bucher to Elizabeth, 14 November 1947, 7901-87-6, Bucher Papers, National Army Museum, London (hereafter NAM).

[104] Nehru's telegrams to Liaquat, 9 and 10 November 1947, *Jinnah Papers*, 8: 376–7.

[105] Extracts from Minutes of an Emergency Meeting of the Cabinet, 10 November 1947, F200/90D, Mountbatten Papers, APAC.

actions were "a clear violation of Pakistan territory and breach of International Law." Liaquat demanded an immediate withdrawal of Indian forces from Junagadh.[106] Nehru replied that the Pakistan government was well aware of Junagadh's thinking. Not only had Harvey Jones travelled to Pakistan to acquaint them with the situation, but Bhutto had informed them before approaching Delhi. India's policy, wrote Nehru, was to ensure a quick stabilization of the situation; to this end it wished to settle the issue by a plebiscite.[107] Thereafter, both sides continued to reiterate their views in sporadic diplomatic exchanges.

Aftermath

On 15 January 1948 Pakistan responded to India's complaint to the UN Security Council on Kashmir by drawing the council's attention to Junagadh as well. The following month a referendum was held in Junagadh by the Indian government. Almost 95 per cent of the 200,000 registered voters exercised their franchise. Only 91 votes went in favour of accession to Pakistan. Referenda were also held in Babariawad, Mangrol, Manavadar, Sardargadh, and Bantwa. Here, too, the people were overwhelmingly in favour of joining India.

The Security Council considered the Junagadh question on 18 and 26 February 1948. Pakistan's representative, Sir Zafrullah Khan, charged India with coercing Junagadh, with abetting the provisional government, and with "a direct act of hostility" by entering Junagadh's territory. The plebiscites, he argued, were a farce. The Indian representative responded with the oft-repeated arguments and declared India's willingness to hold a fresh plebiscite. He urged the council to consider whether it was worth incurring the trouble and expenditure of holding another plebiscite when the result would be nearly the same. The Security Council took no further steps. Although Pakistan did not recognize the legality of Junagadh's accession to India (its maps continued to show Junagadh as its territory until the 1960s), the issue ceased to have traction.

The Junagadh affair was the first international crisis confronted by the Indian government. Far from being a trivial adjunct to Kashmir,

[106] Liaquat to Nehru, 10 November 1947, *Jinnah Papers*, 8: 380–1.
[107] Nehru to Liaquat, 17 November, ibid., 386–8.

it set the tone for India's stance on Kashmir and Hyderabad, especially on the crucial issue of plebiscite. To that extent it had a significant impact on Nehru's foreign policy. But the Junagadh crisis also showcased themes that would recur: Nehru's alertness to domestic opinion and constraints; his worries about the vulnerability of Muslims in India; his concern with the stance of external powers; his desire to adhere to the norms of international politics. Moreover, Junagadh prefigured Nehru's developing approach to crisis management, an approach that laid emphasis on controlling the situation to preclude escalation, on employing the military to demonstrate resolve whilst exploring diplomatic options to avoid war. All of these would influence his handling of the next crisis—over Hyderabad.

3

Hyderabad 1947–1948

Hyderabad was India's largest princely state. Its position, in some ways, was analogous to that of Junagadh. Nizam Osman Ali Khan presided over a population of nearly 16 million, over 80 per cent of them Hindus. But Hyderabad was of much greater interest to the Indian government, for the nizam's sprawling domains squatted at the very centre of India. This accounted both for India's willingness to go the distance to secure Hyderabad's accession and for its eventual decision to annex the state by force.

The state's administrative and security apparatus had largely been the preserve of its Muslim elite. In the late 1930s, after years of insulation, currents of nationalist politics began to circulate in Hyderabad. A non-cooperation movement was launched by the Hyderabad State People's Congress (which had links with the Indian National Congress) and by right-wing Hindu organizations from British India. The nizam quickly clamped down on these groups. But the movement led to the rise of a conservative Muslim party, the Ittehad-i-Muslimeen, geared to protecting the ruling dynasty and Muslim interests. The Ittehad established ties with the Muslim League and soon became a political force to reckon with.[1] This internal configuration of power, as we shall see, would jar on Hyderabad's external relations.

---

[1] For background, see Lucien Benichou, *From Autocracy to Integration: Political Developments in Hyderabad State 1938–1948* (New Delhi: Orient Longman, 2000); Margrit Pernau, *The Passing of Patrimonialism: Politics*

The nizam of hyderabad was a richly eccentric ruler. An accomplished poet, his "perfumed *ghazals*" were often composed at the rate of up to a dozen a day. And yet his favourite pastimes were prowling graveyards at night and watching surgeries in the city hospital. The nizam was easily among the wealthiest individuals of his times.[2] And yet—to put it more delicately than his detractors do—he led rather a niggardly lifestyle. "He wears an extremely dirty old fez," noted a close adviser, "a sherwani (often torn) usually open at the neck (which except in the hottest weather is muffled in a moth-eaten old khaki scarf), a pair of thin white pyjama trousers and yellow socks and yellow bedroom slippers."[3] The nizam's character was a mixed quiver of cleverness and guile, imprudence and mendacity, and all these qualities were evident at various times in his handling of relations with India.

From early 1946 the nizam began jockeying to preserve and advance his position and interests in a decolonized South Asia. His principal counsellor was his constitutional adviser, Sir Walter Monckton. A leading barrister and a prominent Tory, Monckton had been in the employ of the nizam since the 1930s. Monckton's charm and persuasiveness, elephantine patience and voracious appetite for work, percipient intellect and prodigious memory made him a much-sought-after counsellor and negotiator on political and constitutional matters. In 1946–7 he was, as we saw in the previous chapter, constitutional adviser to the sheikh of Mangrol as well; he was also approached by the maharaja of Kashmir—an assignment he wisely declined. During the protracted negotiations with India over the future of Hyderabad, Monckton would play a crucial role, leveraging his familiarity with Mountbatten as well as the nizam, striving tirelessly to reconcile the conflicting interests, and struggling valiantly to avoid a showdown. Indeed, Monckton would, at times, simultaneously draft

---

and Political Culture in Hyderabad 1911–1948 (New Delhi: Manohar, 2001); John Roosa, "Quandary of the *Qaum*: Indian Nationalism in a Muslim State, Hyderabad 1850–1948," PhD thesis, University of Wisconsin-Madison, 1998.

[2] John Zubrzycki, *The Last Nizam: The Rise and Fall of India's Greatest Princely State* (London: Pan Macmillan, 2006), 167; Copland, *The Princes of India*, 11.

[3] "A Strange Client" by Walter Monckton, October 1947, Dep Monckton Trustees 26, Monckton Papers, Bodleian Library (hereafter BL), Oxford.

letters and position papers for both sides. His correspondence and papers, heretofore unused by historians, are invaluable in understanding the course of the negotiations and the crisis.

A month before Partition was announced, Walter Monckton sounded out leaders of the Muslim League and the Congress. Their responses indicated the gulf between their views on the princely states. Jinnah, we may recall, advocated the right of the rulers to decide on accession or independence. Nehru held that the states could not stay independent and that the wishes of the people must be paramount in deciding on accession. In so doing, Jinnah hoped to offset India's strength; Nehru sought to preclude a balkanization of India. Thus, Jinnah told Monckton that "If Hyderabad joined the Hindu Union it would be committing suicide." The state had two "real alternatives:" joining Pakistan's constituent assembly or concluding a "Treaty or Agreement" with Pakistan. In either case, "Pakistan would not thereafter stand by and see the Nizam . . . driven from his throne." Nehru's views were diametrically opposed. "The Nizam," he said, "would be committing political suicide if he did not join the new Union. The great majority of his subjects would wish it." To preserve his position, the nizam should join India and gradually usher in "responsible government."[4] Apprised of these views, the nizam "emphatically agreed that what Mr. Jinnah had suggested was his better course."[5] After the Partition Plan was made public, Jinnah urged Hyderabad to "give a lead to other states by declaring for independence."[6] Consequently, the nizam issued an edict proclaiming that Hyderabad would remain independent after 15 August 1947.

Pakistan *vis-à-vis* Hyderabad

The nizam also penned a piquant letter to the viceroy, remonstrating against "the way in which my state has been abandoned by its old ally, the British Government." He hoped that Hyderabad could establish

[4] Notes on interviews with Jinnah and Nehru, 3 May 1947, Dep Monckton Trustees 29, Monckton Papers, BL.

[5] Note on interview with Nizam, 5 May 1947, ibid.

[6] Note on interview with Jinnah, 4 June 1947, ibid.

direct relations with His Majesty's Government.[7] A delegation from Hyderabad, led by the Nawab of Chhatari, met the viceroy. Mountbatten made it clear that dominion status was impossible. He observed that by refusing to accede the nizam would be doing his state "the greatest possible disservice."[8] In subsequent discussions with the secretary of the ministry of states, V.P. Menon, the Hyderabad delegation expressed interest in a standstill agreement without negotiating accession. Menon refused to consider this.[9]

Thereafter the nizam decided not to accede to either dominion. He was prepared to conclude a "Treaty for purposes of Defence, External Affairs, and Communications" with India. In the event of hostilities between India and Pakistan, Hyderabad would remain neutral. Furthermore, if India opted out of the Commonwealth, Hyderabad could review the treaty. Most important, the treaty would have to recognize the nizam's "full sovereignty and autonomy within his Dominions." The nizam directed his delegation first to obtain Jinnah's approval and then to ascertain if Indian leaders were interested.[10] Meeting the Hyderabad delegation, Jinnah said that at the moment they should only convey to Mountbatten their interest in "cooperating with both new Dominions by treaty." He asked them to put off proper negotiations until 15 August—advice continuous with his suggestion to Junagadh. Jinnah also argued that Hyderabad should not restrict itself to neutrality but "ought to be prepared to come to their [Pakistan's] assistance in time of need."[11]

Monckton felt Jinnah's suggestions were inimical to Hyderabad's interests. In a draft note he observed that the best chance for concluding a treaty was before 15 August 1947, while Mountbatten was viceroy.

[7] Nizam to Mountbatten, 9 July 1947, F200/70A, Mountbatten Papers, APAC.

[8] Minutes of meeting between Viceroy and Hyderabad Delegation, 11 July 1947, ibid.

[9] Menon, *Integration of Indian States*, 319.

[10] Minutes of meeting of Negotiating Committee, 20 July 1947; Nizam's instructions to Negotiating Committee, 24 July 1947, Dep Monckton Trustees 29, Monckton Papers, BL.

[11] Monckton to Nizam, 26 July 1947 (withheld); Telegram from Monckton to Nizam, 24 July 1947, ibid.

Thereafter, Hyderabad would be susceptible to economic and military pressure from India. Jinnah's suggestions would only lead to a "breakdown of negotiations." Pakistan's assurances were beguiling but vague: "we ought to be told by Jinnah in black and white what he could do to come to our aid." Monckton uncovered the nub of the matter with acuity: "If Hyderabad stands out altogether, on Mr. Jinnah's model, the Dominion of India would be thereby in a weaker position and that would suit Pakistan. The advantage would be Pakistan's but the risk would be Hyderabad's."[12]

Monckton, however, pulled his punches and refrained from presenting his views to the nizam in such stark terms. But he drew up a note indicating his concerns and asking Jinnah for clear assurances.[13] At the same time Monckton found himself under increasing pressure from the Ittehad. The leader of the Ittehad, Kasim Razvi, was a lawyer from UP and a devout admirer of Jinnah. According to one observer, Razvi was "the complete fanatic. He stares with eyes that bore holes into you."[14] A more perceptive interviewer found him to be "a fanatical demagogue with great gifts of organization. As a 'rabble-rouser' he is formidable, and even in a *tête-à-tête* he is compelling."[15] By the summer of 1947 Razvi and the Ittehad enjoyed the support of the majority of the state's Muslims: only a minority of educated Muslims disapproved of him but they were unwilling openly to denounce him.[16] Razvi in turn took the cue from Jinnah. As Monckton wrote to Mountbatten, "Ittehad, supported from [*sic*] our mutual friend from Delhi, are attacking me hard. But so far the HEH [the nizam] is not moved by it."[17] This dimension would acquire great importance once the negotiations commenced.

Meantime, a delegation from Hyderabad headed to Karachi. Jinnah goaded the Hyderabad representatives to refuse to join India: "there was something such as standing for one's own right, despite every

---

[12] Monckton to Nizam, 26 July 1947 (withheld), ibid.

[13] Note for Jinnah, 28 July 1947, ibid.

[14] Campbell-Johnson, *Mission with Mountbatten*, 332.

[15] Cited in Guha, *India After Gandhi*, 54.

[16] Benichou, *From Autocracy to Integration*, 179.

[17] Monckton to Mountbatten, 28 July 1947, F200/70A, Mountbatten Papers, APAC.

threat or provocation." Asked how far Pakistan would assist Hydera-bad, Jinnah said that "it was not possible for him at present to give any specific undertaking but that, generally speaking, he was confident that he and Pakistan would come to the help of Hyderabad in every possible way."[18]

On receiving Jinnah's assurances the nizam wrote to Mountbatten that he could not contemplate "organic union" with India or Pakistan. He was willing to conclude a treaty with India on communications, defence, and foreign affairs. There were some caveats, however: neutrality with respect to Pakistan; his right to appoint diplomatic representatives abroad; provisions to reconsider the treaty if India step-ped out of the Commonwealth. He also expostulated against India's refusal to consider standstill arrangements without accession. If Delhi persisted in its recalcitrance, the nizam warned, Hyderabad would mobilize international opinion.[19] By this time Mountbatten had real-ized that the deadline of 15 August could not be met and had per-suaded the cabinet to grant Hyderabad another two months. The cabinet asked Mountbatten to handle further negotiations.[20]

Hyderabad's Negotiations with India:
The First Phase

In Hyderabad the negotiating team considered its options. Monck-ton was clear that Hyderabad would ultimately be unable to resist pressure from India. He argued, therefore, that it would be "foolish not to explore the possibilities of bridging the gulf."[21] Not everyone agreed. Abdur Rahim, minister of commerce and a member of the Ittehad, stated that the reprieve was the "Breathing Time" to make

[18] Note by Ali Yavar Jung on interview with Jinnah, 4 August 1947, *Jinnah Papers*, 9: 25–8.

[19] Nizam to Mountbatten, 8 August 1947, F200/70B, Mountbatten Papers, APAC.

[20] Viceroy's 69th Staff Meeting, 9 August 1947; Mountbatten to Nizam, 12 August, ibid.

[21] Note by Monckton, 13 August 1947; Note by Ali Yavar Jung, 16 August 1947; Note by Monckton, 20 August 1947, Dep Monckton Trustees 26, Monckton Papers, BL.

internal and external arrangements. He recommended negotiating diplomatic treaties with Britain and America. "If we succeed in this attempt, I am sure the Indian Union would be forced to recognize our Independence."[22] In fact Hyderabad had already tried to consolidate its position internationally. In mid-July it had told the French embassy in London that Hyderabad wished to establish in Paris a diplomatic mission for Europe. Scenting trouble, Whitehall had scuppered the move.[23]

Soon, Monckton and Chhatari came under a scalding attack from the Ittehad for ostensibly acting against the interests of the state. Consequently, both submitted their resignations. The nizam, however, was keen to retain the services of Monckton. Interestingly, rather than bringing the Ittehad to heel, he requested Mountbatten to persuade Monckton to stay on.[24] Eventually, at Monckton's insistence, the nizam issued a statement condemning the campaign against his advisers. The contretemps indicated the power play in Hyderabad. The Ittehad was not merely a thorn on the side of the nizam but was adroitly used by him to ensure that his own position was not weakened. As Monckton would subsequently realize, "He gives you his full confidence, but encourages others to attack you lest you be too sure of yourself or too powerful."[25] The puppeteer instincts of the nizam would ultimately prove costly.

Meanwhile, Vallabhbhai Patel wrote to Mountbatten that there was "no alternative" to accession. Anything else would lay him open to "the charge of breach of faith" with those states that had joined India. Besides, the states that were yet to accede would be emboldened to stay out. Inputs from Hyderabad showed that the Ittehad was trying to instil "a feeling of terror amongst the non-Muslim population." Patel had also obtained a copy of Abdur Rahim's note and was convinced that Hyderabad wished to use the two months' time to present India

[22] Rahim to Prime Minister of Hyderabad, 16 August 1947, ibid.

[23] Secretary of State to Viceroy, 19 July 1947, F200/70A, Mountbatten Papers, APAC.

[24] Telegram from Nizam to Mountbatten, F200/70B, Mountbatten Papers, APAC.

[25] "A Strange Client" by Monckton, October 1947, Dep Monckton Trustees 26, Monckton Papers, BL.

with a *fait accompli*. The nizam, he noted, had only two options: accession to India or a referendum.[26]

When Mountbatten relayed the message to Hyderabad, the nizam responded that the negotiations should commence forthwith and that "the question of referendum does not arise."[27] On 8 September the Hyderabad delegation met Mountbatten. Monckton and Chhatari thought they could convince the nizam to offer an agreement "far more like the Instrument of Accession than the original offer of a treaty." It was agreed that they should obtain the nizam's approval for such a document and return at the earliest.[28]

The delegation had been rather sanguine. The nizam refused to countenance any move approaching accession. Monckton bluntly stated that he was "entirely mistaken in being led by Jinnah." The nizam directed Monckton formally to present his offer of a treaty.[29] Nonetheless, Monckton sought to introduce a modicum of flexibility to Hyderabad's stance. In a note to the executive council he claimed that a treaty, as opposed to accession, could be denounced "if Pakistan and Hyderabad grew strong enough to warrant it." On the other hand if Hyderabad was obdurate "there will be a breakdown in negotiations." This would mean internal trouble from the state Congress, external pressure from India, and ultimately an intervention by force.[30] The point went home.

The delegation reached Delhi with a modified letter. Short of accession, the nizam was ready to make a "Treaty of Association." He asked Mountbatten to consider a "first tentative draft Heads of Agreement" on which the treaty would eventually be based.[31] The draft compressed an accordion of ticklish issues. Two proved particularly intractable. It did not give India the power to make laws for Hyderabad on the three subjects. And Hyderabad wanted the right to establish

---

[26] Patel to Mountbatten, 24 August 1947, *SPC*, 7: 109–10.

[27] Mountbatten to Nizam, 27 August 1947; Nizam to Mountbatten, 28 August 1947, F200/70B, Mountbatten Papers, APAC.

[28] Note of interview with Monckton and Chhatari, 8 September 1947, ibid.

[29] Note by Mountbatten, 13 September 1947, ibid.

[30] Note for Council, 15 September 1947, ibid. Monckton sent a copy to Mountbatten.

[31] Nizam to Mountbatten, 18 September 1947, ibid.

diplomatic relations with any foreign power. After weeks of wrangling Monckton proposed a temporary, year-long, accord instead of a full-blown treaty.[32]

Hyderabad's "Standstill Agreement" with India

On 15 October the nizam advanced a draft "Standstill Agreement" with tacit rights to neutrality against Pakistan and to review the accord if India quit the Commonwealth.[33] Despite some revisions to this, Patel found it unacceptable. Although the Indians had agreed to forego the power to legislate for Hyderabad, they wanted the agreement to specify that union laws would be treated as "normative." Further, Hyderabad would be entitled to appoint trade representatives—not political agents, as they demanded—in Commonwealth countries. Finally, the Indians wanted a "positive statement" in the agreement that foreign policy would be entrusted to Delhi. After some heated exchanges Monckton agreed to persuade the nizam on these points.[34] Menon prepared an amended version, cleared it with Patel and Nehru, and handed it to the Hyderabad delegation. A standstill agreement was finally in sight.

The nizam did not like the changes but directed his executive council to consider them. After much deliberation the council voted 6 to 3 in favour of accepting the draft. The dissenting members owed allegiance to the Ittehad. As the delegation prepared to leave for Delhi, the nizam prevaricated. In the early hours of 27 October, the Ittehad's activists threw a vice around the residences of Chhatari and Monckton. According to one observer, "tens of thousands of people . . . covered every inch of the roads around the houses of the delegates."[35] The nizam cabled Mountbatten that the delegation would be delayed by a week.

[32] Monckton to Mountbatten, 12 October 1947, F200/71A, Mountbatten Papers, APAC.

[33] Nizam to Mountbatten, 15 October 1947, ibid.

[34] Note of interview with Menon (and Monckton), 19 October 1947, ibid.; Note by Monckton, 2 November 1947, Dep Monckton Trustees 26, Monckton Papers, BL.

[35] Laik Ali, *Tragedy of Hyderabad* (Karachi: Pakistan Cooperative Book Society, 1962), 73.

Meeting the delegation that afternoon the nizam ostentatiously denounced the Ittehad and Kasim Razvi. But the next morning he summoned Razvi for consultations. Razvi sombrely declared that the agreement would be "the death of Hyderabad." Had the delegation stood its ground, Delhi would have yielded. "As the Indian Union are fully occupied with their troubles elsewhere, they will be in no position to do anything to us or to refuse our demands if we insist." Indian troops had flown into Kashmir the previous day. Razvi asked the negotiating committee to be replaced by another team of his choosing. To this the nizam acquiesced. [36]

He now informed Mountbatten that a new delegation would meet with him. Bolstered by the Ittehad, he claimed that the amended draft "does not do justice" to Hyderabad. If India would not consider his offer of a standstill agreement, it would be "very necessary for me to conclude an agreement of the same kind immediately with Pakistan." Jinnah had asked him to arrive at standstill arrangements with India and enter into "treaty relations" with Pakistan.[37] Indeed, when Mountbatten subsequently met Jinnah the latter rejected the offer of impartial plebiscites in all problematic states: Junagadh, Hyderabad, and Kashmir. Jinnah claimed that he would not compel Hyderabad to abandon its quest for independence.[38]

The new delegation reached Delhi on 31 October. A series of meetings ensued. In the final round, V.P. Menon stood firm that "the Agreement should either be accepted or rejected as it stood". The delegation promised to return with the nizam's "final decision."[39] Mountbatten advised them not to assume that India's hands were full: "India was immensely powerful, and still possessed one of the biggest armies

[36] The developments in Hyderabad are from "Description of Events in Hyderabad, 22 to 30 October 1947"; Monckton to Ismay, 28 October 1947; Interview with Sultan Ahmed and Menon, 31 October 1947, F200/71A, Mountbatten Papers, APAC; Note by Lady Monckton, 27 October 1947, Dep Monckton Trustees 26, Monckton Papers, BL.

[37] Two letters from Nizam to Mountbatten, 30 October 1947, F200/71B, Mountbatten Papers, APAC.

[38] Note of a discussion, 1 November 1947, F200/90C, Mountbatten Papers, APAC.

[39] Summary of discussion with Hyderabad delegation by Menon, 5 November 1947, F200/71B, Mountbatten Papers, APAC.

in the world."[40] Since Mountbatten was going to England for two weeks, the nizam offered to send the delegation on his return. Patel reluctantly agreed. By this time, the Indian government was increasingly concerned about reports of violence against Hindus in Hyderabad. Menon had conveyed these to the Hyderabad delegation. Patel asked Mountbatten to express his concerns directly to the nizam. This was essential not only for the negotiations to succeed, but "in the interests of Hyderabad state itself."[41]

In the interim, the Ittehad strengthened its hold over the Hyderabad administration. Chhatari resigned as head of the executive council, and was replaced by Laik Ali at the behest of Kasim Razvi. A wealthy industrialist and a financial patron of the Ittehad, Laik was serving with Pakistan's delegation to the UN. The Ittehad had originally sought to appoint Pakistan's finance minister, Ghulam Mohammed, as the premier of Hyderabad. Jinnah refused to let go of the latter and allowed Laik to take up the appointment only for a year. From Hyderabad's standpoint Laik was a less-than-satisfactory alternative. As a contemporary noted, "neither politics nor administration was his *metier.*"[42] The Ittehad also insinuated its nominees into the council. On Mountbatten's return the Hyderabad delegation tried its utmost to secure some changes. The governor general insisted on "a completely unchanged document" but agreed to variations in the collateral letter.[43] On 29 November 1947 the nizam signed the standstill agreement and the collateral letter.

Hyderabad and India: The Deepening Mistrust

In a separate letter to Mountbatten the nizam stated that in the event of an India–Pakistan war Hyderabad would remain neutral. He was, of course, worried about the gathering war-clouds over Kashmir.

[40] Note on interview with Moin Nawaz Jung, 6 November 1947, ibid.

[41] Menon to Brockman, 9 November 1947; Mountbatten to Nizam, 9 November 1947, ibid.

[42] Ali Yavar Jung, *Hyderabad in Retrospect* (Bombay: Times of India Publications, 1949), 27.

[43] Mountbatten to Monckton, 29 November 1947, F200/71B, Mountbatten Papers, APAC.

Mountbatten replied that this would create animosity; the nizam insisted that it be shown to the cabinet "as a secret document."[44] Menon, too, felt that it would "only embitter relations." But Hyderabad claimed that it was "better to get any unpleasantness over altogether, and then try to start afresh."[45] The standstill agreement thus began on a less-than-promising note.

Aware of the deep reservations on both sides, Mountbatten suggested that further negotiations on accession be undertaken before he stepped down as governor general in mid-1948. To Mountbatten the nizam responded positively. But in exchanges with Monckton he clarified that that it was "no good . . . hurrying up making long term agreement." He would wait and see how Kashmir and Junagadh were settled by the UN.[46] Unfortunately, copies of these messages found their way to Patel, who concluded that the nizam did not favour "a continued understanding with India."[47]

Several factors contributed to the burgeoning mistrust. First, India's agent general, K.M. Munshi, and the Hyderabad administration failed to hit it off. This was not surprising. For Munshi was aware that "my presence in Hyderabad as agent-general was not going to be hailed with joy. Ten years earlier, when I was home minister of Bombay, I had declined to oblige the nizam by taking action against . . . [Hindu right-wing activists] on their way to Hyderabad to offer *satyagraha*."[48] Moreover Munshi's prickly and imperious demeanour quickly alienated the Hyderabadis. Second, Hyderabad took a series of steps on financial policy that led the Indian government to "lose all faith in Hyderabad's bonafides."[49] The nizam imposed

[44] Nizam's letters, 29 November & 6 December 1947, F200/69, Mountbatten Papers, APAC.

[45] Minute by Erskine Crum, 15 December 1947; Menon to Brockman, 29 January 1948; Record of interview with Laik Ali, 31 January 1948, ibid.

[46] Nizam to Mountbatten, 4 December 1947; Nizam to Monckton, 6 January 1948, F200/72A, Mountbatten Papers, APAC.

[47] Patel to Mountbatten, 12 January 1948, *SPC*, 7: 132–4.

[48] K.M. Munshi, *The End of an Era: Hyderabad Memories* (Bombay: Bharatiya Vidya Bhavan, 1957), 4.

[49] Desai (Ministry of States) to Brockman, 19 January 1948, F200/72A, Mountbatten Papers, APAC.

restrictions on the export of metals to India; declared Indian currency illegal; and advanced a loan of Rs 200 million to Pakistan. Third, Delhi received intelligence that Hyderabad was making "frantic efforts" to obtain arms.[50] Fourth, India was increasingly concerned about the violent activities of the Ittehad, particularly its armed militia known as the Razakar. There were also reports of armed incursions by the Razakar into the neighbouring provinces of Madras and Bombay.[51] Razvi's penchant for inflammatory rhetoric aggravated the tension.

Last, and in hindsight most important, Hyderabad had made no move to reform its government and make it more representative. In consequence, Delhi came under increasing pressure from domestic constituencies for "sacrificing Indian interest to appease Hyderabad."[52] The prime minister responded to these by assuring the provinces that he was "keeping a very close watch on the situation." But Nehru also urged restraint, not least because of Kashmir. "We cannot afford to take precipitate action," especially "when we are heavily committed elsewhere."[53] Nonetheless, as the crisis unfolded domestic pressures would assume increasing importance in India's decision calculus.

Hyderabad, too, had its grievances. Despite the agreement, the import of essential goods was being held up. Hyderabad saw this as an economic blockade to pressurize the state. In fact, these restrictions had been imposed not by Delhi but by the Bombay government.[54] Furthermore, there were delays in the supply of arms and ammunition promised to Hyderabad. In late January 1948 these issues were discussed in a meeting between a Hyderabad delegation and V.P. Menon. Menon pointed out that India's concerns centred on two issues. Hyderabad should retract the recent financial measures and rescind the loan to Pakistan. They should also take steps to rein in the Ittehad and the Razakar. In another meeting Patel made it clear to Hyderabad's

[50] Nehru to Patel, 21 January 1948, *SPC*, 7: 135–6.

[51] Premier Madras to Mountbatten, 29 January 1948, F200/72A, Mountbatten Papers, APAC.

[52] Desai to Brockman, 19 January 1948, ibid.

[53] Letter to Premiers, 17 January 1947, *SWJN-SS*, 5: 310.

[54] See, Intelligence Report, 8 March 1948, subject file 14, D.P. Mishra Papers (I & II Instalments), NMML.

premier, Laik Ali, that internal reform was a prerequisite for a satisfactory relationship.[55]

Monckton, Mountbatten, and Menon

Following Gandhi's assassination by a Hindu extremist at the end of January 1948 the issue of Hyderabad and its potential impact on communal relations acquired renewed urgency. Both Patel and Menon deemed it imperative to reach a final settlement on Hyderabad's status. Mountbatten agreed with Patel that the first step was to get "responsible government introduced in Hyderabad at the earliest."[56] By this time the nizam had summoned Walter Monckton to participate in further negotiations. As earlier, Monckton held that accession was impracticable and "association" inevitable. He concurred with Mountbatten that the immediate aim was to reform the government. But after preliminary discussions in Hyderabad, Monckton was convinced that "parity" between Hindu and Muslim members in the executive council was the utmost possible: it was inconceivable that the regime would cede a majority of positions to the Hindus.[57]

Monckton and Laik met Mountbatten and Menon on 2 March 1948. On being pressed, Laik agreed to consider ways of modifying financial policy and to make interim arrangements with Pakistan on the loan. However, when Mountbatten asked that the Razakar be banned, Laik demurred. Menon thereafter said that they wanted Hyderabad to accede. But if the government was suitably reformed, Delhi would leave the issue of accession to the peoples' discretion. When they met next, Laik claimed to have arranged with Pakistan not to cash the loan for the duration of the standstill agreement. Mountbatten mentioned that Patel wanted "full responsible government." Laik said that introducing such changes at one fell swoop would be risky. Instead, the executive council could be reconstituted to form an interim government.[58] Mountbatten took to the idea of a

[55] Menon, *Integration of Indian States*, 339–41.

[56] Interview between Mountbatten and Patel, 10 February 1948; Menon to Brockman 5 February 1948, F200/72A, Mountbatten Papers, APAC.

[57] Note on Hyderabad by Monckton, 25 February 1948, ibid.

[58] Menon, *Integration of Indian States*, 344–5.

"parity interim government." But Patel insisted that this arrangement should last no longer than a month. And first he wanted the Ittehad banned.[59]

In Hyderabad, Monckton held long discussions with the nizam and Laik. He urged the latter "immediately to broaden the base of his government" and ensure parity. Thereafter he would work out the general lines of a constitution to follow the interim parity stage. When Laik baulked at the suggestion, Monckton told him that "there was danger of too little too late [rather] than too much too soon."[60] Thereafter Laik announced that he proposed to convene a conference of all political parties in the state. The Ittehad brusquely turned down the idea. So did the Hyderabad State People's Congress which insisted on numerous preconditions including the nizam's agreement to accede to India.[61] The initiative proved a non-starter.

Nor could Laik make good on his other assurances: Indian currency continued to be banned; restrictions on the export of metals remained; and there was no announcement regarding the loan to Pakistan. The nizam, Monckton observed, was "resigned to an uncertain and troubled immediate future."[62] The Ittehad turned ever more militant. Kasim Razvi made a rash of incendiary speeches which were blazoned in Indian newspapers. Delhi viewed these with concern. On the one hand they were worried that Razvi's diatribes would strike the match of a communal flare-up. On the other Indian public opinion grew increasingly critical of the government's policy.

In his public and private utterances Nehru sought to balance these considerations by at once urging restraint on domestic audiences and reassuring them that the government was seized of the problem. Addressing a public gathering, he observed that the situation in Hyderabad was "a difficult one" and that he was anxious to solve the problem peacefully. Other methods might yield quicker results but they would

[59] Note of interview with Munshi and Menon, 6 March 1948, F200/72A, Mountbatten Papers, APAC.

[60] Monckton to Mountbatten, 15 March 1948, ibid.

[61] Menon, *Integration of Indian States*, 345–6. Also see, Benichou, *From Autocracy to Integration*, 198–9.

[62] Monckton to Mountbatten, 15 March 1948, F200/72A, Mountbatten Papers, APAC.

come "at a big cost which we would rather not pay." Turning to Razvi's speeches, he conceded that they would be "extraordinary even if they came from a lunatic asylum." Yet it was not an issue over which the people "should grow terribly excited or hysterical." The government confronted several problems, but "India is, has been and will be, strong enough to deal with the Hyderabad problem."[63]

Similarly, he wrote to the provincial governments that "a dismal view" of the situation was unwarranted. The government was not eager "to force an accession or even to expedite it." They were prepared to wait but the people should decide the question. Nor could they let Hyderabad continue as "an autocratic feudal state while the rest of India becomes democratic." For the moment Delhi would be content if the standstill agreement was honoured and if there was no trouble internally or on the borders.[64]

Apprehending a sharp deterioration in the internal situation the government asked the general staff to prepare a contingency plan for intervention. The plan, titled Operation Polo, was ready by mid-March 1948. On being briefed the army C-in-C, General Roy Bucher, felt that the operation would be a serious encumbrance; for the army was already committed to operations in Kashmir, the defence of the country's western borders, and internal security duties.[65] When Mountbatten learnt of this development he panicked. But Nehru assured him that the plan had been prepared "wholly and solely against the extreme emergency of Razvi carrying out his threat of murdering all the Hindus with his Razakar."[66]

Delhi also decided to raise the ante diplomatically. On 23 March the states ministry sent a formal letter to Premier Laik Ali stating that Hyderabad had "failed to carry out the obligations under the standstill agreement." After listing Hyderabad's infractions it demanded that Laik fulfil his undertakings. More important, Delhi wanted the

[63] Speech at Vishakhapatnam, 14 March 1948, *SWJN-SS*, 5: 279–81.

[64] Letter to Premiers, 17 March 1948, ibid., 332.

[65] Bucher to H.M. Patel, 15 March 1948, 7901-87-16, Bucher Papers, NAM.

[66] Note of interview with Nehru, 20 March 1948, F200/72B, Mountbatten Papers, APAC.

Ittehad and the Razakar to be banned.[67] Hyderabad responded tartly. The nizam wrote to Mountbatten that the letter was "in the nature of an ultimatum." He claimed that "economic pressure has . . . been applied on Hyderabad with growing intensity." The nizam warned that if the "policy of attempted coercion" continued, "the peace not only of Hyderabad but of the whole of South India would be endangered."[68] Laik, too, wrote a seventeen-page letter to Nehru, rebutting the charges laid at Hyderabad and levelling others against India. He demanded that both parties submit their differences to arbitration. On the question of Ittehad he adopted an unyielding stance. It was "a matter concerning the internal policy of the state" and there were "no grounds whatsoever justifying proscribing the Ittehad."[69]

Into this combustible situation Razvi threw a Molotov cocktail. In a widely reported speech he urged the Muslims of Hyderabad to undertake a jehad against the enemy, adding for good measure that the Muslims of India would be "our fifth columnists in any showdown." Delhi was startled.[70] Against this backdrop Monckton met the Indian prime minister. Nehru sought to convey both reassurances and risks, invoking to good effect the domestic constraints on his government. He assured Monckton that India was not preparing for a showdown, economically or militarily. But the activities of the Ittehad were creating "a dangerous crisis." Provincial governments had been sending "long lists of border incidents and asking for urgent assistance." Moreover, there was "tremendous apprehension" in parliament. Nehru emphasized his belief that if the "disorder became widespread in Hyderabad" the government "might find their hand forced."

Monckton said if Delhi ensured a free flow of goods he would try to get the nizam both to "broaden government" and to declare that "responsible government would be granted in the near future." Nehru retorted that India could not be expected "to enthuse over steps such as broadening the base of Government and the like." India wanted responsible government and "would not welcome anything else." He

[67] Menon to Laik, 23 March 1949, ibid.
[68] Nizam to Mountbatten, 5 April 1948, ibid.
[69] Laik to Nehru, 5 April 1948, ibid.
[70] Menon, *Integration of Indian States*, 350.

reiterated that the "real crux" of the matter was the "explosive situation" and that unless the nizam took effective steps, India would be in "a very difficult situation."[71]

The next day, 8 April 1948, Monckton informed Nehru that he intended to advise the nizam to take "extremely drastic action against Kasim Razvi." It was decided that Nehru would take up the issue with the provincial governments and that Monckton would make a statement to the nizam emphasizing the need for curbing Razvi and moving towards representative government "as soon and as quickly as possible." A draft of a letter from Mountbatten to the nizam was also finalized. The letter traced the prevailing mistrust to the events of 27 October: "if these methods of coercion had not been permitted" relations between the two sides would have been rather different. To arrest the downward trend the nizam was urged to introduce representative government.[72]

Back in Hyderabad, Monckton implored the nizam and Laik Ali to make a "bold statement" that a new government would be formed.[73] The Hyderabad administration, however, persisted in its refusal to curb the Ittehad. It denied that Razvi had made the jehad speech and claimed that the newspapers had invented it wholesale.[74] Laik sent a telegram along these lines to Nehru and simultaneously released it to the press. Patel was livid. He wrote to Monckton that Hyderabad's efforts to absolve Razvi had filled him with "grave misgivings." Unless the Ittehad was checked and a representative government installed, negotiations could only be conducted in "an atmosphere of make believe."[75]

When Monckton and Laik returned to Delhi, they found the Indians implacable. Nehru made it clear that India could not agree to an intermediate stage unless Hyderabad declared that its objective was a fully representative government and that the interim arrangement

[71] Minutes of meeting between Nehru and Monckton, 7 April 1948, F200/72B, Mountbatten Papers, APAC.

[72] Minutes of meeting between Mountbatten, Nehru and Monckton, 8 April; Mountbatten to Nizam, 8 April 1948, ibid.

[73] Interview with Monckton, 12 April 1948, subject file 97, K.M. Munshi Papers, NMML.

[74] Monckton to Mountbatten, 11 April 1948, F200/72B, Mountbatten Papers, APAC.

[75] Patel to Monckton, 14 April 1948, ibid.

was of a brief duration. Patel was curt: if Razvi continued to call the shots, the future of the nizam and his dynasty would be undermined; Hyderabad had no option but to accede.[76] On 17 April, following consultations with Mountbatten, Menon, and Monckton, Nehru handed a list of points to Laik for the nizam's agreement. First, steps should be taken "at once to control Razvi and the Razakar." Second, members of the Hyderabad State Peoples' Congress who were imprisoned should immediately be released. Third, "genuine reconstruction" of the existing government should be undertaken forthwith. Fourth, responsible government should be introduced and a constituent assembly formed as soon as possible. Fifth, an announcement embodying these measures should be issued no later than 23 April.[77] The date was significant, for the All India Congress Committee was to meet on 24 April. In the last meeting Menon underscored the fact that Hyderabad's choices were accession or transition to responsible government. Neither seemed palatable to Hyderabad.

On reaching Hyderabad, Monckton presented a detailed assessment. The situation was "extremely inflammatory" and could only be controlled by "immediate action." Good relations, he emphasized, were "impossible under the present Hyderabad government." To avoid "serious risk to the dynasty" the government must be replaced by "another broadly based and genuinely representative of both communities on the basis of parity." Monckton warned that repudiating the standstill agreement would "set a match to the fire and could bring down the state."[78] But the nizam chose the path of least resistance. He announced the formation of a committee "with a view to increasing the powers of the Assembly to an appreciable extent." In the interim he hoped that all political parties would join the existing government. In a letter to Mountbatten the nizam was defiant: "It is difficult for me to consider any suggestion . . . [on issues] which should be viewed purely as an internal affair."[79]

[76] Menon, *Integration of Indian States*, 353–4.

[77] Note of conversation between Nehru and Laik, 17 April 1948, F200/72B, Mountbatten Papers, APAC.

[78] Note by Monckton, n.d. (*c.* 18 April 1948), Dep Monckton Trustees 27, Monckton Papers, BL.

[79] Nizam to Mountbatten, 22 April 1948, F200/72B, Mountbatten Papers, APAC.

Inching Towards the Military Option

The nizam's announcement came as "a great disappointment" to Delhi. Besides, not much had been done about the other demands.[80] To avoid further deterioration Mountbatten invited the ruler to Delhi. The nizam declined. Meantime, Menon drew up a note for the cabinet detailing the course of events. The nizam's announcement was "halting and does not satisfy either the legitimate aspirations of the people or the demands we made." Menon concluded that there was no "hope of establishing peaceful conditions with the present set up." He recommended that a firm line be taken, asking Hyderabad to ban the Ittehad and establish representative government. He also suggested that the question be discussed by the Defence Committee.[81]

Even with the negotiations under way, the Indian government had started examining military options. The prime minister sought to yoke military measures with diplomatic moves towards a settlement. A conflict with Hyderabad, he thought, would "not only be bad in itself" but would have "very undesirable consequences" in the rest of India. The underlying concern was that it might spark widespread attacks against Muslims. Yet the situation was "steadily deteriorating" and the government had to be prepared for "any eventuality." Nehru favoured a compellent strategy. The contingency plan envisioned the use of two infantry brigades and one armoured brigade. Infantry units were already present in areas not far from Hyderabad. Nehru now wanted suitably to position the armoured brigade for deployment in an emergency. Such a preparation would show that India meant business and would give Hyderabad pause. Indeed, it might "actually help in preventing any deterioration of the situation." At the same time, Nehru wanted to proceed gingerly: he directed that the move should not be carried out in a hurried fashion, for "any indication of precipitate action might be misunderstood and might bring about a crisis which the move is intended to avoid." The preparations needed to be done "quietly, and without any precipitateness."[82]

[80] Mountbatten to Monckton, 1 May 1948, F200/72D, Mountbatten Papers, APAC.

[81] Note for Cabinet, 4 May 1948, ibid.

[82] Nehru to Baldev Singh, 16 April 1948, *SWJN-SS*, 6: 216–17.

On receiving these orders the acting chief of general staff (CGS), Major General J.N. Chaudhuri, wrote to the army chief setting out his concerns. By moving the armoured brigade down south India's strategic reserves against Pakistan would be "weaken[ed] considerably." Furthermore, the forces for internal security in north and east India were inadequate; the southern and western states would have to make do with police. Finally, if the operation continued beyond the first week of June, the cross-country movement of tanks would be difficult owing to the monsoons. In the light of these Chaudhuri thought the operation should be postponed "for a minimum period of four months."[83] Bucher conveyed these concerns to the defence minister.[84]

Baldev Singh agreed that there would be disturbances across India. Nevertheless he felt the government could not become "helpless spectators" to the events in Hyderabad. If the situation became "intolerable" they ought to meet it. "The risks are there and they will have to be accepted."[85] The deputy prime minister, too, felt that the armed police would suffice for internal duties.[86] To reinforce their point the chiefs of staff submitted a detailed paper prepared by the general staff. After underlining the various commitments and risks the chiefs concluded that an operation against Hyderabad would "for the present" be "a hazardous military gamble, a violation of many principles of war."[87]

By the time the Defence Committee met on 13 May there had been a serious standoff between Hyderabad and Indian forces following the former's refusal to let Bombay officials enter an enclave of Indian territory within Hyderabad's borders. In consequence there was a lengthy debate at the meeting. It was decided that military action would not be undertaken until after the monsoons but the army should be ready to "implement our plans should situation demand it, at ten days' notice." Immediate steps should be taken to stop border

[83] Note by J.N. Chaudhuri, 24 April 1948, 7901-87-16, Bucher Papers, NAM.

[84] Army C-in-C to Minister of Defence, 27 April 1948, ibid.

[85] Baldev to Bucher, 7 May 1948, ibid.

[86] Bucher to Baldev, 5 May 1948, ibid.

[87] Chiefs of Staff Paper (48/1), 8 May 1948, ibid.

incidents. Hyderabad's attention should be drawn to the recent fracas and it be asked to restore normality.[88]

The situation, however, steadily worsened owing to a succession of incidents. On 22 May the Hyderabad police arrested Indian soldiers who were escorting a train of military stores. The same day a train from Madras to Bombay passing through Hyderabad was attacked by an armed mob. Reports stated the presence of Hyderabad police and the Razakar while this incident occurred.[89] In the aftermath both Hyderabad and Indian officials realized that, unless serious efforts were made towards a settlement, the crisis would explode. Well-wishers of Hyderabad, such as its former premier Mirza Ismail, also warned the nizam that to avoid "the impending clash" he must settle with India.[90] Negotiations thus began *in extremis*.

Back to the Table: May 1948

Laik Ali met Nehru and V.P. Menon on 23 May. He continued to oppose accession, claiming that his government would fall and communal riots would erupt.[91] Two days later he held a marathon five-hour meeting with the governor general. Mountbatten described India's military moves and the dangers inherent in the crisis: "did His Exalted Highness not realise how small were his chances of remaining nizam unless he came to terms?" Laik knew that Hyderabad would only last for "a very few days" if India exercised the military option. Yet, "the nizam would prefer to be shot than to accede." Nor would he consider introducing representative government: it would "without doubt lead to accession."

When Menon came in, Laik suggested introducing "responsible" government, "perhaps with a majority of Hindus." But this should be done simultaneously with the conclusion of a "long-term treaty" on

[88] DCC Meeting, 13 May 1948, F200/246, Mountbatten Papers, APAC.

[89] Southern Command to Army Headquarters, 22 May 1948, 7901-87-16, Bucher Papers, NAM; Note on Hyderabad situation, 22–23 May 1948, F200/72E, Mountbatten Papers, APAC.

[90] Ismail to Nizam, 20 May 1948, Mirza Ismail Papers, Reel 2, NMML.

[91] Brief for talk with Laik, 24 May 1948, Mountbatten Papers, F200/72E, APAC.

three subjects. The treaty would provide for "Parallel legislation in emergency." Economically and financially Hyderabad would be "completely free." Menon stated that his government stood for accession. In the alternative option of responsible government, a majority of positions must go to the majority community. Further, in any accompanying agreement India would "insist on the right of over-riding legislation." Laik's proposals, he claimed, "amounted to India acceding to Hyderabad." Menon suggested a third option—a plebiscite. It should be held before the end of 1948, jointly by Hyderabad and India. Prior to the plebiscite, the Hyderabad government should be reconstituted and be fully representative. The administration should also announce its intention to convene a constituent assembly once the question of accession was settled.[92]

Laik and Menon continued the discussion late into the night. Rather than a plebiscite, Laik preferred "a form of association" alongside transition to responsible government. To facilitate negotiations Menon prepared a draft "Heads of Agreement" in two parts. The first dealt with the question of association. It stipulated that on defence, external affairs, and communication Hyderabad would pass legislation requested by India; that Hyderabad would disband all irregular and quasi-military outfits; and that Hyderabad would have no political relations with other countries. The second part concerned the introduction of representative government. As soon as the agreement was inked a new interim government—including at least 50 per cent non-Muslims—would be formed. This government would summon a constituent assembly comprising at least 60 per cent non-Muslims before 1 January 1949. For five years after the new constitution's promulgation relations between Hyderabad and India would continue as set out in Part I.

Menon briefed the prime minister the next morning. As earlier, Nehru was concerned with stabilizing the crisis. Consequently, he felt that "the promise of a plebiscite would leave the present situation doubtful." But he was ready to discuss the document with Laik Ali.[93]

[92] Record of Mountbatten's interview with Laik, 25 May 1948, ibid.
[93] Note of an interview between Mountbatten, Nehru, and Menon, 26 May 1948, ibid.

After another round of negotiations an amended version of the draft was circulated. Laik agreed to the principle of overriding legislation. He also expressed his intention to halve the strength of irregulars (mostly Arabs settled in Hyderabad) to 8000. The Indians consented to this. Owing to Nehru's concerns it was suggested that irrespective of whether Hyderabad opted for the entire proposal or for a plebiscite, Part II should be implemented. In closing Mountbatten emphasized the urgency and "extreme importance of a settlement" on either basis.[94]

When these proposals were discussed in cabinet there was opposition to the provision of 40 per cent representation for Muslims. Patel, who was convalescing in Dehra Dun, conveyed his disagreement. Nehru assured his deputy that the concessions were made in the light of Hyderabad's history and were for a fixed period only. More important, the issue had to be viewed in the wider context. In mid-may 1948 Indian military forces, having consolidated their positions in Kashmir, had launched a "spring offensive" against the tribal invaders. Referring to India's ongoing march, Nehru observed that the military situation in Kashmir was "not so good as we had hoped." The demand for troops was increasing but the reserves were limited. These "just cannot be spared" as long as there was "danger of warlike developments in Hyderabad with other consequences in other parts of the country." He believed it would be of "tremendous advantage to us if we could satisfactorily settle with Hyderabad."[95] Yet Nehru did not repose much faith in Hyderabad. He had received intercepts of Laik's recent telephone conversations which made it "abundantly clear that his one object was to delay matters and to double-cross the Government of India."[96]

As if on cue, Laik wrote to Mountbatten's staff disputing that he had ever agreed to overriding legislation: he had merely suggested that Hyderabad would undertake to introduce parallel legislation.[97] This

[94] Note of an interview between Mountbatten, Nehru, Menon, and Laik, 26 May 1948, ibid.

[95] Doulatram to Patel, 27 May 1948, *SPC*, 7: 209; Nehru to Patel, 27 May 1948, *SWJN-SS*, 6: 222–3.

[96] Record of interview with Nehru, 29 May 1948, F200/72E, Mountbatten Papers, APAC.

[97] Laik to Crum, 29 May 1948, ibid.

volte face was spurred by the nizam's opposition to the idea, which he felt was "equivalent to accession." Further, Laik was unable to persuade the nizam or his ministers to accept 40 per cent representation for Muslims in the constituent assembly: the nizam, backed by the Ittehad, insisted on parity. Monckton knew that Delhi would compromise on neither point. The only chance of breaking the logjam, he concluded, was in "(a) a plebiscite and (b) a radical change in the constitution of the Hyderabad government."[98]

It was a measure of Monckton's persuasive powers that he managed to convince the nizam to accept a plebiscite. But on concomitant issues he failed to make headway. The executive council adopted a resolution on the future course of action, stating that "it may be informally pointed out that Hyderabad will in the near future adopt measures to set up a Constituent Assembly on the basis of Muslim–non-Muslim parity." They were willing to hold a plebiscite provided India halted "subversive activities from outside the state" and lifted the economic blockade. "Thus, when peace is completely restored, Government of Hyderabad will arrange for a plebiscite under its supervision; and the Dominion of India will have no right to interfere directly or indirectly." If India did not accept these proposals, Hyderabad would have no option but to resist.[99]

On the Indian side Patel remained opposed to reservations for Muslims in the constituent assembly. He felt "very keenly" against conceding "a vicious weightage almost at the point of the pistol and under pressure from a militant organisation." Because of the nizam's support for the Ittehad, he felt "very strongly" that India should demand "nothing short of unqualified acceptance of accession and of introduction of undiluted responsible government." Patel was also averse to a further delay: "such delay would only place us in a worse . . . position, both politically and militarily."[100] These views were supported by a report of the Joint Intelligence Sub-Committee, which concluded

[98] Note of interviews on 3 June 1948, Dep Monckton Trustees 32, Monckton Papers, BL. Also, Munshi to Patel, 2 June 1948, *SPC*, 7: 164–5.

[99] Resolution of Council dated 6 June 1948, Dep Monckton Trustees 32, Monckton Papers, BL.

[100] Extract from Patel to Nehru, 4 June 1948; Patel to Nehru, June 1948, *SPC*, 7: 211–12.

that "Ittehad dominates Hyderabad state;" that disturbances in and around the state were "bound to continue until a solution is found to the Indo-Hyderabad issue;" and that the delay in resolution was "resulting in communal tension in India."[101]

The prime minister, however, wanted to move cautiously. He wrote to Patel that the basic requirement was gaining "definite and positive control" over the situation. "Once this is done the crisis is passed." As the internal set-up changed, the Ittehad would "crack up." On other matters, "I would not be uncompromising at this stage." Nehru thought that the consequences of using force would be "full of danger and uncertainty." The possibility of escalation bulked large in his thinking. "Our experience in Kashmir has shown us that it is easier to begin military operations than to end them." There were other repercussions to reckon with. For one thing, the impact on operations in Kashmir would have to be considered. At this point Delhi was already receiving indications that the much vaunted "spring offensive" in Kashmir was unable to make sufficient headway. For another there was the possibility of "far-reaching" effects in the rest of India and Pakistan. All things considered, Nehru felt that it was "unsafe to indulge in a military operation on a big scale unless there is obvious provocation." Meanwhile, if no satisfactory solution emerged India should continue with the coercive strategy: "our pressure should be increased progressively all round Hyderabad." If there was a major provocation, they would be "justified in taking further action."[102]

Hyderabad's tactics in the ensuing negotiations was to uncouple the issues of plebiscite and governmental reform, and to leverage their acceptance of the former to secure concessions on the latter. But Nehru and Menon stuck to their stand that a plebiscite must be accompanied by an immediate change in government.[103] Lucien Benichou has argued that the Indian government's stance reflected their "serious doubts that the population in Hyderabad would decide in favour

[101] JIC Report no. VI enclosed in Brigadier K.B. Singh to Crum, 2 June 1948, F200/72E, Mountbatten Papers, APAC.

[102] Nehru to Patel, 6 June 1948, *SWJN-SS*, 6: 226–8.

[103] Mountbatten's note of interviews with Monckton, Menon, 6 & 7 June, F200/72E, Mountbatten Papers, APAC.

of accession."[104] But there is no evidence to suggest that the Indians harboured such doubts. All along their principal concern was that unless the Hyderabad government was suitably reformed, the situation could not be stabilized.

At the next meeting Mountbatten told Laik and Monckton that, whatever the advantages of a plebiscite, it was essential that "good-will was immediately re-established." After further deliberation a "Draft for Discussion" was prepared by Monckton. The document stated that a plebiscite would be held "as soon as practicable." The plebiscite would be held under a neutral body other than the UN. Meantime, a new interim government would be formed "on a parity basis." The details of the first responsible government and the constituent assembly would be "settled later."[105]

Reviewing the document, Nehru emphasized his "main concern"—that there should be no trouble in Hyderabad in the interim. The Razakar must, therefore, be disbanded. Nehru was also opposed to conceding parity. Menon, who had consulted Patel, stated that the document had "no chance of getting through the Cabinet." Hyderabad had three options: accession; accession pending confirmation by plebiscite; an accord on the lines of his "Heads of Agreement." In the present draft "India got nothing; it might be three years before the plebiscite was held, with all the potentialities of breakdown in the meanwhile." Menon and Monckton decided to prepare yet another draft agreement.[106]

The Last Round of Talks with Hyderabad

Monckton suggested a complex arrangement. The nizam would unilaterally issue an edict committing himself to a plebiscite, and to responsible government and a constituent assembly by early 1949—but there would be no mention of their composition. Simultaneously, both parties would negotiate an interim arrangement on the lines of

[104] Benichou, *From Autocracy to Integration*, 222.

[105] Note of interview between Mountbatten, Laik and Monckton, 7 June 1948; Draft for Discussion, F200/72E, Mountbatten Papers, APAC.

[106] Note of interviews, 8 June 1948, ibid.

Part I of the "Heads of Agreement." Important differences remained. Menon said that the cabinet insisted on banning the Razakar and on reconstituting the government on a popular basis. They also wanted overriding power to legislate on the three subjects. Monckton felt that the nizam would not budge from parity. On the second point a *via media* could be found.[107] The delegation went back to seek the nizam's approval.

Monckton returned to Delhi on 12 June 1948. The nizam had refused to concede the principle of overriding legislation, claiming that it represented "not only the substance, but also the form of accession." Instead he offered, if necessary, to pass parallel legislation himself by ordinance. Moreover, he was unwilling to offer anything more than parity in the constituent assembly. Nehru and Mountbatten went to Dehra Dun to discuss these proposals with Patel. The deputy prime minister was "extremely adamant" but was ultimately persuaded by Nehru to give in on both counts. It was agreed that the composition of the constituent assembly would not be mentioned. Nor would there be a reference to parity in the interim government; instead the nizam would announce its formation "in consultation with the leaders of the major communities." Other ministers assented to these changes.[108]

By this time the rest of the Hyderabad delegation had fetched up. Premier Laik Ali wanted the agreement to specify that Delhi would only ask Hyderabad to pass legislation similar to that extant in India. In other words India could not get them to enact special laws. He also demanded that they be allowed to disband the Razakar over a period of time.[109] That night the Indian prime minister and senior cabinet members accepted these amendments. At a final meeting Laik raised the issue of economic freedom for Hyderabad and of a provision for arbitration. Mountbatten suggested that the former could be included in the collateral letter from Nehru. He told the Hyderabad delegation that the Indians would oblige no more: "There was no question of

[107] Note on Hyderabad Situation, 8/9 June 1948, ibid; Monckton to Mountbatten, 9 June 1948, ibid; Menon, *Integration of Indian States*, 362.

[108] Note on Hyderabad situation, 12/13 June 1948, F200/72G, Mountbatten Papers, APAC.

[109] Note of interview with Hyderabad delegation, 14 June 1948, ibid.

altering the agreement—if it was altered it would not be signed."[110] The delegation went back, leaving Monckton in Delhi.

On the evening of 16 June 1948 the nizam sent a telegram stating that his executive council had advised him not to accept the agreement in its present form. He wanted four further changes. The portion pertaining to the constituent assembly should include the words "on a basis which I shall consider later." The portion dealing with the interim government should omit the words "in consultation with the leaders of the major communities." The question of economic and financial independence should be included in the body of the agreement. And there should be a provision for arbitration.[111] Aghast, Monckton flew down to Hyderabad, but to no avail.

The next afternoon the Indian cabinet met to discuss the situation. Nehru was in a "minority of one," with most members feeling that the terms offered to Hyderabad were "more than generous."[112] At a press conference that evening the prime minister announced that the government would pursue an "open door policy:" the nizam was welcome to accept the draft agreement at any time.

Why did the nizam turn down the agreement? Clearly, the Ittehad and the nizam were loath to forsake their dominance in the Hyderabad government and administration. But their willingness to confront India stemmed from other sources too. The nizam and his advisers believed that Delhi was preoccupied with Kashmir and was unlikely to attack Hyderabad in the near future. For the Pakistan army was now fighting alongside the tribal raiders in Kashmir. As late as 7 September, just two days before the Indian invasion of Hyderabad, they held that India would first want to have "Kashmir off their hands."[113] For another, Hyderabad had begun its own military preparations earlier in the year.

[110] Note on Hyderabad situation, 14/15 June 1948; Note of interview between Mountbatten and Hyderabad delegation, 15 June 1948, ibid.

[111] Nizam to Mountbatten, 16 June 1948, ibid.

[112] Note for Cabinet, 17 June 1948; Note on Hyderabad situation, 17/18 June 1948, ibid; Gadgil to Patel, 18 June 1948, *SPC*, 7: 215.

[113] Colonel Graham to Laik, 7 September 1948, Dep Monckton Trustees 36, Monckton Papers, BL.

In March 1948 Monckton had contacted the Aeronautical and Industrial Research Corporation, owned by an Australian aviator, Sydney Cotton. Cotton had a small fleet of aircraft and a history of smuggling arms. He recalled asking Laik Ali "If his government was prepared to spend £ 20 million to remain free." "You need not ask that question," replied Laik, "the cost will not be counted."[114] Thereafter an agreement had been reached whereby Cotton would procure weapons from various sources in Europe and fly them into Hyderabad. The Pakistan government had allowed Cotton to use Karachi as a staging area. Pakistan had also agreed to provide modest quantities of weapons to Hyderabad. Flights between Karachi and Hyderabad had commenced on 4 June. In all, Cotton carried out 39 sorties ferrying 400 tons of small arms, mortars, 20 mm cannons, grenades, assorted ammunition, and communication equipment. In addition, Hyderabad had appointed a team of former British special service commandos to train and prepare its forces for irregular and guerrilla warfare.[115]

The Showdown

Following the abortive negotiations, Delhi too girded itself for a standoff. Nehru stipulated that, except essentials such as food, salt, and medicines, "all other articles should be denied entry into Hyderabad" and that a "strict blockade should be maintained." The prime minister also authorized "swift action" to repel and punish raiders, including hot pursuit.[116] These decisions also reflected domestic and reputational concerns. The Indians believed that the steps would have a favourable impact on public opinion. Moreover, it would "convince our opponents that we mean business."[117]

Delhi also received intelligence on flights carrying weapons to Hyderabad. After a thorough examination the Indian government

---

[114] Cited in Zubrzycki, *The Last Nizam*, 191.

[115] The details of these preparations are in Dep Monckton Trustees 36, Monckton Papers, BL. Also see, Dep Monckton Trustees 27, which has a fascinating diary detailing the Cotton operations maintained by Colonel Graham.

[116] Note to Ministry of States, 20 June 1948, *SWJN-SS*, 6: 242–3.

[117] Patel to Gadgil, 21 June 1948, *SPC*, 7: 217.

concluded that there were nightly flights from Karachi to Hyderabad. When Delhi lodged a protest the Pakistan government denied complicity.[118] The Indians therefore decided to step up surveillance of airspace. Furthermore they decided to "freeze" Indian securities held by Hyderabad to prevent them from being used for arms purchases.[119] Internal developments in Hyderabad were of greater concern to Delhi. As negotiations ceased, the Razakar grew more aggressive. Reports were received of systematic and murderous violence against Hindus. These became difficult to ignore after the resignation of a Hindu member of the executive council. In his letter of resignation the member denounced the "reign of terror" let loose by the Razakar. The Indian government was equally troubled by the Ittehad's alliance with its erstwhile foes, the communists. Until late 1947 the communists had been engaged in a struggle against the nizam. Early the following year the Communist Party of India decided to oppose the Nehru government and fight for a "democratic revolution." In May 1948 the nizam lifted the ban on the communists. After the break with India the communists were reportedly supplied with weapons too.[120]

Delhi was also faced with increasing domestic criticism for adopting a "soft and appeasement policy." "Action is demanded of us," observed the prime minister, "that action being a military invasion of Hyderabad." Following Mountbatten's departure from India on 21 June 1948 the case for armed action acquired increased vigour within the government. It is seriously misleading, however, to claim that "But for him [Mountbatten] . . . it is almost certain that india would have attacked Hyderabad in the first half of 1948."[121] In fact, even after Mountbatten had left Nehru continued to counsel restraint. Talk of appeasement, he wrote, was "absurd." The government was preparing

---

[118] Note to Secretary General MEA, 2 July 1948, *SWJN-SS*, 7: 183–4; MEA to Indian High Commission, London, 6 July 1948, 7901-87-16, Bucher Papers, NAM.

[119] MEA to Indian High Commission, London, 21 July 1948, F200/72H, Mountbatten Papers, APAC.

[120] Menon, *Integration of Indian States*, 370; Munshi, *The End of an Era*, 178–9. Also see, note titled "Communists in Hyderabad," enclosed in Munshi to Patel, 3 August 1948, *SPC*, 7: 193–201.

[121] Zeigler, *Mountbatten*, 456.

for military action but such a move could not be taken lightly. Nehru's principal concern was the igneous state of inter-communal relations in the country. Whilst India would achieve "victory," it might come at the cost of "great suffering to a large number of people . . . inside or outside Hyderabad." So India ought to take "a long-distance view and not be swept away by some momentary passion."[122] Yet, given the deteriorating situation both inside Hyderabad and along its borders, Nehru felt that they were "heading for a major conflict." All that could be done was "to delay the conflict in the faint hope that something might happen. That delay is becoming more and more difficult."[123]

The Defence Committee met on 6 July to consider the situation. The meeting occurred against the backdrop of Pakistan's open admission that its army was involved in the fighting in Kashmir. The committee, at this point, could hardly have failed to agree that "no definite decisions" for action against Hyderabad could be taken "without a full examination of all our commitments." Of course domestic considerations had also to be weighed. It was pointed out that "not only was delay injurious," but it would be unwise to delude the public about the gravity of the situation in Hyderabad. "If necessary action [must be] taken or begun before the next Assembly session next month."[124] In the event the Indian government managed to hold out longer.

Meanwhile, Hyderabad made frenetic efforts towards external intervention. On Monckton's advice the nizam wrote to Prime Minister Clement Attlee of Britain and President Harry Truman of the United States. India, he claimed, was adopting "a policy of intimidation and coercion perilously reminiscent of that applied by the Nazis against Sudetenland." The nizam urged them to lend their "good offices" in resolving the crisis. Attlee refused to intervene, adding that it was a pity the nizam had turned down India's terms which "offer a good and honourable settlement."[125] The nizam also decided to appeal to the

[122] Nehru to Premiers, 1 July 1948, *SWJN-SS*, 7: 328. Also see Letter to Kher and Shukla, 3 & 4 July 1948, ibid., 187–9.

[123] Letters to Rajagopalachari and Mountbatten, 3 July 1948, ibid., 184–7.

[124] Note to Secretary General MEA, 6 July 1948, ibid., 189–93.

[125] Nizam to Attlee, 4 July 1948; Attlee to Nizam, 27 July 1948, DO 35/3163, TNA. Drafts in Dep Monckton 32, Monckton Papers, BL.

UN. This step was not received well by sections of Hyderabad's elite, which believed that it was tantamount to committing suicide owing to the fear of death.[126] Nehru had anticipated this move. Hyderabad was categorically told that it had no legal right to approach the UN. Nevertheless, the nizam dispatched a delegation at the end of August 1948 to present his case.[127]

The crisis was coming to a boil. On 24 July 1948 Indian troops were ambushed en route to the enclave inside Hyderabad state. Six soldiers were killed and five wounded. Similar incidents occurred in the following weeks.[128] Unchecked by the authorities, the Razakar increased their depredations within the state. "Murder and arson are committed . . . and forcible conversions are taking place," observed the Indian prime minister. These led to "an almost universal" demand in India for the use of force. "It is frightfully difficult for us to look on while this kind of a thing is happening on a considerable scale in Hyderabad," Nehru wrote.[129] By the end of August he was coming around to the view that if the "mounting brutality" of the Razakar was not staunched there might be a "state of lawlessness throughout Hyderabad state."[130]

Nehru's main interest had until this point been to avoid "the possibility of communal troubles in various parts of India." Now, following assurances from premiers of the provinces, he thought that there was "no particular likelihood" of such outbreaks. The situation in Kashmir would certainly have influenced the prime minister's thinking. Pakistani forces having entered the fray in Kashmir, it was important quickly to resolve the crisis in Hyderabad lest it jeopardize India's international security.[131] Nehru concluded that military action must

[126] Jung, *Hyderabad in Retrospect*, 42.

[127] Menon, *Integration of Indian States*, 372–3; Nehru to Patel, 23 July 1948, *SWJN-SS*, 7: 195–6.

[128] S.N. Prasad, *Operation Polo: Police Action Against Hyderabad 1948* (New Delhi: Historical Section Ministry of Defence, 1972), 38–40.

[129] Nehru to Krishna Menon, 15 August 1948, *SWJN-SS*, 7: 207.

[130] Cable to Krishna Menon, 27 August 1948, ibid., 215.

[131] Cf. Taylor C. Sherman, "The Integration of the Princely State of Hyderabad and the Making of the Postcolonial State in India, 1948–1956," *Indian Economic and Social History Review* 44, no. 4 (2007): 495.

be taken "fairly soon and fairly swiftly." Yet this was not an easy choice. "Grave decisions have to be made by us and the alternatives between which we have to choose are equally undesirable. So, as often in life, we search frantically for the lesser evil."[132]

On 31 August 1948 C. Rajagopalachari, who had stepped into Mountbatten's shoes as governor general, sent an ultimatum to the nizam asking him to ban the Razakar and allow Indian troops to be stationed in the state. A week later the nizam replied that India had a "very wrong impression" of the situation in Hyderabad. The idea of stationing Indian forces was "out of the question."[133] On 9 September the Indian government decided to launch Operation Polo, euphemistically termed "police action." The attack commenced on the morning of 13 September. Hyderabad's resistance swiftly crumbled. Four days later the nizam informed Delhi that his government had resigned and that he had taken charge of the political situation. Hyderabad's forces were asked to cease operations and orders were issued to disband the Razakar. The next day the state's forces surrendered unconditionally.[134] A week later the nizam informed the UN that he wished to withdraw the complaint against India.

The Dark Aftermath

The invasion of Hyderabad is often portrayed as an unalloyed political success for India. "There was improvement in public morale and a general lowering of communal tension," writes Sarvepalli Gopal: "secularism had come through its second test."[135] This verdict ignores the dark aftermath of the invasion *within* Hyderabad. If anything, secularism in India had failed a critical test.

Initially, military action appeared to have succeeded in stabilizing the situation. Nehru thought that it had had "a most beneficial result in the whole situation in India. The communal situation has improved tremendously."[136] This assessment was at once partial and premature.

---

[132] Nehru to Mountbatten, 29 August 1948, *SWJN-SS*, 7: 219–22.

[133] Rajagopalachari to Nizam, 31 August 1948; Nizam's reply, 5 September 1948, *SPC*, 7: 229–32. Nehru to Krishna Menon, 29 August 1948, *SWJN-SS*, 7: 222–4.

[134] On the decision to surrender, see Laik Ali, *Tragedy of Hyderabad*.

[135] Gopal, *Nehru*, 2: 42.

[136] Nehru to Monckton, 11 October 1948, *SWJN-SS*, 8: 93.

Before the operation Nehru's principal concern was the possibility of violence against Muslims elsewhere in India. The fatal flaw in his decision calculus was in overlooking the possibility of violence against Muslims in Hyderabad. The focus on atrocities on the Hindus led to the mistaken assumption that order would be restored once the Razakar were tackled. The possibility of reprisals against Muslims was neither envisioned nor provided for. The consequences were calamitous. In the wake of the invasion Hindu mobs systematically targeted and killed Muslims. In places the pogroms continued for nearly twenty days after the attack had commenced. Although the Indian army sought to impose order, there were instances when soldiers looked on or even joined the mobs.[137]

The news of these massacres reached the prime minister only in mid-November. He instructed the states ministry to verify these claims: "We must know the truth." By the time the officials got back Nehru had obtained further information from personal sources. These reports, he wrote, "present a picture which is alarming." The figures of killings mentioned were "so big as to stagger the imagination." If there was "even a fraction of truth in these reports," then the situation was "much worse than we had been led to believe." Nehru made it clear that he wanted "no optimistic account and no suppression of unsavoury episodes." V.P. Menon complacently assured the prime minister that he was "satisfied that while at the initial stages there was some trouble the situation now is entirely under control."[138] Unsatisfied with such responses, Nehru directed two envoys to ascertain the facts and help restore communal amity. The team confirmed his worst fears: "at a very conservative estimate . . . at least 27 thousand to 40 thousand people lost their lives during and after the police action."[139] Patel took strong exception to these conclusions, claiming that detailed official inquiries showed that they "lack balance and proportion."[140]

---

[137] "From the Sunderlal Report," *Frontline*, 18: 5 (3 March 2001). Also see an accompanying essay that provides essential context, A.G. Noorani, "Of a Massacre Untold," *Frontline*, 18: 5 (3 March 2001).

[138] Notes to Ministry of States, 14 & 26 November 1948, *SWJN-SS*, 8: 102–9.

[139] "From the Sunderlal Report", *Frontline*, 18:5 (3 March 2001).

[140] Patel to Abdulghaffar, 4 January 1949, *Sardar's Letters—Mostly Unknown*, 69–70.

The episode substantiated Nehru's concerns over the fragility of communal relations in India and underscored the fact that even the most assured advice on this front was likely to be little more than special pleading. In so doing it pointed to the importance of actively ensuring the security of Muslims. It also bolstered Nehru's belief that the use of force in such a context would be grievously harmful to India's interests. The Hyderabad crisis demonstrated the limits to the exercise of power and the need for ever more circumspection. Its influence would be conspicuous in Nehru's handling of a subsequent crisis—in Bengal.

4

Kashmir 1947–1948

By the end of 1948 Junagadh and Hyderabad had been tackled. Kashmir proved much more challenging. Unlike Hyderabad, or even Junagadh, the contest over Kashmir involved the vital interests of both Pakistan and India. These stemmed from the state's strategic location atop the plains of Punjab, athwart the trade route from Central Asia, and abutting Afghanistan and China. For Pakistan, Kashmir was also important from an economic perspective, not least because its agriculture was sustained by the rivers flowing through the state. Subsequently, Kashmir came to be invested with the hopes and fears of India and Pakistan. In the Stygian darkness after Partition, Gandhi and Nehru regarded Kashmir's accession as a powerful affirmation that India would not become a Hindu Pakistan. As Nehru observed, "If Kashmir went, the position of Muslims in India would become more difficult. In fact, there would be a tendency of people to accept a purely communal Hindu viewpoint. That would mean an upheaval of the greatest magnitude in India."[1] To the Pakistanis, Kashmir's accession seemed but a prelude to the eventual annulment of Partition.

The maharaja of Jammu and Kashmir, Hari Singh, belonged to the Hindu Dogra dynasty that had ruled the state since its creation by the British in 1846.[2] Like many of his contemporaries Hari Singh did not

---

[1] Nehru to Stafford Cripps, 17 December 1948, cited in Brown, *Nehru*, 213.

[2] For the background, see Robert A. Huttenback, *Kashmir and the British Raj, 1847–1947* (Karachi: Oxford University Press, 2004).

take an active interest in governance. Much of his time was spent in hunting and derby. Several months of the year he spent in Bombay, where he maintained a string of excellent race horses. As his son would recall, "my father was much happier racing than administering the state, which chore he largely left to his carefully chosen prime minister and a small council of ministers, mostly from outside Jammu and Kashmir."[3] This aura of feudal shiftlessness could, however, be misleading; for it concealed the prince's sharp, if inflexible, political intellect.

In mid-1947 the maharaja was on the horns of a dilemma. Geographic contiguity and religious composition suggested that accession to Pakistan would be the natural course to adopt; but Hari Singh was loath to join a self-professed Islamic state. Yet if he acceded to India, his subjects might resent the decision.[4] Furthermore, given the Congress Party's stance on the states, he feared that accession to India would result in a haemorrhaging of his own power. The maharaja procrastinated. He signed a standstill agreement with Pakistan and offered one to India but made no moves towards accession. Hari Singh's Micawberism stemmed from his hope that Kashmir might yet manage to stay independent.

Outside the palace the most organized political force in Kashmir was the National Conference led by its charismatic leader Sheikh Mohammed Abdullah. Born in 1905 to the family of a shawl merchant, Abdullah took a master's degree in science from Aligarh University. Despite his qualifications he was denied a position by the state government, which was thoroughly dominated by Hindus.[5] Forced to take up a job as a schoolteacher, Abdullah turned towards political activity, speaking out on behalf of his fellow Muslims and against the maharaja. He played an instrumental role in the creation of the All-Jammu Kashmir Muslim Conference in 1932. Seven years later

[3] Karan Singh, *Autobiography* rev. ed. (New Delhi: Oxford University Press, 1994), 31.

[4] For an excellent study of the formation of a distinctive Kashmiri identity, see Chitralekha Zutshi, *Languages of Belonging: Islam, Regional Identity, and the Making of Kashmir* (Delhi: Permanent Black, 2004).

[5] On Hindu control of the Kashmir state administration, see Mridu Rai, *Hindu Rulers, Muslim Subjects: Islam, Rights, and the History of Kashmir* (Delhi: Permanent Black, 2004).

Abdullah led the transformation of the organization into a secular "National Conference" by including Hindus and Sikhs. During these years Abdullah came to know Jawaharlal Nehru. Their shared commitment to secular values and socialist outlook was matched by mutual personal regard. In consequence, the National Conference drew closer to the Congress. This in turn led to the departure of some of Abdullah's longstanding associates. Ghulam Abbas, a lawyer from Jammu, led the breakaway faction which styled itself the Muslim Conference.

At the time of decolonization, the Muslim Conference favoured accession to Pakistan. However, the popularity of the National Conference and Abdullah far outstripped that of the Muslim Conference, particularly in the crucial valley of Kashmir. Be that as it may Pakistan's leaders were confident that Kashmir had no choice but to join them. Mohammed Ali Jinnah believed that "Kashmir will fall into our lap like a ripe fruit."[6] This was not wishful thinking. The tentative division of Punjab outlined in the 3 June Plan left Kashmir with no real contiguity to India. It was only after the Boundary Award placed parts of the Gurdaspur district within India that Kashmir acquired a tenuous road link to India.[7]

Shortly after the award was announced the Muslim Conference wrote to Pakistan's prime minister, Liaquat Ali Khan, that "the Government and the National Conference are intriguing and any time an announcement is expected declaring Kashmir joining Hindustan." "If, God forbid, the Pakistan Government or the Muslim League do not act," they ominously warned, "Kashmir might be lost to them and the responsibility would be theirs."[8] The Pakistani leaders, of course, realized that the boundary award "was a great blow to us."[9] Given Kashmir's strategic importance they understandably feared that, if the state went to India, Pakistan's security could be jeopardized. Compounding their

[6] Mohammed Ali, *The Emergence of Pakistan* (New York: Columbia University Press, 1967), 297.

[7] Shereen Ilahi, "The Radcliffe Boundary Commission and the Fate of Kashmir," *India Review* 2, no. 1 (January 2003): 77–102.

[8] Note by All-Jammu & Kashmir Muslim Conference, 25 August 1947 enclosed in Mohammed to Liaquat, 25 August 1947, *Jinnah Papers*, 9: 207–16.

[9] Zafrullah Khan, *The Forgotten Years: Memoirs of Sir Muhammad Zafrullah Khan*, ed. A.H. Batalvi (Lahore: Vanguard Books, 1991), 158.

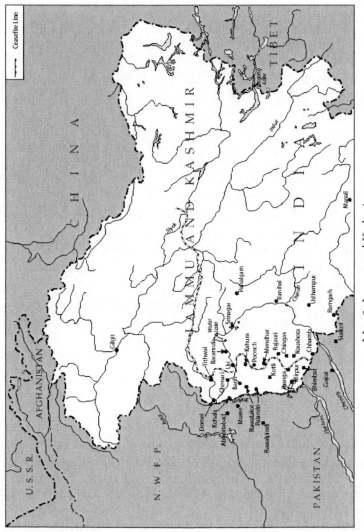

Map 3. Jammu and Kashmir

problems was the fact that the Muslim Conference was a shambles.[10] The Pakistanis were thus faced with two options: entice Kashmir to accede to them; or use force to upend the maharaja and "liberate" Kashmir. Both tracks were set afoot by the end of August 1947.

The Louring Clouds in August–September 1947

The second option was facilitated by the simmering discontent, largely economic, in the Poonch region of Kashmir. The gathering head of steam was used by the local Muslim Conference, led by Sardar M. Ibrahim Khan (later the first president of Azad [Free] Kashmir), to further their campaign for accession to Pakistan. These efforts were invigorated towards the end of August, when Muslim League activists joined in from Pakistan. Soon, the protests turned violent. The maharaja responded with a brutal crackdown: inside a month the incipient revolt was snuffed out.[11]

The rebels now turned to Pakistan for assistance. Sardar Ibrahim met Colonel Akbar Khan of the general staff and requested arms. Akbar was also approached by a senior Muslim League leader, Mian Iftikharuddin, who was proceeding to Kashmir's capital, Srinagar, to assess Pakistan's prospects. If the political situation was unpromising, they would have to take action to prevent the state's adhesion to India. He asked Akbar to prepare a plan for this contingency.[12] This plan and another were discussed at a meeting chaired by Liaquat on 12 September. It was finalized by the end of the month.[13] Khurshid

[10] Mohammed to Khurshid, 25 July 1947; Nasira Siddiqui to Jinnah, n.d. [August 1947], ibid., 184–5, 217–20.

[11] Record of conversation with Major General Henry Scott [Commander of Kashmir State Forces], 8 October 1947, in UKHC Pakistan to CRO, 9 October 1947, IOR L/PS/13/1845b, APAC; TS "Operation in Kashmir" by Richard Powell [Inspector-General of Kashmir Police], Mss Eur D862, Powell Papers, APAC. For an account that claims that the uprising had had early successes, see Sardar M. Ibrahim Khan, *The Kashmir Saga* (Mirpur: Verinag, 1965).

[12] Akbar Khan, *Raiders in Kashmir* (Karachi: Pak Publishers, 1970), 8–14.

[13] Ibid., 15–17; Muhammad Saraf, *Kashmiris Fight for Freedom* (Lahore: Ferozsons, 1977), 2: 858–9, 889; Shaukat Hyat Khan, *The Nation that Lost Its Soul* (Lahore: Jang Publishers, 1995), 214–15.

Anwar of the Muslim League National Guard proceeded to the North West Frontier Province (NWFP) to organize a tribal contingent for the attack. While these levies were being raised, armed bands from across the border launched forays into Kashmir.

Pakistan's assessment that the maharaja would accede to India was correct. By mid-September 1947 the maharaja had fired his prime minister, Ram Chandra Kak, who had wanted Kashmir to remain equidistant from India and Pakistan.[14] The new appointee, a judge from the east Punjab high court (later chief justice of India), M.C. Mahajan, met Patel and Nehru, and informed them that the maharaja was willing to accede but wanted political reforms to be deferred. Nehru insisted that Sheikh Abdullah, who was incarcerated by the Kashmir authorities, should be released and that a popular government be immediately installed; only then should Kashmir declare accession to India.[15] On 29 September Sheikh Abdullah was set free. Soon, emissaries from Pakistan were approaching him; but Abdullah remained noncommittal. In fact he had already decided in favour of accession to India and had begun shaping public opinion.[16]

Jinnah's private secretary reported from Srinagar that these developments unmistakably pointed towards accession to India. "Muslim Conference is now practically a dead organization." Consequently, Pakistan must resort to force. They had only to "supply arms and foodstuffs to the tribes within and without the state." He informed the governor general that preparations were already under way.[17] By this time the governor of the NWFP, Sir George Cunningham, was also alert to Khurshid Anwar's activities. Later, Pakistan's defence minister told him "all the underground history of the present campaign against Kashmir, and brought apologies from Liaquat Ali for not letting me know anything about it sooner . . . Apparently Jinnah himself

[14] "Jammu and Kashmir State in 1946–47" by R.C. Kak, n.d. [c. 1956], Mss Eur D862, Powell Papers, APAC.

[15] M.C. Mahajan, *Looking Back* (London: Asia Publishing House, 1963), 126–7; Nehru to Mahajan, 21 September 1947, *SWJN-SS*, 4: 272–4.

[16] Sheikh Abdullah, *Flames of Chinar* (New Delhi: Viking, 1993), 87–8; Kachru to Nehru, 4 October 1947, *SPC*, 1: 54–5.

[17] Khurshid to Jinnah, 12 October 1947, *Jinnah Papers*, 9: 246–52.

first heard of what was going on about 15 days ago, but said 'Don't tell me anything about it. My conscience must be clear.'"[18]

On 22 October 1947 nearly 5000 tribesmen seized Muzaffarabad, then Domel, Uri; and the raiders surged towards Srinagar. Two days later a beleaguered maharaja formally offered to accede to India and requested Delhi for military assistance.[19] Against this backdrop the Indian Defence Committee met on the morning of 25 October.

Military Intervention

Nehru was certain that the invasion "could not have taken place without 100% assistance of Pakistan authorities." To resist the invasion it was imperative that the maharaja co-opted popular forces in Kashmir. Nehru felt that it was of "little advantage" to talk of accession at this stage. Accession dependent upon the will of the people should be a general principle; but the first step was for the maharaja to secure Abdullah's co-operation. Mountbatten argued that India should counter Pakistan's "political manoeuvre" by allowing Kashmir to accede temporarily, conditional upon the people's will being established once law and order were restored. Thereafter India should afford assistance to Kashmir. Vallabhbhai Patel stated that it was perfectly right for them to provide military support to Kashmir, whether or not the latter acceded. After an inconclusive debate the committee asked the secretary of the ministry of states, V.P. Menon, to fly to Srinagar and discuss these issues with the maharaja. The military chiefs were directed to despatch weapons and ammunition to Kashmir and prepare plans for an intervention.[20]

Back from Kashmir the following day, Menon reported that the situation was parlous. The Defence Committee decided to airlift troops to Srinagar the next morning. It was also agreed that Kashmir's

---

[18] Entry of 26 October 1947, Diary 1947–8, Mss Eur D670/6, Cunningham Papers, APAC.

[19] Andrew Whitehead, *A Mission in Kashmir* (New Delhi: Viking, 2007), 102–3.

[20] DCC Meeting, 25 October 1947, F200/246, Mountbatten Papers, APAC.

accession would be accepted subject to the proviso that the peoples' wishes would be ascertained following the restoration of *status quo ante*.[21] The maharaja in turn appointed Sheikh Abdullah as head of the emergency administration. The question of when exactly he signed the instrument of accession has been the focus of much scholarly debate and has resulted in a literature out of all proportion to the importance of the matter.[22] Suffice it to say that it was almost certainly signed on 27 October 1947—not the 26th as claimed by India.

Although the tribesmen had nipped up the valley of Kashmir, they wasted precious days indulging in an orgy of loot, massacre, and rape in Baramula.[23] Indian forces landed just in time to defend Srinagar. Jinnah was incensed when he learnt of the Indian intervention. Late

[21] DCC Meeting , 26 October 1947, ibid.

[22] The traditional Indian account is laid out in Menon's memoirs, wherein he claims that he had flown to Jammu on the evening of 26 October 1947, obtained the maharaja's signature on the instrument of accession, and returned to Delhi the same day (Menon, *Integration of Indian States*, 399–400). Using British documents, Alastair Lamb irrefutably demonstrates that Menon did not leave Delhi on 26 October. Lamb, however, overreaches himself in contending that the maharaja never signed an instrument of accession (Alastair Lamb, *Birth of a Tragedy: Kashmir 1947* [Karachi: Oxford University Press, 2001], 80–103). He conveniently overlooks a document in a collection that he otherwise relies on. "Sometimes I feel that I should withdraw the accession that I have made to the Indian Union." (Hari Singh to Patel, 31 January 1948, *SPC* 1: 158). Prem Shankar Jha argues that Menon had obtained the maharaja's signature in Srinagar on the night of 25 October or the early hours of the 26th. Menon, with Mountbatten's concurrence, did not produce the instrument at the DCC meeting on 26 October. He was apparently concerned that Nehru would reject it if not accompanied by reforms that catered to the induction of Abdullah into the state government (Prem Shankar Jha, *The Origins of a Dispute: Kashmir 1947* [New Delhi: Oxford University Press, 2003], 64–85). Jha's account relies heavily on the oral testimony of Field Marshal S.H.F.J. Manekshaw who, as a colonel in the Indian army headquarters, had accompanied Menon on his visit to Srinagar. The reliability of the testimony is called into question by the fact that it is incorrect on certain crucial details. Parts of Jha's account are also noisy with the sounds of sawing and stretching as the facts are forced and squeezed into the Procrustean bed prepared for them.

[23] For a first-rate study of these events, Whitehead, *A Mission in Kashmir*.

on the night of 27 October he ordered the acting C-in-C of the Pakistan army, General Douglas Gracey, to rush troops to Baramula, Srinagar, and Mirpur. Gracey, for his part, informed the supreme commander, Field Marshal Claude Auchinleck, who flew to Lahore the next morning. Auchinleck told Jinnah that Kashmir had acceded to India, and that sending Pakistani troops would have dire consequences. Furthermore, he would be compelled to ask British officers to "stand down." This would be doubly disastrous, for the Pakistan army was staffed by British officers in operational as well as higher command appointments. Jinnah fumed; he could do little else.[24]

Jinnah summoned the governors of the NWFP and West Punjab for a meeting at Liaquat's residence. He argued that although the Pakistan army was weak, "he was not at all convinced that Gracey was right in saying that we must not risk war." Evidently Jinnah believed that India's military position in Kashmir was not strong enough. They then discussed the possibility of assisting the invaders with arms and ammunition, short of sending troops. Meanwhile a message was received that the Indians would come for discussions the next day. It was decided that Jinnah should repudiate the legality of Kashmir's accession and demand that a plebiscite be held in the presence of both Indian and Pakistani troops with the army chiefs as plebiscite commissioners.[25]

The meeting, however, was cancelled as Nehru took unwell. Jinnah seized the opportunity to revert to the idea of reinforcing the invasion. He claimed that India had deliberately cancelled the visit to delay matters. "[H]is hands were now free, legally as well as morally" to take any action in Kashmir. He urged the British governors "to enter into the full spirit of this struggle." Cunningham warned Jinnah that if the officials' involvement came to light Pakistan would attract international censure. "Jinnah said he realised this and would take the risk." It was decided that 5000 tribesmen would be maintained at Baramula, with

[24] Auchinleck to Chiefs of Staff in UKHC India to CRO, 28 October 1947, IOR L/PS/13/1845b; Note by Brigadier Scoones, n.d., IOR L/WS/1/1187; Governor General's Personal Report, 5 November 1947, IOR L/PO/6/123, APAC. Also see entry of 9 January 1948, Diary 1947–8, Box 60, Darling Papers, Centre of South Asian Studies, Cambridge.

[25] Entry of 28 October 1947, Diary 1947–8, Mss Eur D670/6, Cunningham Papers, APAC.

regular drafts dispatched for relief. A directing committee of five civil servants would be appointed to continue the recruitment of tribesmen and ensure supplies. At this point Mountbatten called and asked Jinnah to come to Delhi as Nehru was unwell; Jinnah asked him to come to Lahore as Liaquat was unwell. Eventually Mountbatten offered to visit Lahore.[26]

Negotiations in November 1947

Before Mountbatten's departure the Defence Committee decided that he should ask Pakistan to go by the people's wishes and that a joint statement should be prepared. The statement drafted by V.P. Menon read:

> The Governments of India and Pakistan agree that, where the Ruler of a state does not belong to the community to which the majority of his subjects belong, and where the state has not acceded to that Dominion whose majority community is the same as the state's, the question whether the state should finally accede to one or the other of the Dominions should in all cases be decided by an impartial reference to the will of the people.[27]

To ensure impartiality Nehru decided that "it should be held under United Nations' auspices" but not until "complete law and order have been established."[28]

Mountbatten and his chief of staff, Hastings Ismay, flew to Lahore on 1 November. They spent over three hours with Jinnah discussing Junagadh, Hyderabad, and Kashmir. Jinnah, Ismay observed, "was at his most obstinate and on his highest horse."[29] When Mountbatten suggested impartial plebiscites he spurned the proposal, arguing that "it was redundant and undesirable to have a plebiscite when it was quite clear that states should go according to their majority population, and if we [India] would give him accession of Kashmir he would

[26] Entry of 29 October 1947, ibid.

[27] Note for Mountbatten by Erskine Crum, 31 October 1947, F200/90C, Mountbatten Papers, APAC.

[28] Nehru to Mahajan, 31 October 1947, *SWJN-SS*, 4: 293–4.

[29] Note on situation in India, 11 November 1947, 3/7/66, Ismay Papers, LHCMA.

offer to urge the accession of Junagadh direct to India." Mountbatten said that Delhi would not forego the accession unless decreed by the people. Jinnah retorted that he could not accept a formula if it included Hyderabad: the state did not desire to accede to either dominion and he could not be a party to coercion.[30]

Jinnah claimed that Kashmir's accession was the product of a long intrigue and was brought about forcibly. For the fighting to cease, the two sides should withdraw immediately and simultaneously. Asked why he objected "so strongly" to a plebiscite, Jinnah replied that with Indian troops in Kashmir and Sheikh Abdullah in power, "the average Muslim would never have the courage to vote for Pakistan." Mountbatten countered that they could invite the United Nations to conduct and ensure a free and impartial plebiscite. Jinnah claimed that a plebiscite could only be organized by the governors general. Mountbatten explained that this would be unacceptable given his constitutional position. When Mountbatten invited him to Delhi for discussions, Jinnah said that he would consider it after Liaquat had recovered.

Why did Jinnah brush aside the offer of a UN-supervised plebiscite? His implacable stance was driven by two considerations. First, Jinnah believed that despite India's intervention the invasion might yet succeed; this explains his desire to send more tribesmen to Kashmir. Once the Indians realized that their position in Kashmir was untenable, they would accept his offer to swap Junagadh for Kashmir. This would also exempt Hyderabad from a plebiscite and so strengthen its chances of staying independent. These proved major miscalculations. As Cunningham presciently observed: "The tragedy is that Jinnah could, I believe, have got India's agreement to a plebiscite under impartial control, 10 days ago, but as the tribes were then in the ascendant for the time being he thought he would hold out a bit longer for better terms. It looks as if he may now have lost his chance."[31]

Second, Jinnah was not oblivious of the possibility that, owing to the havoc wrought by the tribesmen, Pakistan might lose a plebiscite. "Many people say," noted Cunningham, "that if a plebiscite of Kashmir Muslims were now held they would vote for India, and not

[30] Note of a discussion, 1 November 1947, F200/90C, Mountbatten Papers, APAC.

[31] Entry of 10 November 1947, Diary 1947–8, Mss Eur D670/6, Cunningham Papers, APAC.

for Pakistan, now that they have a taste of what the Pathans can really do." Jinnah was determined, therefore, that if at all a plebiscite was held it should be under circumstances most favourable to Pakistan: Indian forces should be withdrawn and Abdullah should be unseated. As Alastair Lamb delicately puts it, in 1947–8 Pakistan's attitude towards a plebiscite was less than enthusiastic.[32]

Jinnah's demands were entirely unacceptable to India. As the secretary general of the foreign office, G.S. Bajpai, observed, it was tantamount to equating them with the invaders. Besides, there was no certainty that the raiders would not return.[33] Sidelining Abdullah would be a self-confounding move. Not only did he command the greatest following in the valley, he had all along supported accession to India. If he was removed at Pakistan's demand, India's political base in Kashmir would rapidly shrink. Sheikh Abdullah was the linchpin in Nehru's Kashmir policy.

On 8 November Nehru wrote to Liaquat enumerating India's proposals: Pakistan should publicly compel the raiders to withdraw; India would withdraw its troops as soon as the raiders withdrew and law and order was restored; both governments should make a joint request to the UN to hold a plebiscite at the earliest. Nehru wanted the principle of referendum to apply across the board.[34] At this precise time the fate of Junagadh and Hyderabad hung in the balance too. The Indian government, we may recall, had recently taken control of the administration of Junagadh and had been gearing up for an early plebiscite. And the nizam of Hyderabad had not only disavowed accession but had sent a new delegation to negotiate a fresh standstill agreement with India.

Mountbatten was worried that Indian and Pakistani leaders had not yet met to discuss the issue. On 8 November, when a Pakistani official team was in Delhi, he prodded Mohammed Ali (secretary general of the Pakistan cabinet) to sit with V.P. Menon and hammer out an agreement as a basis for further discussion between the principals. Ali was "adamant" that Jinnah would accept nothing but simultaneous

[32] Alastair Lamb, *Kashmir: A Disputed Legacy, 1846–1990* (Karachi: Oxford University Press, 1992), 166–7.

[33] UKHC India to CRO, 18 November 1947, DO 133/68, TNA.

[34] Nehru to Liaquat, 8 November 1947, *SWJN-SS*, 4: 320e–320h.

withdrawal. Both Ismay and Menon pointed out that this would be objectionable to Delhi. Eventually Menon agreed to suggest the following to his government: "Both Governments agree that all forces, whether regular or irregular must be withdrawn from Kashmir soil at the earliest possible moment. The withdrawal will commence on the 12th November and will be concluded by the 26th November." On the issue of plebiscite, Ali took Jinnah's tack. "Surely it was clear that Kashmir must go to Pakistan, so why all this fuss about a plebiscite?" If at all held, it should be left to the governors general. Menon pointed out India's objection. At length, a variant was evolved: "A plebiscite will be held as soon as possible under the aegis of two persons nominated by Governments of India and Pakistan, with a person nominated by the Kashmir Government as observer. The plebiscite will be conducted by British officers." Finally, the draft extended the principle of plebiscite to other problematic states.[35]

Alastair Lamb has claimed that this was "one of the most realistic Indo-Pakistani negotiations ever conducted" and that it was wrecked by Nehru's obstinacy.[36] On the contrary, both Menon and Ismay were rather dubious about the proposals. Their misgivings were confirmed when Nehru told Ali that he could neither agree to simultaneous withdrawal nor to the proposed arrangements for a plebiscite. Writing to Liaquat, Nehru averred that "an essential preliminary is complete withdrawal of all raiders and invaders . . . [till then] we cannot withdraw our troops from Kashmir."[37] Besides Pakistan, too, found portions of the draft uncongenial. On 16 November Liaquat issued a press statement demanding that the UN should halt the fighting in Kashmir, set up an "impartial administration," and conduct a plebiscite. The second point clearly went against the draft; but it was consonant with Jinnah's thinking. Indeed, in his statement Liaquat denounced Abdullah as "a quisling" and an "agent of Congress for many years."[38]

[35] Report on conversation with Ismay, UKHC India to CRO, 10 November 1947, DO 133/68, TNA.

[36] Alastair Lamb, *Incomplete Partition: The Genesis of the Kashmir Dispute, 1947–48* (Hertingfordbury: Roxford Books, 1997), 219–22.

[37] UKHC India to CRO, 10 November 1947, DO 133/68, TNA; Nehru to Liaquat, 13 November 1947, *SWJN-SS*, 4: 323–4.

[38] *Dawn* (Karachi), 17 November 1947.

Military Operations in November 1947

Alongside diplomacy, military operations proceeded apace. By mid-November Indian forces had retaken Uri and secured the valley. The invaders had, however, continued their advance in Poonch and Mirpur areas. With the assistance of the local rebels, now known as the Azad Kashmir forces, they had captured Bhimbar, Rajauri, and Rawalakot. They now posed a serious threat to the state forces' garrisons in Mirpur, Kotli, Poonch, and Naushera. There was a large civilian exodus in the wake of the attacks and thousands sought refuge in the Poonch garrison. In Gilgit the Scouts, led by a British officer, staged a coup and declared their allegiance to Pakistan.[39] In time, joined by the Azad forces, they would capture Baltistan.

From the outset, operations in the Poonch–Mirpur sector had been a matter of debate in Delhi. On 30 October N. Gopalaswami Ayyangar queried whether "it would eventually be *necessary and desirable* for Indian troops to clear the Punch [*sic*] and Mirpur areas." A former prime minister of Kashmir, he knew that the rebels were firmly for Pakistan. Mountbatten pointed out that ultimately the state might have to be divided for a plebiscite, when these areas "might prove a liability to India." The Defence Committee directed the states ministry to examine both these issues.[40] But the questions were rendered somewhat irrelevant by the invaders' subsequent advance.

The Defence Committee met on 14 November to take stock of the situation. The commander of the Jammu & Kashmir Division, Major General Kalwant Singh, outlined his operational intent. In the valley his forces would conduct reconnaissance for an advance from Uri to Domel and Kohala. A column was moving from Jammu towards Mirpur and Poonch to relieve the garrisons still holding out. At an appropriate time another column would be sent down from Uri to Poonch to marry up with the column from Jammu. The committee approved these steps.[41]

[39] Major W.A. Brown, "Gilgit 1947 and After," in Garrett Papers, Centre of South Asian Studies, Cambridge.

[40] DCC Meeting, 30 October 1947, F200/246, Mountbatten Papers, APAC (emphasis added).

[41] DCC Meeting, 14 November 1947, ibid.

The acting army C-in-C, Lieutenant General Roy Bucher, thought that the army should not embark on anything more in the area. "The advent of winter and a lack of means," he wrote to the defence minister, "render wider action impossible." Owing to its many and varied commitments, especially in handling refugees, the army was "very fully stretched." Moreover, the hilly terrain, unlike the valley of Kashmir, was much more suited to the tribesman's tactics. "I cannot overestimate the importance of avoiding any permanent commitment in Poonch."[42] These concerns were not unfounded. The column from Uri came under heavy attack and was forced to move back, though a battalion managed to reach Poonch town. Simultaneously the tribal forces attacked an isolated post across the Jhelum. Its loss, as the official historians note, would have "jeopardised the defence of Uri, with disastrous consequences." In the event the piquet managed to stave off the assault. The garrisons of Naushera, Jhangar, and Kotli were also relieved. But Mirpur, Bhimbar, and Rajauri fell.[43]

Chandrashekar Dasgupta contends that the British officers' attitude towards operations in Poonch was shaped by the views of the British government, who believed that Indian control of this area would pose a grave threat to Pakistan.[44] The argument is contrived. For one thing, these views were expressed by the high commissioner in Pakistan, and there is no evidence that it was swallowed by Whitehall. For another, there were good military reasons for the position adopted by the British commanders. For a third, Bucher was airing these concerns in private too, which suggests that his official arguments were not disingenuous. To his daughter he wrote that the army was overstretched owing to myriad commitments. In another letter Bucher expressed his concerns about Poonch: "India cannot afford a setback."[45]

Following these developments the prime minister, too, became

[42] Bucher to Baldev Singh, 17 November 1947, F200/73B, Mountbatten Papers, APAC.

[43] S.N. Prasad & Dharam Pal, *History of Operations in Jammu and Kashmir (1947–8)* (New Delhi: Ministry of Defence, 2005), 55–63.

[44] Dasgupta, *War and Diplomacy*, 58, 69.

[45] Bucher to Elizabeth, 14 & 24 November 1947, 7901-87-6, Bucher Papers, NAM. Also see Lockhart to Russell, 5 December 1947, 8310-154-102, Lockhart Papers, NAM.

wary. Asked if India was going to maintain garrisons in this area, Nehru replied: "we cannot be strong everywhere but we must be firmly established in such places in Kashmir from where we could attack and take the initiative." Nehru's stance not only acknowledged military realities, but reflected his concern with reputation. Negotiations with Hyderabad were at a crucial stage: the nizam was persistent in his demand to change the previously negotiated draft of the standstill agreement. A setback in Kashmir would enfeeble India's negotiating position *vis-à-vis* Hyderabad. Nehru underlined the "necessity of avoiding all risks," adding that any reversal in Kashmir would have "the most serious psychological repercussions in the whole of India."[46]

The Liaquat–Nehru
Meeting of November 1947

Concurrently, the prime ministers of India and Pakistan met in New Delhi. Eager to prevent further hostilities, Mountbatten took the initiative in facilitating these discussions. At the first session both sides reiterated their positions. India wanted all raiders to withdraw; once the fighting stopped Indian troops would be withdrawn except for small garrisons at vital strategic points to prevent further raids; thereafter a plebiscite would be held under UN auspices. Liaquat sought an impartial administration or alternatively wanted Abdullah to induct members of the opposition party into his government. Pakistan also sought an immediate request to the UN to hold a plebiscite.[47]

The next day Mountbatten yet again asked Mohammed Ali and V.P. Menon to work with Ismay and produce an acceptable formula. The main proposals drawn up by them were: Pakistan would use all its influence to persuade the Azad forces to stop fighting and the tribesmen to withdraw; India would withdraw the bulk of its forces, leaving behind only small detachments of minimum strength; a joint request would be made to the UN to send a commission to hold a plebiscite and advise both governments on the required preliminary

[46] DCC Meeting, 24 November 1947, F200/246, Mountbatten Papers, APAC.
[47] Note of meeting, 26 November 1947, F200/195B, Mountbatten Papers, APAC.

steps.[48] The proposals carefully bridged both sides' positions. By allowing India to retain some troops they acknowledged both its legal position and commitments to Kashmir. By allowing for a UN role at an earlier stage they sought to meet Pakistan's requirements. The subsequent discussion was meandering and inconclusive. Liaquat wanted all Indian forces to be withdrawn. Nehru refused, insisting that some troops were required for internal security. Patel, at one point, offered to withdraw all Indian troops from the Poonch area. This, of course, reflected the internal debates in India about these parts. The Pakistanis seemed to welcome this. But when Nehru pointed out the difficulty of defining the "Poonch area," the discussion petered out. Ultimately, no decisions emerged. Yet the meeting ended on a warm note; both sides agreed to put the proposals to their respective parties in Kashmir. The next meeting would be held in Lahore the following week.[49]

Getting the Kashmir authorities' approval was not a foregone conclusion for Delhi. The National Conference as well as the maharaja had been strongly opposed to a plebiscite. As Ajit Bhattacharjea notes, Abdullah "insisted that the decision to join India had been made when the National Conference supported accession and helped drive out Pathan raiders sent by Pakistan. There was no question of choosing between the two."[50] Abdullah was not worried about losing the vote. Indeed, he believed that owing to the tribal atrocities Pakistan had "not a hope" of winning. Rather, he was worried at the possibility of including his political adversaries in an interim administration: "this would render suitable government impossible."[51] Before meeting Liaquat, Nehru had written a placatory letter to Abdullah, explaining that he could not back out of a plebiscite. Nehru had assured Abdullah that he would not agree to a plebiscite till complete normality was

[48] Hodson, *The Great Divide*, 461–2; Menon, *Integration of Indian States*, 407–8; Campbell-Johnson, *Mission with Mountbatten*, 250–1.

[49] Note of meeting, 28 November 1947, F200/195B, Mountbatten Papers, APAC.

[50] Ajit Bhattacharjea, *Sheikh Mohammad Abdullah: Tragic Hero of Kashmir* (New Delhi: Roli Books, 2008), 139–40.

[51] Note of interview with Sheikh Abdullah, 29 November 1947, Mountbatten Papers, File 195B, APAC.

restored.[52] The National Conference, we shall see, would hold India to this commitment.

Nehru now wrote to the maharaja about the proposals: "time is propitious for a settlement on Kashmir . . . I feel sure that we should try our utmost to achieve it." The alternative was to carry on indefinitely. In particular, it would be difficult to clear the Poonch area. On the political side Nehru observed that in Kashmir and Jammu a majority favoured union with India. In the environs of Poonch "there is little doubt" that the masses were against India. "In the balance probably an overall majority will be in favour of the Union." Nehru also considered the other ideas afloat: independence with guarantees from both India and Pakistan; partition with Jammu going to India and Kashmir to Pakistan; the Poonch area going to Pakistan and the rest to India.

The first idea had originated from Mountbatten, who had suggested it to Sheikh Abdullah prior to the invasion. At the end of November 1947 Abdullah had asked Mountbatten if it was still feasible. Abdullah felt that even if a plebiscite went in favour of India, "Pakistan would never ease up and bitterness would continue." Mountbatten said that true independence was impossible; but Kashmir could accede to both dominions on the three central subjects, provided they acceded to each other on these. If this was unacceptable to both sides, it could be introduced as a third option in the plebiscite.[53]

Nehru thought that independence was "likely to give trouble" for Kashmir might continue as an arena of conflict between India and Pakistan. He stoutly opposed partition along Jammu because it was the "Kashmir [valley] that is of essential value to India." Importantly, he was not averse to letting go of the Poonch area.[54] Whilst Nehru preferred a plebiscite, all these options would be in play over the next year.

In Pakistan the Azad leadership "unanimously and immediately condemned it [the proposals] out of hand." Without a total Indian withdrawal and a new administration they would prefer to continue

[52] Nehru to Abdullah, 21 November 1947, *SWJN-SS*, 4: 336–7.

[53] Note on interview with Abdullah, 29 November 1947, F200/195B, Mountbatten Papers, APAC.

[54] Nehru to Maharaja, 1 December 1947, *SPC*, 1: 101–7.

fighting.[55] More seriously, Jinnah opposed the proposals on the same grounds. As he noted: "Kashmir—no commitment should be made without *my approval of terms* of settlement. Mr. Liaquat has agreed and promised to abide by this understanding."[56] Jinnah, in fact, was open in his opposition and conveyed his views to the British envoy.[57]

Even as Nehru was commending the proposals to the maharaja, Pakistan stepped up attacks in Poonch. By 30 November Indian troops had to abandon Kotli. Mirpur was ransacked by the raiders, who then advanced towards Akhnur. Thousands of inhabitants fled their homes for the safety of Jammu; reports poured in of large-scale massacres and the abduction of women.[58] Reports were received of large concentrations of insurgents particularly at Sialkot, Gujrat, and Jhelum. Nehru excoriated Liaquat for the attacks and massacres. India could not countenance the use of Pakistani territory for launching such raids. "This you will appreciate might involve far-reaching consequences."[59]

At the next Defence Committee meeting Nehru advocated air action against tribal concentrations on the Indian side of the frontier. Patel and Baldev Singh urged stronger measures, demanding the creation of a *cordon sanitaire* ten miles deep, stretching from Naushera to Muzaffarabad, which would be intensely bombarded. The ministers at once overestimated the efficacy of aerial bombardment and underestimated the danger to the civilian populace. Nehru was more cautious and did not lend his support to this idea: "the territory to be bombed should be limited and our object should be to seek out and destroy insurgent concentrations."[60] A subsequent appreciation prepared by the chiefs endorsed Nehru's views.

[55] UKHC Pakistan to CRO, 5 December 1947, DO 133/69, TNA.

[56] Cited in Zaheer, *Rawalpindi Conspiracy*, 120 (emphasis in the original document).

[57] UKHC Pakistan to CRO, 10 December 1947, DO 133/69, TNA.

[58] Mahajan to Nehru, 30 November 1947, *SPC*, 1: 99–100. Also see "A 1947 Tragedy of Jammu and Kashmir State: The Cleansing of Mirpur," Mss Eur C705, Amar Devi Gupta Papers, APAC.

[59] Nehru to Liaquat, 3 December 1947, *SWJN-SS*, 4: 358.

[60] DCC Meeting, 3 December 1947, F200/246, Mountbatten Papers, APAC.

But the military now pressed for the evacuation of Poonch town. Nehru insisted that it be held. Reputational concerns were uppermost in his mind. Withdrawal, he told the army commander, would encourage the enemy at a critical time and the government's prestige would be dimmed. Nehru was also alert to the link between military operations and diplomacy. The negotiations with Pakistan were at an important stage. If an agreement was reached the Poonch issue would be simplified. If not, it was all the more important to reinforce the area.[61]

On 8 December 1947 Nehru and Mountbatten, with Baldev and Ayyangar, met Liaquat and Pakistan's finance minister Ghulam Mohammed.[62] The meeting opened with a pyrotechnic exchange of recriminations. Charges traded, they got down to business. Both sides agreed that the ultimate aim was to hold a plebiscite. The rub lay in the preliminary steps. The Indians wanted a declaration by Pakistan that it would urge the raiders to withdraw and prevent further influx. The Pakistanis reverted to Jinnah's stance: before they could issue such an undertaking India must declare that all its troops would be withdrawn and that there would be an impartial administration prior to the plebiscite. Mountbatten suggested that the UN should be asked to help break the deadlock. Liaquat promptly assented to this. After all, this had been one of his demands in the previous round. Nehru entirely rejected this idea: the UN would be approached only after the cessation of hostilities.

Before the next session Mountbatten sought and obtained Liaquat's "full support" to involving the UN. Mountbatten then attempted to foist the proposal on his prime minister. But Nehru was irate and "extremely adamant." Liaquat reiterated that he supported a reference to the UN—even if India accused Pakistan of assisting the rebels. Liaquat's stance was understandable in the context of the internal differences in Karachi. He knew full well that India would not accept Jinnah's demands. Since Jinnah had forcefully rejected the draft

[61] Prasad & Pal, *Operations*, 81–5. On subsequent military developments in the Poonch area, see Maurice Cohen, *Thunder over Kashmir* (Hyderabad: Orient Longman, 1955; reprint 1994).

[62] Record of meeting, 8 December 1947, F200/195C, Mountbatten Papers, APAC.

agreement, approaching the UN seemed the best way to regain some flexibility. The meeting ended inconclusively.

The Fighting Escalates: Kashmir in November–December 1947

In the following days India's military position in Kashmir steadily worsened. The raiders ratcheted up pressure on Poonch and on the lines of communication from Jammu. In Uri a battalion was ambushed, leaving sixty dead. Nehru began to wonder whether India should continue to acquiesce in Pakistan's support to the invaders. The "obvious course" was to strike at the raiders' bases and lines of communication in Pakistan. From a military standpoint this would be the most effective step. India had refrained from this owing to political considerations. Nehru thought that "We shall have to reconsider this position." Admittedly, this involved a risk of war. "We wish to avoid war, but it is merely deluding ourselves to imagine that we are avoiding war so long as the present operations are continuing on either side."[63]

Hitherto, the prime minister had been anxious to avoid war with Pakistan. During the Junagadh crisis, Nehru had explained his views at some length. A war could destabilize the nascent government; jeopardize the future of the armed forces, which were undergoing reorganization; inflict untold misery on the minorities in both countries; and cast India as an aggressor. In early November he had written that "War is a dangerous thing and must be avoided." Pakistan would be defeated but India would undoubtedly "suffer very great injury." He was certain that "We must do our utmost to avoid war, and this is our definite policy."[64] Nehru was forced to reconsider this position for two reasons. The sharp downturn in the military situation was a catalyst. But he was also under pressure from senior colleagues—including Patel and Baldev Singh—who called for escalation. Yet while Nehru veered towards this option he never lost sight of the costs of war.

At a Defence Committee meeting on 20 December Nehru pronounced the position unsatisfactory. A diplomatic settlement seemed unlikely, though much depended on the next round. In any event India

---

[63] Note, 19 December 1947, *SWJN-SS*, 4: 375–8.
[64] Letter to Premiers, 2 November 1947, ibid., 446–7.

could not allow the present situation to persist. "At the very worst" it might mean having to enter the districts of Sialkot, Gujrat, and Jhelum to deny bases to the raiders. Mountbatten sought to nip the idea in the bud, arguing strongly that India should approach the UN. They had "an iron cast case against Pakistan and must not do anything to weaken it." After some discussion it was agreed that the chiefs should prepare a paper on the eviction of raiders from Pakistan, assuming that the UN would direct India to do so.[65]

The same day the cabinet considered the option of approaching the UN. Thus far, Nehru had been clear that the UN would only be approached after the fighting had stopped. The shift was prompted by four related concerns. First, while the situation was unacceptable, Nehru was still uneasy at the prospect of escalation. As he wrote that very day, "We do not want war and we shall avoid it." Second, Nehru was aware that the operation "would involve aggression on Pakistan." A reference to the UN would ensure that India's actions were "above board and in conformity with international procedure."[66] Third, Nehru was confident of India's case and of its ability to convince "any impartial international body." By so doing he hoped to put the Pakistani leadership in a difficult position.[67] Finally, Nehru realized that the international community, especially the great powers, were already seized of the dispute. Indeed, His Majesty's Government was closely following the developments and was urging both sides to settle the problem amicably. India had "to proceed with great care lest a wrong step might injure our cause."[68] Contrary to conventional wisdom, the internationalization of the Kashmir problem was a cause, as

[65] DCC Meeting, 20 December 1947, F200/246, Mountbatten Papers, APAC.

[66] Nehru to Setalvad, 20 December 1947; Nehru to Maharaja, 21 December 1947, *SWJN-SS*, 4: 379-80, 387-8.

[67] The quote is from Nehru to Attlee, 30 December 1947, ibid., 420. For an excellent discussion of this point, see Andrew Bingham Kennedy, "Dreams Deferred: Mao, Nehru and the Strategic Choices of Rising Powers," PhD thesis, Harvard University (2007), 277–86.

[68] Nehru to Maharaja, 12 December 1947, *SWJN-SS*, 4: 371. Also, Nehru to Abdullah, 12 December 1947, ibid., 369.

well as an effect, of the reference to the UN. Meeting Liaquat the next evening Nehru handed over a note formally requesting Pakistan to pull back the raiders; alternatively, India would approach the UN.

On 24 December Indian forces at Jhangar were evicted by a determined attack. The raiders now had a free run of the road connecting Mirpur–Jhangar–Kotli–Poonch. This opened up several possibilities. They could try and capture Uri; take Poonch; infest Naushera; or attack Jammu. In the immediate aftermath Naushera came under attack, but Indian troops managed to repulse the assault by 27 December.

The fall of Jhangar injected a sense of urgency. Delhi decided to reinforce Kashmir with another brigade, providing a battalion each for Uri and Poonch. The army was also instructed to raise irregular forces. "We should be in full trim by the middle of January," wrote Nehru.[69] It was Uri that the Indians were most concerned about: if it fell, the invaders would yet again course up the valley to Baramula and Srinagar. On 26 December the prime minister and his senior colleagues decided that if Uri fell Indian forces would have to enter Pakistan.[70] Nehru directed the army chief "to be prepared for every contingency and to be prepared soon."[71]

Fearing an all-out war, Mountbatten wrote a long letter urging Nehru "to stop the fighting and to stop it as soon as possible."[72] Nehru replied that unilateral concessions would not lead to peace. Pakistan had high stakes in Kashmir; unless India drove home the costs of continued military action, Pakistan would not desist. Furthermore, India had to create and maintain a reputation for resolve: "I am convinced that any surrender on our part to this kind of aggression would lead to continued aggression elsewhere." He intended to adopt two parallel courses of action: reference to the UN, and "Complete military preparations to meet any possible contingency."[73] Over the next couple

[69] Nehru to Maharaja, 25 December 1947, ibid., 393–4; Prasad & Pal, *Operations*, 100–4.

[70] UKHC India to CRO, 28 December 1947, DO 133/73, TNA.

[71] Nehru to Bucher, 26 December 1947, *SWJN-SS*, 4: 398.

[72] UKHC India to CRO, 28 December 1947, PREM 8/1455/1, TNA (emphasis in the original).

[73] Nehru to Mountbatten, 26 December 1947, *SWJN-SS*, 4: 399–403.

of days the military situation in Kashmir stabilized: Naushera held; and there was no imminent danger to Uri. By the end of December there was no pressing need for an attack into Pakistan.

Dasgupta claims that Mountbatten and Bucher ensured no plans were prepared, and so "thwarted Nehru from ordering the Indian army into Pakistan."[74] The evidence shows that by January 1948 Nehru himself was rowing back from this option. In a meeting with Mountbatten on 22 January he agreed that "planning should not now commence until it was called for afresh."[75] Why did Nehru agree to drop contingency planning? He had all along been aware of the costs of a war. It was India's precarious military position after the fall of Jhangar that led him seriously to contemplate an attack. As the situation improved, the need for escalation dwindled. Indeed, by mid-February he held that the possibility of war had "receded into the background."[76] Nehru felt that a firm plan would act as a spur to escalation. His thoughts seemed to mirror those of Anton Chekhov, the Russian playwright having famously observed that if a gun was introduced in Act I it would certainly be used by Act III. Besides, as the military situation looked up, Nehru could keep his hawkish colleagues at bay. When Baldev protested the decision, Nehru was studiously evasive: "My own impression . . . was that such a plan was being prepared and in fact had been prepared. If that is so, then there was no question of putting a stop to this planning."[77]

Abdullah, Noel-Baker, and the UN
in Early 1948

The Kashmir dispute was referred under Article 35 of the UN charter. India claimed that Pakistani nationals and tribesmen had attacked its state of Jammu and Kashmir. It requested the council to take steps to prevent Pakistan from continuing its actions. Pakistan denied complicity and in turn alleged that India had pocketed the accession of

[74] Dasgupta, *War and Diplomacy*, 108–9.

[75] Governor General's Personal Report, 3 February 1948, Mss Eur D714/86, APAC.

[76] Nehru to Krishna Menon, 20 February 1948, *SWJN-SS*, 5: 223.

[77] Nehru to Baldev, 24 January 1948, ibid., 200.

Kashmir by fraud and violence. Pakistan further charged India with "genocide" of Muslims and aggression against Junagadh. On 20 January 1948 the council passed a resolution establishing a three-member commission to investigate the complaints and make efforts to mediate in the dispute.

The Kashmir dispute was a major cause of concern to countries interested in the subcontinent—Britain, and to a lesser extent the United States. The relinquishment of the Raj did not mean that Britain was ready to accept a smaller role in world affairs. Indeed, the British had no desire either to wind up all their empire or forsake the panoply of a major power.[78] After the Second World War they had wished to rid themselves of the incubus of governing India (and Palestine) and refashion the imperial system. Whitehall's policies on South Asia were mainly influenced by strategic considerations. The large standing army; the vast reservoir of military manpower; India's importance in defending the Middle and Far East: all these had mandated preserving Indian unity and ensuring India's continued presence in the Commonwealth.[79]

But Partition had torn a gaping hole in Britain's plans. London hoped to mend it by drawing both India and Pakistan into the Commonwealth,[80] a task that acquired urgency with the onset of the Cold War. The US shared much of this assessment and, because of Britain's long-standing links, preferred to follow its lead. London and Washington were thus eager to see a speedy resolution of the Kashmir dispute, one which seemed to carry the maximum potential to destabilize the subcontinent and jeopardize their interests.[81]

---

[78] For an overview of these issues, see John Darwin, *Britain and Decolonisation: The Retreat from Empire in the Post-War World* (Basingstoke: Palgrave Macmillan, 1988), 67–166.

[79] Ibid., 89–90; Anita Inder Singh, *The Limits of British Influence: South Asia and the Anglo-American Relationship, 1947–56* (New York: St. Martin's Press, 1993), 16–21; R. J. Moore, *Escape from Empire: The Attlee Government and the Indian Problem* (Oxford: Clarendon Press, 1983), 61–5.

[80] R.J. Moore, *Making the New Commonwealth* (Oxford: Clarendon Press, 1987).

[81] Robert McMahon, *Cold War on the Periphery: The United States, India and Pakistan* (New York: Columbia University Press, 1994), 11–79.

The Security Council's attitude towards Kashmir was largely shaped by the British delegation led by the commonwealth secretary Philip Noel-Baker. Like his counterpart in the foreign office, Noel-Baker believed that Britain's position in the Middle East was doddering: in scurrying from Palestine they had already alienated the Arabs. The latter might be further inflamed if Britain wobbled on Kashmir. "[I]t was important to avoid the danger of antagonising the whole of Islam by appearing to side with India against Pakistan."[82] Besides, Noel-Baker believed that, because it contained a majority of Muslims, Kashmir quite properly belonged to Pakistan.[83] Consequently the British delegation brushed aside India's complaint and asserted that fighting could only stop if arrangements for a fair plebiscite were reached. This would entail the induction of Pakistani troops into Kashmir and the establishment of a "neutral" administration. These ideas, of course, were close to the demands advanced by Jinnah and antithetical to Delhi's stance. Interestingly, Noel-Baker was peddling these proposals without his own cabinet's approval, proposals that could potentially undercut Britain's policy of holding India in the Commonwealth.[84] The Americans realized that the proposals were one-sided but chose to be shepherded by Britain.[85]

Nehru concluded that the UK and the US had "played a dirty role."[86] He asked the Indian delegation to return for consultations. Nehru was aware of London's interests in the subcontinent and pointedly informed Prime Minister Attlee that Noel-Baker's attitude "cannot but prejudice continuance of friendly relations between India and the UK."[87] Thereafter the British cabinet modified the ideas advanced by Noel-Baker: Pakistan should be asked to deny assistance to the raiders without necessarily coupling it to the question of plebiscite; Pakistani

[82] Summary: Kashmir Dispute, March 1948, DO 142/502, TNA.

[83] Noel-Baker to Bucher, 5 February 1952, 7901-87-31, Bucher Papers, NAM.

[84] Dasgupta, *War and Diplomacy*, ch. 10.

[85] Marshall to Austin, 20 February 1948, *Foreign Relations of the United States* (hereafter *FRUS*) *1948*, 5, pt I: 300–1.

[86] Nehru to Vijayalakshmi, 16 February 1948, *SWJN-SS*, 5: 218.

[87] Cable to Attlee, 8 February 1948, ibid., 211.

troops should not be brought into Kashmir; Abdullah's government need not be replaced but should include members of rival parties.[88]

Meanwhile hectic consultations ensued and different options were canvassed. A key issue was the position of Sheikh Abdullah's government. As a compromise India decided to accept a coalition government. Bajpai told the British envoy that this proposal should come, though, from others: if Delhi offered concessions Karachi would ask for more.[89] The Kashmir government released the imprisoned leader of the Muslim Conference, Ghulam Abbas, and permitted him to confer with the Pakistanis. But Nehru was clear that representatives of Azad Kashmir could not be taken on board. This would amount to *de facto* recognition and would render governance "virtually impossible."[90]

When Whitehall aired the idea, Pakistan emphatically rejected it. Liaquat sent a stern missive to Attlee: "the leader of the Muslim Conference will not agree to serve under Abdulla [*sic*] . . . [who] has been a quisling and puppet of the Congress." He insisted that the administration must be taken over by "an independent and neutral body" and that all Indian troops must be withdrawn. He urged Attlee not to "recede or depart" from the stance taken by Noel-Baker: it would be "morally wrong and politically a disaster."[91] To scotch this option Karachi swiftly placed the Azad Kashmir government on a firmer footing and incorporated members of the Muslim Conference. By early April 1948 the Azad government had a rudimentary administrative structure and an "army" with a "general staff."[92]

The other alternative was an independent Kashmir with guarantees from India and Pakistan. Abdullah was especially interested in this. From the outset he had been against a plebiscite. The Security Council debates had confirmed that most members wanted his administration to be replaced. Consequently, he alighted on independence as the best way of ending the conflict without jeopardizing his own

[88] Dasgupta, *War and Diplomacy*, 122–6.

[89] UKHC India to CRO, 21 February 1948, DO 35/3165, TNA.

[90] Cables to Ayyangar, 8 & 14 March, *SWJN-SS*, 5: 253–5.

[91] Liaquat to Attlee, 6 March 1948, DO 133/77, TNA.

[92] Extract from Reed to Deputy High Commissioner Lahore, 11 April 1948, DO 142/495, TNA.

position. Speaking at Lake Success (the temporary home in New York State of the United Nations), where he had gone in late January 1948, Abdullah had claimed that replacing his administration would be deeply resented by the Kashmiris. Hamlet, he argued, could not be staged without the prince of Denmark—the people of Kashmir. "As long as the people are behind me, I will remain there."[93] Abdullah had privately spoken to the Americans of his desire for an independent Kashmir with financial backing from Washington and London.[94] He had also broached the idea with Sardar Ibrahim of Azad Kashmir and Mohammed Ali of Pakistan. Indeed Abdullah recalled that "One reason why I joined the Indian delegation was that I hoped to find the opportunity of privately talking to the member of the Pakistan delegation."[95] Mohammed Ali demurred, arguing that India would "hatch all sorts of plots against us."[96] The Azad leaders echoed these concerns: "independence would be illusory and dangerous."[97] Nehru had felt as much; but, deferring to Abdullah, he had raised this possibility with Liaquat. The latter had rejected the idea "because such a solution would solve nothing and would leave Kashmir as a hot bed of inter Dominion intrigue."[98]

Abdullah was undeterred. Meeting the British minister for commonwealth relations, he raised the idea of independence with guarantees. This would "avoid a plebiscite which he really did not want." He was confident that "The Muslim Conference would accept a joint accession and he could carry his own party."[99] Nehru knew that Abdullah had mooted the possibility. He did not "fancy" it; nor did he

---

[93] Cited in Gupta, *Kashmir*, 160.

[94] Austin to Secretary of State (hereafter SS), 28 January 1948, *FRUS 1948*, 5, pt I: 291–2.

[95] Abdullah, *Flames of Chinar*, 106.

[96] Bilqees Taseer, *The Kashmir of Sheikh Muhammad Abdullah* (Lahore: Ferozsons, 1986), 50–1.

[97] Note of conversation with Ibrahim, 23 January 1948, FO 371/69707, TNA. Also see, *FRUS 1948*, 5, pt I: 293.

[98] Report on meeting with Liaquat, UKHC Pakistan to CRO, 3 February 1948, DO 35/3164, TNA.

[99] Gordon-Walker to CRO, 21 February 1948, DO 35/3165, TNA. Also, Grady to SS, 21 February 1948, *FRUS 1948*, 5, pt I: 303–4.

wish to rule it out. Nevertheless, the option would not be advanced by India "unless circumstances more or less compel us."[100] Nehru did not want to make gratuitous concessions while Pakistan dug in its heels. Further, opinion amongst his colleagues "was against a solution on the lines of independence for Kashmir."[101]

The idea of independence for Kashmir got a fillip from two unexpected sources. Canada suggested that the plebiscite should include a third option of independence with guarantees: this would sidestep much of the controversy surrounding the plebiscite. Mountbatten, too, advocated this to Nehru.[102] Speaking to the Canadian envoy, Nehru agreed that it was "a possible solution and although it would not be liked in India he thought he could put it across."[103] The plan was quashed by the British government. Independence would provide "fresh scope for friction between India and Pakistan, and by setting up a non-viable independent state in an exposed position, would present special scope for Russian intrigue." It would be unwise to pursue this option while there was the possibility of a UN-brokered solution.[104]

The second was a private initiative by Horace Alexander of the Society of Friends, a Quaker organization with links to the Indian and Pakistani leadership. Alexander met Nehru, Mountbatten, and Abdullah. The prime minister was open to Abdullah exploring common ground with the Muslim Conference. The sheikh himself felt that a deal could be cut with Ghulam Abbas if a suitable venue were arranged. Alexander then went to Pakistan and discussed the possibility with Mian Iftikharuddin.[105] Given Pakistan's opposition it is not surprising that the meeting proved difficult to arrange. Eventually, with Nehru's

[100] Nehru to Krishna Menon, 20 February 1948, *SWJN-SS*, 5: 222.

[101] Report on conversation with Bajpai, UKHC India to CRO, 9 March 1948, DO 35/3166, TNA.

[102] Minutes of meeting, 26 February 1948, *SWJN-SS*, 5: 232.

[103] UKHC India to CRO, 10 March 1948, DO 142/504, TNA. Also, Grady to SS, 1 March 1948, *FRUS 1948*, 5, pt I: 310.

[104] Note for Attlee by Gordon-Walker; CRO to UKHCs, 19 March 1948, PREM 8/1455/3, TNA.

[105] On Alexander's initiative, see Duke to UKHC Pakistan, 15 March 1948, Shattock to UKHC India, 17 March 1948; CRO to UKHCs, 23 March 1948, DO 133/77, TNA.

"good offices," Iftikharuddin (on behalf of Abbas) met Abdullah's deputy, Bakshi Ghulam Mohammed. No agreement materialized.[106] The Azad Kashmir leadership continued to insist that Abdullah and his "henchmen" would have to go.[107]

A third alternative was partition-cum-plebiscite. This option gained currency because it seemed clear that certain parts of the state would overwhelmingly vote for Pakistan or India. The Indians were inclined to give this a chance but again would not advance it. As Nehru wrote to Krishna Menon, "If worst comes to the worst, I am prepared to accept Poonch and Gilgit area being partitioned off [after voting], though this would mean a serious blow to the state and would make Srinagar's position insecure."[108] N.G. Ayyangar told Noel-Baker that "in Gilgit, Poonch and Mirpur, no power on earth could prevent the people from voting for Pakistan by an overwhelming majority. It would, therefore, be a great weakness to India to try to keep them within a Kashmir which acceded to India."[109] Besides, the Indians knew that recapturing these parts would be difficult. As Nehru noted, "Poonch will be a hard nut to crack."[110] But Pakistan was opposed to the idea. When the British mentioned it Liaquat tersely replied that "this would be unacceptable."[111]

The Kashmir Imbroglio:
March–April 1948

By the time the Security Council reconvened, none of the alternatives had transmuted into real options. On 18 March China tabled a fresh draft resolution in three parts. The first dealt with the restoration of peace, asking Pakistan to pull back the tribesmen and its nationals. The

[106] UKHC India to CRO, 30 April 1948, DO 142/495, TNA.

[107] Note by Azad Kashmir "Defence Minister" (enclosing memorandum), 20 October 1948, Ali Ahmedshah Papers, Mss Eur D704, APAC.

[108] Nehru to Krishna Menon, 20 February 1948, *SWJN-SS*, 5: 223.

[109] Record of conversation with Ayyangar, 31 March 1948, DO 133/78, TNA. Also see Record of conversation with Bajpai, 4 April 1948, ibid.

[110] Nehru to Krishna Menon, 20 February 1948, *SWJN-SS*, 5: 223.

[111] Gordon-Walker to Noel-Baker, 22 February 1948, DO 35/3165, TNA.

second part focused on the plebiscite. India would create a "Plebiscite Administration" whose directors would be nominated by the UN secretary general and would function as officials of the state. The final part called for an interim government representing all major political groups. This resolution was more attuned to India's concerns. As Nehru observed, it "accepts our general approach and our viewpoint in regard to essentials."[112]

During subsequent discussions the draft was modified considerably, each modification a concession to Pakistan. Despite his new brief Noel-Baker persisted in his partisanship, calling, for instance, for the removal of Abdullah. This drew a reproach from Attlee. But Noel-Baker succeeded in presenting his government with a *fait accompli*.[113] Successive changes to the draft dismayed the Indian prime minister. At one point Nehru felt that "it might be worthwhile considering alternative of guaranteeing independence." In the event he decided against this course for he felt unilateral concessions would only whet Pakistan's appetite for more. [114]

The two-part resolution adopted by the council on 21 April was significantly different from the Chinese draft. The first part increased the commission's strength from three to five members. The second laid out the council's recommendations for restoring peace and order and holding a plebiscite. Pakistan should use its "best endeavours" to secure the withdrawal of the tribesmen and Pakistani nationals. Once a ceasefire was in place, India should progressively reduce its forces to the minimum required for maintaining law and order. If necessary, the commission might employ troops of either dominion subject to both parties' agreement. For the plebiscite India should ensure that the state government invited the major political parties to designate representatives at the ministerial level. A plebiscite administrator would be nominated and given a range of powers, including the authority to deal directly with both countries.[115]

[112] Cable to Ayyangar, 24 March 1948, *SWJN-SS*, 5: 258.

[113] Dasgupta, *War and Diplomacy*, 127–30.

[114] Cable to Ayyangar, 28 March 1948; Mountbatten's interview with Nehru, 30 March 1948, *SWJN-SS*, 5: 259–61.

[115] Gupta, *Kashmir*, 166–7.

Both India and Pakistan rejected the resolution. Delhi had several major objections. First, it felt that in the main the resolution placed India and Pakistan on an equal footing, ignoring its complaint and Kashmir's accession. Second, India was not allowed to retain troops for defence. Third, the Indians thought it preposterous that the other Kashmiri parties should themselves nominate representatives to join the government. "Sheikh Abdullah would be placed in an impossible position in such circumstances."[116] Fourth, the powers conferred on the plebiscite administrator were too wide; some of them, such as the right to appoint special magistrates, undercut the state's sovereignty. Fifth, some provisions, such as that permitting the return of all refugees, were unrealistic. Last, India wanted Pakistan to be excluded from the conduct of the plebiscite. Pakistan mainly opposed the retention of any Indian forces and called for equal representation in the interim administration for Azad Kashmir, the Muslim Conference, and the National Conference. Both sides, all the same, agreed to confer with the UN commission.

The Offensive in Kashmir:
May–June 1948

Meantime, India's military position had improved. Jhangar was captured in March and Rajauri taken next. By early May the threat to the lines of communication from Jammu to Naushera was neutralized. Indian forces were now poised for the "spring offensive." Concurrently, the possibility of military action against Hyderabad came to the fore.

Bucher was clear that the army could only pursue limited objectives: "an advance to Domel and thereafter the removal of non-Muslim population from Poonch city . . . so long as Poonchis, Mirpuris, and Muzaffarabadis offered resistance, it would NOT be possible for India to over-run these areas." The army could not induct more troops into Kashmir without compromising their defence capabilities in East Punjab. The defence minister agreed that "it was not our intention to invade every nook and corner"—Gilgit, for instance, was out of reach.

[116] Minutes of meeting convened by Mountbatten, 19 April 1948, *SWJN-SS*, 6: 159–61.

But, in addition, he wanted Palandri and Mirpur captured. These were "not difficult to achieve with the present strength of our forces."[117]

The general staff examined this in an appreciation. Significantly, it was prepared by Kalwant Singh, now chief of general staff, and his deputy J.N. Chaudhuri, in consultation with the army commander K.M. Cariappa. The paper noted that Cariappa thought he could evacuate refugees from Poonch and advance to Domel. But the available forces did not permit "wide scale operations;" nor could "districts like Mirpur be permanently occupied." For this, "the Army Commander considers that further reinforcements would be required." The general staff were of the opinion that commitments elsewhere in India made it "difficult to reinforce Jammu & Kashmir any further without weakening ourselves in East Punjab."[118]

The matter was considered by the Defence Committee on 13 May. For the past few weeks Nehru had felt that the main military problem was the tactics adopted by the Indian forces. The army sought to undertake ponderous, large-unit operations requiring ever more troops against irregulars "who hover about and make a nuisance of themselves." Operations should aim not to capture and hold ground but to destroy the enemy's will and cohesion. "This requires swift blows at many places and no time given for reformation and recuperation."[119] At the meeting Nehru reiterated that the enemy was likely to "crack up rapidly provided a few successive shocks were administered to them." The prime minister observed that the evacuation of refugees in Poonch was a subsidiary task. But he did not call for an offensive in that sector as Baldev suggested. Rather, Nehru was focused on the Uri sector. He called for a "quick occupation" of Domel and Kohala to "bottle up" the raiders that remained behind. "Mopping up could then follow at leisure."[120]

None of these discussions envisaged that the Pakistan army might be inducted into Kashmir. The possibility was discounted after the face-off between Jinnah and Gracey. In fact by early December the

[117] Bucher to Baldev, 5 May 1948; Baldev's reply, 7 May 1948, 7901-87-16, Bucher Papers, NAM.

[118] Appreciation of General Staff, 8 May 1948, ibid.

[119] Letters to Baldev & Bucher, 22 April 1948, *SWJN-SS*, 6: 177–80.

[120] DCC Meeting, 13 May 1948, F200/246, Mountbatten Papers, APAC.

Pakistan general staff was supporting the operations. In mid-February 1948 the Pakistani brigadier managing the operations in Kashmir wrote bluntly to Liaquat Ali Khan that "our effort has spent its force."[121] Not surprisingly, the following month a mountain battery was in action.[122] As spring approached Gracey grew concerned about possible Indian offensives. In a note he argued that these would create a huge refugee problem. The capture of Bhimbar and Mirpur would enable India to control the headworks on Jhelum; the occupation of Poonch would deal a grave blow to the Azad movement; the fall of Muzaffarabad would unbolt the backdoor to Pakistan. It was "imperative that the Indian army is not allowed to advance beyond the general line Uri–Poonch–Nushahra [sic]."[123]

By late April Pakistani forces began deploying in Kashmir. Whitehall quickly learnt of these developments but decided against action, preferring that the UN commission should discover and handle the matter themselves.[124] Gracey for his part vociferously and repeatedly demanded that in the event of war a "stand-down" order—requiring British officers on both sides to cease performing their duties—should not be issued.[125] Was the Indian army chief, General Roy Bucher, privy to the induction of Pakistani forces? At least one historian strongly suggests that he was.[126] But Bucher's correspondence, thus far overlooked by scholars, shows that he had genuinely misread the situation. At the end of August 1948 Bucher met Pakistan's chief of general staff and complained that he was kept in the dark about the entry of Pakistani forces. Gracey wrote to Bucher: "I did [hint], in so far, as I could." Bucher responded: "You cautioned that certain operations might have serious repercussions. Nevertheless, I did not, for one moment, appreciate you were hinting at opposition to the

---

[121] Note of 19 February 1948, cited in Shuja Nawaz, *Crossed Swords: Pakistan, Its Army, and the Wars Within* (Karachi: Oxford University Press, 2008), 56.

[122] Khan, *Raiders*, 75–80; Internal CRO minute, 31 March 1948, DO 142/495; UKHC Pakistan to CRO, 6 May 1948, DO 35/3163, TNA.

[123] Zaheer, *Rawalpindi Conspiracy*, 125–6; Nawaz, *Crossed Swords*, 62–5.

[124] Carter to Grafftey-Smith, 4 June 1948, DO 133/79, TNA.

[125] Grafftey-Smith to Carter, 23 June 1948, DO 133/80, TNA.

[126] Dasgupta, *War and Diplomacy*, 151–4.

Indian army by stronger elements than those already encountered in Jammu and Kashmir."[127]

On 18 May 1948 India launched a two-pronged offensive: one along the Uri–Domel road, the other towards Tithwal and thence to Muzaffarabad and Domel. The presence of Pakistani forces blunted the offensive by early June. The only significant success was the capture of Tithwal. Further north the raiders attacked and took Kargil and Dras and posed a threat to Srinagar. The army headquarters recommended consolidating positions in the Uri–Tithwal sector with a view to advancing on Muzaffarabad if it was not too risky.

Having closely examined the situation Nehru was convinced that "our defence requirements along East Punjab frontier . . . and need to maintain forces in Hyderabad leave practically no margin for reinforcing troops in Kashmir."[128] Moreover, there was ample evidence that Pakistani forces were ranged against them. So Nehru was cognizant of the risk of all-out war. As the British envoy noted, Bucher had been "advocating a defensive rather than an offensive policy in which . . . he had had considerable success *thanks largely to support from Nehru*."[129]

The UN Commission: July–September 1948

The UN Commission landed in Karachi on 5 July 1948. Foreign Minister Zafrullah Khan threw "the first bombshell"—three brigades of the Pakistan army were fighting in Kashmir.[130] In Delhi the commission found the Indians indignant and opposed to discussing a plebiscite until Pakistan's aggression was condemned. Girja Bajpai bluntly told them: "If the future of Jammu and Kashmir was to be determined by the arbitrament of the sword, then, without in any way

[127] Gracey to Bucher, 30 August 1948, Bucher's reply, 5 September 1948, 7901-87-6, Bucher Papers, NAM.

[128] Nehru to Maharaja of Nepal, 29 June 1948, *SWJN-SS*, 6: 191–2.

[129] UKHC India to CRO, 12 July 1948, DO 35/3163, TNA (emphasis added). Chandrashekar Dasgupta excises the italicized portion of the document and uses it to bolster his case for Bucher's alleged perfidy. Dasgupta, *War and Diplomacy*, 150.

[130] This section draws on Josef Korbel, *Danger in Kashmir*, rev. edn (Princeton: Princeton University Press, 1966), ch. 6.

wishing to utter a threat, or use the language of menace, I should like Commission as realists to recognize that the offer of plebiscite could not remain open." After peace had been restored the Kashmiris would be free to determine their future, "but Pakistan could have no lot or part in the process."[131]

On receiving hints from Karachi the commission explored the possibility of an unconditional ceasefire. Nehru rebuffed it: "you are putting us on the same platform with the other side—the intruder and the aggressor." The commission soon concluded that it might be impossible to hold a plebiscite. Demilitarization seemed a hopeless proposition. Considering Kashmir's topography the "mere technicality of carrying out the plebiscite seemed beyond the scope of reality." Creating a coalition government was "out of the question." The commission therefore contemplated partition.

Prior to the commission's arrival partition had been considered in Delhi. Nehru had been open to it as a last-ditch option. The idea was pushed to the fore by V.P. Menon,[132] and subsequently marketed by Mountbatten. Before departing in late June 1948 Mountbatten had sought to broker a settlement based on partition at an impending meeting between the prime ministers. Ayyangar, too, had lent his support. Partition maps had been marked up and discussed by Nehru and Bucher. But Liaquat had taken ill and the initiative had been shelved.[133]

In discussions with the commission Nehru expressed scepticism about a plebiscite and indicated that he was not opposed to partition. His readiness to consider partition reflected the changed circumstances. The entry of Pakistani forces had at once demonstrated Karachi's interest in retaining the area under the raiders' control, and underlined the difficulty, not to say impossibility, of demilitarization. But the Pakistanis refused to consider partition. The commission reverted to its original mandate.

On 13 August the commission adopted a three-part resolution. Part I called for a ceasefire. Part II outlined the principles for a truce agreement. First, Pakistan would remove its troops from Kashmir and

---

[131] Cited in Gupta, *Kashmir*, 177.
[132] Grady to SS, 18 May 1948, *FRUS 1948*, 5, pt I: 343.
[133] Hodson, *The Great Divide*, 471–2.

secure the withdrawal of tribesmen and Pakistani nationals. The evacuated territory would be administered by "local authorities under the surveillance of the commission." Second, the commission would notify India that the tribesmen and Pakistani nationals had withdrawn and that Pakistani forces were being withdrawn. Thereafter India would withdraw the "bulk of its forces" in stages. Pending agreement on a final settlement India would retain minimal forces to help maintain law and order. Part III stated that, upon acceptance of the truce agreement, both countries would enter into consultations with the commission to determine conditions for settling the future of Kashmir "in accordance with the will of the people."

Unlike the April resolution, this one took into account India's views: Pakistan's "aggression" was indirectly acknowledged; a truce agreement preceded the determination of the people's will. Importantly, the resolution did not state that a plebiscite was the only way to ascertain the people's wishes, and in so doing left open the possibility of exploring other options. India accepted the resolution after obtaining clarifications: the Azad Kashmir government was not recognized, nor would the territory under its control be consolidated in any way during the truce; the strength of the Indian forces should be adequate for external defence too; if a plebiscite was agreed upon, Pakistan would play no part in its conduct.

Pakistan expressed numerous reservations. Among other things it demanded that the Azad Kashmir government be recognized; that a plebiscite be held at the earliest as per the terms of the April resolution; that both governments be accorded absolute equality *vis-à-vis* the plebiscite. The commission ultimately concluded that Pakistan's response was "tantamount to rejection." On 21 September the commission left for Geneva to write its interim report.

Plebiscite, Partition, and Plebiscite-cum-Partition

Faced with an impasse, Nehru urged Liaquat to accept the commission's resolution, highlighting the danger of an "intensification and extension" of the fighting. Liaquat asked India to consent to the terms of the April resolution for a plebiscite and offered an unconditional ceasefire. Nehru replied that India had "objected to certain conditions" in that resolution, but the acceptance of the latest resolution attested its adherence to the principle of self-determination. As for a "simple ceasefire," India had already conveyed its objections. Nehru regretted that his attempt "to explore the possibility of a solution . . . by direct negotiation" was not favoured by Pakistan.[134]

Thereafter the other options began to circulate yet again. The idea of independence had few takers. Pakistan and the Azad leadership had always opposed it. Nehru was now certain that an independent Kashmir would continue to be an area of contention. Sheikh Abdullah's thoughts were pulling in different directions. On the one hand he echoed Nehru's views that an independent Kashmir was not viable.[135] On the other hand Abdullah (and his revenue minister Mirza Afzal Beg) told some members of the UN commission that he favoured independence and was willing to meet Ghulam Abbas (now with the Azad government).[136] In any event rapprochement between the two Kashmiri parties remained a mirage. The Azad leadership would join a coalition only if Abdullah was not prime minister.[137] The commission contemplated inviting Abdullah and Abbas to Geneva. However, the British continued to oppose independence and "poured cold water" on the idea.[138]

In contrast the idea of partition gained ground. Nehru was convinced that "we would never get the conditions which were necessary for a plebiscite. Neither side would give in on this vital issue." So he "ruled out a plebiscite for all practical purposes."[139] Furthermore, Pakistan's refusal to enter into direct negotiations obviated the possibility of finding alternative means of determining the Kashmiris' wishes. Nehru concluded therefore that the only practical solution was a compromise "on the basis of the . . . existing military situation." Patel too

[134] Nehru to Liaquat, 5 October 1948, PREM 8/1455/5, TNA.

[135] Korbel, *Danger in Kashmir*, 147.

[136] Report on conversation with Richard Symonds, UKHC India to CRO, 12 September 1948, DO 35/3167, TNA.

[137] Report on conversation with Richard Symonds, UKHC India to CRO, 29 August 1948, DO 35/3167, TNA.

[138] Record of talk with Korbel on 27 September 1948, DO 134/5, TNA.

[139] Note for Sheikh Abdullah, 25 August 1952, *SWJN-SS*, 19: 323.

felt that partition offered a "permanent, immediate and realistic set-tlement." Parts of Poonch and Gilgit areas could go to Pakistan; but the frontier should cater for "India's strategic and defensive require-ments."[140] The Indians were prepared to let go off western Poonch and Mirpur, and Gilgit, but were loath to give away Muzaffarabad and the surrounding areas.[141] Holding the latter would ensure that India controlled the routes of ingress to the valley. Moreover, it would pro-vide a clear boundary along the Kishanganga River.

The Indians were not the only ones thinking on these lines. After its sojourn in the subcontinent the UN commission unanimously felt that partition was "the only eventual solution." Because Pakistan was resolutely opposed to it and because it was beyond their remit, the commission decided not to recommend it; but they would allude to it in their report.[142]

A variant of partition-cum-plebiscite was also resuscitated. This sought to confine the plebiscite to the valley and to partition the rest of the state. In Delhi V.P. Menon was its principal advocate. The day the UN commission departed he put the idea to the British high commission. Menon said he had brought Nehru and Patel "to the water." He wanted Attlee to suggest this proposal informally to Nehru and Liaquat during the upcoming commonwealth conference. If the idea came from Attlee, Indian leaders might well be receptive; besides, Pakistan would not gratuitously press for more. Menon also asked Mountbatten to work on Nehru.[143] Whitehall felt that this proposal might be acceptable to Pakistan if the plebiscite were held in accordance with the April resolution. They recommended it to Mountbatten, asking him to suggest it to Nehru with "very great cau-tion."[144] The British also mentioned it to the secretary general of the Pakistan cabinet. Mohammed Ali rejected it as "doomed to collapse:" there could be no agreement on "where the dividing lines should be

[140] Report on conversation with Patel, UKHC India to CRO, 11 August 1948, DO 35/3167, TNA.
[141] Nehru to Vijayalakshmi, 21 September 1948, *SWJN-SS*, 7: 694.
[142] Record of talk with Korbel on 27 September 1948, DO 134/5, TNA.
[143] UKHC India to CRO, 21 September 1948, DO 35/3168, TNA. Also, Donovan to SS, 23 July 1948 *FRUS 1948*, 5, pt I: 355–6.
[144] Carter to Mountbatten, 8 October 1948, PREM 8/1455/5, TNA.

drawn." Nor would Pakistan accept partition following an overall plebiscite.[145] The idea fell by the wayside.

The prime ministers met in London on 22 October 1948. Liaquat offered to accept the August resolution provided India agreed to a plebiscite as per the April resolution. Nehru replied that these matters had already been examined in detail. He presented a clear choice to Liaquat: unreserved acceptance of the commission's resolution, or partition with "certain areas in western Poonch and north western territories [Gilgit] being allotted to Pakistan."[146] Neither was acceptable to Liaquat. At another meeting in Paris Liaquat reiterated his views, insisting that India should either accept the conditions for a plebiscite or accord "full powers" to plebiscite commissioners "to lay down any conditions they chose." As Nehru observed, "Differences [are] basically too great to be bridged over."[147] Thereafter Liaquat wrote to Attlee that India sought a military decision and if a wider conflagration were to be prevented the matter must urgently be considered by the Security Council.[148]

Why did Pakistan reject the offer of partition? Obviously they were not prepared to concede the valley. However, Karachi's aversion to partition ran altogether deeper. The reasons can be gleaned from a memorandum prepared by the department dealing with Kashmir affairs, working directly under Liaquat. It examined the question of partition, especially along the river Chenab, which would leave the valley *inside* Pakistan—an idea mooted among others by their erstwhile C-in-C, General Frank Messervy. The memorandum advanced a number of arguments against the proposal—strategic, geographic, and economic. "Jammu in Indian hands would always present a military threat." Both geographically and economically the Chenab valley and areas south of it were "indissolubly linked and connected with Western Pakistan." It was imperative that India should be in no position to interfere with the Chenab, whose waters irrigated the

[145] Minute on talk with Mohammed Ali on 18 October, DO 142/519, TNA.

[146] Nehru to Pai, 22 October 1948; Nehru to Krishna Menon, 15 November 1948, *SWJN-SS*, 8: 42, 46.

[147] Nehru to Patel, 30 October 1948, ibid., 43.

[148] UKHC Pakistan to CRO, 11 November 1948, DO 35/3168, TNA.

Sialkot district. The memorandum concluded that Pakistan could at best agree to examine the possibility of giving up a small strip of the Kathua district.[149]

Back in Karachi, Liaquat met the Indian envoy and proposed an alternative method of conducting the plebiscite. Alastair Lamb claims Liaquat offered a partition-cum-plebiscite and that it fell through because Nehru was "obsessed" with the valley.[150] This is at once erroneous and tendentious. Liaquat made it clear that "he would not tolerate any division of Kashmir" and that he sought a unitary plebiscite. In the valley a proper plebiscite would be conducted. In Gilgit, Poonch, Jammu, and Ladakh the votes would be calculated on the basis of the 1941 census, working on the assumption that all Muslims would vote for Pakistan and all non-Muslims for India. These would be added to the numbers in the valley, so deciding the future of Kashmir.[151] In fact this idea had been advanced to the British by Mohammed Ali.[152] Unsurprisingly, Nehru considered it "a fantastic proposal to which we could never agree." It would be a ringing affirmation of the "Two Nation" theory and would undermine the position of Muslims in India. Moreover, the proposal was based on specious premises. As British officials realized, it would "weigh the scales intolerably against India." Even Noel-Baker admitted that "India will refuse—and rightly: Muslims may (and will) vote for India."[153]

Limited Operations

During the commission's visit operations in Kashmir had continued listlessly. By the time Nehru left for London he concluded that "no

[149] Memorandum by Mainprice, n.d. (end September/early October 1948); Memorandum of discussion between Olver and Mainprice, n.d.; Memorandum by Olver, 25 January 1949; Minute by Aspin, 19 October 1948, DO 142/519, TNA.

[150] Lamb, *Incomplete Partition*, 275–6.

[151] Nehru to Menon, 18 November 1949, *SWJN-SS*, 8: 48–9.

[152] Minute on talk with Mohammed Ali on 18 October 1948, DO 142/519, TNA.

[153] Minute by Rumbold, 21 October 1948, DO 142/519; Minute by Noel-Baker, 20 October 1948, PREM 8/1455/5, TNA.

quick or effective decision was likely." India might push on and gain limited successes but "this would be a long drawn-out affair and would not put an end to the conflict or the problem." To be sure India was militarily superior, but "that superiority was not so great as to overwhelm the enemy." As earlier, Nehru was concerned about escalation to all-out war: "That was not a prospect to be welcomed" for a war would bring "disaster in its train, whatever the result." Besides, the prospect of intervention by the great powers could not be overlooked.[154] Britain and America seemed to have thrown their diplomatic weight behind Pakistan; the former was also tightening military supplies to India.

Before leaving for London, Nehru asked Bucher to prepare an appreciation on the possibility of evicting Pakistani forces and tribesmen. The army headquarters concluded that "an overall military decision is no longer possible."[155] Since Nehru had already reached this conclusion, it appears he wanted the paper to be prepared for the benefit of his colleagues. In Nehru's absence Bucher submitted it to Patel, adding that the only effective measure would be an attack into Pakistan, a course that carried the unacceptable risk of escalation. The deputy prime minister agreed.[156]

The army concentrated on limited offensives in the Ladakh and Jammu sectors. By the end of November 1948 Indian forces recaptured Dras and Kargil, securing the route from the valley to Ladakh. Simultaneously they took Mendhar and linked up with the Poonch garrison, so lifting the year-long siege. The Pakistanis viewed these reverses with trepidation. They thought that India was now poised to launch a major attack to capture the entire Poonch–Mirpur area, so pushing Pakistani forces beyond the Jhelum river. Alarmed, Liaquat wrote to Attlee that India sought to present a *fait accompli* and that unless the impending offensive was halted he would resist it to the

[154] Note for Sheikh Abdullah, 25 August 1952, *SWJN-SS*, 19: 323–4. On the last point, also see Kennedy, "Dreams Undeferred," 292–7.

[155] Report on conversation with Bucher, UKHC India to CRO, 5 November 1948, DO 133/82, TNA; Bucher to Nehru, 22 November 1948, 7901-87-6, Bucher Papers, NAM.

[156] Kennedy, "Dreams Undeferred," 300–1.

hilt.[157] Liaquat was not, however, merely seeking British intercession; he aimed at using this opportunity for diplomatic gains too. He requested Attlee to help Pakistan immediately secure an "unconditional ceasefire." A similar appeal was sent to the Security Council. This was, of course, Liaquat's position since the commission's departure. It would defuse the military threat from India without requiring Pakistan to accept the August resolution.

At a conference in Karachi on 25–26 November, Bucher assured Gracey that India did not intend a large-scale offensive.[158] But Pakistan had already decided that unless the UN ordered a ceasefire, a "counter-offensive" would be launched.[159] The operation would not only result in local military gains but also heighten the sense of urgency for an immediate ceasefire. It would also bring additional pressure to bear on India. As Gracey noted, "A Pak[istan] offensive might put him [Nehru] in a more reasonable frame of mind."[160] The cabinet was initially slated to give the go-ahead on 7 December; but Liaquat decided to wait another four days.

The Ceasefire of 31 December 1948

One reason for postponing the decision was the ongoing discussion between the UN Commission and Indian and Pakistani representatives in Paris. The commission had presented its interim report to the Security Council on 19 November. The UK and the US were agreed that to obtain Pakistan's acceptance of the August resolution it was essential to appoint a plebiscite administrator and draw up the details of a plebiscite. With the council's approval the commission had begun consultations.

The commission was certain that a coalition administration was unworkable. Initially, the Pakistanis were averse to give in on this point. The British delegation managed to persuade them that the plebiscite administrator would be of such standing that Sheikh

---

[157] UKHC Pakistan to CRO, 17 November 1948, DO 35/3168, TNA.
[158] UKHC Pakistan to CRO, 29 November 1948, DO 142/496, TNA.
[159] Zaheer, *Rawalpindi Conspiracy*, 137–8.
[160] Reed to Olver, 14 December 1948, DO 134/5, TNA.

Abdullah could not influence the process (Dwight Eisenhower was their preferred choice). They also urged the Pakistanis to seize the moment for a favourable outcome.[161] Accordingly, Zafrullah Khan and Mohammed Ali recommended to Liaquat that "no large-scale offensive should be launched while Commission is engaged on securing a settlement."[162] Consequently, Pakistan's offensive slated to begin on 11 December was put off.

The Indians were not pleased with the commission's attempt to hammer out proposals for a plebiscite. The August resolution had stated that these discussions would begin only after the conclusion of a truce agreement. India was being asked to make fresh concessions even though Pakistan had rejected the previous resolution. Further, Nehru felt that it was "almost impossible for them [Pakistan] to . . . withdraw all their forces."[163] Abdullah thought that, other difficulties apart, a plebiscite would incite disruptive forces within Kashmir. For instance, if it was agreed that all refugees should return to vote, Pakistan would send as large a contingent as possible. And there would be no way of verifying their citizenship.[164]

The commission's report had conceded the difficulties and left open the possibility of alternative solutions in keeping with the people's wishes. Nehru therefore thought that drawing up detailed proposals for a plebiscite would preclude the consideration of alternatives. As he wrote to Bajpai: "We do not wish to fight shy of a plebiscite provided it is conducted under suitable conditions. But it would be unfortunate to come to [a] decision now which would exclude other methods which might be more feasible." On consideration, Nehru felt that "Election of Constituent Assembly under conditions of voting as [in a] plebiscite might be the best method of considering [the] complicated problem."[165] The assembly so convened could vote on the question of accession. This would not only reduce the political and administrative difficulties associated with a plebiscite, it would enable the issue to be

---

[161] UK Delegation to FO, 5 December 1948, DO 35/3168, TNA.

[162] Zaheer, *Rawalpindi Conspiracy*, 139.

[163] Nehru to Abdullah, 13 December 1948, *SWJN-SS*, 8: 75.

[164] Abdullah to Nehru, 28 November 1948, paraphrased in ibid., 62, fn. 2.

[165] Cable to Bajpai, 29 November 1948, ibid., 59–60.

decided under less impassioned conditions. As Nehru observed, "the type of highly objectionable propaganda which Pakistan and Azad Kashmir are carrying on if permitted in Kashmir itself would produce bloody riots."[166]

But Nehru realized that however unrealistic the option of plebiscite, he could not "just say no the Commission;" for "an adverse decision of the Commission might prove harmful to us."[167] The plebiscite was the one point of agreement amongst all the external players. As Nehru had noticed in Paris, "this business of a plebiscite and the conditions governing it fills peoples' minds."[168] Moreover, whilst Nehru continued to believe that partition was the most practical solution, Pakistan had refused to countenance the idea. So Nehru reluctantly agreed to consider the plebiscite proposals.

In discussions with the commission's representative, he specifically sought and obtained several clarifications: if Pakistan did not implement the first two parts of the August resolution, India would not be bound to the plebiscite; before the plebiscite the Azad forces would be disbanded and disarmed on a "large scale;" any political activity that might disturb the peace would not be regarded as legitimate; the exploration of other methods of ascertaining the peoples' wishes should not be ruled out.[169] In the light of these assurances India accepted the supplementary proposals. The clarifications obtained from the commission were released to the press. By the end of December 1948 Nehru agreed to a plebiscite if appropriate conditions were created, but he was also interested in exploring two alternatives: elections to a constituent assembly, and partition. Nehru's biographer claims that the decision to accept the resolution was "taken on general considerations rather than in India's special interests."[170] However, he underestimates Nehru's concerns about the repercussions of a full-scale war with Pakistan. As seen earlier, Nehru felt that such a war would be ruinous for India. Having ruled out military escalation, it is

[166] Cable to Bajpai, 1 December 1948, ibid., 67.
[167] Nehru to Abdullah, 29 November 1948, ibid., 62.
[168] Nehru to Patel, 27 October 1948, ibid., 285.
[169] Aide Memoire I & II, 20–22 December 1948, *SWJN-SS*, 9: 219–24.
[170] Gopal, *Nehru*, 2: 33.

not clear that India had a better alternative than going along with the UN Commission.

Pakistan too accepted the proposals. Liaquat rightly concluded that with time the military balance would tilt steeply and inexorably in India's favour.[171] Furthermore, in the past few months the Azad Kashmir leadership had grown optimistic about their chances in a plebiscite.[172] As Liaquat told the British envoy, "I have decided to gamble on the United Nations."[173] On the night of 31 December 1948 the guns fell silent in Kashmir.

An Elusive Truce

Six months passed before the "ceasefire line" was delimited. But the truce agreement proved unattainable. The main obstacle was the status of the Azad Kashmir forces. India had agreed that the disbandment and large-scale disarmament of these would occur before the plebiscite, i.e. after the truce agreement had been concluded. In the truce discussions the Pakistanis overreached themselves. They claimed that the agreement should establish a military balance between the two sides. Therefore, Pakistani troops would withdraw only after training the Azad forces to take their place. But India should begin its withdrawal even as the training was under way. Indeed, by this time the Azad forces comprised thirty-two battalions equipped and supplied by Pakistan. In the light of past Pakistani actions the Indians concluded that Karachi was preparing to resume hostilities and consolidate its grip over the Azad territory.[174] Consequently, Delhi demanded that the Azad forces be disbanded and disarmed at the truce stage itself.

To break the deadlock the UN Commission proposed arbitration. But India insisted that this was "not a matter for arbitration but for affirmative and immediate decision." Delhi's stance was considerably influenced by Sheikh Abdullah's staunch opposition to the presence of

[171] Zaheer, *Rawalpindi Conspiracy*, 139–45.

[172] Mudie to Hallett, 26 June 1949, Mss Eur F164/48, Mudie Papers, APAC.

[173] UKHC Pakistan to CRO, 29 December 1948, DO 35/3168, TNA.

[174] IB report, 1 April 1949, cited in Sandeep Bamzai, *The Bonfire of Kashmiriyat* (New Delhi: Rupa, 2006), 240.

Azad forces. The National Conference passed a resolution denouncing arbitration as "appeasement of the aggressor." The dispute was referred back to the Security Council.

Meantime the alternatives to a plebiscite were back on the table. Abdullah considered independence the best option, and said so in a newspaper interview. "Accession to either side cannot bring peace. We want to live in friendship with both the dominions . . . However, an independent Kashmir must be guaranteed not only by India and Pakistan, but also by Great Britain, the US and the UN."[175] The Indian cabinet strongly disagreed and prevailed on him to retract the statement. Since Nehru's preferred solutions seemed to have no purchase on Pakistan, he felt that the best option was to confine the plebiscite to the valley and partition the rest. He conveyed his thinking to the British envoy; Bajpai and Krishna Menon followed it up through official channels. London refused to entertain the idea on the grounds that it would be unacceptable to Pakistan.[176]

The Security Council appointed A.G.L. McNaughton of Canada as an "informal mediator" on demilitarization. McNaughton quickly drew up a set of proposals calling for the withdrawal of regular Pakistani and Indian forces (less those required for internal and external security); and for the disbandment of *both* the Azad forces and the Kashmir state forces and militia. Pakistan accepted it. India held that this was a novel and unacceptable demand. For one thing, it harked back to the April 1948 resolution in equating India and Pakistan. For another, the National Conference was even more vehemently opposed to the idea.[177] On 3 February 1950 McNaughton reported failure. The dispute passed on to a formal mediator—the Australian jurist Sir Owen Dixon.

During this period the internal dimension of the problem underwent significant transformation. Immediately after the ceasefire Abdullah demanded the abdication of the maharaja. The demand was spurred both by a vexatious relationship with Hari Singh and by his

[175] Cited in Bhattacharjea, *Tragic Hero of Kashmir*, 150.
[176] UKHC India to CRO, 9 September 1948; CRO Note, 22 September 1948, DO 142/519, TNA.
[177] Abdullah to Patel, 1 March 1950, *SPC*, 1: 314–16.

desire to shore up his standing with the masses. Nehru advised Abdullah to avoid precipitate action that might undermine India's position in the ongoing negotiations.[178] After all, the instrument of accession had been signed by the maharaja. As a compromise Hari Singh was asked to leave the state "temporarily" and his son Karan Singh was appointed regent. Maharaja Hari Singh would never return to Kashmir.[179]

More important, provisions were written into the Indian constitution according special status to Kashmir and ensuring its autonomy. Article 370 allowed Kashmir to have its own constitution: the Indian parliament could only legislate on Kashmir's defence, external affairs, and communications. The state's constituent assembly would make the final decision on which other subjects it wished to concede. Significantly, the article provided for the state to sever its links with India on the recommendation of its constituent assembly. This was consonant with Nehru's thinking on alternatives to a plebiscite.

The Indian government was also seized of the military aspects of the problem. Contingency plans were drawn up to cater for a surprise attack in Kashmir by Pakistan or Pakistan-abetted forces. These envisaged a counterattack in Punjab as well as defence in Kashmir. Nehru thought that preparations for an attack would themselves have a coercive effect: "troop movements on our part will confirm this fear on their [Pakistan's] part." Besides, they could "throw out this hint to Ambassadors of U.K. and U.S.A."[180] The Kashmir crisis thus reinforced a tendency that was already apparent in Nehru's strategic approach: the preference for coercive as opposed to controlling strategies. More important, this particular strategy would become the cornerstone of India's defence policy on Kashmir. Indeed, its influence would be felt long after Jawaharlal Nehru's years in office.

Interestingly, the first opportunity for Nehru to try such a strategy was provided not by a crisis in Kashmir but by another—the one in Bengal.

[178] Nehru to Abdullah, 12 January 1949, *SWJN-SS*, 9: 196–9.

[179] Singh, *Autobiography*, 92–102.

[180] Note to Defence Minister, 12 June 1949, *SWJN-SS*, 11: 367; Lorne Kavic, *India's Quest for Security: Defence Policies 1947–1965* (Berkeley, LA: University of California Press, 1967), 36–8.

5

Bengal 1950

In the aftermath of Partition and the accompanying bloodbath, relations between India and Pakistan were bedevilled by a host of problems. Principal among these was the cluster of disputes over the fate of the princely states. Nevertheless, there were other issues under contention: the repatriation of property left behind by refugees; the distribution of river waters in Punjab; and trade and monetary questions, including the valuation of currency.[1] The multitude of disputes led the Indian prime minister to propose a "no-war" declaration towards the end of 1949.

Pakistan insisted that a statement abjuring war be accompanied by an agreement to refer outstanding disputes to arbitration or judicial determination, should other peaceful methods of resolution fail. Nehru was prepared to consider this for issues such as evacuee property or canal waters but unwilling to submit the Kashmir dispute to arbitration: this involved the lives and future of a people which could not be considered and decided in this fashion. In any case the issue was being dealt with by the UN Security Council.[2] A "no-war" declaration, Nehru believed, would instil a modicum of mutual confidence, thereby reducing the chance of a stray spark setting alight

[1] For a survey of these issues see J.B. Das Gupta, *India–Pakistan Relations, 1947–1955* (Amsterdam: Uitgeverij Debrug-Djambatan, 1958). On the question of waters, also see A.A. Michel, *The Indus Rivers: A Study of the Effects of Partition* (New Haven: Yale University Press, 1967).

[2] See Nehru's Note to Secretary General of MEA, 4 December 1949; press conference at New Delhi, 6 January 1950, *SWJN-SS*, 14, pt I: 3–4, 15–16.

the tinderbox of India–Pakistan relations. Even as he contemplated this a crisis loomed on the horizon that would bring the neighbours to the brink of war.

The origins of the crisis were murky and the claims of both sides strongly contested. It appears to have been triggered by an incident in a village in the Khulna district of East Pakistan.[3] On 20 December 1949 a police squad went to arrest a suspected communist agent in the village. Unable to trace the person, the police allegedly assaulted some members of this predominantly Hindu village, an action that led to a bigger clash with the local residents. In the ensuing mêlée two policemen were killed. A couple of days later the police, assisted by the Ansar (a semi-official paramilitary force) cracked down on this village and many neighbouring ones largely inhabited by Hindus. The Indian government later claimed the crackdown was aimed deliberately and exclusively against Hindus.[4] The Pakistan government maintained the incident was not communal but had occurred because of an attempt by communists to foment trouble in the area.[5]

Nearly three weeks after these incidents, some of the affected people began trickling into the neighbouring Indian province of West Bengal. By mid-February 1950 Delhi was claiming that over 24,000 had entered West Bengal, with almost 500 migrants streaming in every day.[6] The influx of refugees and their tales of harassment deeply unsettled West Bengal. The simmering discontent against these developments soon assumed the form of anti-Muslim sentiment. The Hindu Mahasabha—the major right wing extremist Hindu organization in India—and its allies seized the opportunity to launch a virulent campaign against Muslims. The mahasabha's president

[3] For an excellent study of the social and political consequences of the partition of Bengal, see Joya Chatterji, *The Spoils of Partition: Bengal and India, 1947–1967* (Cambridge: Cambridge University Press, 2007). Although the book provides an in-depth treatment of the refugee problem, it deals with the crisis of 1950 only in passing.

[4] Statement by Nehru in Parliament, 23 February 1950, *SWJN-SS*, 14, pt I: 56.

[5] Statement by Liaquat Ali Khan, *Dawn*, 14 February 1950.

[6] Statement by Nehru in Parliament, 23 February 1950, *SWJN-SS*, 14, pt I: 56; *Hindu* (*Weekly edn*) (Madras), 5 February 1950.

Map 4. East Pakistan, *c.*1950

advocated a policy of "tit for tat" to counter Pakistan's "policy of genocide towards the Hindus."[7] On 4 February attacks against Muslims began in Calcutta and other parts of the state. They lasted over a week, leaving 72 Muslims dead and almost 250 injured.[8] The violence led to an exodus of Muslims from West Bengal to East Pakistan. This in turn exacerbated the situation in the latter province. Violent anti-Hindu riots erupted in Dhaka on 10 February 1950, forcing large numbers of Hindus to flee. In short, a vicious cycle of violence and retaliation took hold, causing a massive flow of refugees in both directions. The manner in which the crisis developed ensured that its domestic and external dimensions would remain entwined.

A Forgotten Conflagration: Bengal in Early 1950

In early February 1950 India urged Pakistan to take "immediate steps" to dispel fear and restore confidence amongst its Hindus. In his public utterances Nehru was unwilling to comment beyond stating that he took a "very serious view of the situation." He was conscious of the speed with which communal violence could shake both countries and wished to move cautiously. He asked in parliament, "should we in a moment of danger say or do things which may precipitate further crises and disasters?"[9]

Following large-scale violence in West Bengal, Nehru grew "greatly concerned" over the targeting of Muslims. The attacks showed that the canker of sectarian violence could yet afflict India—a perilous prospect given the recent deep cleavages made by Partition. He appealed to the people to act with sobriety and avoid falling "prey to communal passion and retaliation."[10] The government imposed a dawn-to-dusk curfew in the worst-affected areas, authorized the police

[7] *Times of India* (Bombay), 2 February 1950.

[8] Statement by Nehru in Parliament, 23 February 1950, *SWJN-SS*, 14, pt I: 57; *Times of India*, 14 and 15 February 1950; *Hindu* (*Weekly edn*), 12 February 1950.

[9] *Times of India*, 4 February 1950; *Hindu* (*Weekly edn*), 5 February 1950.

[10] Nehru's statement to the press, 10 February 1950, *SWJN-SS*, 14, pt I: 37–8.

to fire on rioting mobs, and employed the army to control the disorder. In order to douse inflammatory news the authorities also instructed the press to submit their reports for scrutiny before publication.[11]

The stern measures taken by Delhi reflected another concern too. The prime minister felt that the targeting of Muslims in India enfeebled his own position *vis-à-vis* Pakistan by depriving him of the moral high ground. "Attempts at retaliation," he argued, "are not only essentially bad from every point of view but also are harmful and weaken the action we might take."[12] Although Nehru was not sure what action could usefully be taken, his thinking was influenced by the experience of the violence over Partition. Nehru had then stated that but for the massacre of Muslims in India he would have sent the army into Pakistan to protect Hindus.[13] Admittedly, such statements were rhetorically employed to mollify tempers in India. Still, Nehru had felt constrained in his dealings with Pakistan on that occasion.

Presently, Pakistan's prime minister Liaquat Ali Khan issued a statement refuting India's account of the events. The Khulna incident, he claimed, was being maliciously tarred with the communal brush. He upbraided the Indian press for "playing up rumours which they must have known to be false." Consequently, "most sanguinary riots" had taken place in Calcutta, resulting in a massive exodus of Muslims to East Pakistan. Liaquat railed against "insinuations" made by Nehru and Patel that the violence in Calcutta was a backlash against events across the border. The very incidence of these riots a month after the disturbances in Khulna showed that the events were unconnected.[14]

The continuing disturbances and the mounting domestic criticism of his "weak policy" towards Pakistan led Nehru to ponder his options before responding to Liaquat's statement. The immediate

[11] Consulate General Calcutta to SS, 11 February 1950, 791.00/2-1150, Record Group (hereafter RG) 59, US National Archives and Records Administration (hereafter USNA), Maryland; *Times of India*, 10 February 1950.

[12] *SWJN-SS*, 14, pt I: 37.

[13] See e.g. speech on 30 September 1947, *SWJN-SS*, 4: 107–9.

[14] *Daily Telegraph* (London), 14 February 1950; *Times of India*, 14 February 1950.

question was obvious: how could the cycle of violence and retribution be arrested? Nehru saw it as a continuation of the problem engendered by the Muslim League's two-nation theory and its demand for Pakistan. The Congress Party had acquiesced in the "painful and injurious" option of Partition hoping to rid the country of this scourge. But the carnage accompanying the event had proved such hopes to be absurdly misplaced. The recrudescence of communal violence showed that the problem lent itself to no easy solution: "it is not quite clear when and how this business will end."[15]

The use of force was an obvious option: most of his critics clamoured for it. Given the magnitude of the crisis Nehru, by his own admission, considered it seriously.[16] Nonetheless, he felt that India's interest in halting the ongoing cycle of violence could not be viewed in isolation: there were greater interests at stake in avoiding a war with Pakistan. Nehru was aware that the military balance rested in India's favour: "From a purely military point of view, I am not afraid of a war." But there were other considerations. For one thing, it was unlikely that a surgical military operation would settle the issue. Any such action would inevitably escalate into all-out war. It would be "a terrible affair and almost an unending thing, bringing ruin to all parties concerned." For another, a prolonged war would amount to "saying goodbye, for a long period, to any real progress of the country." For a third, the possibility of intervention by external powers could not be gainsaid. The costs of war, in short, would be extremely high.

Besides, would going to war provide succour to Hindus in Pakistan? Nehru was convinced it would not. An invasion, however restricted, would channel the wrath of Pakistan's Muslims on its Hindu populace. "They will be completely bottled up in a violently hostile area and there will be no one to protect them."[17] Irrespective of the military outcome, the use of force would lead to "the sacrifice of a large number of those very people, whom we might seek to liberate."[18] "Looking at

---

[15] Letter to Chief Ministers, 16 February 1950, *SWJN-SS*, 14, pt I: 400.
[16] Nehru to Rajagopalachari, 21 February 1950, ibid., 53.
[17] Letter to Chief Ministers, 16 February 1950, ibid., 401.
[18] Nehru to Jogesh Chandra Paul, 17 February 1950, ibid., 43.

the whole picture," then, the prime minister was "convinced that it is our bounden duty to avoid war as far as possible."

Whilst Nehru regarded war as an unsuitable option, he thought that the possibility of one could not be ruled out. The Kashmir issue was still unresolved and Pakistan's leaders were delivering "aggressive and provocative speeches and constantly talking of war." The Pakistani press, too, was pandering to such sentiments. Nehru doubted that Karachi wanted war, for "such a war would be exceedingly injurious to them." Yet he felt that the Pakistani leadership might be forced to launch one despite its obvious costs: "they are creating an atmosphere of war and are becoming more and more prisoners of their own words and exhortations."[19] The communal violence in Bengal and its effect on Pakistani public opinion could egg them on.

Nehru did not consider war inevitable, but the government had to be "fully prepared for any possible development." The next three months, he reckoned, were crucial. Thereafter, with the onset of the monsoon, the chances of military action by Pakistan would reduce.[20] Nevertheless, Nehru did not immediately initiate military preparations—though this perception would influence India's military moves subsequently. Instead, he focused on longer-term measures such as putting on hold the reduction in the military establishment recently announced by his government. This decision was also influenced by his awareness that trimming the armed forces at this juncture would be "strongly resented by Parliament and by the general public in the existing state of affairs."[21]

How, then, should the immediate problem be handled? Nehru claimed that the "only way" to overcome it was "not to do anything which was wrong both in principle and in its practical effects." The government must be prepared, "but at the same time . . . our language should be restrained and our actions firm and peaceful."[22] By urging restraint Nehru sought to avoid increasing the constraints on the Pakistani leadership. This indicated both his cautious approach and

[19] Letter to Chief Ministers, 16 February 1950, ibid., 401–2.

[20] Ibid., 402; Nehru to John Matthai, 17 February 1950, ibid., 326; Nehru to B.C. Roy, 17 February 1950, ibid., 42.

[21] Nehru to John Matthai, 17 February 1950, ibid., 326–7.

[22] Letter to Chief Ministers, 16 February 1950, ibid., 401–2.

his desire not to be propelled by domestic pressures towards any specific course of action.

Proposals Exchanged in February 1950

After evaluating the options the Indian prime minister cabled his Pakistani counterpart suggesting measures to restore confidence in the minority communities of East and West Bengal. He proposed that both governments immediately permit the deputy high commissioners—in Calcutta and Dhaka—to visit the affected areas and ascertain the facts. He also suggested setting up two joint fact-finding commissions, one for each province. These would comprise two representatives from each province, one of whom would be a minister. The commissions would determine the facts, and assess the prevailing condition and prospects for improvement. Nehru wanted the commissions to be appointed forthwith and to begin their task "within a week at the latest."[23] In a letter to Liaquat he emphasized that he was not interested in elaborate enquiries but was suggesting a "fairly quick overall survey." This would in itself allay the fears of the minorities. Nehru also made it clear that he did not share Liaquat's benign reading of the situation in East Bengal.[24] Whilst he was "terribly sorry for what took place in Calcutta," it could not be compared with the happenings in East Bengal. Having outlined proposals which he deemed reasonable, Nehru indicated that he could assume a tougher stance: "If we cannot give that security [to the minorities], then critical conditions continue demanding other action."[25]

Liaquat agreed that immediate steps ought to be taken to restore confidence amongst the minorities. He also directed East Pakistan to help the Indian deputy high commissioner visit the riot-torn areas. Liaquat, however, turned down the proposal of joint fact-finding commissions. Instead, he suggested that both governments declare that they did not support the migration of minorities and that they would take steps to discourage it. Liaquat's rationale was that the migrants

[23] Telegram to Liaquat, 17 February 1950, ibid., 39.
[24] Nehru to Liaquat, 17 February 1950, ibid., 39–40.
[25] Personal letter to Liaquat, 17 February 1950, ibid., 40–1.

invariably carried accounts—at times exaggerated—of dreadful happenings, which aggravated sectarian tensions. The declaration would also contain an assurance that the governments would rehabilitate displaced people and protect their lives and property.[26]

Nehru disagreed. Given the situation in East Bengal, he thought it impractical to prevent the entry of "persons fleeing from terror." He reiterated that the first step should be a quick survey by joint committees. Only if their reports suggested a semblance of normality could he contemplate advising the minorities to stay put. He was "strongly of the opinion that immediate prevention of the movement of refugees at this stage will create still more panic."[27]

Even as telegrams were being exchanged, Nehru's office was inundated with messages from refugees fleeing East Bengal. The details of their travails distressed the prime minister.[28] Nehru was convinced that the situation demanded urgent attention at the highest level. On 20 February 1950 he cabled Liaquat yet again, pressing him to accept the suggestion of joint enquiry commissions. Nehru further proposed that he and Liaquat should together visit the affected areas. This would have "a marked psychological effect" in both countries and would calm the minorities. It would also lay a "sure foundation" for a lasting solution to the problem.[29]

The importance that India attached to these proposals is evident from its attempt to use external influence to prod Pakistan. The secretary general of the MEA, Sir Girja Shankar Bajpai, briefed the British and American envoys, expressing hope that Karachi would accept the proposals. The Indians knew full well where British and American interests lay as far as India–Pakistan relations were concerned. Thus, in order to induce them to lean on Pakistan, Bajpai hinted to the British high commissioner that a joint tour by the prime

[26] Editorial note 2, *SWJN-SS*, 14, pt I: 42; Editorial note 3, ibid., 45; Nehru to Liaquat, 20 February 1950, ibid., 45. Also see UKHC India to CRO, 21 February 1950, FO 371/84246, TNA.

[27] Nehru to Liaquat, 20 February 1950, *SWJN-SS*, 14, pt I: 45–6.

[28] Subimal Dutt, *With Nehru in the Foreign Office* (Columbia: South Asia Books, 1977), 53; Nehru to Liaquat, 18 February 1950, *SWJN-SS*, 14, pt I: 43–4.

[29] Nehru to Liaquat, 20 February 1950, *SWJN-SS*, 14, pt I: 46–7.

ministers could pave the way for further meetings on issues such as Kashmir.[30]

Karachi, however, felt that India's proposals were a "propaganda stunt" to impress world opinion. Pakistan continued to accord the "greatest importance" to its proposal of forbidding migration.[31] There were other considerations as well. An enquiry along the lines proposed by India could be problematic. Liaquat admitted to the British envoy that the local police acted strongly in Khulna and that most of the victims had been Hindus. He argued however that the affair did not have communal overtones;[32] but the Indians could be expected to construe it differently. As for a joint tour, he felt that by the time it could be undertaken the situation would have improved; the visit would only result in more ferment. In any event the experience of such a tour in Punjab, after Partition, had convinced him of its futility.[33]

Of equal importance, if not greater, was Karachi's interest in appearing defiant. For instance, Liaquat told a gathering of students that he would "rather see every one of us die than see ourselves slaves of Hindu India."[34] Pakistan's stance appears to have stemmed from domestic and reputational concerns. The government was still struggling to impose its authority on the provinces. In particular, relations with East Bengal were far from easy.[35] The Pakistan government could hardly wish to be seen by domestic constituencies as obeying Delhi's diktats. Given the manifold disputes with India, Pakistan had good reason to avoid conveying an impression of weakness lest

[30] UKHC India to CRO, 21 February 1950, FO 371/84246, TNA; Ambassador in India to SS, 24 February 1950, *FRUS 1950*, 5: 1389–90.

[31] Australian High Commission (hereafter AHC) to Secretary of State for Commonwealth Relations (hereafter SSCR), 6 March 1950, A1838, TS 169/11/148, National Archives of Australia (hereafter NAA), Canberra; UKHC Pakistan to CRO, 22 February 1950, FO 371/84246, TNA; *Times of India*, 22 February, 1950.

[32] UKHC Pakistan to CRO, 24 February 1950, FO 371/84246, TNA.

[33] UKHC Pakistan to CRO, 24 February 1950, FO 371/84246, TNA (different from the document cited in the previous note); *Times of India*, 22 February 1950.

[34] Speech of 22 February, *Hindu* (*Weekly edn*), 26 February 1950.

[35] Jalal, *The State of Martial Rule*, 106.

Delhi began to expect similar behaviour in other areas of contention. Liaquat, therefore, suggested a different series of steps. These included punishment for all criminal offenders and those propagating hatred, assistance for victims of violence, and an enquiry by the respective governments to suggest measures to preclude such incidents.[36]

Nehru *versus* the Congress Party

By this time a debate was raging in Indian political circles on how best to deal with the crisis. From the outset the Hindu Right had demanded the use of force against Pakistan. Soon, sections of the ruling Congress Party called for a tougher stance and grew censorious of the prime minister's approach. Even the Gandhian, pacifist, wing of the party seemed slumped in despair. J.B. Kripalani, for instance, openly argued that "those who feel that they have right on their side must be prepared for war or martyrdom, but never for cowardly submission."[37] Others mooted the possibility of a large-scale exchange of minorities between East and West Bengal. Still others contended that since the number of Hindu migrants into India would far exceed the Muslims leaving for East Bengal, Pakistan should be forced to give up some territory in the east.[38]

Nehru refused to countenance the argument that the choice was either war or a planned exchange of population. He considered the latter idea particularly pernicious. It would amount to a tacit acceptance of the two-nation theory, a notion that had no place in his pluralist conception of India. Besides, such a measure would pose enormous practical difficulties and stoke more conflict. He deemed the idea of getting Pakistan to cede territory chimerical: "not an inch of territory is going to be given to us by Pakistan, except possibly by war."[39] Having ruled out this option, Nehru saw no alternative other than

[36] Editorial notes 2 and 3, *SWJN-SS*, 14, pt I: 46.

[37] J.B. Kripalani, "Victims of Partition," *Vigil* (New Delhi), 25 February 1950, 7.

[38] Nehru to B. C. Roy, 17 February 1950, *SWJN-SS*, 14, pt I: 42. Also see editorial note 2 in ibid.

[39] Ibid; Nehru to B.C. Roy, 21 February 1950, ibid., 52. Also see, Nehru to B.C. Roy, 28 February 1950, ibid., 213.

insisting that the Hindus of East Bengal be provided security in their own homes.

But the fractious debate within the party left the prime minister distraught. He felt that the party's stance was at variance with his, both on the external and internal dimensions of the problem. Nehru was certain that war would have "disastrous consequences." Furthermore, "there is a constant cry for retaliation and of vicarious punishment of Muslims in India, because the Pakistanis punish Hindus. This argument does not appeal to me in the slightest."[40] The domestic pressures on Nehru were evident from his desire to resign his office and tend to the problem in his private capacity. In so doing he sought to emulate the example of his master, Mahatma Gandhi, who had worked, tirelessly and courageously, to improve communal relations in Bengal before Partition. Such an action would "strike the imagination of people both in West Bengal and East Bengal, and make them pause and think." It might also jolt the party out of its catatonia: "We grow too complacent and smug."[41] At this point, Nehru was awaiting Liaquat's response to his proposal of a joint tour but felt that he should visit East Bengal regardless.

A Letter from Dhaka

Meanwhile, the Indian deputy high commissioner in Dhaka sent a bleak appraisal of the situation in East Bengal. Despite the measures taken by the authorities, he wrote, "extreme panic still prevails." Indeed, the East Bengal authorities had cautioned him not to move about in the city or even go to his office. Nevertheless, he had managed to visit refugee centres in Dhaka. The Hindus believed that the simultaneous outbreak of violence in different areas showed that they "were engineered with active official connivance if not encouragement." The letter concluded on a sombre note: "The minority community feel convinced that it will be impossible for them to stay in this province after what has happened, which is the culmination of the slow process of squeezing out going on some months past."[42]

[40] Nehru to Patel, 20 February 1950, ibid., 47–8.
[41] Nehru to Patel, 21 February 1950, ibid., 50–1.
[42] Deputy High Commissioner in Dhaka to New Delhi, 18 February 1950,

Nehru and Patel discussed the report on 22 February 1950.[43] Delhi took a serious view of this assessment. The Indian defence secretary seemed to echo the prime minister's view when he wrote: "there is a good deal of method in what might at first appear to be madness on the part of Pakistan . . . It is impossible for us to absorb any large number of people and equally it is impossible for us deliberately to adopt a policy of evicting thousands of people just because they are Muslims."[44] By this time, Liaquat's response— turning down Nehru's ideas and advancing his own—was also received.

The confluence of the internal crisis, the report from Dhaka, and Pakistan's seeming recalcitrance, led Nehru to put on hold his plans for resignation. The pressure from the party, however, could not be wished away, more so since the refugee influx was burgeoning. Thus far Nehru had considered avoiding war with Pakistan of paramount interest. Although he still baulked at the possibility he was now convinced that the situation warranted tougher measures. He realized that any solution would entail applying substantial pressure on Pakistan. Considering Pakistan's unyielding stance and its capability to resist or retaliate, pushing it in the desired direction would not be easy. As Nehru explained: "It is natural and right for us to exercise all the pressure we can on East Bengal or Pakistan. But, in the nature of things, this external pressure does not go very far, unless it takes the form of some kind of coercion, when it depends on a balance of various factors."[45]

The first overt indication of the prime minister's changing attitude could be seen in a measured but tough speech delivered in parliament on 23 February. Nehru had originally intended to present the facts of the situation and hint at the possibility of his resignation. In view of Pakistan's rebuff, and at Patel's insistence, he modified the

---

enclosed in Embassy in New Delhi to State Department, 27 February 1950, 791.00/2-2750, RG 59, USNA.

[43] Entry of 22 February 1950, *Inside Story of Sardar Patel: The Diary of Maniben Patel, 1936–50*, ed. P. N. Chopra and Prabha Chopra (New Delhi: Vision Books, 2001) (hereafter *Diary of Maniben Patel*), 347.

[44] H.M. Patel to Bucher, 26 February 1950, 7901-87-32, Bucher Papers, NAM.

[45] Letter to Chief Ministers, 1 March 1950, *SWJN-SS*, 14, pt I: 407.

contents.[46] After detailing the government's version of the events, Nehru informed the house of Liaquat's rejection of his proposals for joint enquiry and tour. Notwithstanding this Nehru advanced yet another proposal. He urged that representatives of the International Red Cross be permitted to visit the affected areas and to ascertain facts, and said bluntly: "It is for the Government of Pakistan to consider seriously what the consequences are likely to be, if they are unable to give peace and security to their own citizens. Those consequences happen to affect India also and we cannot remain indifferent to them." He appealed to the Indian people to eschew retributory violence against the Muslims if they wanted the government to take effective action. In closing he made it clear that "if the methods we have suggested are not agreed to, it may be that we shall have to adopt other methods."[47]

Delhi adopted a strategy of compellence. The objective was to convince Pakistan not to persecute Hindus and agree to a solution suggested by India. As Nehru subsequently explained it to his colleagues, "The threat of war brings some advantages and some pressure and sanctions."[48] The threat to invade East Bengal would force Pakistan to choose between the possibility of war and their acceptance of India's proposals. Compellence at the strategic level would be supplemented by deterrence at the tactical level. As seen earlier, Nehru was concerned that the Pakistani leadership might be impelled by domestic considerations to attack India. This would most likely occur in Punjab; Pakistani troops in East Bengal were barely sufficient for defensive tasks. India, therefore, mobilized the bulk of its forces, including armoured formations, at its borders with West Pakistan. This would at once convey its determination to thwart any aggressive design and willingness to launch a counteroffensive into West Pakistan.

Although Nehru lit upon a coercive strategy, he was still keen to avoid the use of force. Admittedly, there were "some things worse than war and there are occasions when there is no alternative left except war." Yet he believed the costs for India would be unconscionably high.

---

[46] Patel to Nehru, 23 February 1950, *SPC*, 10: 161; Entry of 23 February 1950, *Diary of Maniben Patel*, 347; Gopal, *Nehru*, 2: 84.

[47] Speech in Parliament, 23 February 1950, *SWJN-SS*, 14, pt I: 61–2.

[48] Note to Cabinet, 23 March 1950, ibid., 142.

The prime minister, we may recall, thought a war with Pakistan would be all-out and prolonged, that it would put paid to India's developmental plans, and that the major powers would pass strictures against India or even actually intervene. Indeed, Nehru held that war would be a "disaster of the first magnitude:" it would result in widespread, internecine communal strife within India. Moreover, wars over issues that were "communal or racial" were likely to be fought to the bitter end, leaving little room for settlement.

As in the previous crises, Nehru thought that while the threat of force had to be conveyed to Pakistan, the possibility of escalation to war ought to be minimized: it was important to desist from "talking and encouraging war sentiment."[49] And, as earlier, Delhi tried to carry out these moves unobtrusively. To minimize the pressure from domestic constituencies to actually use these forces the Indian government seems to have convinced the press not to report the mobilization. Indeed, none of the major Indian dailies carried news of troop movements.

The first steps towards mobilization were taken the day Nehru delivered his speech in parliament. But the British chiefs of the Indian air force and navy were anxious to avoid the possibility of hostilities with Pakistan. When Defence Minister Baldev Singh held a meeting to consider the disposition of troops, Air Chief Marshal Thomas Elmhirst and Admiral William Parry counselled caution. Others, however, agreed with the prime minister's approach. The defence secretary thought that India should "avoid taking any precipitate action, while making it clear none-the-less that there is a limit beyond which this country cannot allow things to proceed."[50] Yet Elmhirst and Parry managed to persuade the government to wait at least a week, until they had better intelligence of Pakistani troop locations.[51] But this was only a reprieve, for Delhi was determined to go ahead with the

[49] Letter to Chief Ministers, 1 March 1950, ibid., 409.

[50] H.M. Patel to Bucher, 26 February 1950, 7901-87-32, Bucher Papers, NAM.

[51] UKHC India to CRO, 24 February 1950, FO 371/84246, TNA. The high commissioner concluded with the observation that "senior military officers (British officers) are nevertheless apprehensive that some fresh military disposition might be made." Also see, Note on meeting with Nye by Ambassador Philip Jessup, 24 February 1950, 691.00/2-2650, RG 59, USNA.

mobilization. Baldev Singh voiced the sentiments of the majority when he stated that it was "extremely difficult for any country to go on trying to appease the other without any response from the other side."[52]

The Nehru–Liaquat Correspondence

While military moves were being deliberated, the epistolary exchanges continued. After his speech in parliament Nehru wrote to Liaquat reiterating his proposals and suggesting that, even if Liaquat were unable to accompany him, he was willing to tour the region with any other Pakistani minister.[53] He also assented to the measures suggested by Liaquat. But, in addition, he wanted fact-finding commissions to be appointed. Nehru felt that the range of proposals advanced by him would "go a long way towards controlling the present drift towards catastrophe."[54]

On 27 February Liaquat publicly responded to Nehru's statement and suggestions. A fact-finding commission, he said, would turn into a "fault-finding commission" and would accentuate ill feeling. He also voiced his views on the efficacy of a joint tour, claiming that "we achieved nothing" in Punjab in 1947. As for allowing the International Red Cross to visit, he had "not the slightest objection," but felt "this does not bring us any nearer to the solution of the problem than his [Nehru's] other proposals. The remedy lies with us not with the International Red Cross." The Pakistani prime minister asserted that the only solution to the problem lay in preventing migration and convincing minorities that "it is to their own Government that they should look for the redress of their wrongs, and not to the Government across the border." He called for a declaration by both governments to this effect. Finally, turning to Nehru's reference to "other methods," he declared that Pakistan's policy towards India was "live and let live . . . but if India wants war she will find us fully prepared." He urged the international community to "note the threat."[55]

[52] *Hindu* (*Weekly edn*), 26 February 1950.
[53] Telegrams to Liaquat, 24 February 1950, *SWJN-SS*, 14, pt I: 63-4, 69–70.
[54] Letter to Liaquat, 25 February 1950, ibid., 70–1.
[55] *Times of India*, 28 February 1950; *Statesman*, 1 March 1950. Also see, UKHC Pakistan to CRO, 27 February 1950, FO 371/84246, TNA

Given Karachi's concerns about the domestic audience and reputation, Nehru's tough talk only seemed to have hardened attitudes. The reference to the international community was significant: it foreshadowed the approach Pakistan would later adopt. Liaquat also informed Nehru that his idea of touring East Pakistan by himself was impracticable and likely to embarrass both governments. Besides, any "spectacular action that may prevent emotional temperature from returning to normal should be avoided."[56]

Liaquat's successive rebuffs troubled Nehru. For the present, India had little leverage with Pakistan: military moves were on hold, and, in any event, the mobilization would take a few days. The possibility of bringing external pressure to bear on Pakistan was also explored. Since its earlier attempt to induce Britain to lean on Karachi had not succeeded, Delhi tried to raise the stakes. The Indian high commissioner in London, V.K. Krishna Menon, was instructed to tell the British government that if the situation was not controlled quickly, parliamentary and public opinion might force the Indian government to take steps to protect the Hindus in East Pakistan.[57] Unbeknownst to Delhi, Whitehall was aware that troop movements had been put off, so they chose not to convey a minatory message to Pakistan. Instead, they advised Liaquat to rein in the Pakistani press and prevent the publication of exaggerated accounts of incidents in West Bengal. The British also issued a statement that they would give "immediate attention" to resolving all outstanding disputes between the neighbours.[58]

The situation, however, was rapidly deteriorating. There was news of renewed violence against Hindus in Dhaka; in Calcutta alone there were reportedly almost 50,000 migrants.[59] Nehru was now anxious to take some steps to forestall any further worsening of the situation. On the domestic front, members of the Congress Party were entreated

---

[56] Extracts from Liaquat to Nehru, 28 February 1950 in AHC Pakistan to SSCR, 6 March 1950, A1838, TS 169/11/48, NAA.

[57] Gopal, *Nehru*, 2: 84.

[58] See UKHC Pakistan to CRO, 1 March 1950, FO 371/84246, TNA; *Times of India*, 4 March 1950.

[59] *Times of India*, 27 February, 2 & 3 March 1950; Nehru to Liaquat, 27 February 1950, *SWJN-SS*, 14, pt I: 74–5.

not to "surrender to momentary passion."[60] Provincial governments were enjoined to take firm measures to curb unrest and restrain the press from publishing provocative news.[61]

Given their inability to pressurize Pakistan at this time, it is not surprising that the Indians sought to induce them instead. Nehru assured Liaquat that his statement in parliament was "restrained and there was no element of threat."[62] It was a measure of his desperation that he wrote that it was "urgently necessary that both Governments should make *some declaration* in regard to the Bengal situation." He requested Liaquat to reconsider his suggestions.[63] The Pakistani prime minister agreed with all the points for the declaration, barring the one about appointing inquiry committees. He also insisted that the governments declare that they would make every effort to discourage migration. Nehru, however, stuck to his stand on this point.[64]

Although Nehru's suggestions on a joint declaration failed to elicit a satisfactory response from Pakistan, they served as a focal point for his domestic critics. Members of his cabinet with affiliation to the Hindu Right, such as Syama Prasad Mookerjee (also a Bengali), were chagrined that the government was settling for a mere declaration instead of taking decisive action. Even moderates like Amrit Kaur felt that "things just *cannot* be allowed to go on as they are."[65] Sections of the left called for tougher action, too. The Socialist Party passed a resolution asking both countries to work together to improve the plight of the minorities. If this failed to come about, "India must act on her own" and take the necessary measures to protect the "human rights" of Hindus in Pakistan.[66]

---

[60] Statement drafted by Nehru and issued by the President of the Congress Party, 27 February 1950, *SWJN-SS*, 14, pt I: 75.

[61] Letter to Chief Ministers, 27 February 1950, ibid., 77–9.

[62] Nehru to Liaquat, 27 February 1950, ibid., 73–4; *Times of India*, 1 March 1950.

[63] Nehru to Liaquat, 1 March 1950, *SWJN-SS*, 14, pt I: 79–80 (emphasis added).

[64] Editorial note 2, ibid., 80; Two telegrams from Nehru to Liaquat, 2 March 1950, ibid., 81–3.

[65] Personal letter from Rajkumari Amrit Kaur to P.C. Gordon-Walker (UK SSCR), 6 March 1950, DO 35/2989, TNA (emphasis in original).

[66] *Hindu* (*Weekly edn*), 5 March 1950. Jayaprakash Narayan, a former

Against this backdrop the prime minister's address to the nation was broadcast on 3 March 1950. The speech was carefully crafted. Several audiences had to be simultaneously addressed, demonstrating resolve yet also restraint, conveying a sense of risk yet also reassurance, so that the public would rally around the government, the critics would be persuaded, the external actors made calmer, and Pakistan compelled towards seeking a way out.

Nehru explained that the present situation was the outcome of the very nature of Pakistan: minorities in a religious state were bound to lack a full sense of citizenship and security. Pakistan had criticized him for suggesting the possibility of war: "Anyone who knows me should know that I hate war . . . But to talk complacently of peace, when there is no peace and when something worse than war is possible is to be blind to facts." Turning to his domestic opponents he said that the situation "brooks no delay;" he was trying to find some immediate remedy. This would "necessarily be only a partial one," but it would buy the government the requisite time to arrive at a comprehensive solution. In his peroration Nehru urged the Indian people to exercise restraint: "The strength of a nation ultimately consists in civilised behaviour and not in retaliation on the innocent."[67]

But, privately Nehru conceded that "it has become impossible to remain quiet or even just to protest . . . It is impossible to contemplate 12 million people walking across from East Bengal to West Bengal."[68]

Moves and Missives in March 1950

The mobilization of Indian forces commenced on or around 3 March 1950. Before this, some of the battalions already stationed along the borders with East Bengal were locally redeployed.[69] Now, in this largest movement of Indian forces since Independence, 1 Armoured

---

associate of Nehru and a leader of the Socialist Party, reiterated a few days later that if peaceful methods fail, "the only alternative is to send our forces into East Bengal to protect the minorities there." Reuter's report of Narayan's speech, 7 March 1950, DO 35/2989, TNA.

[67] *SWJN-SS*, 14, pt I: 84–7.

[68] Nehru to Radhakrishnan, 5 March 1950, ibid., 204–5.

[69] UKHC India to CRO, 4 March 1950, FO 371/84246, TNA.

Division was shifted from central India (Jhansi) to an intermediate staging area (Meerut) closer to the western borders. The other mechanized formation, 2 Independent Armoured Brigade, was moved to the concentration area near the border with Pakistan in the Punjab. 4 Infantry Division was also ordered to deploy on the western border, and 5 Infantry Division was kept ready to move at short notice. On 6 March the chiefs of staff were directed to present the contingency plans.[70]

While military moves were afoot, Nehru visited Calcutta. He was aware that tempers were running high in West Bengal and that he would have a tough time placating those advocating stronger measures.[71] Nevertheless the pitch of their emotions would have surprised him. According to an observer, thousands of people had "assembled silently on both sides of the route through which the Prime Minister drove from the airport. Only huge banners and posters demanding immediate action in East Bengal were visible and at places similar slogans greeted the Prime Minister."[72] Nehru spoke to leaders from across the political spectrum, civil society organizations, and editors of newspapers, trying at all times to mollify the malcontents. The last, in particular, were in a militant frame of mind. For instance, just before Nehru's visit the editor of the *Amrita Bazar Patrika*—a leading local daily—had told officials from the US consulate that "The only solution is through [the] force [of] arms."[73] Their strident stance was not surprising; for the Bengali *bhadralok* (upper class, Hindu "gentlefolk") had spearheaded the demand for partitioning Bengal in order to undercut the dominance of Muslims in the province's politics and to restore the primacy of Hindus.[74]

In response to calls for action Nehru explained that military intervention in East Bengal would mean a "war of extermination." At the

[70] UKHC India to CRO, 8 & 9 March 1950, FO 371/84247, TNA; Embassy in New Delhi to SS, 4 and 10 March 1950, 791.00 (W)/3-450 and 791.00 (W)/3-1050, RG 59, USNA.

[71] Nehru to Mountbatten, 5 March 1950, *SWJN-SS*, 14, pt I: 91–2.

[72] *Times of India*, 7 March 1950.

[73] Consulate General Calcutta to SS, 3 March 1950, 791.000/3-350, RG 59, USNA.

[74] Joya Chatterji, *Bengal Divided: Hindu Communalism and Partition, 1932–1947* (Cambridge: Cambridge University Press, 1995).

same time an exchange of population was neither practicable nor desirable. For the time being India's policy was to allow refugees to come in; but soon a solution had to be found for them in Pakistan itself. He stressed the need for India to have clean hands and asked the press to be restrained.[75] The prime minister spoke to this effect to the West Bengal and Assam governments as well.[76] By his own account Nehru was frazzled, "having had to deal for four long days with hysterical people in a highly surcharged atmosphere."[77]

On 10 March the Defence Committee of the cabinet considered the contingency plans. These catered for an entry into East Pakistan to protect the Hindus but not for an attack on West Pakistan. The aim of mobilizing forces in the west was to show that India was ready to meet Pakistani moves in that theatre. Some members of the committee were sensitive to possible international repercussions. Yet they agreed that it was not a bad idea to demonstrate India's preparedness for all eventualities: that alone would rein in extremists in Pakistan. The new air force chief, Air Marshal Ronald Ivelaw-Chapman, underlined the dangers of offensive action and the difficulty of localizing it; the other chiefs concurred with him that any intervention was likely to precipitate full-scale hostilities. The prime minister seemed to agree;[78] after all, it buttressed his own position against the hawks in his cabinet.

The Indian troop movements did not remain concealed from Pakistan for long. The deputy high commissioner in Calcutta informed Karachi about the readjustment of troops in the east.[79] At this stage Pakistan did not have detailed information of the moves. The Pakistani military thought they were a contrivance to provoke Karachi into

[75] UKHC India to CRO, 8 March 1950, FO 371/84246, TNA.

[76] *Times of India*, 8 March 1950.

[77] Nehru to Rajagopalachari, 10 March 1950, *SWJN-SS*, 14, pt I: 97–8.

[78] UKHC India to CRO, 11 March 1950, FO 371/84247 TNA; UKHC India (Military Attaché) to War Office, copied to CRO, 9 March 1950, ibid. The reports were based on the details provided by Admiral Parry and General Dudley Russell (the British adviser at the Indian army headquarters). Although the British were aware of these developments, their envoy felt that India would not resort to aggression. In any event he thought it would be premature to pressurize India at this point.

[79] UKHC Pakistan to CRO, 9 March 1950, FO 371/84247, TNA.

taking some impetuous step, which could then be used to justify an Indian invasion. Such an invasion, they believed, would occur in East Pakistan, which was defended by a mere four battalions. Some officers in the general staff thought that if this happened they should counter-attack in Punjab. But the Pakistan army chief, General Douglas Gracey, deemed such an operation unfeasible both because of the army's existing commitments and because of the substandard condition of its only armoured brigade. Pakistan, he held, should refer the matter to the United Nations. Of course, if India attacked West Pakistan, they would have no option but to fight.[80]

While the military debated these scenarios, Liaquat joined issue with Nehru. He referred to troop concentrations in the east and remonstrated against Nehru's broadcast.[81] In his reply Nehru denied that he had ordered a military build-up on the border with East Bengal; this was narrowly factual as the army had only redeployed existing forces. Defending his remarks in the broadcast, Nehru argued that in some ways the recent occurrences were "worse than war." In these circumstances it would be "unrealistic" for him to say anything more than that he would do his utmost to avoid war.[82]

Concurrently, Delhi sought to influence the UK and the US with a twofold aim. On the one hand India wanted to convince them of the gravity of the situation in the hope that they would urge Pakistan to be more amenable to its proposals. On the other Delhi wanted to reassure them that its military moves were essentially reactive. On 9 March Girja Bajpai met the British envoy and expressed disappointment with the protracted correspondence. He claimed that Liaquat's rejection of a joint tour was a profound error, especially as there were many responsible officials and politicians in India who considered an exchange of population or war as the only alternatives.[83]

Three days later the prime minister himself met the British high commissioner and made it clear that neither war nor a mass transfer

[80] UKHC Pakistan to CRO, 11 March 1950, ibid.
[81] Editorial note 4, *SWJN-SS*, 14, pt I: 93; Editorial note 2, ibid., 102.
[82] Nehru to Liaquat, 10 March 1950, ibid., 103.
[83] UKHC India to CRO, 9 March 1950, FO 371/84247, TNA.

of population was the right solution. The key lay in changing Pakistan's attitude towards its minorities. Nehru hoped that to begin with Pakistan would accept the joint declaration; this would bring down the temperature in West Bengal. Later that evening Bajpai spoke to the British envoy and reiterated Nehru's points.[84] Nehru also met the US ambassador that day, and spoke to the same effect.[85] The following day the chief of the general staff assured the British military attaché that India's military preparations were not aggressive: they had to be prepared in case Pakistan attacked.[86]

Delhi's attempt to communicate a blend of reassurance and risk was only partially successful. Even before these meetings the British and American embassies believed that despite mobilization India would not resort to war. They rightly assessed that the prime minister was averse to this option. The Americans further believed that the Indian army did not possess the requisite equipment to make a lightning thrust into the riverine terrain of East Bengal.[87] Unsurprisingly, the British and American envoys interpreted the new messages to fit their preconceptions, and so underlined the element of reassurance. As a result London and Washington saw no reason for bustle.

With each passing day India's prime minister grew increasingly vexed with Pakistan's reluctance to assent to his suggestions. Since the threat posed by the military moves did not seem to influence Karachi's behaviour, Nehru sought to induce Pakistan towards an understanding and to underscore the danger of procrastination. The declaration, he wrote to Liaquat, was "a very small thing, which hardly scratched the surface of the problem. Even that has not been agreed by you so far." Owing to Pakistan's dilatory attitude it had lost whatever little effect it might have had. "We are on the brink of grave dangers . . . any patchwork remedies are of little use now." Nehru suggested that he

[84] UKHC India to CRO, 12 March 1950, ibid.

[85] Ambassador in New Delhi to SS, 13 March 1950, 791.00/3-1350, RG 59, USNA.

[86] UKHC India (Military Attaché) to War Office, 13 March 1950, FO 371/84247, TNA.

[87] UKHC India to CRO, 11 March 1950, ibid.; Embassy in New Delhi to SS, 11 March 1950, 791.00/3-1150, RG 59, USNA.

and Liaquat meet to consider the problem before it was too late to discuss them.[88] Liaquat, however, ignored the invitation; for he felt that public opinion in Pakistan would disapprove.[89]

At Loggerheads: Nehru and His Cabinet

Nehru left for Calcutta the next morning: the situation appeared to be worsening with an increasing flow of refugees in both directions. There was intense pressure now on Nehru to resort to military means, particularly from newspaper editors.[90] The *Amrita Bazar Patrika* had conducted an opinion poll and claimed that 82.7 per cent of their respondents had voted for military action against Pakistan.[91] Indignant at the press's attitude, the prime minister instructed the West Bengal government to restrain them.[92] Nehru returned distressed. He felt that the propaganda, by both press and extremists, was designed to force him into war with Pakistan.[93] At the same time he believed that "the situation is exceedingly difficult and I cannot just see how we can carry on in the way we have done."[94]

The debate in parliament on 17 March 1950 provided Nehru an opportunity to respond to the mounting pressure. He lambasted the Indian press for its recent coverage, including the opinion poll: they had no business to incite the people or push the government towards military action. Nehru informed the house that he and Liaquat might issue a joint declaration. It would, he conceded, have "no great bearing" on the root causes, but would at least ease the situation. He agreed that because the minorities in Pakistan were in grave danger, it was "impossible for us to remain calm and quiet." Yet only the Pakistan government could protect them. He categorically ruled out an exchange

[88] Nehru to Liaquat, 13 March 1950, *SWJN-SS*, 14, pt I: 111–14. Also see Nehru to Liaquat, 15 March 1950, ibid., 121–2.

[89] UKHC India to CRO, 24 March 1950, DO 35/2989, TNA. The information was based on Liaquat's conversation with the American ambassador in Karachi, who was visiting India.

[90] "Notes on Visit to Calcutta," 14 March 1950, *SWJN-SS*, 14, pt I: 116.

[91] *The Times*, 28 March 1950.

[92] Nehru to Roy, 16 March 1950, *SWJN-SS*, 14, pt I: 123–4.

[93] Nehru to Krishna Menon, 16 March 1950, ibid., 125–6.

[94] Nehru to Rajagopalachari, 16 March 1950, ibid., 126.

of population. Having addressed his domestic constituencies, Nehru turned to the external audience. India, he declared, would have to be prepared for "all contingencies and developments and take such actions as necessity compels us."

The speech drew impassioned rejoinders from the floor, the critics arguing that the prime minister had wholly failed to appreciate the situation. Nehru responded by emphasizing that short of war no solution could be imposed on Pakistan. He hinted at the strategy Delhi was pursuing: "That government [Pakistan] functions according to its own wishes plus according to the circumstances in which it might be placed by other events whatever it may be . . . it may be friendly pressure from us or it may be more than friendly pressure from us."[95] This allusion to his approach eluded his detractors and the press as well. The latter berated him for being out of tune with popular feeling in the country. Even usually sober newspapers like the *Times of India* claimed that the prime minister's "pathetic reliance on Pakistan's promises argues complacency which is dangerous in the extreme."[96] Nor was the speech well received by some members of the cabinet: Vallabhbhai Patel and Syama Prasad Mookerjee among others were rather piqued.[97] The speech thus heightened criticism of the prime minister's handling of the crisis.

Nehru himself felt that matters were coming to a head politically as well as personally. He remained sensitive to the costs of a war with Pakistan, but wondered in moments of despair if the alternative was not worse, confiding to a close associate, "The situation is so complicated and difficult that even I, with all my abhorrence of war and my appreciation of its consequences cannot rule it out completely."[98] More personally, Nehru was anguished by the flight of Muslims from West Bengal. The popular mood in India appeared steadily to eclipse the ideals of pluralism and tolerance: "a cruel destiny seems to pursue us and nullify all our efforts."[99] Criticism from the party hurt deeply, besides. Nehru reverted to the idea of stepping down as prime

[95] *Times of India*, 17 March 1950; *Hindu* (*Weekly edn*), 19 March 1950.

[96] Editorial, *Times of India*, 22 March 1950.

[97] Entries of 17 and 18 March 1950, *Diary of Maniben Patel*, 351.

[98] Nehru to Rajagopalachari, 19 March 1950, *SWJN-SS*, 14, pt I: 126.

[99] Letter to Chief Ministers, 19 March 1950, ibid., 415–18 (quotation on 417).

minister. At a cabinet meeting on 20 March he shared his thoughts with his colleagues; later that day, he informed the president of his desire to relinquish office within a couple of weeks.[100]

Still, the immediate challenges could not be avoided. The earlier efforts to pressurize Pakistan through the UK and the US had not worked. Nehru now wrote directly to Prime Minister Clement Attlee of Britain. After describing in detail the background to the problem he claimed that "it may be said with some assurance that hardly a single Hindu wants to remain there." In all over 200,000 Hindus had arrived while over a 100,000 Muslims had fled to East Bengal. Given the magnitude and complexity of the crisis, mere declarations and reassurances would not suffice. Interestingly, Nehru tried to use the domestic opposition to his handling of the crisis to impel Britain to pressurize Pakistan. He wrote that his government had done its utmost to "stand our ground against heavy pressure for some kind of direct action . . . How long we can stand that pressure will depend on the happenings in East Bengal." So long as Pakistan did not guarantee fair and just treatment to its minorities, there would be an "ever-present risk of sudden conflict." India was thoroughly alive to the perils confronting it and was anxious to avert them. "But success in this extremely difficult task cannot be achieved by us alone."[101]

At a meeting of the Congress Party on 22 March 1950 Nehru came in for a stinging reproach. The critics contended that his speech had provided Pakistan with "material for propaganda" and that it was tantamount to "appeasement."[102] This occasioned an explosion of prime ministerial temper. Nehru reportedly asserted: "Cabinet or no Cabinet. So long as I am the Prime Minister, I will carry on my policy—it will be my policy. I may consult them, but the policy will be mine."[103] Despite the outburst, Nehru was keenly aware of the importance of carrying the cabinet with him. In a note threading to-

[100] Letters to Krishna Menon, Rajendra Prasad, and Vijayalakshmi Pandit, 20 March 1950, ibid., 129–33; Letter to G.S. Bajpai, 21 March 1950, ibid., 138–9.

[101] Nehru to Attlee, 20 March 1950, ibid., 133–8.

[102] Copy of UKHC India to SSCR, 25 March 1950, A1838, TS 169/11/148/14 Part 1, NAA.

[103] Entry of 22 March 1950, *Diary of Maniben Patel*, 351.

gether his thoughts he sought to elucidate his approach and consider the outlines of a solution.

The critics, wrote the prime minister, accused him of not taking "firm action"—a euphemism for war. The only alternative suggested was an organized exchange of minorities. He was opposed to both. He encapsulated his assessment of the costs and claimed he was "more convinced than ever" that war with Pakistan would be disastrous for India. Then again, given the tense situation, not only must India be fully prepared for war but should patently do so. This would help convince Pakistan to arrive at an agreement on the question of minorities. Such an agreement should guarantee full protection and non-discrimination for minorities; cater for punishment of the guilty and compensation for the victims; not encourage migration but provide complete security to those wishing to travel; ensure satisfactory handling of the property left behind by migrants. For its part the Indian government should adhere to its secular mores. In particular, the influence of groups like the Hindu Mahasabha had to be combated.[104]

The View from Pakistan

Karachi, meanwhile, continued to garner intelligence on Indian troop movements. These were discussed at a Defence Committee meeting chaired by the Pakistani prime minister. Hitherto, the military had thought that the moves portended an Indian invasion of East Pakistan. But Liaquat and some of his principal advisers felt that such an invasion would invariably trigger massive retaliation against the Hindus. They found it difficult to believe that India would be willing to jeopardize the lives of 12 million Hindus in East Bengal.[105] As additional intelligence trickled in and as the extent of Indian preparations in the west came to light, Pakistan's assessment turned darker. Yet not everyone interpreted these as indicating a preparation to attack West Pakistan. General Gracey, for one, thought that Nehru was

---

[104] Note to Cabinet, 23 March 1950, *SWJN-SS*, 14, pt I: 141–4.

[105] UKHC Pakistan to UKHC India, 16 March 1950, DO 35/2989, TNA. Interestingly, Liaquat's assessment of the fallout of an Indian invasion was quite similar to Nehru's.

pushing for a settlement backed by a show of superior force; in the event of escalation by Pakistan, Nehru would naturally want sufficient forces to destroy the Pakistan army. Gracey did not, however, rule out the possibility of action in East Pakistan by Hindu "militias" supported by the Indian army.[106]

On 18 March 1950 Liaquat left for East Pakistan on a four-day visit, his first since the outbreak of the crisis. The Pakistani prime minister was perturbed by what he heard and witnessed.[107] In a broadcast from Dhaka he stated that those who had "taken part in the disturbances or even connived at these happenings . . . [have] forfeited the right to be called good citizens." Still, he claimed that the exodus of Hindus was mainly because of the "war mongering" by the press and some leaders in India. Liaquat vowed on several occasions that Pakistan would protect its minorities. But clearly he was unwilling to do so along with India, or indeed under Indian pressure; he could hardly be impervious to domestic imperatives. Liaquat was simultaneously reaching out to audiences at home and abroad when he warned that, if India attacked, Pakistan would "defend every inch and every brick of our homeland."

While Liaquat was touring East Bengal the Pakistani intelligence received inputs indicating that India had stockpiled supplies and ammunition further ahead than necessary for defensive purposes. Karachi now believed, mistakenly, that India had the capability as well as the intention of launching an offensive in the western sector, an assessment that reflected the problem of distinguishing between offensive and defensive intentions based on logistics or weaponry. This misperception was exacerbated by the Pakistanis' apprehension that even if Nehru wanted to avoid war rising domestic pressure could force him into one.[108] Consequently, Pakistan's sole armoured brigade and air force were placed on alert to move within twenty-four hours. The government planned to reinforce East Pakistan by despatching

[106] UKHC Pakistan to SSCR, enclosing memorandum by Assistant Military Attaché, 18 March 1950, DO 35/2989, TNA.

[107] Reports in *Times of India*, 22 March and 23 March 1950.

[108] See the report on conversation with General Wainwright, Military Secretary of the Pakistan Army on 25 March 1950, enclosed in Jasper (UK Military Attaché) to Laurence Grafftey-Smith (UKHC Pakistan), 27 March 1950, DO 35/2990, TNA.

two destroyers and two supply ships to the port of Chittagong. It was further decided that eight air force planes would be flown to East Pakistan without obtaining India's permission to fly over its territory.[109] Nonetheless, the Pakistan government was well aware of its military weaknesses, especially in the east. So Pakistani troops were strictly instructed not to provoke Indian forces across the border. Pakistan also decided to supplement military preparation with manoeuvres on the diplomatic front.[110]

After Liaquat returned on 23 March the Pakistan government sent identical messages to the US, the UK, Canada, and Australia, furnishing details of Indian military dispositions and claiming that these were more "offensive than defensive in view of their locations specially that of the dumps of ammunition, etc." Pakistan urged them to exert their influence on India and persuade it to withdraw its forces.[111]

At the Edge of a Precipice:
The Nehru–Liaquat Pact

Coincidentally, the same morning the British envoy in India, Sir Archibald Nye, met Bajpai of his own accord to discuss the troop movements. In the absence of any indication of Pakistan's offensive designs, said Nye, it was difficult to believe that India had ordered these moves for defensive purposes. He cautioned it would be easy for Pakistan to portray India as the aggressor. Nye requested Bajpai to explore the possibility of at least preventing those moves that had not yet been completed. The secretary general was non-committal and said that he would discuss the matter with Nehru before giving a reply.[112]

[109] UKHC Pakistan to CRO, 22 March 1950, DO 35/2989, TNA; Telegram titled "Indo-Pakistan Tensions," UKHC Pakistan to CRO, 23 March 1950, ibid. Also see Ambassador in Pakistan to SS, 25 March 1950, *FRUS 1950*, 5: 1398.

[110] See the two telegrams from UKHC Pakistan to CRO, 23 March 1950, DO 35/2989; Report on conversation with General Wainwright, in Jasper to Grafftey-Smith, 27 March 1950, DO 35/2990, TNA.

[111] Message from Government of Pakistan, in UKHC Pakistan to CRO, 23 March 1950, ibid.; Chargé in Pakistan to SS, 23 March 1950, *FRUS 1950*, 5: 1394–5.

[112] UKHC India to CRO, 23 March 1950, FO 371/84248, TNA.

He also took the opportunity to inform Nye of Nehru's suggestion to Liaquat (of 13 March) that they meet to discuss a solution to the problem. Such a meeting would help defuse the crisis, he suggested.

After this meeting Nye was convinced that Liaquat should not turn down Nehru's proposal. On receiving Pakistan's message to the British government, Nye immediately wrote to his counterpart in Karachi, Sir Laurence Grafftey-Smith, urging him to ensure that Liaquat accepted Nehru's offer to meet. He insisted that "the door should be kept open."[113] Grafftey-Smith agreed with Nye but doubted if Liaquat would agree to meet under threat from Indian forces. He nevertheless assured Nye that he would try to persuade Liaquat.[114]

The following day Bajpai met Nye and told him that he had discussed the matter with the prime minister. We can only surmise what Bajpai and Nehru had discussed. But with hindsight it seems quite probable that they decided to use the disquiet expressed by Nye to raise the pressure on Pakistan. The secretary general informed Nye that the moves carried out in the west had been planned earlier to cater for a Pakistani misadventure; the recent troubles had only re-affirmed the need to implement them. More interestingly, Bajpai emphasized that, given the domestic political climate in India, if further trouble occurred in East Bengal no government could last for a week without taking active measures. Bajpai was, after a fashion, following the tack taken by Nehru in his letter to Attlee. When queried about cancelling the projected moves Bajpai replied that no such undertaking could be provided; if the situation improved, India could consider it.[115] This interpretation of Indian moves and motives is reinforced by the fact that Bajpai conveyed an identical message to the American and Canadian envoys.[116]

Meantime, Pakistan too had stepped up its diplomatic efforts. On the heels of the message to the British government was a personal one

[113] UKHC India to UKHC Pakistan, 23 March 1950, ibid.

[114] UKHC Pakistan to UKHC India, 24 March 1950, DO 35/2989, TNA.

[115] UKHC India to CRO, 24 March 1950, ibid.

[116] Ambassador in India to SS, 24 March 1950, *FRUS 1950*, 5: 1395; UKHC India to CRO, 25 March 1950, DO 35/2989; UKHC Canada to CRO, 27 March 1950, DO 35/2989, TNA.

from Liaquat to Attlee. The Indian moves, said Liaquat, had created an "extremely grave situation." While the situation in East Pakistan was grim, it was being tremendously exaggerated by India "to create an excuse for aggressive action." Liaquat urged Attlee to impress upon Nehru the tragic consequences of a war. Pakistan believed in peaceful settlement of disputes, but if attacked it would "fight and fight to the last man, regardless of consequences."[117] Later that evening Liaquat told the US ambassador that he hoped Washington would exercise its influence forthwith—independently or along with the Commonwealth countries—to persuade India to remove the military threat.[118] The same day Pakistan's high commissioners in London and Ottawa conveyed similar messages to the countries' foreign ministers.[119]

As the external actor with the greatest interest and influence in the region, Britain was keen to avert war between India and Pakistan. It would spell disaster for the subcontinent, and the ensuing chaos might well be exploited by the communist bloc to make inroads into South Asia. Pakistan's messages led to a short but intense debate within His Majesty's Government. Nye came out in favour of acting as requested by Pakistan.[120] Grafftey-Smith, too, thought that the UK should take immediate steps to control the situation.[121] The chiefs of staff suggested changing the extant orders for British officers on both side to "stand down" in the event of war. India and Pakistan should be told that, if war broke out, Britain would ask its officers serving with the aggressor to step down but would permit the defender to retain British officers. All military supplies would be denied the aggressor, while the other would continue to receive them. Such an announcement, the chiefs claimed, would compel India to pull its troops back.[122]

---

[117] Private and Personal Message from Liaquat to Attlee, 24 March 1950, ibid.

[118] Ambassador in Pakistan to SS, 24 March 1950, *FRUS 1950*, 5: 1396–7.

[119] Record of conversation between Habib Ibrahim Rahimtoola and SSCR, 24 March 1950, DO 35/2989; UKHC Canada to CRO, 25 March 1950, DO 35/2989, TNA.

[120] UKHC India to CRO, 24 March 1950, ibid.

[121] UKHC Pakistan to CRO, 25 March 1950, ibid.

[122] Draft of Minute to Prime Minister, n.d. (25 March 1950?), ibid.

The British cabinet, however, was more cautious and turned down this idea.[123] This was continuous with their desire to keep relations with both India and Pakistan in good repair. They felt that such a move would inevitably be construed as partisan by one of the sides—most probably India—and reduce the prospects of mediation.[124] The option of a joint representation with the Americans was also rejected as Whitehall felt it would be resented by India. Nye was explicitly instructed to restrict his representation to seeking India's "comments" on Pakistan's complaint. He was also told to avoid a joint representation with any other country, especially the US.[125] To Pakistan the British government sent an anodyne response. Attlee wrote to Liaquat that his envoy in India had already taken up the matter with the Indian authorities. They had further directed Nye to convey that the British government viewed these developments with concern and that they "would be glad to receive the observations of the Indian Government on the Pakistan Government's statement."[126]

Washington, too, decided to draw Delhi's attention to Pakistan's note and seek their comments. At Nye's request, Ambassador Loy Henderson agreed to postpone his meeting with Bajpai until Nye had spoken to Nehru. Mirroring Washington's attitude towards South Asian affairs, Henderson considered the problem of greater concern to the Commonwealth than the US and wished not to hamper their efforts.[127] The Canadians acted with still greater discretion: they merely told their envoy to seek assurances from Bajpai that India had no aggressive intent.[128] The Australian high commissioner in India was initially asked not to intervene at all. Canberra felt that it could hinder

[123] Note by the Minister of Defence for the Defence Committee of the Cabinet, 20 April 1950, PREM 8/1450, TNA.

[124] This point is clear from the subsequent discussions of this matter. Memorandum by SSCR, 9 May 1950, ibid.; Minutes of Cabinet Meeting, 19 May 1950, ibid.

[125] CRO to UKHC India, 25 March 1950, DO 35/2989, TNA.

[126] Private and Personal Message from Attlee to Liaquat, CRO to UKHC Pakistan, 25 March 1950, ibid.

[127] Ambassador in India to SS, 25 and 27 March 1950, *FRUS 1950*, 5: 1397–8, 1399–1400.

[128] UKHC Canada to CRO, 26 March 1950, DO 35/2989, TNA.

the forthcoming appointment of the eminent Australian jurist Sir Owen Dixon as the mediator in the Kashmir dispute.[129] On reconsideration, the Australian envoy was instructed to meet the Indian prime minister. Nehru, however, was "discursive," and repeated that the troop movements had been planned months ago.[130]

At this juncture a fresh round of anti-Muslim violence flared up in and around Calcutta. Considering the views being expressed by Hindu extremists, this wave of attacks appears to have been premeditated and aimed at forcing the government's hand.[131] On 26 March the British president of the Bengal and Associated Chambers of Commerce, A.L. Cameron, was killed while attempting to shield his Muslim chauffeur from a violent mob of Hindus.[132] The incident sent shock waves across the country. The prime minister was irate. He directed the West Bengal government to take the strongest measures to curb unrest.[133]

Nehru was convinced that if sectarian violence was not immediately stemmed, the country would career towards catastrophe. The next day the army was inducted in aid of the civil power and given powers approximating to martial law.[134] More important, Nehru resolved to confront his detractors within the government and the Congress Party. Lately he had begun to feel that dissidents were taking their cue from the deputy prime minister. Nehru had been informed of a meeting of Congress MPs convened by Patel, wherein the latter allegedly had

[129] UKHC India to CRO, 27 March 1950, ibid.

[130] AHC India to SSCR, 28 March 1950, A1838, TS 169/11/148/14 Part 1, NAA.

[131] The chairman of the Hindu Mahasabha, Ashutosh Lahiry, claimed that "Muslims are beasts who had to be driven out of Spain and other parts of Europe by the Christians, in order that they could live happily." The programmatic implications were obvious. Lahiry went on to argue that India had had enough of Nehru and that there was "no way out but war." Memorandum of conversation between Ashutosh Lahiry and Henri Sokolove (Labour Attaché), 25 March 1950, enclosed in Embassy in New Delhi to State Department, 3 April 1950, 791.00/4-350, RG 59, USNA.

[132] *Times of India*, 27 March 1950.

[133] Nehru to Roy, 26 March 1950, *SWJN-SS*, 14, pt I: 145–6.

[134] Statement in Parliament by Nehru, 29 March 1950, ibid., 158.

censured the prime minister's policies on Bengal and foreign affairs more broadly.[135] Nehru broached these issues with Patel. The reported meeting with the MPs, wrote Nehru, was "very unfortunate and very extraordinary." Still more dispiriting was Patel's dubious support for Nehru's stance on the internal dimension of the problem. "The belief that retaliation is a suitable method to deal with Pakistan, or what happens in Pakistan is growing. That is the surest way to ruin . . . That is surely not a way to protect minorities." The plans for resignation were shelved and Nehru indicated that he was prepared for a showdown in an emergency meeting of the All India Congress Committee.[136]

Nehru thought that Cameron's murder, apart from besmirching India, would also mute the criticism of his opponents. Hereafter the dissenters would have no moral standing to demand stronger measures against Pakistan.[137] Owing to the barrage of criticism drawn by his speech in parliament, the prime minister had so far refrained from renewing the invitation to his Pakistani counterpart.[138] Now, on 26 March, Nehru wrote to Liaquat that the situation was perilous and he should come to Delhi at the earliest to devise a solution.[139] Almost simultaneously Liaquat sent a letter to Nehru inviting him to Karachi for discussions. Liaquat's move was spurred by two related concerns. The threat posed by the mobilization of Indian troops played an important role—obvious from Liaquat's reference to the "grave situation which the presence of these troops and warlike stores has caused."[140] Furthermore, the reluctance of the US, the UK, and the other Commonwealth countries to lean on Delhi would have convinced the

[135] Editorial note 3, *SWJN-SS*, 14, pt I: 147. At this time, rumours of Patel's criticism of Nehru's policies seem to have been circulating widely in Delhi's political circles. See UKHC India to CRO, 25 March 1950, FO 371/84248, TNA.

[136] Nehru to Patel, 26 March 1950, *SWJN-SS*, 14, pt I: 146–50.

[137] Nehru's letters to Roy and Patel, 26 March 1950, ibid., 146, 149. Nehru's calculation was indeed astute. Syama Prasad Mookerjee later admitted that Cameron's killing had compelled him to give up the idea of war, and thereafter he had begun to support a planned exchange of minorities. See transcript of interview by Taya Zinkin, 27 April 1950, DO 35/2991, TNA.

[138] UKHC India to CRO, 24 March 1950, DO 35/2989, TNA.

[139] Nehru to Liaquat, 26 March 1950, *SWJN-SS*, 14, pt I: 151.

[140] UKHC Pakistan to CRO, 27 March 1950, DO 35/2989, TNA.

Pakistani leadership that they had no option but to parley with India. The decision to invite Nehru was evidently prompted by domestic and reputational concerns: Karachi sought to defuse the crisis without appearing to cave in to Indian pressure.

On receiving news of these developments the British prime minister held a meeting with the high commissioners of India and Pakistan. Attlee emphasized the importance of seizing the opportunity, which presented "the best possible hope" of easing the prevailing tension. He added that Britain was willing to send a cabinet minister to lend his good offices to both sides: Attlee was interested in sending Lord Addison, the Lord Privy Seal. He asked both the envoys to apprise their governments and to obtain their views.[141] Attlee's proposal was motivated by a concern both to grasp the last best chance for a settlement and to ensure that considerations of "face" or prestige would not prevent Liaquat from going to Delhi.

By this time Nehru had replied to Liaquat thanking him for the offer but requesting the Pakistani prime minister to come to Delhi. Nehru wanted some of his cabinet colleagues, who for reasons of health could not travel to Pakistan, to be present during the discussions.[142] He felt that, given the schisms in his cabinet, it would be difficult without Patel's support to implement any agreement concluded with Pakistan.[143] Within a few hours Liaquat announced in the Pakistan parliament that he would be travelling to Delhi to meet Nehru.[144] Liaquat's announcement was received by the prime minister and the official circles in Delhi with palpable relief and satisfaction.[145]

In this scenario, Attlee's offer to dispatch Lord Addison introduced fresh complications. The Indian high commissioner in London, Krishna Menon, was in favour of the idea but Nehru vetoed it. The prime minister was concerned about the domestic fallout of accepting British mediation: "Feelings here are rather excited and touchy and

[141] CRO to UKHC India & Pakistan, 27 March 1950, ibid.

[142] Nehru to Liaquat, 27 March 1950, *SWJN-SS*, 14, pt I: 155.

[143] See report on conversation with Bajpai, Ambassador in India to SS, 28 March 1950, *FRUS 1950*, 5: 1401–3.

[144] *Times of India*, 28 March 1950.

[145] UKHC India to CRO, 28 March 1950, DO 35/2990, TNA; *Times of India*, 28 March 1950; *The Times*, 29 March 1950.

many people accuse U.K. of working against us."[146] Nehru realized, moreover, that Addison's presence would neutralize the coercive leverage which India seemed to possess over Pakistan at that point. As he argued, "The only chance of an agreement is the pressure of events and the realisation of the terrible consequences or the lack of it."[147]

Liaquat, on the other hand, gladly accepted the proposal. Whitehall was in a quandary: having made an offer which was accepted by one side, it felt impelled to pressurize the other to consent. Accordingly, Krishna Menon was asked to urge Nehru to reconsider his decision in the light of Pakistan's acceptance.[148] Nehru stood firm and made it clear that he could not be forced to accept Britain's good offices.[149] In the face of Nehru's unambiguous rebuff the British government backed off. Liaquat was disappointed but decided to go ahead nonetheless.[150]

On 2 April 1950 Pakistan's prime minister arrived in Delhi for talks. Right at the beginning Liaquat referred to India's military build-up along West Pakistan. Nehru assured him that he had no aggressive intent and suggested that the question be discussed after an agreement on the minorities' problem was concluded. The discussions lasted a week; eleven drafts were produced before an agreement was reached.[151] Before departing Liaquat once again raised the issue of troop concentrations. Nehru told him that he could not make any changes at the moment; but if the situation improved and if the flow of migrants reduced, he would be in a position to do so.[152] The mobilization remained in place for a few months after the agreement was reached.

---

[146] Nehru to Krishna Menon, 28 March 1950, *SWJN-SS*, 14, pt I: 155; Record of Conversation between the Prime Minister, Mr Krishna Menon, and SSCR on 29 March 1950, DO 35/3001, TNA.

[147] Nehru to Krishna Menon, 30 March 1950, *SWJN-SS*, 14, pt I: 165.

[148] CRO to UKHC India, 6 May 1950, DO 35/2001, TNA.

[149] Cable and letter to Krishna Menon, 30 March 1950, *SWJN-SS*, 14, pt I:.163, 165–6.

[150] CRO to UKHC Pakistan, 31 March 1950; UKHC Pakistan to CRO, 1 April 1950, DO 35/2001, TNA.

[151] UKHC India to CRO, 8 April 1950, DO 35/2990, TNA; Report on conversation with Mohammed Ali and Ikramullah, AHC Karachi to SSCR, 10 April 1950, A1838, TS 169/11/148, NAA.

[152] Ambassador in India to SS, 8 April 1950, *FRUS 1950*, 5: 1407.

The Nehru–Liaquat pact emphasized the policy of both governments to provide complete equality of citizenship and a full of sense
of security to minorities. Migrants would be provided all assistance
and protection, and continue to remain in legal possession of their
immovable property. The agreement called for punishment of the
guilty, imposition of collective fines, recovery of looted property, and
non-recognition of forcible religious conversions. Both governments
would establish commissions of inquiry to report on the disturbances and despatch a minister to remain in the area until confidence
was restored amongst the minorities. In addition representatives of
the minority communities would be included in the cabinets of East
Bengal, West Bengal, and Assam, and minorities' commissions would
be established.

Predictably, Nehru's opponents pronounced the agreement unsatisfactory. Two of his cabinet colleagues, Syama Prasad Mookerjee
and K.C. Neogy, resigned on this issue. Nehru was aware of the
shortcomings of the agreement but felt that implementing it presented the best chance to root out the problem and improve relations with
Pakistan. As the prime minister told parliament, "We have stopped
ourselves at the edge of a precipice and turned our backs to it."[153]

Aftermath

The Nehru–Liaquat pact was an important step forward in handling
the nettlesome question of religious minorities and refugees. The pact
did not succeed in completely staunching the flow of refugees but it
did ensure that no crisis of similar proportions took hold. Yet the
Bengal crisis had a more insidious impact on India–Pakistan relations.
From Pakistan's perspective the immediate "lesson" of the crisis was its
weakness vis-à-vis India. If the Kashmir problem, in particular, were
to be resolved to Pakistan's satisfaction, India's military superiority
would have to be counteracted.

Within days of concluding the agreement Liaquat dusted off
an earlier proposal,[154] and ventilated the idea of a Commonwealth

[153] Statement in Parliament, 10 April 1950, *SWJN-SS*, 14, pt II: 67.
[154] The proposal was first raised in July 1949. Singh, *The Limits of British
Influence*, 33–4; Jalal, *The State of Martial Rule*, 111.

security guarantee to both India and Pakistan against an attack by the other.[155] The quest for a security guarantee was accompanied by a drive to procure weapons. During his visit to the US the following month, Liaquat met the secretary of defence and the chairman of the joint chiefs of staff and stressed his desire to obtain arms and equipment.[156] He also privately met the navy chief, Admiral Chester Nimitz, and re-emphasized Pakistan's need for arms. Pakistan, he assured Nimitz, would act as a bulwark against a pro-communist India.[157] Although it is not entirely clear how hard Liaquat pushed, both American and British diplomats felt that he "made it clear" where Pakistan stood in the Cold War.[158] The Pakistani prime minister indicated his interest in the matter while interacting with the American press, too. When asked how large an army Pakistan wanted to maintain, he replied, "If your country will guarantee our territorial integrity, I will not keep any army at all."[159]

The Indians were worried. Nehru believed that the arms sought by Pakistan could "only be meant to be used against India, if such an opportunity arises."[160] The Indian government expressed its concerns directly to the US.[161] In the event Washington decided not to supply arms to Pakistan at this stage. This was partly because the Truman administration did not consider Pakistan, and indeed South Asia, of much importance at a time when it was focusing on other problematic

[155] Liaquat's interview with C.L. Sulzberger, *New York Times*, 13 April 1950.

[156] CRO Note on Liaquat's visit, 30 June 1950, PREM 8/1216, TNA. Also see, S.M. Burke and Lawrence Ziring, *Pakistan's Foreign Policy: A Historical Analysis* (Karachi: Oxford University Press, 1990), 124. No American record of these meetings appears to have survived.

[157] Admiral Roger of the US Navy Department conveyed the details of Liaquat's conversation with Nimitz to the Indian embassy. Vijayalakshmi Pandit to Bajpai, 27 May 1950, subject file 56, Vijayalakshmi Pandit Papers, NMML.

[158] McMahon, *Cold War on the Periphery*, 76.

[159] *New York Times*, 5 May 1950. Also see Embassy in Washington to CRO, 1 June 1950, DO 35/2981, TNA.

[160] Nehru to Krishna Menon, 15 May 1950, *SWJN-SS*, 14, pt II: 108.

[161] Nehru to Patel, 9 May 1950, ibid., 104–5; Ambassador in India to SS, *FRUS 1950*, 5: 1408–10; Memorandum of Conversation with the Indian Ambassador by SS, 15 June 1950, ibid., 1412–15.

areas; and partly because the US did not want to alienate India and undercut the prospects for an India–Pakistan détente that the Nehru–Liaquat pact seemed to promise.[162] The caution was justified; for Owen Dixon was making his way to the subcontinent to mediate on Kashmir.

Nehru for his part thought that India's coercive strategy had been important in convincing Pakistan to reach an agreement. "One of them [reasons] certainly is the realisation that things had gone too far and there was no room left for parleying. This, I think, rather frightened them and wisely they decided to make a strong attempt to come to terms."[163] He also believed, wrongly, that the British had exerted "considerable pressure" on Liaquat.[164] The experience of successive encounters had given Nehru confidence in threading his way through a crisis, balancing domestic and international pressures, combining military and diplomatic moves, holding out threats and inducements. Instinct and experience would lead him to rely on this style and technique in subsequent crises with Pakistan and China.

---

[162] McMahon, *Cold War on the Periphery*, 77–9.
[163] Nehru to Vijayalakshmi Pandit, 24 April 1950, *SWJN-SS*, 14, pt II: 67.
[164] Nehru to Roy, 4 April 1950, *SWJN-SS*, 14, pt I: 171.

6

Kashmir—1951 and After

The Bengal crisis had a significant impact on the Kashmir dispute. Sheikh Abdullah, as Girja Bajpai observed, was "profoundly affected" by the attacks on Muslims in India. This strengthened his belief that independence might be the best option for Kashmir, a development that not only led to misgivings in Delhi but also to differences with his colleagues in Kashmir. "Bakshi [Ghulam Mohammad] and . . . a majority of the members of the State Cabinet do not believe in Sheikh Saheb's idea." Nehru went to Kashmir and dissuaded Abdullah from taking this line.[1] But, in time, these differences—internal and with India—would widen into an unbridgeable chasm; for the Sheikh continued quietly to canvass this option. The refugee crisis also had an impact on Delhi's stance *vis-à-vis* Kashmir: an overall plebiscite was now deemed thoroughly undesirable. As Vallabhbhai Patel wrote, "once the talk [of plebiscite] starts the non-Muslims in Jammu and Kashmir would start feeling uneasy and we might be faced with an exodus to India."[2] Partition-cum-plebiscite now seemed the most practical option. The idea of electing a constituent assembly was also open.

The UN mediator, Owen Dixon, reached the subcontinent on 27 May 1950.[3] In initial meetings with him both Nehru and Maulana

---

[1] Bajpai to Vijayalakshmi Pandit, 17 May 1950, subject files 5–6, Vijayalakshmi Pandit Papers, NMML.

[2] Patel to Nehru, 3 July 1950, *SPC*, 1: 317.

[3] This paragraph draws on William Reid, "Sir Owen Dixon's Mediation of the Kashmir Dispute," BA Honours thesis, Deakin University (2000). But my conclusions are different from his.

Azad (minister for education) raised the option of elections to a constituent assembly. Dixon insisted, however, that the people's wishes had to be ascertained by a plebiscite. After a four-day meeting in Delhi with the Indian and Pakistani prime ministers Dixon announced that a state-wide plebiscite was impossible. Thereafter, Nehru proposed a plan for partition-cum-plebiscite: in Jammu the ceasefire line would become the boundary; Azad Kashmir and Northern Areas would go to Pakistan, and Ladakh to India; the plebiscite would be confined solely to the valley. This would minimize refugee movement while simplifying demilitarization and administrative arrangements. When the Pakistanis opposed the plan Dixon offered to throw in "much of Jammu west of the Chenab river." He also assured Liaquat that the voting would be fair: in the plebiscite area, government functionaries would be replaced by UN appointees. Dixon should have known better; for Nehru had explicitly ruled this out during their discussions on an overall plebiscite. Unsurprisingly, Nehru rejected the idea yet again. As he explained to Dixon, if Abdullah's government was superseded the people would see it as an expression by the UN that the government was "not favoured" and would vote accordingly. This was, of course, the reason for Nehru's consistent opposition to any attempt at removing Abdullah. Owen Dixon's impatience and pessimism got the better of him and he refused to mediate further.

Following Dixon's abortive mission, Britain and America grew fretful about the Kashmir problem. Until now, they had tried to avoid overtly supporting either country. Yet they also believed that a solution to the Kashmir dispute was imperative to their interests in a stable and Western-oriented South Asia. More so, since they felt that lack of progress on Kashmir could destabilize the Pakistan government. In March 1951, after a failed attempt at mediation by the Commonwealth, the US and the UK co-sponsored a Security Council resolution calling for arbitration to settle the dispute, should demilitarization fail to take place within three months. Pakistan accepted the resolution; India rejected it. The Security Council nonetheless appointed Frank Graham as the next UN representative.[4]

Meantime, the idea of a constituent assembly ceased to be an alternative to a plebiscite. In July 1950 Sheikh Abdullah had sought to

[4] Gupta, *Kashmir*, 223–35.

introduce far-reaching land reforms in order to implement his pro-gramme for a quasi-socialist Kashmir. The regent, Karan Singh, consulted Delhi, and advised Abdullah against such measures in the absence of an elected legislature.[5] Abdullah was livid, arguing that the Union had no jurisdiction and no business interfering. The Indian government acquiesced. Thereafter, the Sheikh grew insistent on im-mediate elections to a constituent assembly. Eventually, a proclamation was issued in April 1951. It has been argued that Nehru aimed at using these elections to do away with a plebiscite unilaterally.[6] In fact, it was Abdullah who demanded that the assembly should pronounce on the issue of accession. But Nehru publicly declared that the assembly's work would not prejudice the UN's efforts. As he told Abdullah: "to be accused of a breach of faith with them [the UN] and some kind of underhand dealing would be very bad."[7]

Pakistan, however, thought that the assembly would give its im-primatur to Kashmir's accession to India. In consequence Karachi brought this matter to the Security Council's attention. India reiterated its undertaking. Nonetheless the council did refer to this issue in its resolution of March 1951. When the elections were announced Pakis-tan responded with rancour, urging the council to prevent them. India refused to rescind its decision. The National Conference, too, "bitterly opposed this draft and called it an attack on the sovereign rights of the people of Kashmir."[8]

From early 1951 the outlook of the United States and, to a lesser degree, of the United Kingdom towards South Asia began to change. Following the outbreak of the Korean War they became anxious about defending the Middle East from an attack by the communist bloc. Their military establishments knew that India would not par-ticipate in this enterprise; but they thought that Pakistani troops could make a crucial contribution. American officials were certain that Pakistan would get on board only if either the US or the UK guaranteed its security against an Indian attack: indeed, the Pakistani

[5] Singh, *Autobiography*, 119–22.
[6] Lamb, *Kashmir*, 194–5.
[7] Nehru to Abdullah, 29 December 1950, *SWJN-SS*, 15, pt II: 276–7.
[8] Abdullah, *Flames of Chinar*, 115.

prime minister had conveyed as much to the American envoy.[9] The British, however, were more apprehensive about India's reaction. The Truman administration also felt that such a guarantee would blight their relations with India. Both countries were moreover worried about the deleterious impact it might have on India–Pakistan relations.[10] Whilst these deliberations were under way, a crisis flared up.

"Liberating Kashmir": Threats of Jehad 1950–1951

Towards the end of 1950 sections of the Pakistani press and some senior political leaders began to air their dissatisfaction at the lack of tangible progress on Kashmir. Soon these assumed a strident tone. The prime minister of the NWFP claimed that "the day we become desperate and lose all hope of a just solution of the problem, not only the entire Pathan population of Pakistan and tribal areas will rise up for holy jehad in Kashmir but our brothers from across the Afghan frontier will also throw in their lot with us for the cause."[11] The governor of West Punjab said that "if the problem was not settled immediately, the whole of Asia would be engulfed in the flame of war."[12] The calls for a holy war to liberate Kashmir were echoed by many minor political leaders, and soon began to reverberate through the press.

The rising calls for armed action perturbed the Indian government. Their concern was aggravated by the receipt of intelligence suggesting that the calls might not be empty threats. Delhi felt that even if these inputs were wrong, the rising calls for jehad could snowball into some kind of armed action in Kashmir.[13] After all, it was the so-called

[9] On this point, see Ambassador in Pakistan to SS, 15 May 1951, *FRUS 1951*, 6, pt 2: 2204–5.

[10] The views of the US are conveniently summarized in Department of State Policy Statement, 1 July 1951, ibid., 2206–16. For a detailed account, see McMahon, *Cold War on the Periphery*, 130–5. Also see Jalal, *The State of Martial Rule*, 125–8.

[11] *Pakistan Times*, 27 December 1950.

[12] *Pakistan Times*, 10 January 1951.

[13] Report on conversation with Bajpai, UKHC India to CRO, 15 February 1951, FO 371/92865, TNA.

tribal invasion of Kashmir that had originally triggered the problem. In retrospect, it is reasonably clear that at this stage the Pakistan government harboured no intentions of attacking Kashmir, though the Pakistani intelligence was preparing to step up covert action in Indian-administered Kashmir.[14] But observers could not at the time rule out the possibility of some violent move. The British envoy in Karachi, for instance, felt that India's continued obstruction had produced "intense impatience" in Pakistan, and that the likelihood of "some rash action if this provocation is not very soon relieved cannot be excluded."[15]

In mid-February 1951 Delhi decided to draw the attention of the US and the UK to this issue. Bajpai met both the envoys, conveyed India's concerns regarding the war propaganda, and requested them to use their influence on Pakistan to curb it. He told them it would be difficult to continue negotiations on Kashmir or plan a plebiscite when one side was "beating war drums." The British high commissioner felt that, while the Indian government appeared anxious, there certainly was an "element of tactics in raising the matter formally just before Kashmir debate in [sic] Security Council." The US ambassador, too, did not attach much importance to the démarche and instead urged Washington to seek a speedy resolution of the imbroglio.[16] Consequently, the clamour for action continued unabated in Pakistan. As Nehru observed, "Talk of Holy War . . . is as pervasive, persistent and impassioned as ever."[17]

These calls were further energized by the announcement of elections to the constituent assembly. In early June they rose in a crescendo. Nehru felt that the Pakistani press was spewing unprecedented invective.[18] Delhi's dismay was heightened by the Pakistani foreign minister's claim that India was deliberately blocking progress on the Kashmir issue and that it had "no right to complain if it gets

---

[14] Praveen Swami, *India, Pakistan and the Secret Jihad: The Covert War in Kashmir, 1947–2004* (London: Routledge, 2007), 26.

[15] UKHC Pakistan to CRO, 17 February 1951, FO371/9286S, TNA.

[16] Ambassador in India to SS, 14 February 1951, SS to Embassy in India, 15 February 1951, *FRUS 1951*, 6, pt 2: 1729–30; UKHC India to CRO, 15 February 1951, FO 371/92865, TNA.

[17] Cable to Rau, 25 March 1951, *SWJN-SS*, 16, pt I: 361.

[18] Letter to Chief Ministers, 2 June 1951, ibid., 570.

something else."[19] The Indian authorities saw Zafrullah Khan's statement as an unequivocal threat of war.[20] Delhi refrained from making any military moves at this stage, it being not entirely clear that Pakistan's statements portended imminent action. The military did entreat the government to take defensive measures. When the ministry of defence proved unresponsive, the army chief, General K.M. Cariappa, spoke directly to the prime minister. But Nehru too refused to sanction military moves.[21] Despite his reluctance to initiate steps that might be deemed aggressive, Nehru was clear that if Pakistan attacked Kashmir, India would not restrict its actions to Kashmir but respond with a counteroffensive in Punjab.[22] Nehru's thinking was in accordance with the contingency plans developed in 1949 to deal with any future Pakistani incursion or attack in Kashmir. For the present, he opted to wait and watch, focusing on non-operational measures such as holding in abeyance the projected cuts in the armed forces.[23]

Within a couple of weeks a series of developments compelled Delhi to reassess the situation. Between 23 and 26 June 1951 a rash of violent incidents occurred in Kashmir. Two Indian soldiers were ambushed by Pakistani forces, reportedly a mile within the Indian side of the ceasefire line; their bodies were dragged into Pakistani territory and released only after intervention by the UN military observers. Shortly thereafter an Indian patrol was fired upon in the same area, resulting in four casualties. Three more Indian troops were killed by Pakistani firing while patrolling the ceasefire line; one of those injured was captured and held by Pakistani forces for four days. Two further instances of firing on Indian troops near the ceasefire line were reported during this period. The Indian army also received information that a group

---

[19] *Dawn*, 14 June 1951.

[20] Gopal, *Nehru*, 2: 115. Also see Nehru to Liaquat, 24 July 1951, *SWJN-SS*, 16, pt II: 237.

[21] S.P.P. Thorat, *From Reveille to Retreat* (New Delhi: Allied Publishers, 1986), 116. On the Indian army's concerns, see Thorat's comments reported in AHC India to External Affairs Minister, 1 August 1951, A1838, 169/11/148/9, NAA.

[22] Press Conference by Nehru, 13 March 1951, cited in Gopal, *Nehru*, 2: 115; Cable to B.N. Rau, 25 March 1951, *SWJN-SS*, 16, pt I: 361.

[23] Letter to Chief Ministers, 15 June 1951, *SWJN-SS*, 16, pt I: 574–5.

of sixty armed Pakistanis had crossed the ceasefire line on 25 June and raided three villages nearly ten miles inside the line.[24] Concurrently, calls for armed action in the Pakistani press grew ever more shrill. The *Evening Times*, a Karachi newspaper, conducted an opinion poll asking readers whether they approved of war in case the UN failed to resolve the Kashmir dispute. The newspaper claimed that 92 per cent of its respondents favoured the use of force.[25]

Nehru began to sense "real danger of a big-scale conflict between India and Pakistan." Interestingly, he thought that Pakistan's truculence stemmed from Britain and America's renewed support for its stance on the Kashmir dispute.[26] India, therefore, embarked on a concerted attempt to convey a strong message to the major powers as well as to Pakistan. On 29 June Nehru wrote to the Security Council about the recent incidents and the growing war propaganda in Pakistan. These events "justify the suspicion that they are part of a planned programme calculated to lead, if unchecked, to the outbreak of hostilities." He urged the council to pull up Pakistan and warned that if such incidents recurred India might be forced to adopt defensive measures.[27] Delhi also drew the attention of the UN military observers in Kashmir to these occurrences. General Cariappa spent two days in Srinagar discussing them with the chief military observer: the latter agreed to raise India's concerns with the Pakistan army.[28] N.G. Ayyangar—now the minister for states—also visited the valley.[29] In a broadcast on Radio Kashmir on 1 July, Ayyangar voiced Delhi's disquiet over Pakistan's intentions, bluntly adding: "I must warn Pakistan that unless she takes immediate steps to prevent altogether border raids, the responsibility for graver consequences that will follow will be squarely on her shoulders."[30]

These warnings evoked commensurate responses from Pakistan and the situation deteriorated. On the eve of Frank Graham's

[24] *Times of India*, 2 and 4 July 1951.

[25] *Hindu* (Madras), 25 June 1951.

[26] Nehru to Vijayalakshmi Pandit, 25 June 1951, *SWJN-SS*, 16, pt. I: 397–8.

[27] *Times of India*, 4 July 1951.

[28] *Times of India*, 1 and 3 July 1951; *Hindu*, 2 July 1951.

[29] Nehru himself was on a holiday in Kashmir from 26 June to 4 July 1951.

[30] *Times of India*, 2 July 1951.

arrival in the subcontinent, senior Pakistani leaders launched a volley of tough statements. A former president of Azad Kashmir stated that if India persisted with her "uncompromising attitude" the people of Azad Kashmir would be compelled to resume jehad. Almost simultaneously the premier of the NWFP claimed that if the Graham mission failed Pakistan would have to adopt "other effective means."[31] A couple of days later the chief minister of West Punjab said that in view of India's obstinacy there was "no room left for mediation."[32] The rhetoric appeared to be complemented by events on the ground. Delhi received reports that Pakistan was moving an army brigade from Peshawar to Rawalakot, a manoeuvre that could threaten the town of Poonch in Indian-administered Kashmir, which was barely fifteen miles from Rawalakot.[33] This seemed to fit with the intelligence that there was "an organised plan for a big-scale and sudden attack in Kashmir in order to achieve some quick and substantial result." Intelligence reports also pointed to attempts by Pakistan to commit widespread sabotage in the valley.[34]

On 3 July Delhi remonstrated with the UN military observers against the move of the Pakistani brigade. The observers pointed out that Pakistan was at liberty to move its troops behind the ceasefire line so long as it did not augment the forces present at the time of the ceasefire. Since Pakistan had earlier withdrawn a brigade from Azad Kashmir, the move could not be contested.[35] The following day the chief military observer, who had just returned from the Pakistan general headquarters, told the press that he was satisfied there was no danger of a major flare-up in Kashmir.[36] But the Indian prime minister did not have much faith in the UN observers. Most of the American observers, he believed, were brazenly against him, partly due to his opposition to US policies. Indeed, he had recently learnt that one of them had referred to him in a private letter as "Nehru, the prize bastard, whose

---

[31] Ibid.

[32] *Times of India*, 5 July 1951.

[33] Nehru to Liaquat, 4 August 1951; Nehru to Krishna Menon, 5 August 1951, *SWJN-SS*, 16, pt II: 349–54.

[34] Nehru to Mountbatten, 30 July 1951, ibid., 336; Letter to Chief Ministers, 7 July 1951, ibid., 674.

[35] Nehru to Krishna Menon, 5 August 1951, ibid., 352–3.

[36] *Times of India*, 6 July 1951.

stiff-necked attitude has given us so much trouble."[37] Nevertheless, Delhi drew the attention of the Security Council to fresh violations of the ceasefire by Pakistan.[38] Furthermore, there was a renewed outflow of Hindus from East Pakistan to West Bengal. Nehru felt that this was the natural outcome of the importunate calls in Pakistan for action against India.[39]

A Deterrent Strategy: Military and Diplomatic Moves in Mid-1951

The Indian government believed recent events and the intelligence inputs pointed to the distinct possibility of some violent move by Pakistan in Kashmir. Such a move, they assessed, would be aimed at preventing the formation of a constituent assembly. Nehru was right in thinking that Pakistan feared that the assembly would blunt its claim on Kashmir.[40] More important, the military presented a strong case for forward deployment of troops. Heretofore, the civilian leaders had opposed military moves. In light of the latest developments Cariappa and the chief of general staff (CGS), Lieutenant General S.P.P. Thorat, sought an audience with the president of India. Having listened to their case the president requested the prime minister to reconsider their proposal. In the subsequent meeting Nehru was initially reluctant to mobilize troops. Thorat later claimed he had convinced Nehru of the importance of moving the armoured division (the key formation in the contingency plans) across the Beas river in Punjab: not only would the process take time, but at a later stage,

[37] Nehru to Krishna Menon, 7 July 1951, *SWJN-SS*, 16, pt II: 232–3. Also see Nehru to Mountbatten, 30 July 1951, ibid., 339. The official in question was Commander Cadwallader; the Indian government asked the UN to recall him. Nehru to Abdullah, 6 July 1951, ibid., 232; Letter to Chief Ministers, 7 July 1951, ibid., 675.

[38] *Hindu*, 9 July 1951. The matter was brought to the Security Council's notice on 5 July.

[39] Nehru to Abdullah, 6 July 1951, *SWJN-SS*, 16, pt II: 230; Letter to Chief Ministers, 7 July 1951, ibid., 675.

[40] Letter to Chief Ministers, 7 July 1951, ibid., 674; Nehru to Krishna Menon, 22 August 1951, ibid., 323.

should the sole bridge across the river be destroyed, it would be impossible to push the armour ahead.[41] That the prime minister was impressed by this argument is clear from the available evidence.[42]

The army's contention was buttressed by the existing intelligence assessments of Pakistan's intentions. "Pakistan's plan appeared to be to attack us suddenly in Kashmir to begin with, to achieve some results quickly, and then perhaps to stop if the U.N. jumped in and called for a ceasefire."[43] Such an attack was likely "as soon as this Graham mission is over."[44] In this situation Nehru deemed it risky not to take the requisite defensive measures. Interestingly, he thought that "our lack of proper defence on our frontiers would itself be an invitation to attack."[45] Conversely, the presence of Indian troops along the border would make it difficult for the Pakistan army to push across.[46] This, coupled with India's open declarations that an attack on Kashmir would lead to a wider war, would dissuade Pakistan from initiating any action.[47] The deterrent strategy adopted by India was thus a combination of denial and punishment: the mobilization of forces would signal India's determination to foil offensive action by Pakistan; the presence of the armoured division would convey India's readiness to retaliate in Punjab.

For all this, Nehru was aware that the costs of a war with Pakistan would be rather heavy: "war will neither be brief nor gentlemanly . . . It is likely to be a bitter conflict full of suppressed hatred."[48] Nehru believed that a war would divert India's attention from its internal economic concerns and unhinge the recently announced Five Year

[41] Thorat, *From Reveille to Retreat*, 116–17.

[42] Nehru to Mountbatten, 19 July and 30 July 1951, *SWJN-SS*, 16, pt II: 320, 337; Nehru to Krishna Menon, 22 July 1951, ibid., 324.

[43] Nehru to Krishna Menon, 22 July 1951, ibid., 324.

[44] Nehru to Mountbatten, 19 July 1951, ibid., 320.

[45] Nehru to Mountbatten, 30 July 1951, ibid., 337.

[46] Nehru to Krishna Menon, 22 July 1951, ibid., 324.

[47] Speech at Ramlila Ground, New Delhi, 29 July 1951, ibid., 64; Nehru to Mountbatten, 19 July 1951, ibid., 320; Nehru to Krishna Menon, 22 July 1951, ibid., 323; Letters to Chief Ministers, 7 July and 22 July 1951, ibid., 674–5, 683. Also see Gopal, *Nehru*, 2: 115.

[48] Letter to Chief Ministers, 31 August 1951, *SWJN-SS*, 16, pt II: 711.

Plan. More perniciously, it would suck the country into a maelstrom of sectarian violence. So, though Nehru was prepared to implement his threat if Pakistan attacked, he was anxious not to provoke Pakistan. In particular, he sought to obviate the possibility of a clash with Pakistani forces, which might inexorably escalate to war. While agreeing to the proposed moves, the prime minister instructed the military not to deploy forces too close to the border.[49] And the military moves, as earlier, were carried out quietly, unaccompanied by belligerent rhetoric.

The decision to mobilize the army appears to have been taken on 6 or 7 July; the moves commenced on the 10th. These included the move of 1 Armoured Division from Meerut to Punjab, the deployment of 4 Infantry Division and 2 Independent Armoured Brigade along the border in Punjab, and some readjustment of troops in Kashmir.[50] The Indian government also positioned an additional infantry brigade along the borders with East Pakistan. While East Bengal could create trouble, in Nehru's assessment it was "weak and is terribly afraid of our forces entering it."[51]

Presently, India's military moves became apparent to Pakistan. From Karachi's perspective the moves were seemingly aimed at compelling them to acquiesce in the formation of a constituent assembly, thereby relinquishing their claim on Kashmir.[52] Unless the threat posed by India was removed, their room for manoeuvre would be constricted, and they might be forced to accept a *fait accompli*. Given the intensity of public opinion on the emotive issue of Kashmir, there would be serious domestic costs to inaction in the face of Indian

[49] On Nehru's instructions, see Thorat, *From Reveille to Retreat*, 118. Also see report of conversation with Bajpai, AHC India to SSCR, 31 July 1951, A1838, 169/11/148/9, NAA.

[50] K.C. Praval, *Red Eagles: A History of the Fourth Division of India* (New Delhi: Vision Books, 1982), 159–60; S.D. Verma, *To Serve with Honour: My Memoirs* (Kasauli: Published privately, 1988), 76–81.

[51] Nehru to Doulatram, 23 July 1951, *SWJN-SS*, 16, pt II: 329. Also see Embassy in New Delhi to SS, 27 July and 4 August 1951, 791.00 (W)/7-2751 and 791.00 (W)/8-451, RG 59, USNA.

[52] See report of conversation with Liaquat, Ambassador in Pakistan to SS, 26 July 1951, *FRUS 1951*, 6: 1792–3.

provocation. The Pakistanis also sought to avoid conveying an impression of weakness to India. Concerns about reputation would influence their actions as the crisis wore on.

Following a meeting between the Pakistan cabinet and senior military officials, Karachi decided to concentrate its forces on the Punjab border. The decision to adopt civil defence measures also appears to have been taken at this time.[53] In so doing Pakistan sought to deter an Indian offensive in Punjab by threatening to impose substantial costs. Military moves were accompanied by diplomatic ones to secure the withdrawal of Indian forces. Karachi informed America, Britain, and the other Commonwealth countries of India's military preparations and of Pakistan's decision to take "precautionary moves."[54]

The Pakistani prime minister also broached the issue with his Indian counterpart. On 15 July Liaquat cabled Nehru that India's actions were a "great threat to security of Pakistan and to international peace," and that India should remove the threat immediately. Pakistan, he asserted, had no aggressive intentions. The reason for the current tension was India's "persistent refusal" to settle disputes, while Pakistan had made "every effort for just and peaceful settlements."[55] The same day, Liaquat called a press conference and announced that India had concentrated 90 per cent of its armed forces along the borders with Pakistan. He claimed that the move of the armoured formations attested to India's aggressive designs. Pakistan was fully prepared to meet any eventuality. He informed the press about the approach to the UK, the US, and the others, and also released the contents of his message to Nehru.[56]

Liaquat's statement appears to have been prompted by the experience of the Bengal crisis when Pakistan had sought, with little success, to influence external actors through diplomatic channels alone.

---

[53] *Times of India*, 16 July 1951.

[54] Department of External Affairs (hereafter DEA) note on "The Kashmir Situation," 25 July 1951; Pakistan High Commissioner in Australia to Minister for External Affairs, 18 July 1951, A1838, 169/11/148/9, NAA.

[55] Editorial notes 2 and 3, *SWJN-SS*, 16, pt II: 317–18. Also see *Hindustan Times* (New Delhi) and *Times of India*, 16 July 1951.

[56] *Times of India*, 16 July 1951.

Evidently, Karachi now tried to prod them by bringing to bear the pressure of public opinion. It was a shrewd move aimed at portraying India as the aggressive party. It also attempted to present a resolute image to the Pakistani people and so rally them round the flag while conveying to Delhi that Pakistan would not be cowed down.

India too was influenced by the experience of the last crisis, especially in assessing Pakistan's likely response to its military moves. Liaquat's slick public diplomacy caught Delhi off-guard. The Indian prime minister was impelled to counter it in a speech the very next day.[57] Nehru claimed that the mobilization was a defensive measure taken in response to the ceaseless calls for jehad in Pakistan, and to the increasing instances of raids and violence in Kashmir. These had continued despite several representations to Pakistan and the UN, forcing India to take precautions. Nehru was astute in realizing that this was an opportunity not only to refute Pakistan's claims but also to reinforce India's deterrent threat. So he declared: "we shall commit no aggression on Pakistan on any account, but if Pakistan attacks any part of the Indian union territory we shall repel this attack with all our strength."[58] The speech was followed by a similar message to Liaquat, asking him to stem the war propaganda as a first step towards repairing relations.[59] The communication was promptly released to the press.

Simultaneously, the Indian government tried to counter Pakistan's approach to the external powers. Delhi was interested not merely in elucidating its intentions but also in influencing them to dissuade Pakistan from any misadventure. The officiating foreign secretary, Subimal Dutt, met the US chargé d'affaires and explained the reasons for India's decision to mobilize its forces. He made it apparent that while India's intentions were purely defensive, if Pakistan attacked it would result in an all-out war—on all fronts.[60] Dutt conveyed a similar

[57] See Nehru to Rajagopalachari, 15 July 1951; Rajagopalachari's reply, 16 July 1951, subject file 61, C. Rajagopalachari Papers (IV Instalment), NMML.

[58] Nehru's speech at a public meeting in Bangalore, 16 July 1951, *SWJN-SS*, 16, pt II: 311–17 (quotations on 313).

[59] Nehru to Liaquat, 17 July 1951, ibid., 317–18.

[60] Chargé in India to SS, 16 July 1951, *FRUS 1951*, 6, pt 2: 1775–6.

message to the British envoy.[61] India also took steps to forestall adverse action by the UN. The Indian representative at the UN, B.N. Rau, met the American delegation and explained India's moves and defensive intentions. To make them more pliable, Rau confided that Nehru was much impressed by Frank Graham and that he had instructed his officials to facilitate Graham's mission in every way.[62]

International Diplomacy: The USA, the Commonwealth, and Kashmir

Meanwhile, London began considering ways to defuse the crisis. The best option, it reckoned, was to convene a Commonwealth conference in Colombo and invite the prime ministers of India and Pakistan. In fact, this had been discussed and agreed upon as a contingency plan by all the Commonwealth countries (except, of course, India and Pakistan) in the summer of 1950. In the aftermath of the Bengal crisis these countries, especially Britain, felt a war between India and Pakistan would "strike a crippling blow at the whole structure of the Commonwealth." A Commonwealth summit, it was thought, would be more effective than action by the Security Council in preventing an imminent conflict. Utmost secrecy was maintained about the idea, which was not shared even with Washington.[63] Although the option of invoking this plan existed, the British government felt that the situation had not worsened to that extent.[64]

But the Americans were keen to take some measures. The state department thought that the most effective action would be "a request by the Security Council for explanations from the Governments of India and Pakistan followed by a resolution expressing the hope that

[61] Memorandum of conversation with First Secretary, British Embassy, by Acting Deputy Director of the Office of South Asian Affairs, 18 July 1951, ibid., 1778–9.

[62] US Representative at the UN to SS, 18 July 1951, ibid., 1780–1.

[63] Aide Memoire, June 1950, CAB 21/3375, TNA. It was circulated to all Commonwealth countries barring India and Pakistan on 6 July 1950.

[64] CRO to UKHCs of Commonwealth countries, 17 July 1951, ibid; Aide Memoire for Prime Minister from UKHC Australia, 21 July 1951, A1838, 169/11/148/9, NAA.

both Governments would create an atmosphere favourable to the settlement of the current dispute." But they felt that Britain should take
the lead as this was a Commonwealth problem, and that Washington
should closely co-ordinate its efforts with them.[65] Britain's reluctance
both to take the UN channel and to divulge the Commonwealth plan
caused some consternation among the Americans. The ambassador in
London said he was "convinced" that Whitehall was "completely
devoid of ideas as to possible solution."[66] The British, for their part,
continued to prevaricate.

It was Australia which first leaped into the fray. On 17 July Prime
Minister Menzies wrote to Nehru: he was "greatly disturbed" by the
recent events and hoped Graham's efforts for a settlement would not
be undermined. He offered his good offices to help resolve the crisis.[67]
Nehru brushed this aside, insisting that since India's intent was defensive there was "nothing really that need be done so far as India is
concerned."[68] The Indian prime minister realized that other countries
would go on trying to pressurize India and Pakistan in order to ease the
situation, particularly since the crisis turned on Kashmir. Nehru's
assessment of their motives was interesting. He thought the American
and British stances on Kashmir were dictated not by legal or moral
considerations but by their desire to make Pakistan the mainstay of
their defence of the Middle East. Moreover, they wanted Kashmir to
be with Pakistan so that its borderlands abutting the Soviet Union
would be under their control. Nevertheless, he believed that a non-
aligned India had enough leverage with these powers: "In the final
analysis, however, it is thoroughly understood in the U.K. as well as the
U.S.A., that India counts far more than Pakistan."[69] Two conclusions
flowed from this analysis: first, there were limits beyond which the UK

[65] Memorandum by Assistant Secretary of State for Near Eastern, South
Asian and African Affairs to SS, 19 July 1951, *FRUS 1951*, 6, pt 2: 1781–2. Also
see Embassy in Washington to DEA, 28 July 1951, A1838, 169/11/148/9,
NAA.

[66] Ambassador in the UK to SS, 18 July 1951, *FRUS 1951*, 6, pt 2: 1779.

[67] Government of Australia to CRO, 17 July 1951, FO 371/92865, TNA.

[68] Nehru to Menzies, 19 July 1951, *SWJN-SS*, 16, pt II: 319. Also available in A1838, 169/11/148/9, NAA.

[69] Letter to Chief Ministers, 1 August 1951, *SWJN-SS*, 16, pt II: 691–3.

and the US would not push India; second, Pakistan would be more responsive to their pressure.

Nehru believed the present tension arose from Pakistan's desire to prevent the convening of a constituent assembly, a desire shared by London and Washington; but he was determined to go ahead. "No amount of pressure or threats from Pakistan or the U.K., or the U.S.A., or the U.N., will stop us from having constituent assembly elections in Kashmir." India would not remove its troops from the Pakistan border until it was satisfied that there was no danger of attack.[70] Nor was Nehru prepared to accept Liaquat's assurances of Pakistan's benevolent intentions. India's deterrent strategy was yielding results and the chances of an attack had diminished for two reasons: "(1) Pakistan knows very well that we are fully prepared and is not likely to incur the grave risk of attack on us, and (2) the attention of the world has been drawn to this crisis and that itself has a certain deterrent effect."[71] The second point was influenced by his experience of the previous crisis: the importance of external pressure in convincing Pakistan to come to terms.

Liaquat kept up his defiance. In his reply he contested India's professions of peaceful intent by citing its use of force over Junagadh, Kashmir, Hyderabad, and Bengal. He claimed that Nehru was deliberately construing "a national desire for liberation of Kashmir as propaganda of war against India." He reiterated his demand that India remove its troops from the borders.[72] Liaquat's message was dismissed as propaganda in the official circles in Delhi.[73] Nehru made it clear that he would settle for nothing short of a declaration by Pakistan that "on no account will they attack or invade Indian territory." If the militant propaganda against India were checked, it would not just reduce tension but create conditions for an amicable settlement of disputes.[74]

By this time large-scale preparations for civil defence were under

[70] Nehru to Krishna Menon, 22 July 1951, ibid., 325.

[71] Letter to Chief Ministers, 22 July 1951, ibid., 683.

[72] Text of letter to Nehru dated 19 July 1951, *Times of India*, 21 July 1951.

[73] Note of interview with Bajpai, 27 July 1951, enclosed in AHC India to Minister for External Affairs, 1 August 1951, A1838, 169/11/148/9, NAA; *Times of India*, 22 July 1951.

[74] Nehru to Liaquat, 24 July 1951, *SWJN-SS*, 16, pt II: 236–9.

way in Pakistan. The Pakistani prime minister held a security conference attended by the premiers of the provinces as well as the military top brass. Consequent upon this the major cities of Pakistan began to observe black-outs, air-raid drills, and so-called "Defence Days;" civil defence organizations reportedly began to train in the use of small arms and guerrilla tactics. The decision to call-up reserves also seems to have been taken around this time.[75] The military utility of these measures was dubious but they played an important role in mobilizing the public behind the government's policy.[76] They also conveyed a sense of urgency to the external actors. The quasi-military measures were accompanied by a palpable surge in anti-India sentiments in the press and public discourse.

On the Indian side, according to the American envoy, the atmosphere was "one of calm determination or resignation [rather] than anger but seems none-the-less dangerous if dangerous [*sic*] incidents of violence should occur."[77] The situation appeared brimming with risks now, so the US made simultaneous diplomatic approaches to India and Pakistan, pointing out that a single spark—a violent communal incident or a misperception—could lead to a conflagration. Both governments were urged to pull their troops back and tone down the rhetoric. To the Indian government the US also suggested that if India refused, its actions would seem contradictory to its repeated calls for a peaceful resolution to international problems.[78]

Liaquat told the American ambassador that India's intention was to force Pakistan either to accept the constituent assembly or fight. The move was timed to impress upon Graham that the situation along the ceasefire line was grim: India could not, therefore, withdraw its troops from Kashmir. Liaquat argued that on no account would Pakistan agree to the election; but he was open to a simultaneous withdrawal of troops from the border.[79] Nehru, for his part, dwelt on the reasons

[75] *Times of India*, 23 and 27 July 1951. AHC Pakistan to Minister for External Affairs, 3 August 1951, A1838, 169/11/148/9, NAA.

[76] Ibid.

[77] Ambassador in India to SS, 20 July 1951, *FRUS 1951*, 6, pt 2: 1786.

[78] SS to Embassy in India (copy to Embassy in Pakistan), 24 July 1951, ibid., 1791.

[79] Ambassador in Pakistan to SS, 26 July 1951, ibid., 1792–3.

why he had decided to mobilize troops: if a war had been averted it was because of the forward deployment of Indian troops. As for the seeming inconsistency in Delhi's attitude, he retorted that India was engaged in a defensive operation being painted as aggressive by Pakistani propaganda. He did not comment on the suggestion of pulling the troops back.[80]

Shortly thereafter the British independently approached Delhi and Karachi. They too said "a small incident on either side of the frontier may set in motion a train of events leading to active hostilities." Both governments were exhorted to arrive at an agreement to withdraw troops from the border to a distance sufficient to "minimise the risk of any unpremeditated incident."[81] But Whitehall was reluctant to make any further moves—such as a personal appeal by the British prime minister to Nehru and Liaquat—at this stage.[82] Both Bajpai and Zafrullah Khan made polite and equivocal responses to the effect that their own positions were unassailable and the other side needed to make the requisite concessions.[83] The Canadian government expressed similar concerns to Delhi but to no avail.[84]

Nehru and Liaquat: Inconclusive Epistolary Duelling

Notwithstanding their defiant stance, the Pakistani leadership appreciated that securing the withdrawal of Indian troops was in their best interests. Since Delhi seemed impervious to American and British efforts, Pakistan tried directly to induce India to come to terms. Then

[80] Ambassador in India to SS, 26 July 1951, ibid., 1793–4.

[81] CRO to UKHC India and UKHC Pakistan, 28 July 1951, CAB 21/3375, TNA.

[82] CRO to UKHCs Commonwealth countries, 28 July 1951, ibid. The British government requested the Canadians to offer mediation, if required, at a later stage, in view of the good personal rapport between Prime Minister St Laurent and Nehru. Also see UKHC Australia to Prime Minister Menzies, 1 August 1951, A1838, 169/11/148/9, NAA.

[83] Ambassador in the UK to SS, 1 August 1951, *FRUS 1951*, 6, pt 2: 1804–5.

[84] Embassy in New Delhi to SS, 17 August 1951, 791.00 (W)/8-1751, RG 59, USNA.

again, domestic political and reputational considerations could not be cast aside. Pakistan's initiative was consequently threaded with ambivalence.

Liaquat's message to Nehru opened with a fusillade of criticism and accusations. But he also proposed a five-point plan to alleviate the tension and invited Nehru to visit Karachi to discuss them. The plan called for the withdrawal of troops on the border; a reaffirmation that the accession of Kashmir to India or Pakistan would be decided through a plebiscite held under UN auspices; a declaration that both governments would renounce the use of force in settling disputes and would refer these to arbitration or judicial determination if they could not be resolved by negotiation or mediation; a reiteration of their commitment under the Delhi Agreement of April 1950 to clamp down on offensive propaganda; and a declaration by both sides that they would not invade the other's territory. Pakistan's prime minister stipulated that "the first and foremost essential step" was for India to withdraw its troops; Pakistan would follow suit. He also made it clear that the invitation to visit Pakistan was conditional on the removal of troops.[85]

The next day Liaquat addressed a "Defence Day" rally attended by over a 150,000 people. After denouncing India's aggressive moves he raised his clenched fist and proclaimed that henceforth this would be Pakistan's national symbol. "If the enemies of Pakistan," declared Liaquat, "have any ideas that 80 million Pakistanis can be coerced they are sadly mistaken." The Pakistan government promulgated a civil defence special powers ordinance and announced the induction of four National Guard battalions into the army.[86] They also sought to get the US to intercede with India. But the American secretary of state, Dean Acheson, was noncommittal.[87] Acheson's stance reflected their ambassador's assessment that Pakistan's proposal was "advanced for the record only and not with any idea that it would be accepted."[88]

[85] Text of letter to Nehru dated 26 July, *Times of India*, 27 July 1951.

[86] *Times of India*, 28 July 1951; AHC Pakistan to Minister for External Affairs, 3 August 1951, A1838 169/11/148/9, NAA.

[87] Memorandum of Conversation (with Ambassador of Pakistan) by SS, 30 July 1951, *FRUS 1951*, 6, pt 2: 1798–1800.

[88] Ambassador in Pakistan to SS, 27 July 1951, ibid., 1795.

Unsurprisingly, the peace plan and invitation were viewed by Delhi as a publicity stunt; Liaquat's other actions were deemed provocative. The Indian press was equally dismissive. An editorial in the *Times of India* drew a parallel to Hitler's invitation to the Austrian premier and his demand for the unopposed entry of German troops into Austria.[89] In his reply to Liaquat Nehru wrote that in view of the precondition, which was so obviously unacceptable to India, the invitation was meaningless. India had compelling reasons to retain its troops on the border. "With a clenched fist raised against us, do you seriously expect us to leave our frontiers unguarded and open to aggression?" Nehru in turn invited Liaquat to Delhi. He also addressed the other points in Pakistan's proposal. On Kashmir, he reiterated India's oft-repeated claim that it was the presence of Pakistani forces that hindered a plebiscite. The Indian government had already said the question of arbitration would have to be decided from case to case. Nehru was ready for a joint declaration eschewing the use of force but demanded that it explicitly cover Jammu and Kashmir.[90]

As seems clear, much the same ground was being endlessly covered and re-covered to little avail, and Nehru had grown weary of the correspondence with Liaquat. Privately, he admitted to being convinced that "most of the leaders of Pakistan are crooked in their dealings."[91] His attitude towards the UK and the US on this issue was also hardening. To an extent he was reacting to the Western press's chiding response to India's concentration of troops.[92] Nehru felt these were of a piece with Britain and America's consistent support to Pakistan on the Kashmir dispute, a stance that had encouraged and fostered

[89] *Times of India*, 28 July 1951.

[90] Nehru to Liaquat, 29 July 1951, *SWJN-SS*, 16, pt II: 331–5 (quotation on 333).

[91] Nehru to Mountbatten, 30 July 1951, ibid., 338.

[92] The *Manchester Guardian* wrote on 24 July, "India has made a deplorable impression by its troop movements . . . the world has not forgotten Hyderabad." The *Daily Telegraph* on 19 July: "It is surely unwise, if one has no intention of drawing the sword, to rattle it loudly in the scabbard." The *New York Herald Tribune* on 17 July: "India imperils peace." The *Economist* (London) claimed on 21 July that Nehru was "the prime and obstinate source of trouble" in the Kashmir dispute.

Pakistan's obduracy and belligerence, leading to the current situation. He considered the recent démarches by Britain and America as wholly unwarranted.[93] But the prime minister's attitude was also governed by reputational concerns: giving in to external pressure would convey an impression of weakness, and so set expectations for the future. He wrote to Mountbatten: "They seem to forget that we are not some little Central American Republic or some Balkan country which can be cowed down."[94]

At the same time Nehru avoided needless confrontation. With London he played the Commonwealth card, reminding Attlee of how despite domestic opposition he sought to maintain this tie with Britain.[95] Simultaneously, he sought to bring pressure to bear on Pakistan. He let it be known that he would not withdraw troops till the elections were held and that "any encouragement of Pakistan at this juncture means encouragement of war."[96] These moves were occasioned by Nehru's assessment that, apart from India's preparedness, Pakistan's inability to muster "as much support as they wanted and expected" from the UK and the US played an important role in restraining it from offensive action.[97]

Although Nehru adopted a tough stance against Pakistan and refused to be influenced by the major powers, he was alive to the possibility of a war being triggered by communal violence or other forms of provocation in India. In a major speech to a gathering of over a 100,000 people he contrasted Pakistan's belligerence with India's calmness and urged the people to maintain it; communal violence would not only affect India but strengthen Pakistan's hands. India was fully prepared for a war should one be thrust upon it. Indeed, owing to the steps taken by India the prospect of a war had receded.[98] Yet, despite criticism from some quarters, Nehru refused to adopt civil defence measures. These, he thought, would generate unnecessary

[93] Letter to Chief Ministers, 1 August 1951, *SWJN-SS*, 16, pt II: 690-3. Also see Nehru to Krishna Menon, 22 July 1951, ibid., 233–5.

[94] Nehru to Mountbatten, 30 July 1951, ibid., 340.

[95] Nehru to Attlee, 3 August 1951, ibid., 341–4.

[96] Nehru to Krishna Menon, 5 August 1951, ibid., 354.

[97] Ibid., 353; Nehru to Abdullah, 4 August 1951, ibid., 347.

[98] Speech in Delhi, 29 July 1951, ibid., 61–9; *Times of India*, 30 July 1951. Also see Ambassador in India to SS, 26 July 1951, *FRUS 1951*, 6, pt 2: 1794.

excitement among the people and create an impression that war was imminent. In any event Pakistan did not have the kind of air force against which air-raid precautions were necessary.[99]

In a lengthy response to Nehru, Liaquat turned down the invitation. "It is too much for me to undertake an annual trip to Delhi each time you decide to threaten the security of Pakistan." Clearly, Karachi did not want to acquire a reputation for crumbling under India's threats. It also indicated its sensitivity to repercussions on the domestic front. Two more points stood out. First, realizing the weakness of its bargaining position and the costs of a full-fledged war, Karachi scaled down its demands and offered a further concession. Liaquat now wanted both sides to withdraw their troops simultaneously. Second, Liaquat rejected Nehru's demand that a no-attack declaration include Jammu and Kashmir. Arguing that "this begs the very question at issue," he asked Nehru to reconsider his five-point proposal.[100]

The Indians predictably seized on the second point. According to one observer, the "dominant reaction" in Delhi was that it "conclusively establishes that Pakistan had deliberately created tension and the crisis."[101] Nehru considered it obvious that Pakistan reserved the right to use force in Kashmir. He felt "dead certain" that if he had not made the military moves, Pakistan would have attacked Kashmir.[102] In response, Nehru unequivocally stated that an attack on Kashmir was "an attack on Indian territory which will have to be met fully." He dismissed the suggestion of withdrawing troops from the border: the Indian forces were at a distance safe enough to avoid mishap. Nehru yet again emphasized his demands and argued that "peace is not offered with clenched fists nor with threatened aggression and resounding cries of jehad."[103] The following day the Indian government published a compilation of the exchange between the prime ministers,[104] indicating its reluctance to indulge in further correspondence.

---

[99] Letter to Chief Ministers, 1 August 1951, *SWJN-SS*, 16, pt II: 689–90; Nehru to Medhi, 4 August 1951, ibid., 345–6.

[100] Text of telegram to Nehru dated 2 August, *Times of India*, 3 August 1951.

[101] Dispatch from New Delhi dated 3 August, *Hindu*, 5 August 1951.

[102] Nehru to Krishna Menon, 5 August 1951, *SWJN-SS*, 16, pt II: 352–3.

[103] Nehru to Liaquat, 4 August 1951, ibid., 351.

[104] *Times of India*, 5 August 1951.

Diplomacy or War?
Kashmir in August–September 1951

A month after the mobilization, Nehru felt the situation had not substantially improved: at best, India's actions had arrested further deterioration. He still refrained from taking civil defence measures but asked the state governments to prepare plans for maintaining security and order in the event of an emergency. Nehru's assessment of the risk of war stemmed from his concern that the Pakistan government might not act rationally. In particular he was worried that domestic imperatives might force Karachi to attack India despite the obvious dangers. A logical analysis indicated that war was not likely, but "we cannot base our activities on pure logic."[105]

This consideration also lay behind his categorical warning to Pakistan in a large public meeting: "if Kashmir is attacked the war will not be confined to the hills of Kashmir but will spread to the whole of Pakistan."[106] Nehru believed that Britain and America's stance would play an important role in the resolution of the crisis: "if they make it perfectly clear to Pakistan that it must not indulge in its warlike activities, then there would be no war, since Pakistan has been depending a great deal on such direct or indirect support it might get from them."[107] He desisted from taking any step that might ratchet up the tension and even sought to counter demands for additional measures, such as economic sanctions, against Pakistan—steps that he considered short-sighted and provocative.[108]

Washington and London were by now seriously apprehensive about the turn of events in Pakistan. The American ambassador considered

---

[105] Letter to Chief Ministers, 9 August 1951, *SWJN-SS*, 16, pt II: 697–700. Also see Nehru to Karan Singh, 3 August 1951, in Jawaid Alam (ed.), *Jammu & Kashmir 1949–64: Select Correspondence between Jawaharlal Nehru and Karan Singh* (New Delhi: Penguin Viking, 2006), 27. This view was shared by many of Nehru's colleagues. See AHC India to Minister for External Affairs, 8 August 1951, A1838, 169/11/148/9, NAA.

[106] Speech in New Delhi on 9 August 1951, *Times of India*, 10 August 1951.

[107] Letter to Chief Ministers, 9 August 1951, *SWJN-SS*, 16, pt II: 698.

[108] Speech in Parliament, 11 August 1951, ibid., 577–94.

the propaganda in the press "inflammatory" and the organization of mass rallies with the attendance of frontier tribesmen "dangerous."[109] The British high commissioner felt that Liaquat's clenched fist speech was "foolish" and incendiary; though there was no "immediate risk" of an attack by Pakistan, "it now seems generally to be taken for granted that Pakistan will be forced to go to war" if there was no progress on the Kashmir issue.[110] Yet both countries were unwilling to move too quickly; for they wanted to keep this matter out of the Security Council until the completion of Graham's mission, lest it damage his prospects. Should the crisis appreciably worsen, Washington decided to issue an appeal from President Truman to the Indian and Pakistani prime ministers. The Americans were also interested in arranging a meeting between the two prime ministers and looked to the British to take the lead. The British government contemplated similar action by Attlee at a later stage, if necessary. The other suggestion was politely turned down.[111] As earlier, London was unwilling to disclose to Washington its plans for a Commonwealth conference.[112] Throughout August 1951, then, there was no collaborative action from the US and the UK.

Washington's call for energetic measures by the British was echoed by some sections of His Majesty's Government, which thought that a Commonwealth conference was "hardly likely to prove effective" when war was imminent. An alternative floated by desk-level officials was a "Locarno guarantee" of the frontiers between India and Pakistan: the British would guarantee both India and Pakistan against aggression by either party. But this had already been ruled out: it was felt that such a move would result in India's departure from the Commonwealth.

[109] Ambassador in Pakistan to SS, 1 August 1951, *FRUS 1951*, 6, pt 2: 1803–4.

[110] UKHC Pakistan to CRO, 6 August 1951, FO 371/92865, TNA. The Australian government thought the same. Internal DEA Minute, 10 August 1951, A1838, 169/11/148/9, NAA.

[111] Memorandum for SS, 2 August, *FRUS 1951*, 6, pt 2: 1805–7; SS to Representative at UN, 6 August, ibid., 1810–11; Chargé in the UK to SS, 8 August 1951, ibid., 1811–12.

[112] Scott to Pritchard, 20 August 1951, FO 371/92865, TNA.

The only other option was for either the UN or the Commonwealth to impose some form of sanctions, economic or otherwise.[113] While sanctions theoretically seemed a good option, Whitehall feared they would drive India into the arms of the Soviet Union. For this reason the Americans too would oppose sanctions.[114]

Karachi, in the meantime, grew increasingly concerned with America and Britain's unwillingness to lean on India. The domestic pressure to confront India militarily was also rising. Foreign Minister Zafrullah Khan considered war almost inevitable before the end of the year.[115] This seems to have led the Pakistani leadership briefly to contemplate a pre-emptive strike. Indeed, the civilian leadership was initially optimistic about the chances of success in a military encounter, placing it at "fifty-fifty."[116] According to the Pakistan army chief General Ayub Khan, Liaquat told him that he was "tired of these alarums and excursions. Let us fight it out." Ayub, however, dissuaded him from such a move owing to India's military preponderance. The Pakistan army had only thirteen tanks with a mere forty to fifty hours of engine life with which to face the Indian army.[117] Liaquat appears to have been sensible to the other costs of a war as well, realizing it would "also cause destruction of civilian lives and devastation of private and public property on a scale unprecedented."[118]

Having rejected this option, Karachi redoubled its diplomatic efforts. The secretary general of Pakistan's foreign office told the French ambassador that the crisis held "the most dangerous potentialities . . . only a very rapid and very firm taking of position by the UN or at least by the Western nations could yet avoid a conflict which

[113] Memorandum by Olver, 11 August 1951, FO 371/92865, TNA; remarks by Murray, 14 August & Scott, 15 August 1951, ibid.

[114] Minutes, 14 and 15 September 1951, ibid.

[115] Report on conversation with Zafrullah, AHC Karachi, 3 August 1951, A1838, 169/11/148/9, NAA.

[116] On the odds for success, see ibid.

[117] Ayub, *Friends not Masters: A Political Autobiography* (London: Oxford University Press, 1967), 40.

[118] Sarwar Hasan, "The Foreign Policy of Liaquat Ali Khan," *Pakistan Horizon* 4, no. 4 (December 1951), reprinted in *Liaquat Ali Khan: Leader and Statesman*, ed. Ziauddin Ahmed (Karachi: The Oriental Academy, 1971), 180.

once begun could be neither restrained nor even controlled."[119] Pakistan was obviously trying to manipulate France's perception of the risk of war. The French sounded out the British and the Americans on the possibility of a joint approach to India. Both London and Washington were uncomfortable with this idea.[120] American officials reckoned that France's interest arose from a wish to assert its position as a great power and enhance its prestige in the Muslim countries by supporting Pakistan. Any association with the French on this issue was "undesirable." Paris was informed that while their support in the Security Council would be welcome, a joint approach would be seen by the Indians as Western powers "ganging up" on them.[121]

Pakistan's discontent with Anglo-American lassitude was also evident in its leaders' utterances. In a major public speech Liaquat said that should war occur the responsibility would rest with India and the members of the Security Council.[122] Zafrullah similarly stated that if the Commonwealth countries did not act to prevent a war, the very idea of a Commonwealth would be rendered redundant.[123] These statements also indicated Pakistan's perception of the sources of urgency of the crisis. Broadcasting from Radio Kashmir on 15 August, Sheikh Abdullah had affirmed his determination to convoke a constituent assembly: "intimidation and threats of jehad cannot deter us from proceeding." His deputy, Bakshi Ghulam Mohammad, had declared that there was no question of revoking Kashmir's accession; the constituent assembly would merely ratify it. He claimed that Pakistan's calls for plebiscite were a hoax.[124] These pronouncements naturally caused disquiet in Karachi.

[119] Note by High Commissioner for Indochina to the French Government, 7 August 1951, enclosed in American Legation Saigon to State Department, 7 August 1951, 791.00/8-751, RG 59, USNA.

[120] Note titled "Indo-Pakistan Relations," 8 August 1951, FO 371/ 92865, TNA; SS to Embassy in Pakistan, 11 August 1951, *FRUS 1951*, 6, pt 2: 1813–14. Also see editorial note 4, ibid., 1814.

[121] Memorandum by William, 22 August 1951, ibid., 1820–1. Also see, Embassy in Washington to DEA, 16 August 1951, A1838, 169/11/7, NAA.

[122] *Dawn*, 22 August 1951.

[123] UKHC Pakistan to CRO, 21 August 1951, FO 371/92865, TNA.

[124] *Hindustan Times*, 17 August 1951, *Indian News Chronicle* (New Delhi), 17 August 1951.

Towards the end of August 1951 the British government concluded that the crisis would peak in late September or early October. By this time Graham's mission would have failed and the elections for the constituent assembly would have been held. If these occurred simultaneously it was probable that Pakistan would initiate some action in Kashmir.[125] The US state department assessed that the Pakistan government was "under pressure to resort to war to prevent a *fait accompli* in Kashmir." Only if Graham's recommendations held out the possibility of a settlement would Liaquat be able to resist the hawks "who favour gambling all on a military adventure." The situation was discussed at a meeting of the National Security Council presided by Truman but no decision was reached.[126] A national intelligence estimate presented in mid-September argued that as long as effective UN action was possible, Pakistan seemed unlikely to precipitate a war. "It is possible, however, that the GOP [Government of Pakistan] would deliberately launch or sponsor local action in Kashmir, as it did in 1947. This possibility will be greatest during and immediately after the Constituent Assembly elections (roughly 15 September to 1 November)."[127]

American officials still looked to Britain to take the lead although they believed that the situation was fraught and that "we cannot acquiesce in inaction or weak action if hostilities are to be averted." They were concerned that Britain had "not yet given any clear indication of new measures which it believes would be helpful."[128] On 10 September 1951 the foreign ministers of the UK and the US met and discussed the situation. At last, the British disclosed the outlines of their plan for action by the Commonwealth.[129]

---

[125] Report by CRO titled "Present State of Tension between India and Pakistan," 31 August 1951, FO 371/92865, TNA.

[126] Memorandum for SS, 21 August 1951, *FRUS 1951*, 6, pt 2: 1817–18. Also see editorial note 1, ibid., 1817.

[127] Memorandum by the Central Intelligence Agency (hereafter CIA), 14 September 1951, ibid., 1850–9.

[128] Paper Prepared in the Bureau of Near Eastern, South Asian and African Affairs, 28 August 1951, ibid., 1825–7.

[129] US Delegation minutes, 10 September 1951, ibid., 1837.

Resolution by Assassination: The Death
of Liaquat Ali Khan

But events on the ground outpaced diplomacy as Graham departed from the subcontinent the following day. The Pakistan government now shifted its focus to getting the Security Council to take swift action towards holding a plebiscite; the withdrawal of troops by India would be an obvious prerequisite. As before, Karachi was also reacting to developments in Kashmir. By early September the results of the elections to the constituent assembly had been announced: the National Conference had practically carried all before it.[130] Soon afterwards Liaquat made it clear to the American envoy that the domestic pressure on him was mounting and he could only withstand it if the Pakistanis were convinced that the Security Council would not act sluggishly.[131] While the message was undoubtedly aimed at imparting a sense of urgency, there was a measure of truth in it. Zafrullah Khan met senior state department officials, including Secretary Acheson, and re-emphasized the need for immediate action by the Security Council. He told them that the "tribal leaders" had given assurances to Graham's delegation that so long as the UN was taking positive action, they could restrain their tribes.[132] Nevertheless it would be a month before Graham finally submitted his report.

In the following weeks the rhetoric emanating from Pakistan was slightly muted. Nehru felt that Pakistan "by its continuous cursing and shouting has overshot the mark . . . the chances of conflict are much less now, though they cannot be ruled out."[133] He told the army chief that the troops would remain deployed "so long as there is the slightest danger."[134] Liaquat was growing impatient at the delay in

[130] *Hindustan Times*, 1 September 1951.

[131] Ambassador in Pakistan to SS, 11 September 1951, *FRUS 1951*, 6, pt 2: 1838–9.

[132] Memoranda of conversation, 13 and 14 September 1951, ibid., 1845–9.

[133] Nehru to Biswas, 6 October 1951, *SWJN-SS*, 16, pt II: 361; Letter to Chief Ministers, 4 October, ibid., 723.

[134] Nehru to Cariappa, 5 October 1951, ibid., 303.

the submission of Graham's report and conveyed his displeasure to the US ambassador.[135] The Pakistan government also issued a press communiqué registering its dissatisfaction. The next day the newspapers carried protests by several leaders of the Muslim League decrying the government's "wait and see foreign policy." The press reported the start of another mass campaign for action in Kashmir. The American envoy thought that if the government encouraged popular feelings at this stage it would be running an "uncalculated risk of war."[136]

On 15 October 1951 Graham presented his report to the Security Council. The report indicated persisting differences on the question of demilitarization. Graham, however, recommended a continuation of his efforts. In fact this had been urged upon him by the Americans and the British, who felt that there must be some UN activity in order "to give Pakistan sufficient hope of a reasonable settlement so that it will not in desperation resort to armed force."[137]

The next morning Liaquat Ali Khan was scheduled to address a large public gathering. As the Pakistani prime minister rose to deliver his speech, he was cut down by an assassin's bullets. The latter, a refugee from Afghanistan, was immediately killed by the frenzied crowd. The motive behind the assassination could never clearly be established; nor is it known what Liaquat proposed to say at the meeting.

In due course the Pakistani press censured Graham's report as "responsibility shirking" and as "deepen[ing] the prevailing sense of frustration."[138] Indeed, external observers wondered if the new Pakistani prime minister could resist "popular pressure . . . to take direct action in Kashmir which would lead to hostilities with India."[139] Delhi had similar concerns. As Girja Bajpai wrote, "I am not without fear that wild men may take charge [in Pakistan] . . . and lead into dangerous adventures, India being the first target."[140]

[135] Ambassador in Pakistan to SS, 10 October 1951, *FRUS 1951*, 6, pt 2: 1879–80.

[136] Ambassador in Pakistan to SS, 11 October 1951, ibid., 1880.

[137] SS to US Representative at UN, 8 October 1951, ibid., 1877–8.

[138] Cited in Gupta, *Kashmir*, 242.

[139] Memorandum by SS, to the President, 22 October 1951, *FRUS 1951*, 6, pt 2: 2224–5.

[140] Bajpai to Vijayalakshmi Pandit, 17 October 1951, subject file 56, Vijayalakshmi Pandit Papers, NMML.

These fears proved ill-founded, for Liaquat's assassination shook the Pakistani people as well as the leadership.[141] In retrospect it is clear that both Delhi and Karachi used this opportunity gradually to back off from the crisis. Speaking a day after the tragedy Nehru called on both sides "to hush the voice of controversy and disputes" and establish "real peace."[142] Cariappa corresponded with his Pakistani counterpart Ayub Khan regarding measures to reduce tension.[143] From Pakistan there was a marked toning down of statements and actions. The assassination had had a sobering effect on the crisis. The Kashmir constituent assembly was convened on 31 October 1951; Graham's efforts on behalf of the UN continued. By early 1952 both armies were pulled back from the Punjab border.

To the extent that Pakistan did not use force to disrupt the elections, Nehru's management of the crisis may be considered successful. What contributed to Pakistan's restraint? The threat of retaliation by India was certainly an important consideration, as was its expectation that efforts by the external powers might yield results. Yet the chances of Pakistan resorting to force appear to have been highest after the failure of Graham's mission was announced. Britain and America's desire to extend the mission together with the convening of the constituent assembly could have greatly increased the domestic pressure on Karachi. Would deterrence then have worked? Liaquat's assassination makes this a tantalizing counterfactual question in the history of India–Pakistan relations.

The Aftermath: Sheikh Abdullah's Incarceration in 1953

A second coercive encounter in less than two years convinced the Pakistani leadership of the need to obtain arms and external security guarantees. This was essential to avoid being steamrolled by India in all areas of contention, particularly Kashmir. Indeed, even as the crisis raged Karachi had decided to intensify efforts in this direction. On 25 August Liaquat had written to Acheson indicating Pakistan's desire

[141] See, for example, Ayub, *Friends not Masters*, 41–2.

[142] Speech, 16 October 1951, *SWJN-SS*, 16, pt II: 363.

[143] See Ayub Khan to Cariappa, 4 December 1951, Part I, Group XXXIII, Cariappa Papers, National Archives of India, New Delhi.

to procure arms.[144] A few weeks later Pakistan's foreign secretary told the American ambassador that the two countries should commence discussions on the defence of the Middle East.[145]

Two days after Liaquat's assassination a Pakistani military mission arrived in Washington. The leader of the delegation explained that his aim was "to get as much military equipment as he could." The list included a request for 250 tanks. He also expressed Karachi's willingness to participate in arrangements for defending the Middle East, even if the US was unwilling to guarantee Pakistan's security against India. In November 1951 Washington approved for sale to Pakistan a portion of the equipment requested,[146] a decision that marked an important step towards Pakistan's eventual membership in anti-Communist alliances.

In retrospect it is also clear that the crises of 1950–1 left a deep imprint on the Pakistani official mind.[147] By indicating boundaries that could only be crossed at their peril, the experience of these crises led Pakistan to eschew overt use of force to wrest Kashmir. This is not to claim that their restraint was shaped by the fear of Indian retaliation alone. But it was undoubtedly an important consideration. Indeed, as late as September 1960 President Ayub Khan was reminding Nehru about India's "aggressive" behaviour during these crises.[148] Following the crisis of 1951 Karachi began to focus on covert measures to foment unrest in Indian-held areas.[149] Subsequent developments created conditions that seemed ideal for such a strategy.

---

[144] See summary of Liaquat's letter of 25 August 1951, *FRUS 1951*, 6, pt 2: 2219.

[145] McMahon, *Cold War on the Periphery*, 140.

[146] *FRUS 1951*, 6, pt 2: 2220–9.

[147] The concept of "official mind" is from Ronald Robinson and John Gallagher, *Africa and the Victorians: The Official Mind of Imperialism* (London: Macmillan, 1961). They define the official mind as comprising the routine assumptions, preferences, and calculations on which officials draw in formulating policy. It embodies the "cold rules for national safety" handed down by one generation of officials to the next.

[148] Ayub, *Friends not Masters*, 124.

[149] Swami, *Secret Jihad*, 34ff.; Nehru to Ayyangar, 27 August 1952, *SWJN-SS*, 19: 154.

The most important development was the fallout between Nehru and Abdullah, culminating in the latter's dismissal and imprisonment in August 1953. The rift was owing to three factors: first, the mutual mistrust between Sheikh Abdullah and the ministry of states dating back to the early days after accession. Vallabhbhai Patel's private secretary recalled that "Sardar [Patel] did not trust the Sheikh nor did he share Pt. Nehru's assessment of his influence in the State . . . he did not want to put all eggs in the Abdullah basket."[150] The contretemps over land reforms in the summer of 1950 accentuated both sides' misgivings. Abdullah wrote to Nehru that there were "powerful influences" in India which sought to undermine Nehru's ideal of secularism and thwart his internal Kashmir policy.[151] The second factor was the rise of regional dissensions within the state. Ever since the maharaja had been forced to decamp, the Hindus of Jammu had been disgruntled. This led to the creation of the Praja Parishad (Subjects' Committee), a party with links to the Hindu Right in India. Their resentments were aggravated by the land reforms in the valley, which had affected the big landowners, most of whom were Hindu. These measures were also viewed with disfavour in Ladakh, where much of the land was controlled by the Buddhist ecclesiastical order. Sheikh Abdullah, however, was notoriously intolerant of dissent and opposition. A contemporary was not exaggerating much when he wrote: "During his [Abdullah's] seven years' rule thousands of political workers were consigned to prison, mostly without trial, for varying periods extending to three years, merely because they held views unpalatable to the government."[152] In the elections to the constituent assembly, 45 out of the 49 Praja Parishad candidates were disqualified on flimsy technical grounds.[153] The Parishad boycotted the elections and commenced mass agitation once the constituent assembly convened. The third factor was Sheikh Abdullah's continued interest in an independent Kashmir. Abdullah was aware that the idea was not supported by the majority of his

---

[150] Cited in Bhattacharjea, *Tragic Hero of Kashmir*, 135–6.

[151] Cited in Gopal, *Nehru*, 2: 119.

[152] Prem Nath Bazaz, *Kashmir in the Crucible* (Bombay: Pearl Publications, 1969), 82.

[153] Navnita Chadha Behera, *State, Identity and Violence: Jammu, Kashmir and Ladakh* (New Delhi: Manohar, 2000), 83.

colleagues and strongly opposed by Delhi. So, during the inaugural session of the constituent assembly in November 1951 he declared that independence would only open them up to further aggression. But in the next round of discussions at the Security Council he privately mooted the idea of independence.[154]

These three hitherto separate issues converged in mid-1952. Early that year the Praja Parishad began protests demanding an end to Kashmir's special status and full integration with India. The Abdullah government came down heavily and imprisoned hundreds of agitators. Fearing a wider Hindu backlash Delhi asked Srinagar to release the Parishad's leaders. This at once stoked the Sheikh's fears about Hindu communalism in India and his ire at Delhi's interference in the affairs of Kashmir. Furthermore, by obliging Delhi, Abdullah's standing with his constituency of Kashmiri Muslims was affected. In consequence he grew increasingly censorious of India in his public pronouncements. The Sheikh also sought to take a spectacular step to shore up his position in the valley. He wanted to depose the maharaja and end dynastic rule in Kashmir. Such a move would, of course, add to the farrago of resentments in Jammu. A cycle of protest and reaction had commenced which would drag the state into a downward spiral.

Nehru considered the Praja Parishad an odious, reactionary, and communal organization. But the move to depose the ruler raised serious constitutional issues; for the maharaja was recognized by the president of India. More important, it underscored the need to settle the broad principles governing the relationship between Kashmir and India. This was necessary to ensure that Kashmir's constitution consorted smoothly with that of India.[155] Nehru therefore told Abdullah to let the maharaja abdicate rather than insist on his ejection. The question of transition to an elected head of state should be handled after an agreement on principles was reached. Following intense negotiations the two sides concluded an accord in July 1952.

Under the Delhi Agreement the union's authority would be confined to the three subjects of accession; the residuary powers would be vested in the Kashmir government. The residents of the state would be

[154] Bajpai to Rajagopalachari, 13 February 1952, C. Rajagopalachari Papers (V Instalment), NMML.
[155] Note, 3 July 1952, *SWJN-SS*, 18: 423–5.

citizens of India but the state legislature would define and regulate their rights and privileges. The head of state would be recognized by the president of India on the recommendation of the state legislature. Delhi could only exercise emergency powers on the request of the state government.

A.G. Noorani has claimed that in concluding the Delhi Agreement Nehru actually wanted to finalize Kashmir's accession to India. This argument is evidently intended to buttress Sheikh Abdullah's retrospective claim that "The final break in our relations came in 1953 when Pandit Jawaharlal suggested that I should get the accession ratified by the Kashmir Constituent Assembly. This change in his attitude baffled me for he had himself opposed it in the past . . . I strongly advised him against such a step. This led to my removal from the premiership of the State and long imprisonment without trial."[156] There is no evidence to support this contention in the copious exchanges between Nehru and Abdullah. Noorani quotes Nehru telling Kashmiri delegates (before negotiations on the agreement began) that "even before they finalised their Constitution, the relationship of Kashmir to India must be fully clarified."[157] Nehru was not referring, however, to the issue of accession. As he wrote in the same letter his concerns were: "What was the position of Jammu & Kashmir State in the Indian Union? Was it a federal unit of the Union? Were Kashmiris citizens and nationals of India, using Indian passports? What was the position of our President who was the symbol of the entire Union? Where did the Supreme Court come in and the flag?"[158] These were the issues negotiated in the Delhi Agreement. To be sure, Abdullah came to *perceive* the agreement as an attempt by the central government to erode Kashmir's special status. But the claim that Nehru wanted to use it to undermine Kashmir's autonomy or finalize accession to India simply does not wash.

After the agreement was concluded Sheikh Abdullah continued to press Nehru for a presidential order under Article 370, providing for

[156] Cited in A.G. Noorani, "Brought to Heel," *Frontline*, 25, no. 18 (30 August 2008). Also see Abdullah, *Flames of Chinar*, 116.

[157] Cited in A.G. Noorani, "The Legacy of 1953," *Frontline*, 25, no. 17 (16 August 2008).

[158] Nehru to Azad, 19 June 1952, *SWJN-SS*, 18: 402–3.

an elected head of state in Kashmir. The Delhi Agreement had made room for this principle. But in the circumstances Nehru felt it was best to give effect to it once the entire constitution was drawn up: "we should, as statesmen, disarm as much opposition as possible . . . One step at a time is better because that enables us to fashion the next step more easily."[159] When Abdullah insisted, the Indian prime minister had to give in.

Jammu became convulsed yet again in demonstrations. The Hindu Right in other parts of India capitalized on this situation. At the helm was Syama Prasad Mookerjee, an erstwhile member of the Indian cabinet who had resigned in protest after the Bengal crisis. In October 1951 Mookerjee had launched a new political party, Bharatiya Jan Sangh. His party performed poorly in the general elections of 1952, securing only three seats in parliament. The upheaval in Kashmir came in handy for the Jan Sangh.[160] Mookerjee now adopted the cause of the Hindus of Jammu and launched a vociferous campaign against Kashmir's special status. Soon, protests began to rock other parts of North India. These ramified Abdullah's suspicion that powerful sections of the Indian polity were ranged against him. He began to impute sinister motives to Delhi's actions, claiming, for instance, that N.G. Ayyangar had said Article 370 could be "wiped off" the constitution. Abdullah should have known better: the article could only be removed on the constituent assembly's recommendation and its removal would sunder Kashmir from India. Beset by the protests in Jammu and the reactions in Kashmir, Abdullah steadily moved in the direction of independence for the valley.

Nehru was aware of this shift. In a lengthy note to Abdullah he discussed the options for Kashmir. The talks with the UN had not yielded any results. "Throughout this period, my old conviction has taken root in my mind that the only feasible solution . . . was the acceptance of the *status quo*, more or less." Over time Pakistan would acquiesce. The prime minister made it clear that independence for the state, much less for the valley, was utterly unviable and unacceptable to India.[161] Nehru discussed the note with Abdullah and his colleagues.

[159] Nehru to Abdullah, 14 August 1952, *SWJN-SS*, 19: 317.
[160] Guha, *India After Gandhi*, 250.
[161] Note for Abdullah, 25 August 1952, *SWJN-SS*, 19: 322–30.

As he informed N.G. Ayyangar, "it was firm opinion of all concerned that idea of independence for whole State or part of it [was] completely unpractical and should be resisted. Kashmir leaders [are] also entirely opposed to limited plebiscite in Valley."[162] Clearly, Abdullah was faced with a situation where his stance was opposed by his colleagues and his popularity was dwindling in the valley.

As the protests coursed through northern India, Nehru simultaneously urged Abdullah to defuse the agitation by implementing the Delhi Agreement and appealed to others to cut Abdullah some slack. But the Sheikh was recalcitrant. By February 1953 he was telling Indian officials that the problem of accession had to be revisited: Jammu was not with him; many Indians were unhappy with Kashmir's status; Pakistan would never leave the state alone. By April he was advancing a variety of alternatives including independence or a condominium of India and Pakistan for the whole state or the valley. On 24 May the working committee of the National Conference considered the list of options proposed by Abdullah. The majority of his colleagues opposed a change of course.[163] Visiting Kashmir at this time, Nehru reiterated the view that India could not abide an independent Kashmir. It would be a cockpit of "international intrigue" and detrimental to India's interests.[164] It would have "tremendous consequences" for the secular fabric of the country.[165] Nehru urged Abdullah to rethink his position.

Abdullah appointed a subcommittee to consider alternatives. By 8 June the options had narrowed down to four: overall plebiscite with the option of independence; independence with, and without, joint control of foreign affairs by India and Pakistan; Dixon's plan with the option of independence for the plebiscite in the valley.[166] The working committee disagreed with these.[167] In the prevailing circumstances the last was the only plausible option; and it would inevitably lead to an independent valley. At Nehru's request Maulana Azad visited Srinagar. Abdullah "pointedly ignored" Azad and continued to espouse

---

[162] Cable to Ayyangar, 31 August 1952, ibid., 355–6.

[163] Bamzai, *Bonfire of Kashmiriyat*, 177–9, 184–7.

[164] Mir Qasim, *My Life and Times* (New Delhi: Allied, 1992), 61.

[165] Nehru to Abdullah, 8 July 1953, *SWJN-SS*, 23: 284–6.

[166] Cited in Abdullah to Sadiq, 26 September 1956, Mridula Sarabhai (ed.), *Sheikh–Sadiq Correspondence* (New Delhi: Privately published, 1956), 18.

[167] Nehru to Bajpai, 11 June 1953, *SWJN-SS*, 22: 191.

independence for the valley.[168] The Kashmir valley was loud with rumours about dissensions between Abdullah and some of his colleagues. As a close associate of both Abdullah and Nehru wrote to the prime minister, "The common man . . . seems to be quite confused about the Kashmir question at present and generally speaking the doubts seem to have risen about Kashmir's future relationship with India."[169] Towards the end of June 1953 Nehru entreated Abdullah to come for discussions.

By this time the crisis had been given a grim twist. Syama Prasad Mookerjee, who had been incarcerated in Srinagar, had died in prison on 23 June. The agitation escalated and assumed a pronounced anti-Abdullah character. The Jan Sangh organized a massive procession in Delhi, with the marchers calling for revenge and insisting that "Kashmir shall be ours."[170] Increasingly isolated, the Sheikh went about making astringent speeches, declaring his willingness to break with India. He declined to come to Delhi, claiming that "no useful purpose" would be served.[171] His colleagues, especially Bakshi Ghulam Mohammad and G.M. Sadiq, went public with their opposition to independence. Something had to give.

On 31 July Nehru decided that "The present drift and the resulting confusion cannot be allowed to go on."[172] Following his instructions the dissidents conveyed their lack of confidence in Abdullah's leadership to the head of state, Karan Singh. Soon after Abdullah was dismissed and imprisoned on the night of 9 August 1953.[173] Bakshi Ghulam Mohammad took over as the prime minister of Jammu and Kashmir. Nehru's role in Sheikh Abdullah's internment has occasioned much

[168] Singh, *Autobiography*, 155–6; Azad to Abdullah, 9 July 1953, *SWJN-SS*, 23: 287, n. 3. The IB director, B.N. Mullik, claimed that on returning Azad advised Nehru to dismiss Abdullah. B.N. Mullik, *My Years with Nehru: Kashmir* (Bombay: Allied Publishers, 1971), 37.

[169] Mridula Sarabhai's letter cited in Aparna Basu, *Mridula Sarabhai: Rebel with a Cause* (New Delhi: Oxford University Press, 1996), 157.

[170] Guha, *India After Gandhi*, 254.

[171] Cited in Bamzai, *Bonfire of Kashmiriyat*, 188.

[172] Nehru's instructions, 31 July 1953, *SWJN-SS*, 23: 303–5.

[173] Two letters from Karan Singh (head of state) to Nehru, 9 August 1953, *Select Correspondence between Jawaharlal Nehru and Karan Singh*, 118–21.

controversy.[174] On balance the evidence suggests that the decision was taken by the Kashmiri authorities and Nehru was not directly involved. Yet inasmuch as it flowed from the prior decision to dismiss Abdullah, Nehru's responsibility cannot be gainsaid. Certainly, the Indian prime minister did nothing to secure Abdullah's release. The decision looked almost as bad in prospect as it does in retrospect. "Not to take any steps was to court disaster. To take them, was also to invite a break with all its difficulties and unknown consequences."[175] Ironically, the downturn occurred just when India–Pakistan relations began to look up. Pakistan's governor general, Ghulam Mohammed, and the new prime minister, Mohammed Ali Bogra, sought to improve ties with India and settle the Kashmir dispute. Abdullah's imprisonment raised a furore in Pakistan and Bogra asked for a meeting with his Indian counterpart.

Given India's abridged authority in Kashmir, Nehru had to reconsider his position that the *status quo* was the only solution. He reckoned that the outcry in Pakistan would give a fillip to the pro-Pakistan and pro-Abdullah groups in the valley. Nevertheless, if Bakshi could implement a sound developmental programme the situation might be remedied to an extent. Consequently, Nehru decided to propose that a plebiscite administrator be appointed in six months. Meantime, both countries would try to settle the preliminary steps. Two years, if not more, would pass before a plebiscite was held. The plebiscite would be held in all regions, and based on the results the state would be partitioned. In short, Nehru was inclined to a variant of partition-cum-plebiscite. Nehru conveyed his views to Bogra and a joint communiqué was issued.[176] It has been argued that Nehru was devious and merely sought to "fool" Bogra.[177] This seems implausible for there was always the possibility that he might not be able to wriggle out of the commitment. Equally, it was not a firm decision, as others have argued,[178]

[174] For a useful summary of the various accounts, see Bhattacharjea, *Tragic Hero of Kashmir*, 182–94.

[175] Nehru to Bakshi, 15 August 1953, *SWJN-SS*, 23: 327–30.

[176] Ibid.; Note of conversation with Bogra, 17 August 1953, ibid., 331–6.

[177] A.G. Noorani, "Kashmir: Bridge, not a Battle Ground," *Frontline* 23, no. 6 (30 December 2006).

[178] Gopal, *Nehru*, 2: 182–3.

but rather a working assumption. The road to a plebiscite was still strewn with impediments.

Later that year, as the US–Pakistan alliance crystallized, Nehru warned Bogra that it would bring the Cold War "to the very frontiers of India" and that the Kashmir dispute would have to be seen in that light. It can be argued that these developments came handy to Nehru in stalling the move towards a plebiscite. But the Indian prime minister's concerns about the alliance were deep-seated. Even before this had transpired, Nehru had been firmly opposed to letting Chester Nimitz continue as the plebiscite administrator. He had written to Bogra, "For any great nation . . . to be brought into the Kashmir picture, would be to make Kashmir a part of this world conflict arousing rivalries between great powers."[179] Besides, Nehru was well aware that, for all its anti-communist rhetoric, Pakistan's moves were essentially directed against India—a fact that undoubtedly hardened his stance.

Although the accord of 1953 fell through, the Pakistanis continued to look for a favourable deal on Kashmir. In early 1955 Ghulam Mohammed, using a back channel, proposed to Nehru that Poonch and part of Jammu (north of the Chenab) should go to Pakistan, and that the valley should be jointly controlled, both politically and militarily, pending a plebiscite in the next five to twenty years. This was followed by a visit by Bogra and the Pakistani defence minister to Delhi. Pakistan's governor general was evidently under some misapprehension: Nehru was not prepared for anything more than the transfer of the Poonch and Mirpur areas. The prime minister told the visitors that their terms "amounted to a surrender by India which might perhaps follow a complete defeat." The Pakistanis in turn claimed that "their government would fall if India's proposal was accepted."[180] The two sides parted amicably.

Eight years would pass before India and Pakistan negotiated again on Kashmir. Curiously, these negotiations would follow an Indian defeat: against China in 1962.

[179] Nehru to Bogra, 3 September 1953, *SWJN-SS*, 23: 361–8.
[180] Talks with Bogra and Iskandar Mirza, 14–17 May 1955, *SWJN-SS*, 28: 247ff.

7

The Disputed India–China Boundary 1948–1960

In the closing years of the 1940s and in the early 1950s Prime Minister Nehru was, as we have seen, focused on India's problems with Pakistan. Yet relations with China increasingly drew his attention and gradually occupied the centrestage of foreign policy, culminating in the India–China war of 1962. The origins of this conflict lay in two intertwined issues: the boundary dispute and Tibet.

The Sino–Indian boundary is usually divided into the western, middle, and eastern sectors. The western sector encompasses the area of Ladakh; the middle sector the boundary of Himachal Pradesh and Uttar Pradesh (UP) with Tibet; and the eastern sector the area called North Eastern Frontier Agency (NEFA)—now Arunachal Pradesh. In contrast to the western and eastern sectors, the dispute in the middle sector was a minor one.[1] The status of the boundaries at the time of Independence is clear from the maps produced by Delhi as late as

[1] There is a substantial literature on the historical aspects of the boundary dispute, but most of it relies on British and Indian sources. The most important works are Alastair Lamb, *The China–India Border: The Origins of the Disputed Boundaries* (London: Oxford University Press, 1964); idem, *The McMahon Line*, 2 vols (London: Routledge and Kegan Paul, 1966); idem, *The Sino–Indian Boundary in Ladakh* (Columbia: University of South Carolina Press, 1975); Parshotam Mehra, *The McMahon Line and After* (New Delhi: Macmillan, 1974); idem, *An "Agreed" Frontier: Ladakh and India's Northernmost Borders, 1846–1947* (New Delhi: Oxford University Press, 1992); idem, *Essays in Frontier History: India, China and the Disputed Border* (New Delhi: Oxford University

1950. The boundary in the western and middle sectors was marked "undefined." In the western sector the British had toyed with a variety of boundary alignments in keeping with their perceived security requirements. The central concern of the Raj was to ensure that its northern boundary abutted an area that was not under the control of Czarist Russia, a power whose steady march towards the northern boundaries of Afghanistan engendered much apprehension in British India. To forestall this possibility the British sought to conclude a frontier agreement with China that would at once delimit India's northern boundary and encourage the Chinese to take effective control of the areas that fell under its sovereignty, so denying these parts to Russia. But in so doing the British also sought to obtain a boundary that would be militarily defensible.

Thus, in 1897, the chief of British military intelligence in London, Major General Sir John Ardagh, suggested to the Indian government a boundary that ran along the Kuen Lun range of mountains in the north and north-east, and that included the Aksai Chin area within India. The Ardagh alignment was based on an earlier alignment of 1865, drawn by the Survey of India explorer W.H. Johnson. The Indian government rejected the Ardagh alignment, deeming it too ambitious. In consequence a different boundary alignment was proposed to the Chinese foreign office in March 1899. The line presented by

Press, 2007); Karunakar Gupta, *The Hidden History of the Sino–Indian Frontier* (Calcutta: Minerva Associates, 1974); Margaret Fisher, Leo Rose, and Robert Huttenback, *Himalayan Battleground: Sino–Indian Rivalry in Ladakh* (New York: Praeger, 1963); Dorothy Woodman, *Himalayan Frontiers: A Political Review of British, Chinese, Indian and Russian Rivalries* (New York: Praeger, 1969); G. Narayana Rao, *The India–China Border: A Reappraisal* (New York: Asia Publishing House, 1968); John Lall, *Aksai Chin and Sino–Indian Conflict* (New Delhi: Allied Publishers, 1989). An important collection of sources can be found in *The North-Eastern Frontier: A Documentary Study of the Internecine Rivalry between India, Tibet and China*, ed. Parshotam Mehra, 2 vols (New Delhi: Oxford University Press, 1979–80). For a rare study drawing on Chinese sources, Hsiao-Ting Lin, "Boundary, Sovereignty, and Imagination: Reconsidering the Frontier Disputes between British India and Republican China, 1914–47," *Journal of Imperial and Commonwealth History* 32, no. 3 (September 2004): 25–47.

the British ambassador to China, Sir Claude MacDonald, placed almost all of the Aksai Chin area inside China. But the Chinese were cagey and refused to be drawn into any discussion of boundaries with the British. China's refusal to respond to the MacDonald offer led the British to make further unilateral alterations as mandated by their changing perceptions of security. Following the revolution in China of 1911 and the resultant weakness of the Chinese state, the Government of India reverted to the Ardagh alignment as its pre-fered northern boundary. The "undefined" boundary in the western sector reflected the failure of British attempts to secure a frontier agree-ment with China

In the eastern sector Indian maps showed the boundary as conform-ing to the alignment formalized in the tripartite conference between India, China, and Tibet held at Simla in 1914. The McMahon Line, as it came to be called after the foreign secretary of India at the time, was defined in a set of notes exchanged between Henry McMahon and the chief Tibetan delegate, Lonchen Shatra, on 24–25 March 1914. Accompanying the notes was a map that delineated the border along the highest line of the Assam Himalaya, and that outlined the bound-aries and buffer zones between Tibet and China. These were also mark-ed on the map of the draft convention which was initialled on 27 April 1914 by the Chinese as well as the British Indian and Tibetan repre-sentatives. The Simla convention was initialled yet again by the British Indian and Tibetan plenipotentiaries on 3 July 1914. They also signed a joint declaration stating that the convention was binding on both parties, irrespective of Chinese agreement.

The Chinese government, however, repudiated the Simla convention owing to their disagreement *vis-à-vis* the boundaries between Tibet and China, and their desire to curb British attempts at enhancing Tibet's autonomy. The Chinese would later insist that Tibet had no right to conclude an agreement with India, for this would amount to accepting that Tibet had *de facto* independence in 1914. In the after-math of the Simla conference the Indian government, too, did not make efforts to extend its administrative control up to the McMahon Line. Republican China was a shambles and posed no significant threat in the Assam Himalaya. Besides, British policy was influenced by the international context (including Russia's problematic stance in

1914 towards the Simla convention) and bureaucratic politics in London, Delhi, and Assam.

The McMahon Line came to the forefront in 1935, following the contretemps involving a British botanist studying the frontier tracts and Tibetan officials who controlled the area surrounding the Buddhist monastery in Tawang. Between 1938 and 1944 the Indian government belatedly sought to make good on the McMahon Line; but to no avail. Lhasa refused to withdraw its personnel from Tawang; and the British were chary of offending the Chinese—now their ally in the struggle against the Axis powers. Consequently, the Raj's administrative control could not be extended to Tawang. British policy at the time of decolonization was that "The Government of India stand by the McMahon Line and will not tolerate incursion into India . . . They would however at all times be prepared to discuss in a friendly way with China and Tibet any rectification of the frontier that might be urged on reasonable grounds by any of the parties to the abortive Simla Conference of 1914."[2]

Closely related to the boundary issue was the question of Tibet. During their rule in India the British had sought to maintain Tibet as a buffer state free of external influence, particularly Russian. They had only acknowledged China's "suzerainty"—as opposed to sovereignty— over Tibet. In practice this meant that British India maintained direct diplomatic ties with Lhasa and enjoyed other privileges, such as trading rights and armed detachments, in Tibet.

Independent India's policy towards Tibet was under sporadic consideration even before the Chinese civil war ended. The contours of official thinking can be discerned from a note prepared in June 1948 by the Indian ambassador in Nanjing, K.M. Panikkar. It stated that following British withdrawal India had become "in law the successor to British rights in Tibet." "The first and most important" of India's interests was the McMahon Line. Panikkar observed that though the Chinese had accepted the Simla convention of 1914 they had refused to ratify it. China's control over Tibet would mean "the immediate revival of claims against Nepal, Bhutan and Sikkim and also the

2 Fry to Hopkinson, 6 April 1947, *Transfer of Power*, 10: 156–7.

Map 5. Sino–Indian Boundary: Western Sector

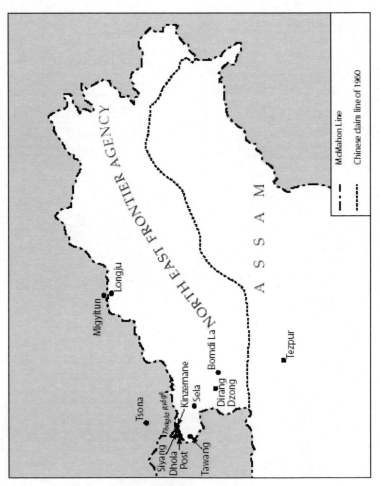

Map 6. Sino–Indian Boundary: Eastern Sector

denunciation of the Macmahon [*sic*] line."³ The assumption that a strong Chinese government would seize Tibet and advance claims to the region below the McMahon Line appears to have been widely accepted.⁴

The Invasion of Tibet

No sooner had the communists taken control of China than they announced their intention to "liberate" Tibet. India's policy was to avoid provoking China; but India would not give up its rights in Tibet and would provide moral and material support to Lhasa. As Secretary General Bajpai put it: "Chinese Communists, like any other Communists, reacted well to firmness but would exploit any sign of weakness."⁵ This attitude would underpin subsequent Indian policy on the boundary.

India was among the first countries to accord recognition to the People's Republic of China (PRC). The Indian prime minister eagerly looked forward to close cooperation between the Asian giants. Bajpai wryly observed: "I have to work hard to control his [Nehru's] enthusiasm when, in my own rather conservative judgement, caution seems to be necessary [in dealing with China]."⁶ For all this, the Chinese invasion of Tibet in late 1950 was viewed with concern in Delhi. Bajpai felt that India would now have on its northern frontiers a "militaristic and aggressive nation."⁷ Nehru's senior cabinet colleagues shared these apprehensions. In a note to Nehru, Vallabhbhai Patel said Chinese control over Tibet threw "into the melting pot all frontier and commercial settlements." Among other things, he warned of a weakly held northeastern frontier with "unlimited scope for infiltration," adding that "the people inhabiting these portions have no established loyalty to India." Patel suggested a range of issues to be considered, including

³ Note by K. M. Panikkar, 9 June 1948, FO 371/70042, TNA.

⁴ See, for example, Embassy in Nanking to FO, 18 August 1948, FO 371/70043, TNA.

⁵ UKHC India to CRO, 2 December 1949, FO 371/76317, TNA.

⁶ Bajpai to Vijayalakshmi Pandit, 10 September 1950, subject file 53, Vijayalakshmi Pandit Papers, NMML.

⁷ UKHC India to CRO, 26 October 1950, FO 371/84456, TNA.

redeployment of the army to protect likely areas of dispute; India's defence requirements; administrative steps to strengthen the frontier provinces; and policy regarding the McMahon Line.[8]

In the aftermath of the invasion Nehru too began to have "considerable doubts" about Chinese intentions; but was not prepared to go too far in condemnation, "making it inevitable that a break should take place."[9] Nehru elaborated his ideas in an important note. He conceded that neither India nor any other external power could prevent the Chinese takeover of Tibet. However, he discounted the possibility of an invasion of India as "exceedingly unlikely," for any such invasion would "undoubtedly lead to a world war." At the same time there were "certainly chances of gradual infiltration across our border and possibly of entering and taking possession of disputed territory, if there is no obstruction to this happening." India had to prepare to counter the "infiltration of men and ideas." In the ultimate analysis, wrote Nehru, "the real protection we should seek is some kind of understanding with China."[10]

Nehru's note delineated the various strands of India's policy towards China in the subsequent years. Underlying these was the realization of the disparity in power between the two countries. India would strive for a peaceful relationship whilst simultaneously taking the necessary steps to safeguard its fundamental interest: the preservation of its frontiers. This entailed taking measures to prevent gradual occupation of territory rather than preparing to meet an invasion. The assumption that infiltration would be the *modus operandi* of the Chinese gained currency because the peoples of India's frontier regions had ethnic, religious, and cultural ties with Tibet and had remained outside the pale of administration during the Raj. It was felt that their loyalties could be susceptible to the lures of communism or kinship: both of which could be exploited by China. Hence, it was important not just

8 Letter to Nehru, 7 November 1950, *SPC*, 10: 335–41.

9 UKHC India to CRO, 26 October 1950, FO 371/84456, TNA; Nehru to Rajagopalachari, 1 November 1950, *SWJN-SS*, 15, pt II: 338–9.

10 Note, 18 November 1950, ibid., 342–7. Also see OHT K.P.S. Menon, 20, NMML; Nehru's talk to an Indian delegation to China, Entry of 25 April 1952, China Diary, PPMS 24, Box 1, File 2, Frank Moraes Papers, School of Oriental and African Studies, London.

to establish checkposts to prevent infiltration but also to integrate the peoples of these areas with India. The economic and political advantages of being with India would have to be brought home to them. To examine these issues the government decided to form a committee under the deputy defence minister, M.S. Himmatsinhji.

Presently Nehru declared India's stance on the boundary in a statement in parliament. The frontier from Ladakh to Nepal was defined "chiefly by long usage and custom." In the east it was "clearly defined by the McMahon Line which was fixed by the Simla Convention of 1914 . . . that is our boundary—map or no map." This categorical pronouncement was spurred by Delhi's concern to adopt a robust posture in defence of its interests: any sign of weakness, as Bajpai had observed, would be exploited. The emphasis on the McMahon Line stemmed from two considerations. It is evident from Nehru's statement that India was surer of its rights in the eastern sector than in the west. Further, from the standpoint of security Nehru felt that the "main frontier was the Assam frontier."[11] The importance attached to this sector led to the decision to occupy Tawang. As Nehru wrote later, "It was on our side of the McMahon line, but it had not been occupied by us and was practically under Tibetan control till then."[12] In February 1951 an Indian political officer took control of Tawang amidst the clamorous ululations of Tibetans.[13] Beijing did not respond in any fashion.

Securing the Eastern Frontier

The Himmatsinhji Committee submitted its report in two parts in April and September 1951. On its recommendation the government sought to extend administrative cover into the remote tribal areas of NEFA, and to introduce economic and welfare measures. A road-building programme was initiated and checkposts established close

[11] Statement, 20 November 1950, *SWJN-SS*, 15, pt II: 348; Nehru to B.C. Roy, 15 November 1950, ibid., 341.

[12] Note, 27/29 October 1952, *SWJN-SS*, 20: 161.

[13] Nari Rustomji, *Enchanted Frontiers: Sikkim, Bhutan and India's North-Eastern Borderlands* (Calcutta: Oxford University Press, 1973), 126; Sitaram Johri, *Where India, China and Burma Meet* (Calcutta: Thacker Spink, 1962), 146.

to the frontier.[14] The committee also seems to have suggested that, in the sectors where the boundary was undefined, India should decide its claims, if only as a basis for negotiations. Having decided on its claim line, effective steps should be taken to prevent unilateral occupation of these areas by Chinese or Tibetans. In disputed areas, armed police might have to be stationed to prevent infiltration or intrusion.[15]

These measures apart, the Indians felt that they should try and obtain Beijing's acceptance of the frontier. Bajpai and Foreign Secretary K.P.S. Menon thought that China's recognition of the frontier should form part of an overall settlement on Tibet: India should not withdraw its armed parties from Tibet without securing this. In January 1952 instructions on these lines were issued to Ambassador Panikkar. When Panikkar met the Chinese premier the following month, Zhou Enlai spoke only about trade and cultural issues. Panikkar felt Zhou was anxious not to open wider issues, and ignoring his instructions remained silent about the frontier. In their next meeting, too, Zhou was reluctant to talk about India's interests in Tibet. He stated that they had been in Tibet for a short duration and had not yet thoroughly studied the problem. Instead, Zhou sought facilities to transport food supplies to Tibet via India.

Menon thought that China's attitude was "cunning." He wondered if the Chinese were "waiting to be free from their preoccupations in the North to be able to enforce a settlement in Tibet after their own hearts?" "Irredentism," wrote Menon, "has always played a part in the policy of the Chinese Government, whether Imperial, Kuomintang or Communists." He recalled "seeing, on the walls of the Military Academy in Chengtu, a map, showing China as it was and ought to be and including large portions of Kashmir and areas to the south of the McMahon Line. This is perhaps the real reason for the Chinese reluctance to discuss the problem of Tibet with us." Menon recommended

14 B.N. Mullik, *My Years with Nehru: The Chinese Betrayal* (New Delhi: Allied Publishers, 1971), 125–7; Embassy in India to SS, *FRUS 1951*, 7, pt II: 1692.

15 D.R. Mankekar, *The Guilty Men of 1962* (Bombay: Tulsi Shah, 1968), 137. Also see Steven Hoffmann, *India and the China Crisis* (Berkeley: University of California Press, 1990), 24.

that "we must firmly adhere to our decision that any such proposal . . . can only be considered as part of a general settlement on Tibet."[16] Nehru agreed with Menon that Zhou's response "does not carry conviction." He wrote to Panikkar that the request could only be considered in the context of a general settlement of India's interests, which were "not confined to trade relation but involve political interests such as affirmation of the Frontier."[17]

Following another meeting with the Chinese premier, Panikkar reported that the "question of boundary was not touched and no allusion made to any political problems." Zhou, Panikkar argued, knew India's declared position; his persistent silence should, therefore, be treated as acquiescence in—if not acceptance of—India's view. India should stick to the stand that the frontier had been defined and that there was nothing to be discussed. Nehru initially agreed that it would not be desirable to raise the matter "at this stage." Soon, he began to doubt the wisdom of such a course: "I am beginning to feel that our attempt at being clever might overreach itself. I think it is better to be absolutely straight and frank."[18] Nehru's thinking was apparently influenced by a Chinese note which stated that the existing arrangement on Tibet was a "scar" left by British imperialism. More important, Girja Bajpai, now governor of Bombay, wrote to the new secretary general, N.R. Pillai, contesting Panikkar's stance. Bajpai argued that the McMahon Line might well be one of the scars: China "may seek to heal or erase this scar on the basis of frontier rectifications that may not be to our liking."[19]

By this time Panikkar had completed his term in Beijing and returned to Delhi. He managed to convince the prime minister of the soundness of his point.[20] Reviewing the decision in March 1953, Nehru felt that the time was not yet suitable to raise this question. "But

16 Note by K.P.S. Menon, 11 April 1952, subject file 24, Vijayalakshmi Pandit Papers (II Instalment), NMML.

17 Cables to Panikkar, 12 April & 24 May 1952, *SWJN-SS*, 18: 471–3.

18 Cable to Panikkar, 18 June 1952, ibid., 475; Note to Foreign Secretary, 25 July 1952, *SWJN-SS*, 19: 585.

19 Quoted in Maxwell, *India's China War*, 76; Gopal, *Nehru*, 2: 179, n. 64.

20 Note, 29 July 1952, *SWJN-SS*, 19: 651.

if occasion offers itself and especially if any challenge to the frontier is made, then we shall have to make this perfectly clear."[21] Nehru persisted with this attitude at the eve of negotiations with China over Tibet. The officials representing India suggested that the boundary issue be raised in India's general statement. Nehru declined, but importantly added that "this will have to be brought in in a larger settlement. In that settlement I should like to make clear our special position in the border States."[22]

Panikkar's advice and Nehru's acceptance of it have been sharply criticized by scholars. Even a historian as sympathetic to Nehru as Sarvepalli Gopal agrees that the prime minister succumbed to ill-considered advice. Nevertheless, Panikkar was not, as Gopal contends, rationalizing "a shirking of unpleasantness." Nor was he trying to be clever, as Nehru had put it earlier. Panikkar's point was that China was unlikely to accept the McMahon Line since successive governments had repudiated the Simla convention. In such a situation the Chinese might offer to negotiate a fresh boundary, which "would not be advantageous to us." On the other hand if China raised the issue, India could stick to its stated position that the McMahon Line was the boundary and there was nothing to discuss.[23] This last point has led most scholars to overlook the nub of Panikkar's argument: so long as China was unwilling to rake up the matter, India should use the time to make its position effective in the frontier areas, where its administrative hold was weak and its political position fledgling.[24]

In retrospect this decision was lamentable, for India passed up an opportunity to settle the boundary issue. But in 1952–3 this argument would have appealed to Nehru for a variety of reasons. For one thing, it was widely held that China had latent claims towards territory along India's frontiers. For another, Delhi had received reports from its mission in Lhasa suggesting that the Chinese were indulging in a "whispering campaign" to the effect that, after Tibet, Sikkim, Bhutan, and areas

[21] Note, 5 March 1953, *SWJN-SS*, 21: 555–8.

[22] Note, 30 August 1953, *SWJN-SS*, 23: 484.

[23] Quoted in Maxwell, *India's China War*, 77.

[24] OHT R.K. Nehru, 17–18, 31, NMML. Also see, Karunakar Gupta, *Sino-Indian Relations 1948–52: Role of K. M. Panikkar* (Calcutta: Minerva, 1987), 64–5.

south of the McMahon Line would be "liberated." Nehru himself thought that India had to be on guard "for some kind of gradual spreading out or infiltration."[25] For a third, although various steps were initiated in accordance with the Himmatsinhji report, there was not much progress.

The listless implementation of these measures was the cause of periodic concern to Nehru. Since October 1951 the UP government had been writing to him about the possibility of Tibetan incursions abetted by the Chinese and of the need to expedite the requisite steps. As late as February 1953 the issue remained mired in financial and bureaucratic delays. Nehru reminded the home minister that the matter had been "delayed very greatly."[26] The following month the UP chief minister G.B. Pant wrote directly to Nehru about disconcerting reports of likely infiltration. Pant knew of the existing proposals but observed that there had been "no visible progress."[27] Subsequently Pant met Nehru and conveyed his apprehensions. The lack of progress in NEFA was also underscored by Joint Secretary T.N. Kaul following his tour of the region. Throughout, Nehru continued to issue instructions emphasizing the urgency of the problem.[28] In these circumstances it is not surprising that he sought to avoid pushing the boundary question to the fore. India was far from consolidating its influence in the border regions and ill-prepared to counter any efforts by China to take possession of these parts. If the issue became an openly contested one, India might be unable to defend its claims.

A crucial component of India's frontier policy was to adopt a robust stance and eschew any move indicating doubt or weakness. As Nehru explained it to his ambassador in Beijing, "If we show weakness

25 Note by K.P.S. Menon, 11 April 1952, subject file 24, Vijayalakshmi Pandit Papers (II Instalment), NMML; Letter to Chief Ministers, 2 August 1952, *SWJN-SS*, 19: 695; Note, 25 October 1953, *SWJN-SS*, 24: 596–8.

26 Nehru to Sampurnanand, 31 October 1951, *SWJN-SS*, 16, pt II: 541; Nehru to Katju, 13 February 1953, *SWJN-SS*, 21: 305.

27 Pant to Nehru, 3 March 1953, in B.R. Nanda (ed.), *Selected Works of Govind Ballabh Pant* (New Delhi: Oxford University Press, 1994–2003; hereafter *SWGBP*), 18 vols, 18: 396.

28 Note, 9 March 1953, *SWJN-SS*, 21: 308. Note by Kaul, 21 April 1953, File 2, Bisnuram Medhi Papers, NMML. Nehru's response, 24 April 1953, *SWJN-SS*, 22: 235–6.

advantage will be taken of immediately. This applies to any development that might take place or in reference to our frontier problems . . . In regard to this entire frontier we have to maintain an attitude of firmness. Indeed there is nothing to discuss there and we have made that previously clear to the Chinese Government."[29] As part of this posture (and probably in pursuance of the Himmatsinhji Committee's recommendations) it was decided in 1953 to publish new official maps which would show the boundary between India and China as unambiguously delimited.[30] The crucial decision, in retrospect, lay in the Ladakh sector. Here Delhi decided neither on the ambitious Ardagh Line nor on the MacDonald Line, but a "compromise line which had some plausibility."[31] This line placed Aksai Chin within Indian territory. The foreign secretary at the time, R.K. Nehru, later recalled that "in 1953, our experts had advised us that our claim to Aksai Chin was not too strong." The prime minister was "agreeable" to adjustments in "Aksai Chin and one or two other places" being made "as part of a satisfactory overall settlement."[32]

Panchsheel and After

In keeping with his approach Nehru instructed the Indian delegation not to raise the boundary question during the negotiations over Tibet: "If the Chinese raise it, we should express our surprise and point out that this is a settled issue." He publicly stated that "our people have not gone there to discuss the frontier problem. It is not an issue at all to be discussed."[33] The agreement on Tibet was signed on 29 April 1954. India gave up its rights in Tibet and recognized it as a "region of

[29] Cable to Raghavan, 10 December 1952, *SWJN-SS*, 20: 488–9.

[30] Hoffmann, *India and the China Crisis*, 25.

[31] J.S. Mehta, "India-China Relations: Review and Prognosis", in Surjit Mansingh (ed.), *Indian and Chinese Foreign Policies in Comparative Perspective* (New Delhi: Radiant Publishers 1998), 468. Mehta was the leader of the Indian team which examined the evidence on the boundary dispute in 1960.

[32] Confidential Note, "Our China Policy: A Personal Assessment," 30 July 1968, R.K. Nehru Papers, NMML.

[33] Note to Secretary General, 3 December 1953, *SWJN-SS*, 24: 598–9; Reply in Parliament, 24 December 1953, ibid., 577–8.

China." These, as R.K. Nehru explained, were "a concession only to realism."[34] Delhi was also keen to include the five principles of peaceful coexistence, or Panchsheel, in the text of the treaty. Nehru hoped that the acknowledgement of these would lay the foundation for peaceful Sino-Indian relations. But Nehru was not naïve. "In the final analysis," he said, "no country has any deep faith in the policies of another country, more especially in regard to a country which tends to expand . . . But whatever its urges might be, we can, by our policy, strengthen our own position and even curb to some extent undesirable urges in the other country."[35]

After returning from Beijing T.N. Kaul wrote a preliminary note on the negotiations wherein he recorded his misgivings. Kaul thought that the Chinese would attempt pushing their claim lines along the frontier within the next five years: it explained their insistence on this duration for the agreement. India should therefore establish checkposts at important points on the frontier to prevent Chinese encroachment. Such checkposts should particularly be installed in areas like Demchok, on which China's attitude had aroused suspicion.[36]

Nehru was already worried by the torpid implementation of these measures. A few months earlier the UP government had drawn his attention to it and the chief minister, Pant, had written to him about the apathy of the relevant ministries. The prime minister had enjoined his officials to delve into the bureaucratic mess and "get this moving."[37] In this context Kaul's note amplified Nehru's anxiety about the frontiers. Nehru agreed that India should establish checkposts at all disputed points and extend its administration to the border provinces. "We should find out how matters stand and try to do something to expedite decisions and action."

After the Panchsheel agreement was signed, Zhou Enlai visited India from 25 to 28 June 1954. The talks between the prime ministers

34 UKHC India to CRO, 14 May 1954, FO 371/110647, TNA.

35 Nehru to Chettur, 9 May 1954, *SWJN-SS*, 25: 479.

36 The contents are inferred from T.N. Kaul, *A Diplomat's Diary* (Delhi: Macmillan, 2000), 64, and Nehru's note, 12 May 1954, *SWJN-SS*, 25: 469–70.

37 Pant to Nehru, 17 February 1954, *SWGBP*, 18: 407–8. Note to Secretary General & Foreign Secretary, 20 February 1954, *SWJN-SS*, 25: 204.

mainly pertained to international issues; neither of them raised any point about differences on the frontier. After Zhou's departure Nehru read the detailed report on the negotiations in Beijing and issued an important directive. He remarked that he was generally in agreement with the approach suggested by Kaul. On the crucial issue of the frontier, he wrote:

7. All our old maps dealing with this frontier should be carefully examined and, where necessary, withdrawn. New maps should be printed showing our North and North-East frontier without reference to any "line." These new maps should also not state there is any undemarcated territory . . .
8. Both as flowing from our policy and as a consequence of our Agreement with China, this frontier should be considered a firm and definite one which is not open to discussion with anybody . . . It is necessary that the system of check-posts should be spread along this entire frontier. More especially we should have check-posts in such places as might be considered disputed areas.[38]

Revisionist scholars have argued that this directive conclusively proves Nehru wanted to settle the boundary issue unilaterally. To Neville Maxwell, Nehru's intention is clear: "India should fill out what she considered her proper boundaries, and then decline to discuss them with China."[39] Maxwell reached these conclusions based on a partial reading of the directive; he had access only to paragraph 8 of the document.[40] Read in the light of preceding developments it is clear that the intentions behind this directive were quite different. The disputed areas which Nehru had in mind, as he revealed in the next paragraph, were Demchok and Tsang Chokla: areas over which Chinese intentions, according to Kaul, were suspect. Nehru also wanted checkposts along the UP–Tibet border, which reflected his prior concerns regarding possible Chinese intrusions there. Moreover, Nehru carefully defined the tasks of these checkposts as being to "control traffic, prevent unauthorized infiltration and act as symbols of India's frontier." The intent was prophylactic: to preclude the Chinese from

[38] Note to Secretary General & Foreign Secretary, 1 July 1954, *SWJN-SS*, 26: 481–4.
[39] Maxwell, *India's China War*, 80.
[40] Ibid., 13. Also see Mankekar, *The Guilty Men of 1962*, 138.

infiltrating and occupying territory, so presenting a *fait accompli* to India. His wider concern was to develop the frontier areas and integrate them with India. Nehru's policy, in short, was to implement a hearts and minds programme whilst simultaneously taking measures to ensure India was not caught unawares.

What about the revisionist claim that Nehru had shut the door to discussions on the boundary? We now know that Nehru had already been thinking in terms of a "larger settlement," entailing some concessions by India. It had suited Delhi to wait for Beijing to raise the issue. The agreement on Tibet seemed to indicate that the Chinese had implicitly accepted the existing frontier; yet the negotiations suggested that they held a different conception of some parts of the boundary and that they might attempt to seize these. The situation confronting Indian decision-makers was thus one of great uncertainty about China's claims and intentions. There was a need to adopt a commensurately unambiguous and resolute public posture by issuing new maps clarifying India's claims and treating the frontier as "firm and definite." Nonetheless, at the end of the note the prime minister directed that if Chinese maps continued to depict large swathes of territory claimed by India within their boundaries, Delhi would have to join issue with Beijing. If Nehru was indeed determined not to discuss the boundary issue, why then would he think of raising the question of maps?

Shortly after the 1954 agreement the two sides began to contest the ownership of a grazing ground called Bara Hoti in the middle sector. In talks with Zhou Enlai in Beijing later that year, Nehru indirectly referred to the boundary alignment in Chinese maps. Zhou replied that China had been reprinting old maps. They had not undertaken surveys, nor consulted neighbouring countries, and had no basis for fixing the boundary lines. Nehru replied that he was not worried about these maps: "Our frontiers are clear." Despite the air of nonchalance, Nehru's unease was obvious: "Supposing we publish a map showing Tibet as part of India, how would China feel about it?"[41] Interestingly, Zhou did not raise any question about the new Indian maps. The following summer the Hoti problem cropped up again. G.B. Pant—now the Indian home minister—felt that the Chinese had "their eye on Hoti." He wrote to Nehru that the issue of defining the boundary in

41 Minutes of talk with Zhou, 20 October 1954, *SWJN-SS*, 27: 17–20.

the area might have to be taken up, "but there is no urgency and it can well wait for easier days."[42] Pant's comments reflected the consensus within the government that the issue was best left for consideration later.

By early 1956 there were reports that the Chinese were constructing roads on their side of the India–Tibet frontier. The Indian mission in Lhasa wrote that these roads could be used to access border areas and take possession of these parts. To counteract this it was essential to accelerate the existing measures to "develope [sic] areas along our border, make roads, educate people and make them conscious of India." The mission also called for checkposts closer to the border and mobile patrols to "ensure that the Chinese will not encroach on our areas."[43]

Nehru's principal concern was with the Chinese maps, which claimed "quite a good part of Assam . . . Also, a bit of U.P." He was apparently not much bothered about the western sector. Nehru, we may recall, was amenable to compromising here. He now began to reconsider the wisdom of waiting for China to raise the issue. Zhou had not explicitly accepted India's version of the boundary. The continued publication of old maps together with petty border incidents and the construction of roads produced "a sense of disquiet." Ambassador R.K. Nehru advised that Delhi bide its time, but the prime minister felt "we shall have to take up this matter some time or the other."[44] Later that year when Premier U Nu of Burma requested India's help in their boundary dispute with China, Nehru agreed to write to Zhou. He thought India should not directly bring up the question of its own frontiers, but it might come up indirectly as the McMahon Line encompassed a part of Burma's northern boundary too.[45]

[42] 3 July 1955, *SWGBP*, 16: 267.

[43] "Recent Developments in Tibet and their Effects on the Security of India" by S.L. Chibber, in P.N. Menon to Apa Pant, 3 February 1956, subject file 3, Apa Pant Papers, NMML.

[44] Note to Krishna Menon, 6 May 1956; Note, 12 May 1956, *SWJN-SS*, 33: 475–8.

[45] Note to Foreign Secretary & Commonwealth Secretary, 26 August 1956, *SWJN-SS*, 34: 385–7.

During a visit to India in January 1957 Zhou referred to the McMahon Line in the context of the Sino–Burmese boundary. Although China had never recognized the line, they thought "now that it is an accomplished fact, we should accept it." They had not consulted the Tibetan authorities, and would do so. Nehru took this as clear acceptance of the McMahon Line. He suggested that minor border issues such as Hoti could be settled by discussions between officials. Zhou agreed but the discussions did not commence until April 1958.[46] Zhou still did not question Indian claims in the western sector though the Chinese were constructing a highway linking Xinjiang and Tibet passing through Aksai Chin. China, of course, regarded Aksai Chin as its territory. But in retrospect Zhou's silence on this occasion had deleterious repercussions: it lent credence to Delhi's perception that China had occupied Aksai Chin furtively and treacherously.

In September 1957 the embassy in Beijing drew Delhi's attention to an official announcement of the completion of the Xinjiang–Tibet road. A small-scale map was also published which suggested that the road might run through Aksai Chin. Years later the director of the IB at the time, B.N. Mullik, wrote that he had provided "enough information" about the construction of the road from 1951 onwards.[47] Whilst information was certainly received, the available evidence suggests it may not have been as definitive as Mullik claimed. The main sources were reports from Indian representatives in Tibet who were aware of the road under construction. Nevertheless, as late as February 1956 their assessment of roads being constructed did not suggest that the Xinjiang road might cut through Aksai Chin. Other sources like traders, travellers, and Tibetan émigrés may have provided clearer inputs. But in general these sources were not deemed reliable.[48] The

[46] Record of conversation, 31 December 1956/1 January 1957, *SWJN-SS*, 36: 600–1; Subimal Dutt, *With Nehru in the Foreign Office*, 116–17.

[47] Mullik, *Chinese Betrayal*, 196–9.

[48] "Recent Developments in Tibet and their Effects on the Security of India" by S.L. Chibber, in P.N. Menon to Apa Pant, 3 February 1956; Subimal Dutt (Foreign Secretary) to Apa Pant, 1 May 1956; Apa Pant to Dutt, 7 May 1956, subject file 3, Apa Pant Papers, NMML.

Indians' awareness that their claims to Aksai Chin were not definitive would have further inhibited them from acting on uncertain intelligence. In September 1957 it was thought the alignment had to be ascertained before any steps could be taken.[49]

Early next year an intelligence patrol reported additional signs of Chinese activity near Aksai Chin. The IB recommended that a protest be lodged. Officials in the MEA thought that since the boundary in this area had not been delimited a protest would not be on firm grounds. The army took the view that the road was of no strategic importance; besides, they could not oust the Chinese from Aksai Chin.[50] Nehru did not consider it feasible to protest without being surer about the alignment of the road: "What we might perhaps do is that in some communication with the Chinese government in regard to the points in dispute which have to be decided we should mention the Aksai Chin area."[51] Clearly, Nehru did not believe that Aksai Chin "belonged" to India and that it was not open to discussion. He was willing to treat it on a par with other minor areas in dispute like Hoti. In June 1958, following further reports, the government decided to send two patrols to verify the alignment of the road.

Negotiations on Hoti were held in April–May 1958. The Chinese were implacable and refused to provide the information that would have enabled headway. The Indians got the impression that the Chinese were unwilling to negotiate a minor issue or even make their claims clear.[52] In July 1958 the *China Pictorial* published a small-scale map depicting a large portion of NEFA, Ladakh, and some parts of UP within the "approximate boundaries" of China. Delhi now sent a formal protest note.

---

[49] Nehru's statement, 31 August 1959, *Prime Minister on Sino–Indian Relations* (hereafter *PMSIR*): *Parliament* (New Delhi: Ministry of External Affairs, Government of India, 1963), 1: 100.

[50] Mullik, *Chinese Betrayal*, 200–1, 205. R.K. Nehru also recalled that "the experts were doubtful whether a protest should be lodged at all." Confidential Note, "Our China Policy: A Personal Assessment," 30 July 1968, R.K. Nehru Papers, NMML.

[51] Note, 4 February 1958, cited in Gopal, *Nehru*, 3: 79.

[52] Dutt, *With Nehru in the Foreign Office*, 117; Hoffmann, *India and the China Crisis*, 35.

In October 1958 one of the parties returned from Aksai Chin and confirmed that the road cut through Indian-claimed territory; the other was intercepted. Accordingly, the Chinese ambassador was given an informal note. Besides asking for information about the patrol, the note expressed surprise at China's construction of a road on what was "indisputable Indian territory." It concluded by stating that India was "anxious to settle these petty frontier disputes." Although India's claims were asserted, Delhi considered Aksai Chin a minor issue and indicated its willingness to deal with it. In reply Beijing asserted that the road lay within their territory and said the patrol had been detained and sent back through the Karakoram Pass. India, in turn, expressed shock at the treatment meted out to the patrol. As for China's claim over the area, the Indian response read: "The question whether the particular area is in Indian or Chinese territory is a matter in dispute which has to be dealt with separately. The Government of India proposed to do so."[53]

The Chinese also handed a reply to India's protest about their maps. It reiterated what Zhou Enlai had told Nehru in 1954, adding that in time, and after consultations with neighbours and surveys, a "new way of drawing the boundary'" would be decided. In the context of recent developments Nehru was unwilling to abide by tenuous reassurances and decided to write directly to the Chinese premier. Nehru's intention was not to force Beijing to accept India's conception of the boundary, but to get confirmation they were not claiming the vast areas shown by their maps.[54] Nehru recalled that Zhou had told him in 1954 that the Chinese maps were old. In 1956 Zhou had made it "quite clear" that China proposed to accept the McMahon Line. China had now published a map depicting "A large part of our North-East Front-ier Agency as well as some other parts" as Chinese territory and had given an evasive reply to India's note. Nehru felt "puzzled" since he had thought that there was "no *major* boundary dispute." He would no longer be satisfied with an assurance that these were old maps: "There

[53] *Notes Memoranda and Letters Exchanged and Agreements Signed between India and China: White Papers* (New Delhi: Ministry of External Affairs, 1959–66), 8 vols, 1: 26–9. Unless indicated, all subsequent references to official and prime ministerial correspondence are from these volumes.

[54] Hoffmann, *India and the China Crisis*, 36.

can be no question of these *large parts* of India being anything but India" (emphases added). Evidently, Nehru was only troubled by the "large" areas shown within China's boundaries particularly south of the McMahon Line. There was no mention of Aksai Chin, for India had already stated it could be resolved through discussions.

In his reply of 23 January 1959 Zhou said that the entire boundary had never been formally delimited by any treaty or agreement. The matter had not been raised "because conditions were not yet ripe for its settlement." He averred that Aksai Chin had "always been under Chinese jurisdiction." Nor would he accept the McMahon Line since it was a product of British imperialism and was illegal. Nevertheless, China found it necessary to "take a more or realistic attitude" towards the line; it also had to "act with prudence" and needed time. Since the boundary was not delimited there were bound to be discrepancies in maps. China did "not hold that every portion of this [Chinese] boundary line is drawn on sufficient grounds." For the first time, Zhou questioned Indian maps, "particularly its western section." To avoid border incidents he proposed that both sides maintain the status quo.

The Indians were surprised but not alarmed by the letter. Apart from Ladakh the Chinese had not explicitly claimed any area included in their maps. Yet the letter suggested the belief that their boundary line was drawn on "sufficient grounds" at least in some sector, probably the western, where their line ran much further west of Aksai Chin. Zhou's disavowal of the McMahon Line coupled with his guarded assurances would have seemed a slight retraction, for Nehru believed that Zhou had clearly accepted it in 1956. Most important, the thrust of Zhou's letter was that the entire boundary was undefined and in need of negotiation afresh.

The Indians did not think the boundary drawn by them had no basis at all. Nehru's response of 22 March 1959 set forth the historical and geographical basis for India's conception of the boundary. It is evident from this note that Delhi considered its case for the McMahon Line unassailable and that it attached greater importance to this sector. In the western sector a nebulous treaty of 1842 was cited in support of India's claims. On Zhou's suggestion to maintain the status quo Nehru wrote that neither side should take unilateral action in support of its claims: "Further, if any possession has been secured recently, the position should be rectified." Nehru wrote this in connection with Hoti, which he claimed had recently been occupied. The note did not explicitly state that this proposal applied to Aksai Chin, though India would do so at a later stage.

Why did Nehru claim a definite boundary in the western sector instead of acknowledging that the boundary had not been delimited? For one thing, his letter sought only to explain the basis on which India had drawn the boundary; it did not claim that there was nothing further to discuss. Indeed, India had already admitted that the owner-ship of a part of this sector, Aksai Chin, was disputed. Nehru was aware all along that he might have to compromise on the area but would have concealed this for tactical reasons. The talks over Hoti had shown that any negotiation with the Chinese would be prolonged and tough. It would have seemed imprudent to display any eagerness to make concessions upfront for that would encourage the other side to press for more.

The Uprising of 1959 in Tibet

In the following months the relationship between India and China deteriorated sharply owing to the rebellion in Tibet—a large-scale up-rising that underscored the tenuousness of China's hold on the region. For some time past Beijing strongly suspected that India harboured designs on Tibet. The available evidence suggests that this perception was ideological rather than factual. China's suspicions began with their belief that India had assisted the Khampa uprising in Tibet in 1956. Some Khampas had indeed fled to India and had established contact with Guomindang agents in the border town of Kalimpong. But the rebels had not sought any assistance from the Indian authorities. As a prominent rebel leader had told the Indian political officer in Sikkim, Apa Pant, "We are not asking you for arms or ammunition . . . We want him [Nehru] to help us morally."[55] During his visit in 1957 Zhou had asked Nehru to curtail hostile activities by Tibetan émigrés in Kalimpong. Nehru in turn had told the Dalai Lama that an armed

55 Apa Pant to Kaul, n.d. (c. April 1956), subject file 3, Apa Pant Papers, NMML. Pant told him "categorically that India can do nothing for them."

struggle would be futile and that he would not permit any activity in India.[56] Furthermore, the émigrés had unequivocally been told that the idea of assisting them in any manner was "abhorrent to India."[57]

Prior to the outbreak of the rebellion in 1958, the American Central Intelligence Agency (CIA) had begun assisting Tibetan rebels. India's role in these efforts has been widely speculated. S.M. Ali argues that since 1947 India was in a covert "alliance" with the US, initially to help the Guomindang, and then the Tibetans. But the evidence he presents is far from convincing.[58] A recent study drawing on Chinese sources concludes that "there is little evidence to support Beijing's claims that New Delhi inspired and colluded with the rebels in Tibet."[59] Nor does the available evidence suggest that the Indian government co-operated with the US after the Dalai Lama fled to India. In fact, from April 1959 the Americans took care not to give India reason to believe that they were instigating the revolt. In September 1959 the CIA base for these operations was shifted from East Pakistan to northern Thailand to avoid the need to over-fly Indian territory.[60] There is, however, some fragmentary evidence that from 1960 Delhi might have known about the CIA's assistance to the Tibetans, and that it chose to turn a blind eye as long as this was not carried out on Indian soil and the Indian government was not implicated.[61]

[56] Gopal, *Nehru*, 3: 36; Dutt, *With Nehru in the Foreign Office*, 140–3.

[57] Report on the visit of the Dalai Lama, n.d. (*c.* March 1957), subject file 3, Apa Pant Papers, NMML.

[58] S.M. Ali, *Cold War in the High Himalayas: The USA, China, and South Asia in the 1950s* (New York: St Martin's Press, 1999); for a clinical dissection, see John Garver, "Review Essay: India, China, the United States, Tibet, and the Origins of the 1962 War," *India Review* 3, no. 2 (April 2004): 171–82.

[59] Chen Jian, "The Tibetan Rebellion of 1959 and China's Changing Relations with India and the Soviet Union," *Journal of Cold War Studies* 8, no. 3 (Summer 2006): 54–101 (quotation on 100).

[60] Kenneth Conboy and James Morrison, *The CIA's Secret War in Tibet* (Lawrence: University Press of Kansas, 2002), 96, 117.

[61] The US ambassador, Ellsworth Bunker, reported in late 1960 that the Indian foreign secretary, Subimal Dutt, had remonstrated about an American aircraft straying into Indian airspace. The Indians had initially assumed it was a Chinese aircraft and had accordingly protested; Beijing had replied that it was an American plane from Taiwan dropping supplies in Tibet. Dutt told Bunker

In the event the confluence of the boundary dispute and the rebellion in Tibet gravely impaired Sino-Indian relations. India's decision to grant asylum to the Dalai Lama in March 1959 catalysed the deterioration. The Indians, however, were determined not to "break the bridges," for they believed that only by maintaining good relations could they influence the Chinese on Tibet.[62] As Nehru told the Dalai Lama, "at the moment our relations with China are bad. We have to recover the lost ground."[63]

But Beijing worked these developments into a more sinister tableau. Mao Zedong urged the *People's Daily* to criticize Nehru and the "Indian expansionists" who "want ardently to grab Tibet." The chairman himself revised a draft of this article.[64] Mao's perceptions were refracted through the prism of ideology. Thus the article claimed that "the Indian big bourgeoisie maintains innumerable links with imperialism . . . Moreover, by its class nature, the big bourgeoisie has a certain urge for outward expansion . . . it more or less reflects, consciously or unconsciously, certain influences of [an] imperialist policy of intervention."[65] The same day, Zhou Enlai told ambassadors of

---

that while he was not aware if US had dropped supplies in Tibet, any future drops should not cross Indian territory. Dutt informed him that India planned to shoot down any planes violating its airspace. Embassy in India to State Department, 26 November 1960, *FRUS 1958–1960*, 19: 814. Also see Kenneth Knaus, *Orphans of the Cold War: America and the Tibetan Struggle for Survival* (New York: Public Affairs, 1999), 248. For a judicious examination of all the pertinent sources, see Steven Hoffmann, "Rethinking the Linkage between Tibet and the China–India Border Conflict: A Realist Approach," *Journal of Cold War Studies* 8, no. 3 (Summer 2006): 165–94.

62 UKHC India to CRO, 21 April 1959, FO 371/141592, TNA.

63 Record of the Prime Minister's Talk with the Dalai Lama, 24 April 1959, subject file 9, Subimal Dutt Papers, NMML. Also see, OHT Dalai Lama, 7–9, NMML.

64 John Garver, "China's Decision for War with India in 1962," *New Directions in the Study of China's Foreign Policy*, ed. Alastair Iain Johnston and Robert S. Ross, (Stanford: Stanford University Press), 93–4; Chen, "The Tibetan Rebellion of 1959," 86–8.

65 "The Revolution in Tibet and Nehru's Philosophy," *People's Daily*, 6 May 1959, cited in Gopal, *Nehru*, 3: 93, n. 104.

the communist bloc countries that Nehru's policy, deriving from his class nature, was to make Tibet a "buffer" state: "This is the centre of the China–India dispute."[66] This ideological perception of India's stance would play an important role in shaping the outcome of the incipient crisis.

The Skirmish at Longju: August 1959

To subdue the Tibetan rebellion China moved its forces to the frontier with India. The Indians too were engaged in fortifying their presence in these parts. Unsurprisingly, there were clashes. The first of these took place at Longju towards the end of August 1959 with both sides accusing the other of provocation. Beijing rightly pointed out that the Indian posts at Longju and two other points lay north of the McMahon Line as marked on the original maps of 1914. Delhi's view was that whatever the disputes about the alignment of the line the use of force was gratuitous. Nehru considered it "the culmination of progressive Chinese unfriendliness towards India."[67] In exchanges with China, India insisted that the McMahon Line was the boundary but expressed its readiness to discuss the alignment at contested places. Subsequently, India withdrew a post, agreeing it lay north of the boundary.

When the clash occurred the Indian government was already being questioned about the frontier on the basis of newspaper reports and leaks. The prime minister was asked in parliament whether China had refused to accept the McMahon Line. In keeping with his policy of not publicizing these issues, Nehru was evasive. Queried about the road through Aksai Chin, he conceded that China had built a road but said that though Indian maps showed the area within their territory the boundary was not clear. He distinguished between the McMahon Line and the boundary in Ladakh, which was not defined: "Nobody had marked it." It was an issue for discussion between the two sides.[68] At this point Delhi was prepared to discuss specific areas "in dispute or as yet unsettled," but not the "considerable regions" claimed

66 Garver, *Protracted Contest: Sino-Indian Rivalry in the Twentieth Century* (Seattle: University of Washington Press, 2001), 61–2; Garver, "China's Decision for War," 95.

67 Nehru to Macmillan, 30 September 1959, FO 371/141271, TNA.

68 *PMSIR: Parliament*, 1: 70, 85–6.

by Chinese maps. The Indians held NEFA to be "indisputably Indian territory." Whilst they also claimed Aksai Chin, they regarded the area "very remote and uninhabited" and pondered what steps to take regarding it.[69] They were also awaiting a reply to Nehru's letter of 22 March.

By this time several MPs thought the government had not been alert to China's activities and that important information was being withheld. To allay parliament's concerns the prime minister made detailed statements.[70] Nehru revealed his evolving position when he repeatedly stated that the boundary in Ladakh was not sufficiently defined and that Aksai Chin was a disputed area. He described it as a "barren uninhabited region without a vestige of grass," "peculiarly suited" for discussions. The road was admittedly "an important connection" for the Chinese. Ladakh was different from NEFA. The dispute in the former was a "minor" thing. India was prepared to discuss it on the basis of treaties, maps, usage, and geography.[71] Following a request he also agreed to release a white paper on these issues.

On 7 September the first white paper was published. The decision to release it was taken to stem the tide of criticism, and to demonstrate that the government had not been complacent. This proved a major miscalculation on Nehru's part; the paper served only to inflame parliamentary and public opinion and brought the government under intense, unremitting pressure. Nehru was pushed to a position were his diplomatic manoeuvrability was severely curtailed. Thenceforth he had to assess constantly what the political marketplace would bear, and to adopt only those policies which could conceivably be sold to the public.

The Longju incident also drew the attention of the external powers to the boundary dispute. On 6 September Beijing briefed the Soviet chargé d'affaires, Sergei Antonov, insisting that the Indians had initiated the clash.[72] The Soviet embassy, however, considered it "logical that the Chinese side had started the skirmishes:" Chinese actions

69 Report on conversations with secretary general and foreign secretary, UKHC India to CRO, 1 September 1959, DO 35/8819, TNA.

70 Hoffmann, *India and the China Crisis*, 67.

71 *PMSIR: Parliament*, 1: 101–4, 107–9, 123–4.

72 Chen, "The Tibetan Rebellion of 1959," 92.

during the Taiwan Straits crisis suggested as much.[73] From Moscow's standpoint the incident was most inopportune: Nikita Khrushchev was keenly looking forward to his impending visit to the US; and the Sino–Indian clash could undermine his tour. The Russians realized that if Moscow adopted a pro-China stand the Eisenhower administration would be cool towards Khrushchev.[74] Furthermore, Khrushchev wished to avoid rupturing ties with India, which had grown strong over the previous few years. He believed that Nehru, whilst not a communist, was certainly a force for progress.[75]

Consequently, Moscow decided to issue a statement adopting a neutral stance and calling on both the countries to resolve the dispute peacefully. As Khrushchev later explained it: "If we had not issued the TASS declaration, there could have been an impression that there was a united front of socialist countries against Nehru."[76] On 9 September Antonov handed Beijing a copy of the statement that would be released the following day. The Chinese responded that there was no need for Moscow to take a public stance. The Soviets would not be dissuaded, however.[77] Nehru welcomed the statement, describing it as very fair and unusual.[78]

Immediately after his American tour Khrushchev visited Beijing. The Sino–Indian dispute figured prominently in his discussions with the Chinese leadership. Indeed, Moscow's stand on the dispute opened a crevice in the Sino–Soviet relationship. Khrushchev squarely blamed

[73] Alexei Brezhnev, *Kitai* (Moskva: Mezhdunarodnye Otnosheniye, 1998), 70.

[74] Mikhail Kapitsa, *Na raznykh parallelyakh* (Moskva: Kniga i biznes, 1996), 63–4.

[75] Nikita Khrushchev, *Khrushchev Remembers: The Last Testament* (London: Andre Deutsch, 1974), 306.

[76] Roderick MacFarquhar, *The Origins of the Cultural Revolution 2: The Great Leap Forward, 1958–1960* (Oxford: Oxford University Press, 1983), 266.

[77] Chen, "The Tibetan Rebellion of 1959," 93–4; MacFarquhar, *Origins 2*, 259.

[78] Gopal, *Nehru*, 3: 99. In fact, the Soviets had already told the Indian ambassador in Beijing that they were going to issue a statement to this effect. Interview with Mira Sinha Bhattacharjea, 12 May 2005, New Delhi. Bhattacharjea was then serving in the Indian embassy in Beijing.

China for the events in Tibet: "If you allow him [the Dalai Lama] an opportunity to flee to India, then what had Nehru to do with it?" "The Hindus acted in Tibet as if it belonged to them," retorted Mao. The Chinese leaders accused Khrushchev of opportunism in supporting India: "The Tass announcement made all imperialists happy." Mao, however, told Khrushchev that China would respect the McMahon Line and that the boundary issue would be resolved by negotiations.[79]

In fact, on 8 September 1959 Mao had convened a politburo meeting to discuss the boundary dispute with India. According to one participant, the politburo agreed that China should seek a negotiation settlement and that prior to holding negotiations the status quo should be maintained.[80] The same day Zhou Enlai wrote to Nehru. He correctly argued that the boundary in the west had never been formally delimited. But Zhou claimed that the boundary shown by Chinese maps was in accord with "a customary line drawn from historical traditions" up to which China exercised administrative control. This last point would be strongly contested by India. Zhou contended that Nehru had misunderstood his statements on the McMahon Line. He had only stated that to maintain amity and facilitate negotiations Chinese troops would not cross the line. He also asserted that the boundary in this sector as shown in Chinese maps was a "true reflection" of the customary boundary before the so-called McMahon Line came up. Zhou wrote that he sought a settlement fair and reasonable to both sides but would not let India impose its one-sided claims on China.

Nehru was taken aback. He thought that China's claims in the east were "fantastic and absurd." Having given evasive answers about maps and having told him they accepted the McMahon Line, Beijing was not playing fair. It produced a "lack of confidence" in China's words and assurances. Indeed, China's claims were still unclear and open to the possibility of further extension. On Ladakh he told parliament on

---

[79] "Memorandum of conversation, 2 October 1962," *Cold War International History Project* (hereafter *CWIHP*) *Bulletin* 12/13 (Fall-Winter 2001), 266–70.

[80] M. Taylor Fravel, *Strong Borders, Secure Nation: Cooperation and Conflict in China's Territorial Disputes* (Princeton: Princeton University Press, 2008), 83.

two more occasions that the boundary was unclear. Yet in his reply to Zhou Nehru adopted a firm line. After laying out India's case for a "historical frontier" in all the sectors, he clarified that India would not entertain the latest Chinese claims. He also stated that talks could begin only after the Chinese withdrew their posts "opened in recent months" at certain places. The letter did not call for a Chinese withdrawal from Aksai Chin.

Nehru's main concern was China's "demand for considerable areas, *more especially in the NEFA.*" Their claims implied that they wanted to establish a presence on the Indian side of the Himalayan barrier. If they managed to do so, India's "basic security" would be "greatly endangered." Furthermore, the Himalaya were the most "vital part of India's thought and existence," and could not be gifted to the Chinese, a point he had also made in parliament.[81] Nehru's rejection of Chinese claims was thus based on considerations of security and nationalism. He and his advisers thought Beijing had advanced these claims with the aim of realizing "at least substantial parts of them." Officials in the MEA confided to the British envoy that Nehru's "uncompromising reply" was more "a bargaining position." Delhi was willing to make "some adjustments and concessions at various points."[82] Nehru turned down the Burmese premier U Nu's offer of mediation on the same grounds: India would not agree to "absurd" Chinese claims, and an effort by U Nu might suggest that India was anxious for a settlement, so hardening China's stance.[83]

Nehru's advisers differed in their assessment of Chinese behaviour. Some felt that it arose from the events in Tibet: China was behaving "aggressively without any long-term plan of aggression." The majority held a darker view. They feared that this might well be the "first stage in long-term Chinese ambitions to expand south of the Himalayas." These differences apart, the Indians were convinced that they had been "wantonly tricked" and that Beijing could "never again be

---

[81] 1 October 1959, G. Parthasarathi (ed.), *Letters to Chief Ministers 1947–1964* (New Delhi: Jawaharlal Nehru Memorial Fund, 1985–9), 5 vols, 5: 288 (emphasis added).

[82] Report on conversations, UKHC India to CRO, 10 October 1959, DO 35/8819, TNA.

[83] Nehru to U Nu, 29 September 1959, cited in Gopal, *Nehru*, 3: 98.

trusted." Any settlement might only be temporary as the Chinese were likely to revive their claims at a later date, whenever it suited them.[84]

The Clash at Kongka Pass: October 1959

The pessimistic appraisal came to prevail after the Kongka Pass incident. On 21 October 1959 an Indian police patrol was apparently ambushed near the pass, leaving five dead, four injured, and ten captured. Delhi's appreciation was that the Chinese had crept forward and occupied empty areas in Ladakh (beyond Aksai Chin) over the summer of 1959. Privately, Nehru still maintained that this was an "indefinite border." But he was now convinced that India had to face "a powerful country bent on spreading out to what they consider their old frontiers, and possibly beyond. The Chinese have always, in their past history, had the notion that any territory which they once occupied in the past necessarily belonged to them subsequently."[85] MEA officials thought Beijing wanted to annex areas up to its claim line in the western sector. They were doubtful that the Chinese would want to "shoot their way through;" it seemed more likely that they would seek to fill any vacuums in Ladakh.[86]

The Chinese claimed Kongka as a border pass and their version of the incident was diametrically opposed to India's. On 26 October Beijing issued a statement that if India continued to send its forces across the boundary claimed by China in the west, the Chinese would have reason to come south of the McMahon Line. In a note to his ambassadors abroad Nehru interpreted this as a warning that unless India made a territorial concession in Ladakh, China would start trouble in NEFA.[87] In the aftermath of the incident Nehru grew defiant: "we cannot agree to or submit to anything that affects India's honour and self-respect, and our integrity and independence."[88] His

[84] "Sino-Indian dispute" by UKHC India, 21 October 1959, FO 371/141272, TNA.

[85] Nehru's letter, 26 October 1959, *Letters to Chief Ministers*, 5: 303–13.

[86] Report on conversations with Secretary General, Deputy Secretary Eastern Division MEA, UKHC India to CRO, 3 November 1959, FO 371/141273, TNA.

[87] *Times of India*, 30 October 1959.

[88] Nehru's letter, 4 November 1959, *Letters to Chief Ministers*, 5: 322.

attitude also reflected the increasing pressure of public opinion. Addressing a public meeting after the incident he referred to the remarkable record of friendship with China and said it had been "vitiated a little of late." India could not take any steps in "anger or passion" and had to bear in mind the long-term consequences.[89] The speech drew the ire of the opposition and the press; a torrent of criticism descended upon Nehru.[90] In a speech delivered the next week, the placatory accent was muted. Nehru now spoke of Chinese arrogance and declared: "We will defend our country with all our might."

Nehru was confronted with increasing disapproval from his own party too. On 4 November 1959 he met over a hundred Congress MPs who exhorted him to take a stronger line. Nehru explained that this would not just increase tension but would make any agreement with China all the more difficult. The MPs were not satisfied with these explanations.[91] Nehru could hardly remain immune to the mounting deprecation. He wrote to Vijayalakshmi that the main newspapers were taking advantage of the "high pitch of excitement" on the border issue "to attack all our policies internal and external, and to make me a target of attack." Criticism by erstwhile colleagues like Jayaprakash Narayan and Rajagopalachari also stung.[92] In parliament he rejected calls for strong action against China and urged restraint: a showdown with China would be disastrous for it would entail great focus

[89] *Times of India*, 25 October 1959.

[90] The *Hindustan Times* (26 October) wrote: "to go on talking of our desire for friendly and peaceful relations is to compromise the nation's honour, so brutally tattered already." According to the *Indian Express* (Bombay) (26 October), Nehru's attitude had begun "increasingly to dismay the Indian people and embolden the Chinese." The *Times of India* (26 October) called upon Nehru to remove "any Chinese impression of Indian appeasement." On 28 October the *Hindustan Times* bemoaned "the present spectacle of our helplessness" and went on to say: "Mr. Nehru has been a great symbol of national stability, but we must have real fears that his capacity to unite the nation behind him can in certain circumstances be seriously impaired."

[91] Note on conversation with H.C. Heda, 5 November 1959, FO 371/141273, TNA.

[92] 3 & 7 November 1959, subject file 61, Vijayalakshmi Pandit Papers, NMML.

on military measures, and so divert resources from pressing domestic concerns. But India would not be cowed down by China. Nor would it abandon non-alignment and seek military assistance. The country's emphasis had to be on building the requisite industrial base for military strength. Nehru would reiterate these points on numerous occasions in the years ahead. Nonetheless, the prime minister was coming under increasing strain. According to one perceptive observer, "Much confidence had manifestly been lost in Nehru's conduct of foreign policy; his monopoly was cracked. By 1960 his monopoly was broken."[93]

On 3 November 1959 Mao convened an informal working meeting of senior leaders to consider the situation along the Sino–Indian borders. The Chinese military commanders in Tibet were raring to go by assaulting Indian positions. Mao refused their requests. Instead, he asked Zhou Enlai to advance two new proposals to India.[94] Four days later Zhou wrote to Nehru that pending delimitation of the border the status quo should be maintained. To obviate further clashes both sides should withdraw twenty kilometres from the McMahon Line in the east, and from "the line upto which each side exercises actual control in the west." Zhou also proposed talks at the prime ministerial level in the immediate future.[95]

China's proposal for a demilitarized zone was unacceptable to India on several grounds. The army argued that pulling back twenty kilometres from the McMahon Line was "absurd and unrealistic." The Chinese could approach the border by roads while the Indians had to traverse several mountain ridges; pulling back would amount to handing over control of the passes to the Chinese.[96] Delhi also felt that Beijing sought to equate India's possession of NEFA with Chinese control over Ladakh. They believed that the Chinese had come west of the Indian-claimed boundary in Ladakh only between 1956 and 1959.

---

[93] Walter Crocker, *Nehru: A Contemporary's Estimate* (London: George Allen and Unwin, 1966), 100. Crocker, then Australian high commissioner, was considered closest to Nehru among the western envoys in New Delhi.

[94] Fravel, *Strong Borders*, 84–5.

[95] Zhou to Nehru, *White Papers*, 3: 45–6.

[96] Report on conversation with CGS, 10 November 1959, DO 35/8820, TNA.

Moreover, they had not yet reached the line claimed by their maps. Beijing's idea of a "line of actual control" had no historical basis, nor did it accord with ground realities.[97] Besides, a mere twenty-kilometre withdrawal would leave the Chinese in effective control of most of the occupied territory.

In response Nehru suggested that patrolling be suspended in NEFA. In Ladakh, India should withdraw to the west of China's claim line and China to the east of India's claim line. He would meet Zhou only if these measures were implemented. This proposal was unacceptable to Beijing. It would imply the evacuation of nearly 20,000 square miles and abandonment of the road, whereas India would only have to give up about fifty square miles. Nehru was aware of the importance of the road to China and was interested in coupling his proposal with an offer to let China use the area through which the road ran. Because of opposition from the home minister, G.B. Pant, the offer had to be withheld.[98] Within a few days Nehru managed partially to convince his colleagues. In a press conference and in parliament he announced that as an interim measure India was prepared to allow the use of the Aksai Chin road for civilian traffic.

Nehru's proposals indicated a gradual hardening of India's stance on Aksai Chin. Hitherto, he had openly voiced his doubts about the strength of India's claims. After the clash at Kongka Pass, Nehru was disinclined to concede anything to China under duress. This attitude was bolstered by the growing pressure of parliamentary and public opinion. At this juncture the director of the MEA's historical division, Sarvepalli Gopal, returned from London where he had been studying the basis of India's claims in British archives. Gopal thought that India had a sound historical case for Aksai Chin and conveyed it to Nehru; but it was only in February 1960 that Gopal took Nehru through all the evidence and finally convinced him that India's claims to Aksai Chin were strong.[99] The available evidence suggests that until this point Nehru was thinking of Aksai Chin as a bargaining counter.

---

97 Hoffmann, *India and the China Crisis*, 80–1; Dutt, *With Nehru in the Foreign Office*, 124–5.

98 Gopal, *Nehru*, 3: 103.

99 Hoffmann, *India and the China Crisis*, 82–3.

THE DISPUTED INDIA–CHINA BOUNDARY 1948–1960   261

As R.K. Nehru recalled, "until 1960, we ourselves were not sure that the territory belonged to us and we were thinking in terms of giving up our claims as part of a satisfactory settlement."[100]

The Nehru–Zhou Delhi Summit of April 1960

Towards the end of January 1960 Nehru agreed to meet Zhou. The Indians thought that the correspondence was getting nowhere while a thick tension prevailed on the frontiers. As Nehru told Khrushchev, "Although for the moment there is no basis for negotiations, a personal meeting will generally be helpful . . . It will be unfortunate if tensions were to continue indefinitely."[101] Writing to Zhou, Nehru said there could be no negotiations on the ground that the entire boundary was undelimited: "Such a basis for negotiations would ignore past history, custom, tradition and international agreements." Underlying this position was the apprehension that if India gave up its stance that the boundary was a traditional one delimited by geography, custom, and treaty, the entire border would be up for bargaining. It would open the sluice gates to completely arbitrary and variable Chinese claims all along the frontier. In view of past Chinese conduct Delhi felt that it could ill afford to run the risk.[102] The earlier concerns about China's intentions were now buttressed by the conviction that the Chinese could not be trusted. These perceptions were accentuated by Nehru's belief that the Chinese leadership had personally deceived him. As Mountbatten observed, Nehru "was greatly shaken by their duplicity."[103]

From the end of 1959 Delhi felt that Beijing might come up with a proposal whereby China would forsake claims south of the McMahon

---

100 "India & China: Policy Alternatives," n.d., R. K. Nehru Papers, NMML.

101 Record of talk between Khrushchev and Nehru (in New Delhi), 12 February 1960, subject file 24, Subimal Dutt Papers, NMML.

102 Dutt, *With Nehru in the Foreign Office*, 131; Hoffmann, *India and the China Crisis*, 87.

103 Record of talks with Nehru, 13–15 May 1960, DO 35/8822, TNA. Also see OHT R.K. Nehru, OHT Kingsley Martin & Dorothy Woodman, NMML.

Line in return for India accepting its claims in Ladakh.[104] From India's standpoint this would entail giving up not just Aksai Chin but the entire area incorporated by the customary line up to which the Chinese claimed to exercise control. This solution was deemed unacceptable for a host of reasons. First, the idea of "barter," as it came to be called, was stoutly opposed by public opinion. Nehru acknowledged this when he reputedly stated: "If I give them that I shall no longer be Prime Minister of India—I will not do it."[105] It is difficult to judge whether an embattled Nehru was overreacting to public opinion. But we now know that his senior cabinet colleagues and officials also thought that he would be "out of office as Prime Minister" if he ceded territory.[106] Domestic pressures on Nehru can be gauged from the virulent reaction in parliament and in the press to his invitation to Zhou for talks. These were amply underscored by protests from the non-communist opposition parties prior to Zhou's visit, including the organization, by the right-wing Hindu party Jan Sangh, of a "no surrender week" and of a massive demonstration outside Nehru's residence. Second, Nehru himself felt that bartering would be incorrect given the manner in which the Chinese had used deceit and force to occupy the area.[107] From February 1960 onwards the Indian government was convinced that it had a strong case. Delhi saw no reason to relinquish its claims in a deal, particularly when public opinion was "passionate against any concession whatsoever." Third, in March 1960 the Indian Supreme Court pronounced on the government's boundary agreement with Pakistan over the Berubari enclave, involving transfer of some territory to East Pakistan. The ruling stated the executive did not have the authority to cede or accept territory: it would have to seek an amendment of the constitution on each occasion. This would require approval of a two-thirds majority in parliament and at least

104 Report on conversation with S. Gopal, 9 January 1960, UKHC India to CRO, FO 371/150440, TNA.

105 Maxwell, *India's China War*, 161.

106 Reports of conversations with Secretary General N.R. Pillai, 17 March 1960; Finance Minister Morarji Desai, 5 April 1960, UKHC India to CRO, DO 35/8822, TNA.

107 Ibid. Also see N.R. Pillai's views in Hoffmann, *India and the China Crisis*, 86.

half of the fourteen state legislatures. Given Nehru's enfeebled political position on China, securing an amendment would have been rather difficult. Last, and perhaps most important, the Indians had completely lost trust in their Chinese interlocutors. They believed that even if they acceded to China's claims in Ladakh, it would not be a "final settlement." The Chinese would only be emboldened to advance additional claims later. As the finance minister, Morarji Desai, told the British envoy, the cabinet was not prepared to allow Ladakh to become "the thin edge of a wedge."[108]

During this period the Indians were considering other alternatives too. These discussions were held very discreetly and were confined to Nehru, his senior cabinet colleagues, and some MEA officials. The Indians sought to come up with compromise solutions that would not involve formal relinquishment of territory. The outlines of such an idea did not crystallize until a few days before Zhou's arrival on 20 April 1960. As late as 1 April, the vice president Sarvepalli Radhakrishnan told the British high commissioner, Malcolm MacDonald, that there would be "a breakdown'" in talks.[109] The internal discussions seemed to have proceeded apace in the next few days. On 5 April Morarji Desai informed MacDonald that the Indian government "fully appreciated" the importance of the Aksai Chin road to the Chinese and that India was prepared to assure them continued use of the area. "But this would have to be done without any surrender of Indian sovereignty over the region."[110]

When Radhakrishnan met MacDonald a week later, Nehru's thinking on these lines had evolved further. Radhakrishnan made it clear that Nehru could not cede territory. India would want China to accept the McMahon Line. In Ladakh, if the Chinese accepted Indian sovereignty "in theory," the Indians would "agree to them remaining in practical occupation of the territory which they now occupied." They

108 Report on conversation with Morarji Desai, 5 April 1960, UKHC India to CRO, DO 35/8822, TNA. Also see Dutt, *With Nehru in the Foreign Office*, 131; Gopal's views in Hoffmann, *India and the China Crisis*, 87.

109 Record of conversation with the Vice President by MacDonald, 1 April 1960, FO 371/150440, TNA.

110 Report on conversation with Morarji Desai, 5 April 1960, UKHC India to CRO, DO 35/8822, TNA.

realized that the Chinese had established themselves there and were unlikely to get out; hence they had to "face facts." The right solution, therefore, was for "the Chinese to concede to us the shadow whilst we concede to them the substance" of sovereignty in Ladakh. This was a significant shift in the Indian position. As MacDonald wrote, "This shook me." Asked if India would station any administrative personnel in support of its sovereignty, Radhakrishnan replied in the negative. When MacDonald expressed "great surprise and disappointment" at India's changed stance, Radhakrishnan said that the whole idea was a "face saving" one. He reiterated that all faces could be saved if the Chinese yielded the "shadow" while the Indians yielded the "substance." Such an agreement may not be reached at this summit, but the Indians could reach a "tacit understanding" with the Chinese.[111]

The talks between Nehru and Zhou were held over several sessions but got nowhere.[112] The Indians understood that Zhou wanted to reach an agreement whereby China would recognize the status quo in the east, and in turn India would accept Chinese claims in the west. In the crucial western sector Zhou was unwilling to concede anything. He insisted that they had all along been in effective control of the area shown by their claim lines—a point strongly contested by Nehru. Delhi rejected such a bargain.[113] As Secretary General N.R. Pillai explained, public opinion apart, "if they [India] gave way now on this matter, it would only encourage the Chinese to feel that they were weak and to press even more ambitious claims later on."[114] In this scenario the Indian idea of ceding control of occupied areas in Ladakh to China in return for an acknowledgement of Indian sovereignty was

111 Record of conversation with Radhakrishnan by MacDonald, 12 April 1959, DO 35/8822, TNA.

112 Records of talks between Nehru and Zhou, 20 April to 25 April 1960, subject files 24 and 25, P.N. Haksar Papers, NMML. These files also contain records of discussions between the Chinese leaders and their Indian counterparts. For an unofficial contemporary account, see K. Natwar Singh, *My China Diary, 1956–88* (New Delhi: Rupa & Co, 2009), 89–110.

113 Foreign Secretary to Heads of Missions, 27 April 1960, subject file 25, P.N. Haksar Papers, NMML.

114 Report on conversation with N.R. Pillai, 25 April 1960, UKHC India to CRO, FO 371/150440, TNA.

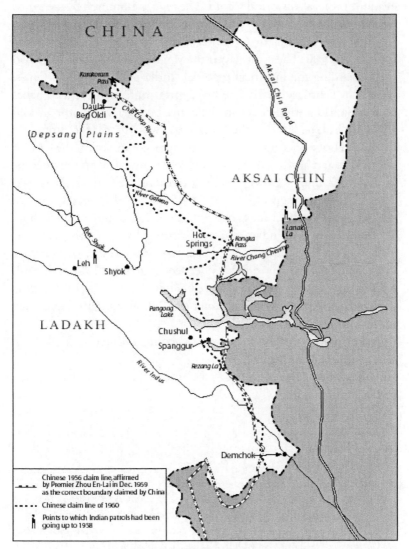

Map 7. China's 1956 and 1960 Claim Lines

a non-starter. The only point on which India assented to the Chinese proposals was on appointing a group of officials on both sides to examine the legal-historical record. The report submitted by the teams would then be considered by the prime ministers.

The teams met for three rounds of discussions between June and December 1960. These displayed the yawning gulf between the two sides regarding the historical material. India published the officials' reports in February 1961.[115] The reports confirmed Nehru's belief that India had a strong case on the entire boundary, including Aksai Chin. Indeed, he felt that the Indian case was "almost foolproof."[116] China did not evince interest in resuming negotiations on the basis of the reports and apparently continued to favour a deal on the lines indicated by Zhou.[117] During these discussions the Chinese produced a map depicting their claim line in Ladakh further to the west of the line shown in their maps of 1956, so incorporating an additional 2500 square miles of Indian-claimed territory. In fact Zhou had previously written to Nehru that the 1956 map was authoritative. Beijing insisted that there was no disparity between its maps of 1956 and 1960, a claim that only served to reinforce Delhi's opinion that the Chinese were untrustworthy. By the summer of 1960 meaningful diplomacy juddered to a halt.

But events on the ground began to acquire momentum.

[115] *Report of the Officials of the Government's of India and the People's Republic of China on the Boundary Question* (New Delhi, Ministry of External Affairs, 1961). For transcripts of the meetings, see Parshotam Mehra, *Negotiating with the Chinese, 1846–1947* (New Delhi: Reliance Publishing House, 1989). Also, Jagat S. Mehta, *Negotiating for India: Resolving Problems Through Diplomacy* (New Delhi: Manohar, 2006).

[116] Speech in Parliament, 20 February 1961, cited in Gopal, *Nehru*, 3: 206.

[117] Fravel, *Strong Borders*, 95–6.

8

China 1961–1962

I n the decade preceding the war with China, the Indian military
system underwent an important transition. The role of British
officers in command and advisory functions dwindled. In April
1954 the air force got its first Indian chief of staff; as did the navy four
years later. By the time the dispute with China came to the fore, the
Indian armed forces were staffed entirely by Indian officers. In retrospect it is clear that this transition was not unproblematic. Not because
Indian officers were in any way less capable than their British counterparts, but because several of them had less than adequate preparation
for higher command particularly at the strategic level. Owing to the
delayed "Indianization" of the officer corps during the Raj, the pool
of Indian officers with the requisite experience had been limited. In
consequence, several officers had had rapidly to climb up the chain of
command in independent India's armed forces.

Unsurprisingly, the transformation of the command structure did
not lead to any significant change in operational outlook. Indeed,
Indian military strategy *vis-à-vis* China until the late 1950s was marked more by continuities than ruptures. Until the clash at Longju,
India's frontiers with China continued to be manned by civilian border
police and the Assam Rifles. The army headquarters maintained that
"The Army should not be committed . . . for day to day border security . . . When, however, a situation arises on a particular border which
civil border police cannot cope with, the Army should assume overall
responsibility."[1] So in the wake of the Longju incident the army was

[1] Minutes of Meeting to consider the Blue Print drawn by the Army, 20 May
1959, subject file 79, Subimal Dutt Papers, NMML.

given control of the frontier areas. Military options to deal with the emerging Chinese threat also began to be debated.

But these debates were overshadowed by a sensational offer of resignation by the army chief, General K.S. Thimayya, and its subsequent withdrawal.

According to traditional accounts, Thimayya's resignation was sparked off by a disagreement with the defence minister, Krishna Menon, over the promotion of senior officers. Menon apparently wanted to promote officers who were close to him. Professional differences were aggravated by Menon's irascible personality.[2] A recent biographer claims that Thimayya was also worried about Menon's imperviousness to the need for raising and equipping additional forces to meet the threat from China.[3] All existing accounts agree that Nehru cleverly persuaded Thimayya to retract the resignation in order to protect Menon. But the evidence now available from Thimayya's own papers shows that the reasons for his resignation went rather deeper. In a sententious note on his conversation with Nehru towards the end of August 1959 Thimayya recalls discussing the "apathetic attitude of the Minister of Defence regarding Chinese moves" as compared to his "war-psuchosis [sic] against Pakistan." More important, he mentions Menon not wanting Nehru to meet President Ayub Khan of Pakistan,[4] a point requiring explanation. Thimayya raised it in connection with Ayub's proposed stopover at Delhi airport on 1 September. Earlier in the year, when Sino–Indian relations grew strained, Ayub proposed joint defence arrangements between India and Pakistan to counter China. Nehru brusquely turned this down for it would imply forsaking India's policy of non-alignment.[5] During Ayub's proposed meeting with Nehru it was believed that Pakistan's president would renew his offer.[6]

[2] Maxwell, *India's China War*, 189–91; Apurba Kundu, *Militarism in India: The Army and Civil Society in Consensus* (London: I.B. Taurus, 1998), 104–5.

[3] C.B. Khanduri, *Thimayya: An Amazing Life* (New Delhi: Knowledge World, 2006), 251.

[4] Note on conversation, n.d., Correspondence with J. Nehru, Thimayya Papers, NMML.

[5] Gopal, *Nehru*, 3: 91–2.

[6] As he reportedly did. *Statesman*, 2 September 1959.

Menon apparently thought that since the proposal was unacceptable Nehru should avoid meeting Ayub. Thimayya, however, felt that the problem with China had begun to assume alarming proportions and so regarded Ayub's idea favourably. The prime minister naturally deemed this an attempt by the army chief to interfere in matters of policy.[7] Nehru told Thimayya he would speak to Menon on all the issues. A few days later Menon reproached Thimayya for directly approaching the prime minister and suggested they resolve the differences themselves. When matters did not improve Thimayya sent his resignation to Nehru, claiming that it was "impossible" for him to function under Menon.[8] Nehru considered this a step to force his hand on Menon and on questions of policy. Without giving any assurances he convinced Thimayya to withdraw the resignation. By this time the matter had reached the press. When questioned in parliament Nehru played it down as arising out of temperamental differences. Nonetheless, the prime minister's concerns were obvious when he stressed that "civil authority is and must remain supreme."[9]

The Thimayya affair, then, was not so much about civilian interference in professional matters as about military intrusion into the realm of policy. The episode underlined the dilemma confronting the military leadership. On the one hand Thimayya was acutely aware of the threat which China could pose. On the other he thought India could never meet a major military challenge from China. Thimayya continued to hold this view even after retiring from office. As late as July 1962, a few months before the war, he wrote: "I cannot even as a soldier envisage India taking on China in an open conflict on its own . . . It must be left to the politicians and diplomats to ensure our security."[10] Given this attitude it is not surprising that the general staff failed to take steps towards adequate military measures.

[7] Report prepared on the eve of Thimayya's retirement titled "Krishna Menon & the Generals," by High Commissioner in India, 5 May 1961, DO 196/209, TNA.

[8] Kavic, *India's Quest for Security*; Thimayya to Nehru, 31 August 1959, Correspondence with J. Nehru, Thimayya Papers, NMML.

[9] *Hindu*, 3 September 1959.

[10] Thimayya's article in *Seminar*, cited in Guha, *India After Gandhi*, 330.

Military Preparations in 1960–1961

In September 1959 the director of military intelligence prepared an appreciation stating that a "major incursion" by the Chinese was unlikely. Based on an appraisal of Chinese military deployments he recommended positioning a brigade in Ladakh, a division with armour in Sikkim, and a division in NEFA. This would entail not only raising new formations but also surmounting logistical problems in redeploying troops; despite efforts dating back to the early 1950s, roads and communications along the frontiers had remained underdeveloped.[11]

The strategy envisioned by the general staff was to offer only token resistance at the frontier and prepare to confront the Chinese deep inside Indian territory. As an appreciation put it, "We will not rush forward to the border but fight from the ground of our own choosing, easily defensible and sustainable." At a briefing on 28 October 1959 the army chief stated that "in case of war, the government may have to accept loss of some territory initially but could rely on the army's ability to blunt major offensives in depth."[12] The prime minister concurred with his military advisers that the lack of communications was a serious problem. He also agreed it would not be possible "wholly [to] prevent incursions" along the entire frontier. Nehru was, however, given to understand that in the event of an attack "the balance of advantage progressively tilts in our favour."[13]

Considering the state of communications, this strategy made much sense. But it did not cater for alternative scenarios such as an attempt by the Chinese to grab chunks of territory close to the frontier without coming up to the main line of Indian defences; after all, this was a boundary dispute. Moreover, the force levels projected by the general staff assumed a limited attack of some kind. Thimayya himself admitted that "the measures would not be adequate to contain a major invasion."[14] The requirements for a larger invasion were apparently

[11] P.B. Sinha and A.A. Athale, *History of the Conflict with China, 1962* (New Delhi: History Division, Ministry of Defence, 1992), 65.

[12] Cited in Khanduri, *Thimayya*, 227, 273.

[13] Nehru's letter, 4 November 1959, *Letters to Chief Ministers*, 5: 326–8.

[14] UKHC India to CRO, 21 October 1959, FO 371/141272, TNA.

neither considered nor projected by the military. This was consonant with the military's belief that it was up to the politicians to ensure that such an attack did not occur.

After the clash at Kongka, the army decided to pull out 4 Division from Punjab and redeploy it in NEFA. In order to expedite the construction of roads, a Border Roads Organization was created in 1960. In NEFA, Operation Onkar was launched, which aimed at substantially increasing the number of paramilitary posts under command of the army. In Ladakh two militia battalions were inducted in April 1960; but a regular battalion was not stationed until a year later.[15]

Following the abortive summit with Nehru, Zhou Enlai wrote to Mao Zedong on 5 May 1960. He noted that since no agreement had been reached on suspension of patrolling in disputed areas, it was imperative to strengthen China's military presence in the western sector. Zhou suggested that Chinese force should seize the opportunity and the favourable weather to establish additional posts inside China's claim line. Mao approved the plan, which was then implemented under the supervision of Deng Xiaoping.[16]

From May 1960 onwards the IB periodically reported Chinese activity in Ladakh: "reconnaissance, probing, surveys and road-building much beyond the line claimed by them in 1956."[17] In consequence the government decided to set up additional posts and patrol unoccupied areas; but troops were enjoined to avoid clashes.[18] The army headquarters, however, refrained from giving firm orders for patrolling. The reasons for their caution were explained by the chief of general staff (CGS), Lieutenant General L.P. Sen, in a letter to the ministry of defence. Sen wrote that owing to logistical difficulties additional troops had not been inducted into Ladakh. If patrolling were intensified the Chinese might react sharply; and the army might be unable to counter a large-scale incursion. Civilian officials thought the army was

[15] Sinha and Athale, *Conflict with China*, 66–7. On the Border Roads Organization, also see, OHT, Kaul, 93–6, NMML.

[16] Fravel, *Strong Borders*, 177.

[17] Mullik, *Chinese Betrayal*, 306.

[18] Note for Prime Minister, 28 May 1960, subject file 42, Subimal Dutt Papers, NMML; Note for Director (North), 29 May 1950, subject file 43, ibid.

tardy in implementing important decisions. When asked for an explanation the general staff reiterated the problem of logistics.[19]

The civilians certainly underestimated the logistical constraints; but part of the problem lay with the military too. The latter's approach to their tasks is clear from the chiefs of staff paper of January 1961, which spelt out the overall requirements of the armed forces.[20] Regarding China the paper noted that they were required to "resist to the full *and evict* any further incursions or aggressions by China." The chiefs recommended an increase of two infantry divisions (one each for NEFA and Sikkim) and one infantry brigade (for the middle sector). These figures took into account the fact that the projected deployment of September 1959 had not yet been completed. After spelling out their requirements the chiefs added: "Should the nature of the war go beyond that of a limited war . . . and develop into a full-scale conflagration amounting to an invasion of our territory, then it would be beyond the capacity of our forces to prosecute war . . . beyond a short period, because of limitation on size, the paucity of available equipment and the lack of adequate logistical support."

As earlier, the military assumed that they would only have to cater for a limited conflict; the question of preparing to counter threats across a spectrum was overlooked; the strategic problem of dealing with territorial incursions was blithely evaded. The chiefs evidently sought to wage the kind of war with which they were most comfortable. Even here, scant thought was given to logistical requirements. The assessment of threats and counter-measures was crude: no effort had been made to forecast likely Chinese troops and logistics build-up. Assuming that they would have to prepare for a limited war, the chiefs projected only a modest increase in resources. But instead of asking for more they went on to claim that limited resources were a constraint in waging a higher intensity conflict—indeed in implementing existing orders. The paper showcased a remarkable lack of strategic judgement on the part of the professional military.

[19] Maxwell, *India's China War*, 201–2; Mankekar, *Guilty Men of 1962*, 144.

[20] This paragraph and the next draw upon D.K. Palit, *War in High Himalaya: Indian Army in Crisis, 1962* (London: Hurst, 1991), 79–83 (emphasis in the original).

The chiefs' paper was prepared at a time of rising concern over the People's Liberation Army's (PLA) activity in Ladakh. Intelligence reports in September and November 1960 had indicated that the Chinese were trying to move west of their new circular road. Inputs were also received about intrusions in south-east Ladakh and south of the river Chang Chenmo, and about the PLA's efforts to reroute a road via Hot Springs, west of the Kongka Pass. Krishna Menon wanted to prevent further advance by the Chinese in this area. An army post was installed at Hot Springs and other steps taken. Yet by the end of 1960 only Hot Springs and parts of south-east Ladakh were deemed adequately secure.[21]

India's "Forward Policy" in Late 1961

The chiefs' inability to formulate specific proposals to meet such incursions left the initiative for planning in the hands of civilians. The issue was discussed in January or early February 1961 at a meeting of the cabinet's Foreign Affairs Committee. Krishna Menon suggested the idea of "zigzagging:" if the Chinese placed their posts further within Indian-claimed areas, the Indians could place posts behind them in areas which were claimed by China but unoccupied.[22] This would prevent the Chinese from establishing another "line of control" west of the existing one. But no action was initiated, presumably because of the logistical difficulties cited by the army.

In September 1961 Delhi discovered that the PLA had already established a post in the Chip Chap valley a mere four miles east of the Indian post at Daulat Beg Oldi. Vehicular traffic was observed close to the Chinese post and their troops attempted to capture an Indian patrol.[23] The MEA concluded from these reports that China was pushing forward towards its 1960 claim line, thereby occupying further Indian-claimed territory. The foreign secretary, M.J. Desai, took up the matter with the army.

A few months earlier, a new team of officers had taken over at the army headquarters. Thimayya had retired and been replaced by

---

[21] Mullik, *Chinese Betrayal*, 307–9.
[22] Hoffmann, *India and the China Crisis*, 95.
[23] Mullik, *Chinese Betrayal*, 312; Palit, *War in High Himalaya*, 95.

General P.N. Thapar; B.M. Kaul had taken over as his CGS. Thapar and Kaul are often portrayed as "courtier soldiers" in contrast to the "old-guard professionals" they had replaced.[24] The distinction is at once superficial and misleading. For one thing it obfuscates the continuities with the previous dispensation. Thimayya's CGS, L.P. Sen, for instance, would play a crucial role in the unfolding drama as the eastern army commander. More important, while it is possible that the government chose its senior military advisers for political pliability, it was the military system that had pushed officers like Thapar to the top. Thapar was the seniormost amongst the candidates for the slot: he had served as independent India's first director of military operations (DMO) and performed well subsequently. Besides, the appointment of the army chief had always been driven by political considerations. Thimayya himself had been chosen because of his acceptability to the political leadership.[25] In any event, the new team was more cooperative with Menon and established additional posts in Ladakh.[26]

Following the Chip Chap valley incident, the foreign secretary, Desai, wanted the army to take a more robust stance and reinforce the deterrent effect of Indian posts by active measures. He suggested that "one of the most effective methods of stemming Chinese policy of gradually creeping westwards across our borders in Ladakh would be to give them an occasional knock during these chance encounters . . . [and] to engage them in a short offensive action aimed at inflicting casualties and/or taking prisoners." The DMO, Brigadier D.K. Palit, explained to Desai that if Indian troops got engaged in action in such places they could not be reinforced or replenished owing to poor logistics. Eventually the IB was asked for an assessment of Chinese capabilities and intent.[27]

[24] For instance, Neville Maxwell, *China's "Aggression" of 1962 and the Unresolved Border Dispute* (Oxford: Court Place Books, 1999), 15.

[25] These facts were drawn to Neville Maxwell's attention while he was researching his book *India's China War*. His informant was General Roy Bucher, the British officer who served as India's army chief in 1948–9. Maxwell, however, chose to suppress this information. See Bucher to Maxwell, 4 June 1969, and Maxwell's reply, 19 June 1969, 7901-87/29, Bucher Papers, NAM.

[26] Mullik, *Chinese Betrayal*, 310–11.

[27] Palit, *War in High Himalaya*, 95–6.

On 26 September 1961 the IB submitted a comprehensive paper stating that "the Chinese would like to come right up to their claim of 1960 wherever we ourselves were not in occupation. But where even a dozen men of ours are present, the Chinese have kept away." The IB recommended opening posts in the unoccupied areas of Ladakh and filling gaps along the McMahon Line.[28] The tenor of the paper was that China would not react sharply to these moves. This assumption soon became an article of faith for military as well as civilian officials in Delhi. CGS Kaul wrote to the ministry of defence elucidating the logistical challenges involved in setting up new posts;[29] but the general staff did not question the IB's assumption about benign Chinese reaction. In October, Krishna Menon held several meetings with Thapar and Kaul, taunting them about the army's torpidity. Menon seems to have been concerned both by briefings from the director of the IB, B.N. Mullik, and by the tough questioning in parliament regarding the latest Chinese intrusions.[30]

Mullik was conveying his assessment to the prime minister, too. Over three meetings he explained the extent of Chinese penetration since October 1959 and the areas where gaps existed into which they "might intrude any moment."[31] Inactivity at this stage would not only result in a *fait accompli* but also have serious domestic repercussions. On 2 November 1961 Nehru held a meeting with his civilian and military advisers to discuss measures to meet the developing situation. The following directive was issued:

(a)   So far as Ladakh is concerned we are to patrol as far forward as possible from our present positions towards the international border. This will be done with a view to establishing our posts which should prevent the Chinese from advancing any further and also dominating from any posts which they may have already established in our terri-

---

[28] Ibid., 97–8.

[29] Ibid., 103.

[30] Hoffmann, *India and the China Crisis*, 97; Mullik, *Chinese Betrayal*, 314. Moreover, in a secret meeting leaders of the parliamentary opposition had caustically remonstrated with Nehru about the situation in the frontier. See B.M. Kaul, *The Untold Story* (New Delhi: Allied Publishers, 1967), 279.

[31] Mullik, *Chinese Betrayal*, 314.

tory. This must be done without getting involved in a clash with the Chinese unless this becomes necessary in self-defence.

(b) As regards U.P. [middle sector] and other northern areas there are not the same difficulties as in Ladakh. We should, therefore, as far as practicable, go forward and be in effective occupation of the whole frontier. Where there are any gaps they must be covered either by patrolling or by posts.

(c) In view of the numerous operational and administrative difficulties, efforts should be made to position major concentrations of forces along our borders in places conveniently situated behind the forward posts from where they could be maintained logistically and from where they can restore a border situation at short notice.[32]

The "forward policy," as it came to be called, aimed at deterring further Chinese incursions by installing posts and ensuring patrolling. By so doing, India sought to convince China that any fresh advance would be resisted. The directive reflected Nehru's cautious approach and his desire to control escalation. It was in marked contrast to M.J. Desai's suggestion, which undoubtedly carried a higher risk of escalation.

The directive acknowledged the problems voiced by the military during the meeting and gave them adequate leeway in implementation. Nehru had been told that owing to numerical and logistical problems India could not keep up in a race with the Chinese; ultimately, the PLA's superiority could render the Indian posts operationally untenable. Thapar had observed that the new posts could be supported neither tactically nor logistically. The prime minister had remarked, however, that he did not expect a battle with the Chinese. And the military leaders had not pressed their point.[33]

The directive was shown in draft by MEA officials to Kaul and was issued with his approval. Kaul felt that the army headquarters had the whole winter to create sufficient logistical back-up using airlift. He also appears to have drawn comfort in Mullik's assurance during the meeting that China would not contest Indian moves with force.[34] The

[32] Maxwell, *India's China War*, 221–2; Palit, *War in High Himalaya*, 107. Also see Sinha and Athale, *Conflict with China*, 86–7, nn. 89, 92.

[33] Kaul, *Untold Story*, 280; Palit, *War in High Himalaya*, 106; Hoffmann, *India and the China Crisis*, 98.

[34] Palit, *War in High Himalaya*, 105, 110.

army chief was not quite convinced by Mullik's assessment. In a letter to the defence minister Thapar registered his concerns; yet he was prepared to execute the strategy.[35] Furthermore, in his instructions to the operational headquarters the point about troop concentrations in the rear was not mentioned. The available evidence shows the omission was deliberate,[36] though the rationale remains unclear. Whatever the general staff's reasoning, it ran counter to the prime minister's thinking. Nehru's statements in parliament confirm that the concentrations of forces were integral to his conception of the forward policy. The army headquarters' instructions contravened his directive, and apparently did so without his knowledge.[37]

Kaul and Thapar went along with civilian advocates of the forward policy despite initial reservations. In this instance, as in subsequent ones, personality and proximity to political leadership only partly account for their stance. The nub of the problem was that the military leadership had no alternatives to offer, no unanimous "professional judgement" that applied to the situation. This vacuum was best illustrated by the DMO, Brigadier D.K. Palit, who proposed to Kaul that in light of the logistical problems it would be best for the army to hand back control of the frontiers to the IB.[38] Criticism of the top military commanders for not "standing up" to the civilians—a recurrent theme in writings on the war—largely misses the point.[39]

[35] Sinha and Athale, *Conflict with China*, 86, n. 91.

[36] Thapar later wrote that such a build-up would have taken years, by which time the Chinese would have occupied large parts of Indian territory. See P.N. Thapar, "The Chinese Invasion," *Statesman*, 9 January 1971. Palit claims that Nehru had not mentioned this point in his instructions; it was added as an afterthought by the MEA to hedge their bets and was credulously accepted by Kaul. But Palit's testimony is dubious. His own account states that when informed of the necessity for tactical support, Nehru had asked what exactly was meant by it. He was told that it was the availability of reserves and reinforcements in case of a firefight: Palit, *War in High Himalaya*, 106. This was the point mentioned in the final paragraph of the directive.

[37] Gopal, *Nehru*, 3: 208–9; Maxwell, *India's China War*, 223–4.

[38] Palit, *War in High Himalaya*, 109.

[39] This angle is explored in Srinath Raghavan, "Civil–Military Relations in India: The China Crisis and After," *Journal of Strategic Studies* 32, no. 1 (February 2009), 149–75.

Another criticism commonly levelled at Nehru and Krishna Menon is that they ignored the military's demands for purchasing weapons and equipment from other countries and that the military budget was actually reduced in the years 1960–2. There is force to this argument. Indeed, after the war broke Nehru himself acknowledged lapses on this count. As he wrote to Menon, "we have been found lacking and there is an impression that we have approached these things in a somewhat amateurish way."[40] Nevertheless, in evaluating the procurement policy three factors need to be considered. First, while the overall budgetary allocation for the military was marginally reduced, this did not necessarily impact on the military's projected requirements to meet the Chinese threat. As seen earlier, even in 1961 the chiefs of staff were only asking for modest increases for this purpose, which could have been met from within the existing defence budget. Second, Thapar and Kaul did make efforts to draw the political leadership's attention to the shortages in weapons and equipment, particularly in the spring and summer of 1962. But the urgency of these warnings would have been considerably diluted by the drift of other reports sent by the army headquarters. For instance, in June 1962 Kaul wrote: "I am convinced that the Chinese will not attack any of our positions even if they [Indian posts] are relatively weaker than theirs."[41] Third, and perhaps most important, at this time India faced a potentially grave balance of payments situation. As a trusted adviser on financial policy wrote to Nehru: "the need for immediate tightening up of all expenditure of foreign currency of any massive kind is very great. It is also necessary to take stock of position as it is today. All this will need some kind of freeze."[42]

The forward policy decision also indicated serious flaws in the assessment and utilization of intelligence. In asking the IB for an evaluation of likely Chinese reactions the MEA and army headquarters overlooked a basic tenet of intelligence assessment: the reporting agency should not be asked to assess its own reports. This task fell under the purview of the JIC, which was a sub-council of the chiefs

---

[40] Gopal, *Nehru*, 3: 224.

[41] Cited in Sinha and Athale, *Conflict with China*, 82, n. 59.

[42] Krishnamachari to Nehru, 13 June 1962, Correspondence with Nehru (1962), T.T. Krishnamachari Papers, NMML.

of staff committee. The JIC, however, was defunct.[43] Its chairman, K.L. Mehta, a senior MEA official, had no prior exposure to intelligence, and by his own admission he was unable to get the committee to function in a co-ordinated manner.[44] The directorate of military intelligence was a key component of the JIC. But it neither possessed independent intelligence sources nor was effective in producing threat assessments.[45] In this situation the IB was asked both to gather intelligence and generate assessments.

The prime minister's views on the unlikelihood of an armed confrontation with China were based on political calculations; the IB's assessments only supplemented them. At least since the end of 1950 Nehru had discounted the possibility of a major attack by China owing to international factors. He thought an attack on India would invariably carry the risk of great power intervention.[46] Back in the mid-1950s Nehru may have thought India's friendship would act as an additional restraint on China. But from late 1959 Nehru no longer set much store by Beijing's good will. Still, he believed that "an out-and-out Chinese invasion" was improbable. As he told a meeting of the Congress Party, "the Chinese are unlikely to invade India because they know that this would start a world war, which the Chinese cannot want."[47]

Nehru reiterated this point in interviews and speeches when the forward policy was being set in motion. He told the *Guardian* that any major Chinese aggression would trigger a wider war, which would not be fought on India's frontiers alone.[48] For the same reason, he

[43] K. Subrahmanyam, "Nehru and the India-China Conflict of 1962," in B.R. Nanda (ed.), *Indian Foreign Policy: The Nehru Years* (New Delhi: Vikas, 1976), 122–3.

[44] K.L. Mehta, *In Different Worlds: From Haveli to Head Hunters of Tuensang* (New Delhi: Lancer, 1985), 168.

[45] Only after the war did the chiefs start paying greater attention to the military intelligence organization and the JIC. See Minutes of discussion between Military Affairs Committee and Lord Mountbatten, 1 May 1963, subject file 27, T.T. Krishnamachari Papers, NMML.

[46] See, for example, Note, 18 November 1950, *SWJN-SS*, 15, pt II: 342–6; Letter to Chief Ministers, 1 December 1953, *SWJN-SS*, 24: 680–1.

[47] UKHC India to CRO, 21 October 1959, FO 371/141272, TNA.

[48] Interview with Nehru in the *Guardian*, 23 October 1961.

told parliament that China would not resort to large-scale military action: "one must not go by all the brave words that are said in these communications to us by the Chinese Government. But other factors work also."[49] These assumptions were evidently shared by the prime minister's most senior and closest advisers. R.K. Nehru, for instance, told Zhou Enlai that "war between two countries like India and China could not be a small affair. It would involve the whole world."[50] Looking back after the war Krishna Menon observed: "I am not even now sure that the Chinese did not think we were much more powerful than we were (in 1962)—that the whole of America would be behind us with the threat to invade China from its underbelly. It may have been a foolish idea—but it was there."[51]

Among the "other factors" Nehru alluded to was the role of the Soviet Union. In his assessment this was of greater significance. As early as 1949 Nehru had thought that despite being a communist state China would not be subservient to the USSR. As Nehru told Liddell Hart, whatever the short-term behaviour, in the long run the attitudes and the policies of the PRC would be moulded by Chinese nationalism rather than communism.[52] Subsequently, Nehru was impressed by reports from the Indian ambassador in the USSR that Mao had negotiated on equal terms with the Soviet leaders while concluding the 1950 Sino–Soviet agreement. "He was in no sense a subordinate."[53] From the early 1950s Nehru had thought that a Sino–Soviet split was likely to occur. This stemmed from his belief that nationalism was a stronger force in international politics than ideological solidarity. The interests of two major powers like the Soviet Union and China

---

[49] Speeches in Parliament on 5 and 6 December 1961, cited in Gopal, *Nehru*, 3: 209.

[50] Record of conversation between R.K. Nehru, and Zhou Enlai and Chen Yi, 21 April 1960, subject file 26, P.N. Haksar Papers, NMML.

[51] Michael Brecher, *India and World Politics: Krishna Menon's View of the World* (London: Oxford University Press, 1968), 152.

[52] Talk with Nehru, 25 April 1949, LH 11/1949/15, Liddell Hart Papers, LHCMA.

[53] Report of conversation with Indian Ambassador-elect to China, N. Raghavan, British Legation to the Holy See to Foreign Secretary, 30 May 1952, DO 35/8817, TNA.

would collide at some point: "China was a great power and was bound to function as such."[54]

The Tass statement after the Longju incident convinced Nehru that the USSR had its own interests in not overtly supporting China. The Soviets, he told the British envoy, were by no means pleased at the prospect of China growing stronger; this was one of the reasons why Khrushchev sought to improve relations with the US. More important, Nehru thought that the USSR had begun to regard India as "a balancing force in relation to China in Asia."[55] A corollary to this was that "the Soviet Union cannot wish to see Chinese action drive India right into the western camp."[56] The ambassador in Moscow, K.P.S. Menon, later recalled that following the Longju incident he was certain that the USSR preferred a friendly India to a cantankerous China.[57]

This reading of the situation was strengthened by Khrushchev's visit to India just before Nehru met Zhou in 1960. In discussions Khrushchev told Nehru that the Soviet Union "took no definite stand [on the Sino–Indian dispute] and will do our best to hold that line . . . This conflict is a sop to aggressive forces and is against the interest of the forces working for peace."[58] Nehru subsequently told Mountbatten that the visit was "clearly support for India and a slap in the face for China."[59] Nehru's thinking would have been buttressed by the

[54] Nehru's note on conversation with US ambassador, Loy Henderson, 15 September 1951, subject file 56, Vijayalakshmi Pandit Papers, NMML. Also see Nehru to Vijayalakshmi Pandit, 30 August 1950, subject file 60, ibid.; and Gopal, *Nehru*, 3: 80.

[55] Record of conversation with Nehru, 17 October 1959, FO 371/141272, TNA.

[56] UKHC India to CRO, 21 October 1959, ibid. Nehru subsequently reiterated his view that the Soviet Union would exercise a restraining influence on China. See entry of 4 January 1960, MS Macmillan dep. c.21/1, Harold Macmillan Diaries, Bodleian Library, Oxford. Similar views were also expressed by Secretary General Pillai. UKHC India to CRO, 3 November 1959, FO 371/141272, TNA.

[57] K.P.S. Menon, "India and the Soviet Union," in *Indian Foreign Policy: The Nehru Years*, 144–5.

[58] Record of talk between Khrushchev and Nehru, 12 February 1960, subject file 24, Subimal Dutt Papers, NMML.

[59] Record of talks with Nehru by Mountbatten, 13–15 May 1960, DO

dispatches from Moscow. K.P.S. Menon wrote in detail about the Sino–Soviet ideological controversy, which came to the fore in 1960 especially at the congress of the Romanian Workers' Party in Bucharest; the PRC's opposition to Khrushchev's policy of peaceful coexistence; and the withdrawal of Soviet advisers and technicians from China. Menon, moreover, reported that Khrushchev had assured him that "so far as Indo–Soviet friendship was concerned there was not a single cloud on the sky. Even the clouds which have settled on our [India's] frontier . . . left no shadow on the sunny landscape of Indo-Soviet friendship."[60]

Nehru did not prematurely conclude that Sino–Soviet relations had fractured and that the USSR would militarily assist India. Rather, he thought that such a split would not occur for a few years. Although fundamental differences were crystallizing, the Soviet Union and China still needed to act in concert.[61] In this scenario the Soviets would have greater interest and leverage in preventing the Chinese from launching a war with India. During his visit to the US in November 1961 Nehru privately reiterated his belief that "Khrushchev sees India as a future bulwark against China and that it is in Soviet interest to help restrain Peking."[62] The Australian high commissioner in Delhi, Walter Crocker, astutely observed that Nehru regarded the Soviet Union as the "best insurance" in dealing with the PRC.[63]

These calculations were central to Nehru's conception of the forward policy as a form of deterrence: they led him to believe that China would not overreact to India's moves. The military chiefs had earlier

---

35/8822, TNA. On China's reaction to Khrushchev's visit, Chen, "The Tibetan Rebellion of 1959," 97–8.

[60] Annual Report for 1960 from Indian Ambassador to USSR, n.d., subject file 5, K.P.S. Menon Papers, NMML.

[61] Nehru's remarks at Commonwealth conference, 3 May 1960, cited in Gopal, *Nehru*, 3: 141; Report of conversation with Nehru by Averill Harriman, 24 March 1961, *FRUS 1961–63*, 19: 30–1.

[62] Selig S. Harrison, "South Asia and US Policy," *The New Republic* (Washington, D.C.), 11 December 1961, 11–16.

[63] "Ten Years Observing India," Walter Crocker to Garfield Barwick (Australian Minister of State for External Affairs), 6 February 1962, DO 196/211, TNA.

stated that they could only handle a limited war with China; the prime minister did not foresee a major conflict. The forward policy, then, was based on loose assumptions by the civilian and military leadership which were mutually reinforcing. Adding to its precariousness was the absence of functional institutional mechanisms to subject inchoate ideas like "limited conflict" and "major invasion" to tough-minded analysis, and to consider the gamut of courses open to both sides and their likely consequences.

Deterring piecemeal advances by the PLA was only one component of Nehru's approach. The problem, he thought, could only be solved through a negotiated settlement. As Krishna Menon recalled, "We expected negotiation and diplomacy to play their part."[64] The pressure of international opinion together with a demonstration of India's resolve would help create the conditions for such a settlement. But this would have to be done cautiously to obviate the possibility of escalation. As Nehru told parliament, "it would be an utter absence of prudence to rush into some step, the end of which we cannot see."[65] The diplomatic steps towards a settlement began to be considered in early 1962. Delhi hoped to convince the PRC of the strength of India's claims on the basis of the officials' reports; China's interest in Aksai Chin could then be accommodated without formal transfer of sovereignty. This accorded with Nehru's thinking prior to the summit of 1960.

Apart from persuading the Chinese, the major problem was domestic opinion. Nehru knew that any overtures on his part prior to conciliatory moves by Beijing would strongly be resented. China should at least indicate willingness to pull back from Ladakh, though India would not insist on a physical withdrawal. Nehru asked the Burmese premier, U Nu, to convey his thinking to the Chinese leadership. But Beijing did not respond.[66] Delhi continued to think that even a "token withdrawal" by China could pave the way for a settlement.[67] An alternative being considered was that both sides would withdraw

[64] Brecher, *India and World Politics*, 151.

[65] Speech, 19 March 1962, *PMSIR: Parliament*, 2: 82–3.

[66] Note of discussion with U Nu, 13 January 1962, cited in Gopal, *Nehru*, 3: 210.

[67] Report of conversation with joint secretary MEA, 17 March 1962, UKHC India to CRO, FO 371/164910, TNA.

behind the boundary claimed by the other in Ladakh, which would create an administrative no-man's land. China could continue using the road, and the question of sovereignty could be held in abeyance.[68]

In early 1962 Beijing, too, was reconsidering its foreign policy. These deliberations were prompted by the calamitous failure of the Great Leap Forward. Wang Jiaxiang, a former ambassador to the Soviet Union, suggested that the government should focus its energies on critical domestic problems and adopt more placatory foreign policies to preclude crises with the US, the USSR, and India. With regard to India, Wang appeared to advocate at least a partial revival of the "Bandung line" of the mid-1950s, i.e. to consider non-communist Third World countries as allies in the struggle against imperialism. This policy had been discarded because of the 1959 border clashes with India and the Sino–Soviet dispute. Wang also called for new methods to break the impasse over the boundary dispute.[69]

Between February and June 1962 Wang presented his ideas to several Chinese leaders, including Liu Shaoqi, Zhou Enlai, Deng Xiaoping, and Chen Yi. During this period Mao had temporarily withdrawn from day-to-day government affairs, leaving Liu in charge. Wang's ideas—later dubbed "the three reconciliations and the one reduction"—were fully endorsed by Liu and Deng.[70] But these ideas would come under increasing strain because of India's forward policy, important developments *vis-à-vis* the US, and Mao's return to the helm in August 1962.

The Indian Forward Policy in Ladakh

Before establishing posts in Ladakh, the army headquarters asked the western command to submit an assessment of force requirements. The latter placed its requirements at a full division with artillery, and also "expressed alarm" at having to take on additional tasks without an

[68] Report of conversation with secretary general MEA, 19 March 1962, UKHC India to CRO, FO 371/164911, TNA.

[69] Roderick MacFarquhar, *The Origins of the Cultural Revolution 3: The Coming of the Cataclysm 1961–1966* (Oxford: Oxford University Press, 1997), 269–73; Niu Jun, "1962: The Eve of the Left Turn in China's Foreign Policy," *CWIHP Working Paper* 48 (October 2005), 28–9.

[70] MacFarquhar, *Origins 3*, 270–1.

increase in logistical resources.[71] The army headquarters, however, decided to establish posts in "penny pockets [*sic*] rather than wait for substantial build-up."[72] In March–April 1962 posts with barely 10–20 troops were sited in the Depsang plains and the Chip Chap valley.

Beijing thought the Indians were "nibbling" at Chinese territory; if they did not contest these moves it would result in a new line of control favourable to India. The PRC decided to counter-coerce India by establishing posts encircling the new Indian ones. Mao called this a policy of "armed coexistence." Yet the Chinese were mindful of the potential costs of a major offensive against Indian positions. The PLA was instructed to avoid skirmishes and not open fire without permission from higher quarters. Mao knew that the military balance strongly favoured China but thought that the PLA could not "blindly" take on the Indian forces: "We must pay attention to the situation."[73] Beijing was already feeling "severely threatened on their southern border" by American involvement in Laos and Vietnam. Their concerns were amplified by the Kennedy administration's announcement in May 1962 that US troops would be stationed in Thailand. Chinese leaders were also concerned about their south-east coast. They believed Jiang Jieshi (Chiang Kai-shek) would try to take advantage of the mainland's economic problems and launch a military attack along with the US.[74] Mao was, in consequence, cautious of using force against India.

Towards the end of April, after several notes protesting Indian moves, Beijing announced the resumption of forward patrolling in Ladakh and warned that it would be extended to the entire frontier. Despite inducting an additional battalion into Ladakh the Indians could not match the PLA's numerical and logistical superiority. By September 1962 they could install only 36 posts as against 47 Chinese posts. The latter were also qualitatively superior; for they were sited on dominating heights whilst the Indians had to establish their posts on valley floors where dropping zones were available.[75]

[71] Palit, *War in High Himalaya*, 155–7.

[72] Sinha and Athale, *Conflict with China*, 69–70.

[73] Garver, "China's Decision for War," 107–8.

[74] Niu "1962," 24–5, 27.

[75] China's note, 30 April 1962, *White Paper*, 6: 37–40; Sinha and Athale, *Conflict with China*, 69–70; Hoffmann, *India and the China Crisis*, 104.

On 6 May about 100 Chinese troops, in "assault formation," advanced towards an Indian post in the Chip Chap valley. The western army commander, Lieutenant General Daulet Singh, sought the army chief's permission immediately to pull back the post. Thapar and DMO Palit felt that if they withdrew the first post to be threatened, it would signal a lack of resolve. Furthermore, it would encourage the PLA to adopt similar tactics against all other posts and so unravel the forward policy. The prime minister thought China's menacing move was "a show of force" to test India's resolution. He directed that the post should stand firm and be reinforced: this was necessary to study the "behaviour pattern of Chinese aggression [*sic*]." In the event the Chinese backed off without attacking.[76]

The army chief and the CGS concluded that the incident vindicated their assumptions about Chinese reactions, and that the forward policy could be pursued without much risk.[77] Nevertheless, it was a minor escalation and cause for concern to Nehru. Delhi now sought to offer an inducement to China. The Indian government called for both sides to withdraw behind the line claimed by the other in Ladakh, and offered the use of the Aksai Chin road for civilian traffic. Nehru knew that this would entail "a very small" withdrawal for India and "a large withdrawal" for the PRC; but he emphasized the continued use of the road by China.[78] Not only had this idea been under consideration in Delhi, it had been discussed by Krishna Menon, Chen Yi, and the Soviet foreign minister Andrei Gromyko. They had agreed that this proposal would create a suitable environment for further negotiations.[79] Beijing, however, rejected the offer. Aksai Chin was their territory, they said, and it was preposterous to suggest that they needed India's permission to use the road: "Is China a defeated country?"[80]

[76] Palit, *War in High Himalaya*, 173–4. Also see Maxwell, *India's China War*, 237.

[77] Palit, *War in High Himalaya*, 175–6.

[78] India's note, 14 May 1962, *White Paper*, 6: 41–3; Nehru's statement, 14 May 1962, *PMSIR: Parliament*, 2: 94.

[79] P.K. Banerjee, *My Peking Memoirs of the Chinese Invasion of India* (New Delhi: Clarion Books, 1990), 40.

[80] China's note, 2 June 1962, *White Paper*, 6: 56–8.

The next flashpoint in this war of nerves was the Galwan valley. On 4 July 1962 a platoon of Gorkhas established a post in the upper reaches of the Galwan. The Chinese construed it as a premeditated attempt to cut the lines of communication of their post nearby; their reaction was "immediate and violent." By 10 July the PLA had surrounded the post, sealed off all possible withdrawal routes, and advanced within a hundred yards of the post.[81] The *People's Daily* carried a lurid headline: "The Indian Government Should Rein in on the Brink of the Precipice."[82] The MEA warned the Chinese ambassador of grave consequences should their troops come any closer to the post.[83] Following a cabinet meeting on 13 July, instructions were issued to the post to fire if the Chinese crept ahead. The same day the MEA reiterated to the Chinese envoy that India was determined to hold the post at all costs. The PLA pulled back slightly the following day but continued to surround the post. The Indian press and some politicians portrayed the outcome as a major triumph. The foreign and defence ministries, however, took a grim view of the incident.[84] The Galwan confrontation triggered further moves by the PLA to surround Indian posts and isolate them from the dropping zones, actions that led to a rash of shooting incidents.[85]

Diplomacy and Domestic Politics

The Galwan incident and the subsequent escalation in violence worried the Indian prime minister: the situation was "drifting badly" and could lead to war.[86] Nehru now redoubled efforts to allay China's concerns and offer additional inducements. At a farewell lunch on 13 July 1962 the Chinese ambassador told Nehru that India's hostile

---

[81] Palit, *War in High Himalaya*, 178–9.

[82] Cited in Allen Whiting, *The Chinese Calculus of Deterrence: India and Indochina* (Ann Arbor: Center for Chinese Studies, University of Michigan, 1975, reprint 2001), 78.

[83] Indian note, 10 July 1962, *White Paper*, 6: 79–80.

[84] UKHC India to CRO, 17 July 1962, FO 371/164912, TNA.

[85] Palit, *War in High Himalaya*, 181.

[86] Speech, 14 August 1962, *PMSIR: Parliament*, 2: 116.

attitude to the PRC was harming the solidarity of the Asian peoples. Nehru expressed concern and urged China to avoid such incidents. The prime minister also proposed that both the governments take up the officials' reports for consideration.[87] Significantly, Nehru did not suggest even a token Chinese withdrawal in Ladakh. Indeed, his remarks presaged an important shift in India's negotiating stance.

Delhi also initiated a series of diplomatic moves apparently facilitated by Moscow. Krishna Menon and Chen Yi met at Geneva prior to the signing of the Laos Accord on 23 July. The agreement between Laos and fourteen states (including the US, the USSR, the PRC, and India) guaranteed the neutrality of Laos and catered for the withdrawal of all foreign troops and military assistance.[88] Nehru had instructed Menon to use this opportunity to convey his concern to the Chinese delegation. Zhou Enlai had similarly directed Chen Yi to meet Krishna Menon and find ways of arresting the deterioration. This was in keeping with the policy of "the three reconciliations and the one reduction."[89] Over three sessions the delegations negotiated seriously. The Indian side sought to arrive at an arrangement whereby clashes could be avoided and China's interests in Aksai Chin accommodated. The Chinese gave clear indications that they would not disturb the McMahon Line. At the final session Chen Yi suggested a joint press communiqué proposing further talks. The Indian side sought Nehru's approval of this. But owing to a delay in communication the approval did not arrive until after Chen had left Geneva.[90] The Chinese, of course, were unaware of this.

---

[87] "The Afterthoughts of Premier Chou" (an interview with Neville Maxwell), *Sunday Times*, 19 December 1971; Belcher (Deputy high commisioner in India) to Paul Gore-Booth (British high commisioner in India), 16 July 1962, Mss Gore-Booth 85, Gore-Booth Papers, BL.

[88] Lawrence Freedman, *Kennedy's Wars: Berlin, Cuba, Laos, and Vietnam* (Oxford: Oxford University Press, 2000), 293–304, 340–50.

[89] *PMSIR: Parliament*, 2: 116; Garver, "China's Decision for War," 111; MacFarquhar, *Origins 3*, 301, 590, n. 29.

[90] Arthur Lall, *The Emergence of Modern India* (New York: Columbia University Press, 1981), 155–7. A senior official in the ministry of defence, Lall was present during these negotiations. Also see "The Afterthoughts of Premier Chou," *Sunday Times*, 19 December 1971.

After these seemingly nugatory discussions Beijing concluded that India was not sincere about finding a peaceful solution. Whilst they had strived hard for one, the Indians had persisted with their forward policy. The Chinese premier decided that the matter ought to be discussed with the chairman.[91] By this time Beijing had good reason to believe that a war against India would not draw in other powers, principally the US. For one thing, the Geneva agreement on Laos mandated the removal of all foreign troops from that country, and so precluded a US-led or backed attack on China via Laos. As John Garver points out, this "increased the prospect that a war between China and India would remain limited." For another, the US had given the PRC adequate assurances that they would not support an invasion of the mainland by Jiang Jieshi.[92]

Since early 1962 Jiang had been contemplating major military action against the PRC. The generalissimo was encouraged both by the acute economic crisis in the mainland and by the Sino–Soviet estrangement. In June Jiang told the Americans that he had "a military machine capable of exploiting the deterioration of Communist control on the Mainland."[93] But the Kennedy administration felt these arguments mirrored the debates preceding the Bay of Pigs fiasco and were loath to support any such misadventure by Jiang. The situation was complicated by large-scale troop movements by the PRC across the Taiwan Straits. To restrain both sides Washington assured Beijing it would not support an attack on the mainland. The message was conveyed through the Soviets and the British. Meantime the Chinese ambassador in Warsaw, Wang Bingnan, was directed by Zhou to meet his US counterpart to probe America's stance.[94] On 23 June Wang met John Cabot and expressed Beijing's concerns at the US military build-up in South Vietnam, Thailand, and, most important, the Guomindang's preparations for an invasion. Cabot emphatically stated: "we had no intention of committing or supporting aggression

[91] Garver, "China's Decision for War," 111–12.

[92] Ibid., 110.

[93] Conversation of McCone with Chiang, 5 June 1962; McCone meeting with Kennedy, 18 June 1962, *FRUS 1961–63*, 12: 241–4, 246–7.

[94] MacFarquhar, *Origins 3*, 272; Garver, "China's Decision for War," 110.

against his side anywhere."[95] A few days later President Kennedy declared at a press conference that the US was opposed to the use of force in the Taiwan Straits area. Wang later recalled that these "had a great impact on policy decisions at home."[96] Indeed, the conjunction of India's seeming obduracy and these international developments led Beijing to reassess its interest in seeking a peaceful resolution of the border crisis.

Following Krishna Menon's return from Geneva, Delhi decided to open negotiations with Beijing without attaching any preconditions. This was a major departure from India's stand. This shift also seems to have been influenced by the Soviet Union. The deputy chairman of the Soviet council of ministers, Anastas Mikoyan, was visiting Delhi, and might have conveyed Moscow's desire for a negotiated solution.[97]

Heretofore, to assuage domestic opposition, Nehru had wanted China at least to indicate willingness to withdraw. The prime minister was well aware that if this latest move became public he would be under tremendous pressure from domestic constituencies to repudiate it. So Delhi set afoot diplomatic moves on two tracks. First, the chargé d'affaires in Beijing, P.K. Banerjee, was instructed "immediately [to] see Chou and inform him that the Government of India would be prepared to send a ministerial-level delegation to Peking to discuss, without preconditions, all bilateral problems and disputes."[98] Second, the Chinese embassy in Delhi was given an official note on 26 July which did not call for a withdrawal from Ladakh but merely asked Beijing to restrain its forces from going beyond China's 1956 claim line "which is capable of easy and quick verification." As soon as tensions were eased discussions on the boundary question could commence on the basis of the officials' reports.[99]

Beijing, however, had lost trust in Delhi, and therefore rebuffed the new proposal conveyed by Banerjee. Chen Yi informed him that China would not assent to it unless India "unequivocally and public-ly withdrew all fictitious and false claims on Chinese territory. The

[95] Embassy in Poland to State Department, 23 June 1962, *FRUS 1961–1963*, 22: 273–5.

[96] Freedman, *Kennedy's Wars*, 254–5; MacFarquhar, *Origins 3*, 272–3; Garver, "China's Decision for War," 110.

[97] On the Soviet role, see Banerjee, *Peking Memoirs*, 52.

[98] Ibid., 51.

[99] India's note, 26 July 1962, *White Paper*, 7: 3–4.

present proposal was loaded with ammunition for Indian propaganda against the Chinese. It was a trap and therefore not acceptable."[100] Before replying to the formal note Zhou Enlai told Banerjee that China would agree to hold talks, but not on India's terms. As for defusing tensions, he argued that "India should withdraw from Chinese territory and not make further excuses." Zhou went on claim that India was colluding with the CIA in arming Tibetan rebels against China: the Indian prime minister was either unaware or pretended not to know about this. Nehru, he averred, had lost control over the Indian government.[101] The ideological view that a "bourgeois" Nehru would act in league with the imperialists was first articulated in the spring of 1959. Zhou's remarks indicate that Beijing had begun to link the forward policy with India's perceived efforts to make Tibet an independent "buffer" state.[102]

In its official reply to the note the PRC brusquely turned down India's suggestion: "The basic way to ease tension is not for the Chinese side to withdraw to whatever distance within its own territory, but for the Indian side to withdraw." China agreed to discussions on the basis of the report, but there should not be "any preconditions for such discussions."[103] Beijing's call for talks was clearly for the consumption of the international audience. India's note of 26 July was roundly denounced at home. It was derided in parliament as "a most shocking and surprising document." The press accused the government of embarking on the road to dishonour and of breaking faith with the people of India.[104] In the light of China's rejection as well as the acrimonious domestic reaction, the Indian government reverted to its earlier stance. Nehru told parliament on 13 August that until the status quo prior to Chinese occupation was restored in Ladakh there could be no discussions on the boundary issue. The gridlock was complete. Hereafter the Indians would insist on a Chinese withdrawal as the first step towards negotiations. The Chinese would respond with a

[100] Banerjee, *Peking Memoirs*, 51–2.

[101] Ibid., 53–4.

[102] John Garver argues that this linkage was one of the main reasons why China went to war, but he overlooks the underlying ideological factor. Garver, "China's Decision for War."

[103] China's note, 4 August 1962, *White Paper*, 7: 17–18.

[104] Maxwell, *India's China War*, 244.

disingenuous reasonableness—by calling for talks "without preconditions," which they had categorically rejected—aimed at convincing the international community of India's intransigence.

From 6 to 26 August the Chinese leadership met at a working conference in Beidaihe to discuss economic issues. The conference was part of a series of meetings, since early 1962, to cope with the failure of the Great Leap Forward. In these discussions the criticism of economic policies fanned out to other policy areas as well. Wang Jiaxiang's proposals for a conciliatory foreign policy were a part of this critique.[105] By the time the Beidaihe conference began, Mao was convinced that these criticisms had far exceeded the limits he deemed acceptable. The chairman therefore overthrew the scheduled agenda in Beidaihe. He wanted to discuss the question of class struggle and fervently attacked criticisms of the Great Leap Forward.[106] Mao also singled out Wang's ideas for censure.[107] It is not clear if he dealt with them at length, especially as they pertained to India. Nonetheless, as MacFarquhar argues, Zhou and his colleagues would have realized the implications of Mao's strident stance for the conduct of foreign policy: at the very least it meant the end of "the three reconciliations and the one reduction." In retrospect it is evident that after the Beidaihe conference there was a decided change in Beijing's approach to managing the crisis with India. From 27 August Chinese diplomatic notes and actions on the ground turned more truculent. Two days later the major buildup of material and troops began.[108]

India's Forward Policy in NEFA

Between May and July 1962 India established an additional 34 paramilitary posts close to the McMahon Line. The army did not cater for "major concentrations" behind the outer string of posts. In fact 4 Division had only two brigades—7 and 5 Infantry Brigades—in NEFA. The divisional commander, Major General Niranjan Prasad, considered

[105] Niu, "1962," 31–2.

[106] For details of Mao's speeches, see MacFarquhar, *Origins 3*, 274–81.

[107] Odd Arne Westad, "Introduction," in *Brothers in Arms: The Rise and Fall of the Sino-Soviet Alliance, 1945–1963*, ed. Odd Arne Westad (Stanford, CA: Stanford University Press, 1998), 27.

[108] MacFarquhar, *Origins 3*, 302–3.

the operation "somewhat unrealistic." The platoon-sized posts were of little tactical value; it would be more sensible to establish company- or battalion-sized positions further to the rear, from where regular patrols could be sent out to the McMahon Line. Moreover, given the lack of roads and the requisite airlift capability, supporting the forward posts would be a logistical nightmare. Prasad's immediate superior, the commander of 33 Corps, Lieutenant General Umrao Singh, concurred with his assessment. During a visit by the CGS, Prasad voiced his misgivings. Kaul retorted that the prime minister himself had ordered the establishment of these posts and that army headquarters would brook no dragging of heels.[109]

As part of this precipitate drive to "plug gaps" a piquet, called Dhola post, was situated near the NEFA–Bhutan–Tibet trijunction, in the valley of the Namkachu, over which lay the Thagla ridge. This was a sensitive area. During the officials' discussions in 1960 the Chinese had contested India's interpretation of the alignment of the McMahon Line in the area. According to the treaty map of 1914 the McMahon Line ran south of the Thagla ridge. The Indians held that if the boundary was supposed to follow the watershed, and if the Thagla ridge had not been explored at that time, then the line lay on the Thagla ridge despite its erroneous depiction on the map. (The area under contention was about sixty square kilometres.) Prasad thought that if the area did belong to India it made better tactical sense to occupy the Thagla ridge itself. He sought permission for a pre-emptive occupation of the ridge.[110] By the time the army headquarters obtained a clarification from the MEA's historical division and passed it on, the PLA had occupied the Thagla ridge on 8 September.[111] The following day Eastern Command ordered 7 Brigade to prepare to move ahead within forty-eight hours and deal with the PLA's investment of Dhola.[112] The focus in Delhi was on the political implications of China's move. The

---

[109] Niranjan Prasad, *The Fall of Towang* (New Delhi: Palit & Palit, 1981), 16–18. Also see Prasad's views as conveyed to the DMO. Palit, *War in High Himalaya*, 187.

[110] Prasad, *Fall of Towang*, 22–5.

[111] Hoffmann, *India and the China Crisis*, 110–11; Palit, *War in High Himalaya*, 188–91.

[112] Prasad, *Fall of Towang*, 25–8; J.P. Dalvi, *Himalayan Blunder* (Bombay: Thacker, 1969), 169–70, 177–8. Dalvi was the commander of 7 Brigade.

occupation of Thagla forced the Indian government to reconsider the interests at stake. Delhi saw it as foreshadowing a Chinese strategy of responding to the forward policy in Ladakh by opening a new front in the east. To deter further incursions in NEFA, India had to demonstrate resolve in the Thagla area. If not, the PRC would be emboldened to conduct piecemeal intrusions all along the McMahon Line. As Steven Hoffmann puts it, the Indians believed that they were faced with a "no alternative situation."[113]

Chinese presence south of the Indian-claimed boundary was fraught with domestic implications too. Nehru was in London for a Commonwealth prime ministers' meeting. Krishna Menon apprised him of the situation on the phone, suggesting that the government should "play it cool" and not give publicity to China's move. The prime minister agreed.[114] Underlying this decision was the concern that if the matter became public there would be intense pressure on the government, specially as they had given an impression to the public that India's position in NEFA was stronger than in Ladakh. When news reports of Chinese presence south of the boundary began to circulate, the government tried to muzzle them; but with little success. Soon the main opposition parties were railing against the government's complacency: the Swatantra Party, led by Rajagopalachari, called for Nehru's resignation; the right-wing Jan Sangh demanded that an ultimatum be issued to China.[115]

At a meeting chaired by Krishna Menon on 10 or 11 September 1962 the government decided to use force to expel the Chinese from south of Thagla. The army chief, and the eastern army commander L.P. Sen, thought that the PLA's strength near Dhola approximated 600, whereas India would soon have a brigade in the area. They also felt that adequate supplies were available and that the brigade could be maintained by air. In consequence they believed that the Chinese could be evicted.[116] The defence minister and the civilian officials were

---

[113] Hoffmann, *India and the China Crisis*, 127.

[114] Interview with Romesh Bhandari, New Delhi, 9 May 2005. A foreign service officer, Bhandari was then private secretary to Krishna Menon.

[115] Maxwell, *India's China War*, 311–12.

[116] Kaul, *The Untold Story*, 355–6; Palit, *War in High Himalaya*, 196; Hoffmann, *India and the China Crisis*, 131–2. Both Maxwell and the official

under the impression that in NEFA, unlike Ladakh, the army was in a position to take action if necessary.[117] As earlier, they took little interest in operational or logistical questions, being content to accept the top military leaderships' opinion.

The commanders down the military echelon considered the operation utterly infeasible. On 12 September the corps commander Umrao Singh told Sen that the PLA could easily outstrip any effort to push Indian troops into the Thagla area. Logistically, too, they were in a much superior position, with a roadhead only a few miles short of the Thagla ridge. Umrao recommended pulling the Dhola post back south of the map-marked McMahon Line.[118] Sen insisted that the government was "not prepared to accept any intrusion of the Chinese into our territory and if they come they must be thrown out by force."[119] After a heated exchange Sen demanded that Umrao and his subordinate commanders produce an operational plan with "utmost speed."[120]

On 17 September, at another meeting presided by Krishna Menon, Thapar queried the danger of all-out war if the army used force near Dhola. The foreign secretary, M.J. Desai, said that since the operation would be carefully circumscribed, escalation was unlikely, though Indian posts at one or two places could be threatened, this being indicated by the pattern of Chinese behaviour.[121] Desai's confidence stemmed from yet another source. The MEA's China division and the DMO had together tried to assess the PLA's logistical capabilities based on estimates of the road networks close to the frontier. They had

history date the decision as 9 September, presumably because the Henderson-Brooks report on the war (the principal source for both accounts) dates it accordingly. However, it is clear from the references cited by the official history that no record of the purported 9 September meeting was available to its authors. See Sinha and Athale, *Conflict with China*, 94; Maxwell, *India's China War*, 303–4.

[117] Ibid., 297; Hoffmann, *India and the China Crisis*, 121.

[118] Maxwell, *India's China War*, 305.

[119] Sinha and Athale, *Conflict with China*, 141, nn. 2 and 3. The date is misprinted as 13 September.

[120] Prasad, *Fall of Towang*, 32; Sinha and Athale, *Conflict with China*, 97.

[121] Mullik, *Chinese Betrayal*, 345. At this time, Mullik himself believed that the Chinese were unlikely to cross into Indian territory in large numbers. Palit, *War in High Himalaya*, 204.

concluded that the infrastructure was incapable of supporting a full-scale invasion deep into Indian territory. The joint secretary recalled this belief holding sway in the MEA "till the last moment."[122]

Alongside military moves, diplomatic exchanges continued. On 13 September Beijing warned India to stop pursuing a policy of "sham negotiations and real fighting." The note called for a twenty-kilometre withdrawal in NEFA by both sides and for negotiations without preconditions. The Chinese proposed to hold these discussions on 15 October in Beijing. Importantly, China's concern about influencing international opinion was visible for the first time.[123] Delhi agreed to talks on the date suggested but insisted that these should focus on measures to restore *status quo ante* in Ladakh and to reduce the prevailing tension. Once these measures were implemented, discussions on the boundary issue could commence.[124]

On the night of 20 September firing broke out in the Dhola area; spasmodic exchanges continued for the next ten days. These pushed to the fore the army chief's latent yet lingering concerns about Chinese retaliation. On 22 September Thapar presented his appreciation of the PRC's likely reaction to the operation in Dhola. He noted that the PLA could reinforce their troops opposite Dhola; retaliate elsewhere in NEFA; and/or retaliate in Ladakh. He considered the last option most likely, as by attacking Indian posts in Ladakh the Chinese could move up to their 1960 claim line. The Indians were, he observed, "much weaker" and could not resist a determined effort. Desai said that the government would not accept any encroachment in NEFA. When the army was ready, the PLA should be evicted from Dhola, even at the cost of losing additional territory in Ladakh. India's interest in preventing incursions in NEFA had evidently superseded its earlier interest in curbing Chinese advance in Ladakh. Thapar then asked for written instructions to expel the PLA. Despite his concerns, Thapar did not challenge the decision, but played safe by asking for formal confirmation. Indeed, the instructions were drafted in the meeting itself.[125]

[122] Hoffmann, *India and the China Crisis*, 244; Mehta, *In Different Worlds*, 168.

[123] China's note, 13 September 1962, *White Paper*, 7: 71–3.

[124] India's note, 19 September 1962, ibid., 77–8.

[125] Record of meeting on 22 September 1962, reproduced in Palit, *War in High Himalaya*, 213.

Meantime, in response to the pressure from Sen, the divisional and brigade commanders prepared a plan to dislodge the Chinese from Thagla. Incredibly, the plan was a make-believe one, expressly designed to show the impossibility of evicting the Chinese. The logistical requirements projected were well beyond what could be built up before the onset of winter. Umrao considered even this plan too ambitious.[126] An upgraded version calling for a division with full artillery and logistical support was handed to Sen. Umrao added for good measure that the operation was totally infeasible.[127] Sen retorted that the field commanders "seemed to have gotten cold feet." He refused to accept that the projected logistical build-up was truly necessary, and argued that airlift could be used to improve the current situation.[128] Reviewing the situation on 2 October, Sen held the corps commander responsible for the delays in launching the operation, and called for his removal. Thapar agreed and sought the defence minister's permission to replace Umrao.[129] The following day an extraordinary set of decisions was taken. Instead of sacking Umrao, 33 Corps would be divested of responsibility of NEFA; a new formation, 4 Corps, would take over. B.M. Kaul would command the new corps and would continue to function as the CGS.[130] He would have no additional troops apart from two brigades of 4 Division: his sole task would be to force out the PLA from Thagla.

Nehru, meanwhile, had returned to Delhi and met the CGS on the evening of 3 October. According to Kaul's account the prime minister said that India must contest the claims that China sought to establish in NEFA by intruding into Thagla: "we must take —or appear to take a strong stand irrespective of consequences." He hoped that the Chinese would see reason and withdraw. If not, India would have no option but to evict them *"or at least try to do so to the best of our ability."*[131] Clearly Nehru attached great importance to demonstrating resolve. This was entirely consistent with his earlier thinking on deterring Chinese intrusions in Ladakh. Such action was also essential

[126] Dalvi, *Himalayan Blunder*, 233–41.
[127] Prasad, *Fall of Towang*, 40.
[128] Hoffmann, *India and the China Crisis*, 147.
[129] Mullik, *Chinese Betrayal*, 355–6; Maxwell, *India's China War*, 321–2.
[130] Sinha and Athale, *Conflict with China*, 97.
[131] Kaul, *Untold Story*, 367–8 (emphasis in the original).

to fend off domestic criticism and retain diplomatic flexibility in dealing with China. Nehru told Kaul that if the government failed to take these steps, it would completely lose public confidence.

Diplomacy and War:
September–October 1962

By this time crucial developments had occurred in China. At the Central Committee's Tenth Plenum, which commenced on 24 September, Mao stepped up the attacks initiated in Beidaihe, denouncing the criticism of the Great Leap Forward as "Chinese revisionism," accusing "rightist" leaders such as Liu Shaoqi of being "Chinese revisionists." Revisionism at home, he argued, was connected to revisionism abroad. In two sessions he castigated the ideas of Wang Jiaxiang. In Mao's reading the problem was not just the policy implications of these ideas but their ideological basis, which ran counter to his conception of the ultimately revolutionary purposes of foreign policy.[132] The chairman believed that the sand castles of imperialism were being eroded by the rising tide of revolution. By seeking a détente with the US and supporting India, Khrushchev had forfeited the mantle of revolutionary leadership. Beijing, hereafter, would lead the struggle against the imperialists, the revisionists, and the anti-revolutionists.[133]

Mao and other leaders thought that the policy of "armed coexistence" had failed to prevent Indian intrusion. Their "little blows" would not help: to punish India and halt its aggression, China would have to strike hard. This would ensure that the Indians would never again commit aggression against the PRC.[134] Beijing firmly believed that the forward policy stemmed from India's designs on Tibet. As late as 16 October an internal Chinese report claimed that India's aggressive posture reflected its desire to make Tibet an Indian "colony or protectorate."[135] India's forward policy certainly played a role in Beijing's decision to go to war. But it was ideology that gave an edge to China's assessments of India's actions. More important, Mao's return

[132] Niu, "1962," 33–5; MacFarquhar, *Origins 3*, 283–5.

[133] Cf. Westad, "Introduction," 27–8.

[134] Garver, "China's Decision for War," 114–15.

[135] Ibid., 120; Fravel, *Strong Borders*, 194.

to centrestage and the subsequent ideological turn in foreign policy led to a greater emphasis on the use of force in dealing with India.

On 3 October Beijing replied to India's note of 19 September. It observed that India had yet again rejected its proposal for discussions without preconditions. Turning to the international audience, the note claimed that "it is not difficult for the Asian countries and all peace loving countries" to see that while China wanted a peaceful settlement India was setting unacceptable preconditions and creating tensions on the border. The note declared: "Whenever India attacks, China is sure to strike back." The Chinese proposed that the talks might cover whatever issues both sides wanted to raise. Beijing would raise the eastern sector, which was the "most pressing question."[136] As Allen Whiting observes, the note was "little more than an exercise to influence foreign opinion and to set the stage for subsequent fighting."[137] Delhi for its part reiterated its earlier stance.

On 6 October Mao and the central military committee decided on a major punitive attack on India. The same day the PLA received a directive authorizing a "fierce and painful" attack: "If they attack, don't just repulse them, hit back ruthlessly so that it hurts." The directive also called for a co-ordinated assault in the western and eastern sectors. It was decided that the main assault would be in the east: India had a larger number of troops here, and the PLA could inflict a massive blow. Moreover, it would conclusively demonstrate that China would never accept the McMahon Line.[138]

In tandem with military measures, Beijing intensified its diplomatic efforts. Zhou Enlai told the Soviet ambassador on 8 October that he had intelligence that India was about to launch a massive attack. In the event of such an attack, China would resolutely defend itself. Zhou also expressed pique at Soviet military supplies to India. At the end of August 1962 the USSR had finalized an agreement to supply Mig-21 fighters, transport aircraft, and helicopters to India. Whilst they had not yet provided the fighters, some transport planes and helicopters had been sent. Zhou remarked that the PLA had spotted these

[136] China's note, 3 October 1962, *White Paper*, 7: 96–8.
[137] Whiting, *Chinese Calculus of Deterrence*, 108.
[138] Garver, "China's Decision for War," 117–19; MacFarquhar, *Origins 3*, 307.

along the borders. Their appearance, he said, "has a certain effect on the mood of our soldiers."[139] Khrushchev had anticipated the PRC's reaction to the sale of Soviet aircraft to India. The Soviet ambassador told Zhou that Moscow was prepared to offer licences and technical assistance to manufacture a modified Mig-21 aircraft in China. But Beijing chose not to take it up.[140]

The presidium of the Communist Party of the Soviet Union (CPSU) discussed the Sino–Indian crisis on 11 October. Khrushchev said that they must "look for measures for peacemaking." He conceded that it would be "difficult [for India] to get an agreement with China." Nevertheless, the Chinese proposal about troop withdrawals was "sensible."[141]

By this time General Kaul had taken charge in NEFA. Despite strenuous objections from the divisional and brigade commanders, he made so bold as to send a patrol across the Namkachu on 9 October.[142] Early next morning, as more troops were preparing to cross the river, the Chinese attacked and almost wiped out the patrol. Kaul immediately informed the army headquarters that "a grave situation" had developed and that he wanted to fly to Delhi to present his case. On receiving approval he departed, instructing Prasad to hold the positions along the Namkachu.[143]

The CGS reached Delhi the following day. The same evening a meeting was held, chaired by the prime minister, with Krishna Menon, Mullik, Thapar, Sen, and other officials in attendance. Kaul began with a detailed briefing of the situation at Namkachu. He underscored

[139] Record of conversation between Stepan Chervonenko and Zhou Enlai, 8 October 1962, cited in Sergey Radchenko, "The China Puzzle: Soviet Policy Towards the People's Republic of China, 1962–1947" (PhD thesis, London School of Economics and Political Science, 2005), 28–9. Also see, *People's Daily*, 2 November 1963, cited in John Gittings, *Survey of the Sino-Soviet Dispute: A Commentary and Extracts from the Recent Polemics, 1963–1967* (London: Oxford University Press, 1968), 178.

[140] Radchenko, "The Chinese Puzzle," 29–30.

[141] Meeting of CPSU Presidium, 11 October 1962, *Prezidium TsK KPSS 1954–1964: Chernovye Protokolnye Zapisi Zasedani, Stenogrammy, Postanovleniia*, ed. Aleksandr Fursenko (Moscow: Rosspen, 2003), 596.

[142] Prasad, *Fall of Towang*, 47–9; Dalvi, *Himalayan Blunder*, 282–6.

[143] Sinha and Athale, *Conflict with China*, 100.

the numerical superiority of the PLA in the area, and the tactical and logistical problems that his troops faced. Kaul later claimed to have offered three alternatives: attack despite Chinese superiority; abandon the idea of an attack but hold on to present positions; withdraw to better positions in the rear. Nehru said he did not want to jeopardize troops and asked the military to make the choice. Kaul argued against persisting with an attack, but it is not clear which of the other two alternatives he favoured. In any event Thapar and Sen felt that a brigade could hold the existing defensive positions against an enemy division. They urged that the positions along the Namkachu be held, even if an attack was not mounted anytime soon. The prime minister accepted their views.[144]

En route to Colombo on 13 October Nehru was asked by the press about the orders given to the army in NEFA. "Our instructions are to free our territory," he replied, "I cannot fix the date, that is entirely for the Army." He pointed out that wintry conditions were already setting in, that the PLA's positions were numerically and tactically superior, and that the main Chinese bases were located nearby.[145] Nehru was indicating that no action could be taken for the present. But the press publicized his comments as saying that the army had been asked to "throw out" the Chinese from NEFA. Nehru's purported remarks were seized by Beijing as proof of Indian aggression. An editorial in the *People's Daily* on 14 October declared that a "massive invasion of Chinese territory by Indian troops . . . seems imminent."[146]

At this juncture, the USSR tilted further towards the PRC and away from India. Khrushchev's stance is often portrayed as tactical, dictated by the need for Beijing's support in Cuba.[147] However, the Soviet offer of Migs to China shows that his attitude had begun to

[144] My account is based on a number of versions of this meeting. Kaul, *Untold Story*, 385–6; Mullik, *Chinese Betrayal*, 361–4; S.S. Khera, *India's Defence Problem* (Bombay: Orient Longman, 1968), 225; Palit, *War in High Himalaya*, 226–7; Maxwell, *India's China War*, 340–1; Hoffmann, *India and the China Crisis*, 153–4; OHT B.M. Kaul, 147, NMML.

[145] *Statesman*, 13 October 1962; *Times*, 13 October 1962.

[146] MacFarquhar, *Origins 3*, 308.

[147] Gopal, *Nehru*, 3: 221; MacFarquhar, *Origins 3*, 314, 317; Mikhail Prozumenshchikov, "The Sino-Indian Conflict, the Cuban Missile Crisis, and the

shift well before the Cuban missile crisis. Besides, during this period Khrushchev was confident that missiles could be placed in Cuba without being detected by the Americans. He planned to announce their presence in November, after the US congressional elections. It is unlikely that Khrushchev would have felt a pressing need for Chinese support at this stage. The change in Khrushchev's stand was guided not by realpolitik but ideology. Since the summer of 1962 he had been exercising restraint in the Sino–Soviet dispute. As Sergey Radchenko argues, to Khrushchev the split with China was "simply inexplicable;" he believed that as socialist countries they were natural allies. On several occasions he admitted to being confounded by China's refusal of a rapprochement. In October 1962 Khrushchev sought to show Beijing that, disagreements notwithstanding, they remained in the same camp: "they were class allies whose close relationship was not based on calculations of political expediency but on scientific principles of Marxism."[148]

When the departing Chinese ambassador Liu Xiao paid his last call on 13 October, Khrushchev waxed nostalgic, recalling Sino–Soviet solidarity before 1958 and asking: "What is preventing us from having the same relations now? We do not see any obstacles to this on our part." He went on to claim that "our parties have a responsibility . . . to create a common monolithic world Communist front." Khrushchev averred that the Chinese were "our brothers," the Indians merely "friends." If India attacked, the USSR would stand by China: "in relations between us there is not place for neutrality. This would be a betrayal . . . We shall always be in one camp and share joys and sorrows."[149] Khrushchev explained that thus far he had tried to be even-handed because he wanted "to keep India out of the arms of imperialists." He trivialized the military equipment provided to India, arguing that "this sale did not affect the balance of power between

---

Sino-Soviet Split, October 1962: New Evidence from the Russian Archives," *CWIHP Bulletin* 8/9 (Winter 1996–7), 253.

[148] Radchenko, "The China Puzzle," 26, 34.

[149] Record of conversation between Khrushchev and Liu Xiao, 13 October 1962, cited in ibid., 26–7, 30–1. Also see Gittings, *Survey of the Sino–Soviet Dispute*, 178.

Indian and the PRC in the border conflict."[150] The next day Khrushchev proposed to the CPSU presidium that they "delay the dispatch
of Mig-21 aircraft to India." The ambassador in India should convey
Moscow's disappointment to Nehru: "Do they have any idea when the
conflict will end?" He must emphasize that the McMahon Line was a
hangover from the past: "The conditions have changed." China's
proposal for a twenty-kilometre withdrawal was "reasonable" whereas
India's call for further withdrawal was "humiliating to the PRC." The
USSR, Nehru must be told, was for defusing the crisis because "it was
not doing any good to anybody. India will hardly gain anything from
the conflict."[151] At a farewell dinner that evening Khrushchev informed Liu that the sale of Mig-21s to India would be postponed until the
settlement of the boundary issue.[152]

Khrushchev was performing a delicate balancing act. On the one
hand he realized that if the USSR openly supported the PRC, India
might look to the West for countervailing assistance. This would be
undesirable, for Khrushchev disagreed with China's views on India
and Nehru. On the other hand a break with socialist China was inconceivable: hence the efforts to facilitate a negotiated settlement between India and China. But the steadily rising tension along the
borders forced the issue. Given his ideological desire to strengthen the
Sino–Soviet alliance, Khrushchev decided to favour Beijing. He might
well have hoped that the situation would not be so desperate as to
compel Delhi to turn to the Western countries for assistance.

Kaul returned to his headquarters on 13 October. Two days later
Prasad requested that 7 Brigade be withdrawn from its positions along
the Namkachu. Prasad's contention was backed by Kaul's staff.[153]
On 16 October Kaul sent a signal to army headquarters, arguing that
the positions along the Namkachu were untenable. The army chief
was rather agitated and himself drafted a reply to Kaul. Thapar ordered
Kaul to reinforce the area and carry out "aggressive patrolling." Kaul

[150] Cited in Radchenko, "The China Puzzle," 29.

[151] Meeting of the CPSU Presidium, 14 October 1962, *Prezidium TsK KPSS*, 616.

[152] For an account based on Liu Xiao's memoirs, MacFarquhar, *Origins 3*, 312–13.

[153] Prasad, *Fall of Towang*, 74; Maxwell, *India's China War*, 353.

was asked to forward, at the earliest, his recommendations and requirements for the operation to evict the Chinese.[154] Clearly, despite the discretion vested in him by the prime minister, Thapar was eager to get on with the offensive.

That same evening Krishna Menon, Thapar, Mullik, and Sen flew to Kaul's headquarters. Kaul strongly argued that the Namkachu positions were untenable. Menon responded that public opinion would not tolerate any further loss of territory. After nearly three hours of discussion the civilians left room to let the military commanders confer among themselves and arrive at a decision. Considering Thapar's orders to Kaul the previous day, it is not surprising that the generals decided against any withdrawal. Thapar agreed to provide additional supplies, equipment, and troops.[155]

Even as these discussions were under way, the PLA was given the operational order to "liquidate the invading Indian army."[156] On 18 October, the Central Military Committee met formally to approve the decision for a "self defence counterattack war." The decision was also endorsed by an expanded politburo meeting. The PLA's operational plan was approved and the date was set for 20 October.[157] The Indian troops could only watch as the PLA openly prepared for the attack. On the night of 19 October, Chinese troops began to infiltrate Indian positions along the Namkachu. At the crack of dawn the onslaught commenced.

The Debacle of Winter 1962

In concert with the operations in NEFA, the PLA began an offensive in Ladakh. Here they sought systematically to eliminate Indian posts ahead of their claim line. The puny forward policy posts stood no chance and were rapidly wiped out. By 24 October the Chinese effectively controlled the area up to their 1960 claim line in northern and central Ladakh. In NEFA they swiftly overran Indian positions along the McMahon Line.

---

[154] Palit, *War in High Himalaya*, 232; Sinha & Athale, *Conflict with China*, 101.

[155] Mullik, *Chinese Betrayal*, 369–72; Kaul, *The Untold Story*, 388–9.

[156] MacFarquhar, *Origins 3*, 308; Garver, "China's Decision for War," 121.

[157] Garver, "China's Decision for War," 121–2.

Until 22 October both the army commander and chief were keen to defend Tawang. The divisional commander, however, was convinced that Tawang was untenable. Concurrently, at the army headquarters, DMO Palit sought to convince his superiors of the imperative of evacuating Tawang and concentrating at the rear, at the dominating Sela massif. But Thapar felt that the government would not accept abandoning Tawang. At a meeting presided by Nehru on 23 October Thapar asked Palit to explain his views. Briefing from a map, Palit pointed out that the Chinese could use numerous tracks to bypass Tawang and head straight for the plains of Assam. So it was important to pull back from Tawang and hold Sela. Nehru unhesitatingly left the decision to the army chief: "It is a matter now for the military to decide—where, how they should fight . . . I cannot lay down conditions about Towang [*sic*] or any other place on grounds other than military."[158] The Indian government decided to evacuate Tawang and concentrate their forces further to the rear at Sela and Bomdila. Two days later the PLA entered Tawang unopposed. There they paused and began improving their lines of communication for the next phase.

By this time the Indian prime minister was under increasing pressure to remove the defence minister. Shortly after the war began there was a groundswell of criticism of Krishna Menon, who was regarded as culpable for the early reverses.[159] Nehru was compelled to accept Menon's resignation and assume charge of defence himself. Speaking to the chiefs of staff shortly afterwards, the prime minister explained that "Our broad strategy must be governed by political factors, but detailed strategy—and tactics especially—have to be judged by military considerations."[160]

Nevertheless, the political leadership was involved in a decision that proved disastrous—to reinstate Kaul in command of 4 Corps. A few days into the war Kaul had been persuaded to step down and Lieutenant General Harbaksh Singh was appointed instead. Just as Harbaksh had settled down and set in motion his plans, Kaul was abruptly restored as corps commander. The role played by Nehru in

---

[158] Palit, *War in High Himalaya*, 246.

[159] Krishnamachari to Nehru, 30 October 1962, Correspondence with Nehru (1962), T.T. Krishnamachari Papers, NMML.

[160] Palit, *War in High Himalaya*, 278–9.

reinstating Kaul is unclear; but the decision could not have been taken without his consent. Following Kaul's return the momentum built up by Harbaksh slackened. Worse still, Kaul refused to be briefed and tampered with the defensive plan drawn up by Harbaksh. Yet it would be less than fair solely to blame Kaul for the ensuing defeat. For both his subordinates and superiors in the chain of command failed to get to grips with the developing military situation.[161]

On the diplomatic front Beijing claimed that it was India that had launched massive attacks in both sectors: China had been forced to strike back in self-defence.[162] On 24 October Zhou advanced a three-point proposal to Nehru. Both sides should withdraw their troops twenty kilometres from the "line of actual control;" if India agreed, Chinese forces would be pulled back north of the McMahon Line; the prime ministers should meet to find a solution. Beijing defined the "line of actual control" as that on 7 November 1959.[163] Read in conjunction with China's assertions that this line was identical to its 1960 claim-line, Zhou's proposal meant that China would retain the areas it currently occupied in the west, but India should forsake the areas where it had sited posts. Delhi refused to acquiesce in the claims that China had established by force.

Meanwhile Khrushchev had written to Nehru, rebuking him for failing to show a "due urge for reconciliation" and advising him to agree to the PRC's proposals for negotiations without preconditions. The Indian prime minister had responded that it was futile preaching moderation to the victim of aggression.[164] On 25 October *Pravda* commended China's three-point proposal as "constructive." It noted that the McMahon Line had been imposed on both the countries and

[161] For a short account of the military operations, see Srinath Raghavan, "A Bad Knock: The War with China, 1962," in Daniel Marston and Chandar Sundaram (eds), *A Military History of India and South Asia* (Westport, CT: Praeger, 2006).

[162] China's note, 20 October 1962, *White Paper*, 7: 123; *The Sino-Indian Boundary Question* (Beijing: Foreign Language Press, 1962).

[163] Zhou to Nehru, 24 October and 4 November 1962, *White Paper*, 8: 1, 7–10.

[164] Khrushchev to Nehru, 20 October 1962, and Nehru's reply, 22 October 1962, cited in Gopal, *Nehru*, 3: 221–2.

that it had never been recognized by China. The editorial reaffirmed Sino–Soviet friendship "based on an identity of aims . . . and a joint ideology, Marxism-Leninism."[165]

The *Pravda* editorial elicited a sharp response both from the Indian government and from the Communist Party of India (CPI). Nehru stated that he was "very pained" and that the article had considerably damaged Indo–Soviet relations. The pro-China faction of the CPI welcomed the editorial; but the party as a whole was acutely embarrassed. Finding itself under attack by anti-Communist groups, the CPI sent a telegram requesting the CPSU to retract some of the statements in the article.[166] The party's general secretary E.M.S. Namboodiripad told the Soviet ambassador Ivan Benediktov that "this publication in all probability will inaugurate a new period of anti-Soviet hysteria in India."[167] The party's chairman Shripad Dange warned Benediktov that the article "offended the Indian people."[168] During the lull in battle Delhi also approached several Western countries, mainly America and Britain, for military equipment. By early November the first consignment of weapons started arriving from the UK and the US; but the bulk of Western assistance would only come after the ceasefire.

Moscow viewed these developments with consternation. Khrushchev wrote to Nehru, urging him "to show courage and rise above the heat of passion and hurt feelings by accepting an immediate cease-fire." Nehru replied that "shorn of its wrappings . . . [Beijing's proposal] is in effect a demand for surrender."[169] Consequently, *Pravda* published another editorial claiming fraternal relations with China "based on the common fundamental aims of building socialism and communism," but also speaking of "good friendly relations" with India "which we prize highly." *Pravda* called on both sides to find a "mutually acceptable

---

[165] Cited in Whiting, *Chinese Calculus of Deterrence*, 131–2.

[166] Prozumenshchikov, "The Sino-Indian Conflict," 253.

[167] Note of conversation with Namboodiripad by Benediktov, 26 October 1962, in "New East-Bloc Documents on the Sino-Indian Conflict, 1959 & 1962," *CWIHP Bulletin* 8/9 (Winter 1996), 263–4.

[168] Record of conversation between Benediktov and Dange, 4 November 1962, cited in Radchenko, "The China Puzzle," 32.

[169] Paraphrase of Khrushchev to Nehru, 31 October 1962; Nehru's reply, 5 November 1962, Gopal, *Nehru*, 3: 223, 226.

solution."[170] Four days later Khrushchev assured the Indian ambassador that "the second *Pravda* editorial . . . represents their correct
position." Other senior Soviet officials "were very friendly towards
India and almost apologetic in their inability to take our side openly."[171]
At the same time the Soviets kept Beijing informed of the exchanges between Khrushchev and Nehru, and even shared intelligence on
India. The USSR also appealed to the PRC to end the fighting.[172]

On 16 November the PLA launched the second phase of operations.
Whilst the Indian forces put up a staunch resistance in Ladakh, those
in NEFA ignominiously collapsed, virtually without a fight. By the
evening of 19 November the Indian army was helpless to withstand
further onslaughts. In the west the Chinese seemed likely to advance
to Leh; in the east they were poised to enter the plains of Assam. Nehru
now approached the US for air cover. Writing to President Kennedy
he described the situation as "really desperate" and requested immediate
despatch of at least twelve squadrons of fighter aircraft.[173] In the event
it was not American aircraft but the cessation of hostilities by the PRC
that precluded further disaster. On 21 November Beijing announced
a unilateral ceasefire to be followed by the withdrawal of Chinese
troops to the north of the McMahon Line. But China would retain
control up to its 1960 claim-line in Ladakh—a situation that persists
till today.

Back to Kashmir

Despite the military debacle India's diplomatic position improved
after the war. Not only did the West support Delhi, the USSR too came
round to its side. On 24 November 1962 Khrushchev told the Indian
envoy: "We hope India will continue to follow its policy on non-alignment. Our policy towards India will continue to be one of strong

[170] Whiting, *Chinese Calculus of Deterrence*, 141.

[171] T.N. Kaul to Nehru, 16 November 1962, Correspondence with
J. Nehru, T.N. Kaul Papers (I-III Instalments), NMML.

[172] Radchenko, "The China Puzzle," 33; Westad, "Introduction," 45,
n. 100.

[173] Nehru to Kennedy, 19 November 1962, India Nehru Correspondence,
11 November 1962 to 19 November 1962, NSC Box 111, JFKL.

friendship and we will fulfil all our obligations . . . We may be able to supply you the Migs even in December."[174] By mid-December Khrushchev was openly stating that China's attack on India had been unnecessary.[175] Khrushchev's volte-face was driven by two considerations. First, the border war had had exactly the upshot that he had wished to avoid. Indeed, Anglo-American military assistance to India was well under way. Second, Khrushchev was irked and disappointed by Beijing's attacks and accusations that he had backed down in Cuba and appeased the imperialists.[176] Nehru for his part took care to ensure that India was not locked in an embrace with the West. He firmly rejected proposals advocating a military alliance with the US and the UK as the best insurance for India. "That guarantee will be purchased at the expense of giving up our basic policy of non-alignment."[177] As he explained to his ambassador in Washington: "The attitude of the Soviet Union in this matter has been and will continue to be of great importance . . . It is, we think, of the utmost importance that the Soviet Union maintains this attitude [of support to India] in the Sino-Indian conflict . . . Even if there were no other valid reasons, our maintaining our policy of non-alignment is essential for this purpose."[178]

The crisis of 1962 led India to enhance its military capabilities *vis-à-vis* China. Eventually, the Indian army increased in strength to over 21 divisions and the air force to 45 squadrons. The China crisis thus set India on the road to military pre-eminence in South Asia. But there were immediate political costs to seeking military aid from America and Britain. As equipment and advisers trickled into India, President Ayub Khan of Pakistan grew nervous. He wrote to Kennedy, insisting that that if the US was arming India they should also nudge

[174] Record of talk between Khrushchev and Kaul, 24 November 1962, Correspondence with J. Nehru, T.N. Kaul Papers (I-III Instalments), NMML.

[175] Robert H. Donaldson, *Soviet Policy toward India: Ideology and Strategy* (Cambridge, Ma.: Harvard University Press, 1974), 165–6.

[176] Radchenko, "The China Puzzle," 36–9.

[177] Nehru to Sudhir Ghosh, 5 January 1963, India 1961–1963, Robert Komer Papers, JFKL.

[178] Nehru to B.K. Nehru, 8 March 1963, Correspondence with Jawaharlal Nehru, 1963, T.T. Krishnamachari Papers, NMML.

Delhi towards a settlement on Kashmir. Kennedy and his advisers had already been thinking along these lines. At an Anglo-American conference in late December it was decided that time was propitious for a renewed effort to resolve the dispute.

Under pressure from this quarter, the Indians agreed to begin negotiations. In the years since the last bilateral talks, the dispute with China had crowded out most other items in the foreign policy agenda. Consequently, no fresh thought had been given to Kashmir. In the run-up to the negotiations Indian officials sought and obtained Nehru's approval for plans to partition Kashmir. These envisaged alterations to the ceasefire line that would be favourable to Pakistan. The Indians were clear that there could be no compromise on the valley, for the lines of communication to Ladakh passed through it.

The talks began on 26 December 1962 on a tense note, as Pakistan and China announced that they were set to sign a boundary agreement. The areas covering the agreement were, of course, claimed by India as part of Kashmir. The Pakistanis were agreeable to partition but claimed the entire state barring the Kathua area. They had evidently gone back to the partition memorandum of late 1948. As their foreign minister Zulfikar Ali Bhutto candidly told the Indian foreign secretary, Y.D. Gundevia, "You are a defeated nation, don't you see."[179] Matters were made no easier by Washington and London's decision to hand both sides a paper calling for the partition of the valley. After six rounds the negotiations ended in a deadlock on 16 May 1963.

[179] Y.D. Gundevia, *Outside the Archives* (New Delhi: Sangam Books, 1984), 246.

Conclusion

February 1964 was very like February 1950. Both Kashmir and the refugee problem in Bengal were back in the news. Worse, the two issues were now linked. In the second week of December 1963, a holy relic—believed to be the hair of the Prophet—went missing from Hazratbal, the most important of mosques in the Kashmir valley. The sacrilege unloosed an avalanche of anger in the valley that quickly acquired political overtones. "The huge anti-government demonstrations which were held all over the valley paralysed the administration. For days, members of the state cabinet had to remain confined within the four walls of their homes."[1]

Indian intelligence operatives managed to trace and restore it in a week.[2] But the valley was astir with suspicion about its authenticity. When the Kashmir government obtusely refused to permit verification by leading clerics, widespread agitation commenced. The movement was spearheaded by an action committee formed by the supporters of Sheikh Abdullah. Eventually, at Nehru's intervention, a special examination was held the following February and the relic was declared genuine.

Meanwhile, in response to these events large-scale anti-Hindu violence had erupted in East Bengal. As in 1950, streams of refugees poured into West Bengal resulting in retributory attacks and an outflow of Muslims from the latter province. By the end of March 1964 an estimated 125,000 Hindus had sought refuge in India. In correspondence with Pakistan, Delhi suggested a meeting between the home

---

[1] Bazaz, *Kashmir in the Crucible*, 94. Also see, Singh, *Autobiography*, 262–3.
[2] Mullik, *My Years with Nehru: Kashmir*, 127–54.

ministers of both the countries. Pakistan refused, insisting that India take active measures to restore tranquillity in West Bengal.[3] The Indian government sent a detailed memorandum on 19 March, with a letter from Nehru to Ayub. Expressing India's distress and anxiety, it recalled the Nehru–Liaquat pact and urged that measures along those lines be taken immediately. India called for a meeting of the home ministers at a location of Pakistan's choosing. Ayub's response, as the Indian foreign secretary of the day recalled it, was "remarkable." Pakistan's president expressed satisfaction that India had at last accepted *his* suggestion for a meeting of the home ministers.[4] Evidently, neither side had forgotten the crisis of 1950.

As Delhi scrambled to manage the situation, Nehru's thoughts drifted back to the dark days after Partition. The latest crisis was proof that despite the passage of time communal violence could yet devour the country. That Kashmir was triggering these upheavals was deeply unsettling. Furthermore, it was amply clear that the protests in Kashmir were a manifestation of the people's resentments against a government that was seen as a satrapy of the Indian government. At the crossroads of these developments Nehru decided that, rather than continuing to accept and work within the established policy consensus, it was imperative to rethink and change the approach to Kashmir. As a first step he reached out to Sheikh Abdullah, who had been languishing in prison for much of the past decade. Nehru forced the home ministry to drop charges against the Sheikh and release him.[5]

Even before Abdullah was freed, Nehru invited him to Delhi for discussions. Realizing that this might be the last best chance for a settlement, Abdullah rose to the occasion. The prime minister's moves did not go down well with many of his cabinet members, who issued statements insisting that the Kashmir dispute was "closed." Not

---

[3] See correspondence between the presidents in *Recurrent Exodus of Minorities from East Pakistan and Disturbances in India: A Report to the Indian Commission of Jurists by its Committee of Enquiry* (New Delhi: Indian Commission of Jurists, 1965), 40–6.

[4] Gundevia, *Outside the Archives*, 396.

[5] This paragraph and the next draw mainly on Ramachandra Guha, "Opening a Window in Kashmir," *Economic and Political Weekly* 39, no. 35 (28 August 2004).

surprisingly, the Jan Sangh too fulminated against this measure. And Nehru faced some tough questioning in parliament. Abdullah stayed with Nehru for several days and discussed the issue at some length. He also met other ministers and prominent political leaders such as Jayaprakash Narayan and Rajagopalachari.

Many of the options considered by Abdullah, Nehru, and his advisers were old ones: overall plebiscite, partial plebiscite, and partition. There were others that had been mooted earlier by Abdullah but had never been discussed seriously: an India–Pakistan condominium on Kashmir, and a confederation between India, Pakistan, and Kashmir. The Sheikh himself favoured a confederation. Nehru felt that talk of a confederation might be premature and unpalatable to Pakistan. Nevertheless, he agreed that Abdullah should go to Pakistan and probe Ayub's mind. Nehru's instincts were right: it was too much. He may not have realized that it was also too late.

Abdullah met Ayub Khan on 25–26 May. The Pakistani president summarily rejected the idea of a confederation. In his memoirs Ayub sardonically claimed that whilst he was seeking to liberate Kashmir, Abdullah was paving the way for the enslavement of Pakistan.[6] But Ayub did agree to meet Nehru in Delhi the following month. The next day, 27 May 1964, Jawaharlal Nehru was dead, leaving behind the question of whether, had he lived, he would have surmounted or succumbed to the constraints of the past.

The Dutch historian Pieter Geyl observed that history is "argument without end." Indeed, over four decades after Nehru's death historical judgements on his long years in office remain at once divided and disputed. In particular, the debacle of 1962 has marred all subsequent assessments of his foreign policy. The traditional accounts attribute the failure to his idealistic assumption that India and China, as ancient Asian civilizations, were destined to a fraternal future, and hence a war was inconceivable. Revisionist scholarship ascribes it to his arrogant intransigence, and to his propensity to use force whenever he thought

---

[6] Ayub, *Friends Not Masters*, 128.

he could get away with it; against China he obviously could not. Both the traditional and the revisionist accounts, then, underline the lack of realism in Nehru's handling of international affairs.

The failure against China should not make us oblivious of the sophistication of Nehru's approach to strategy and crisis management. Military measures were initiated to demonstrate commitment without risking full-scale war, while diplomatic settlements were pursued to the extent that domestic opposition could be contained. Unsurprisingly, this meant that Nehru, at times, seemed to deny the necessity for choice, to assume that contrary courses could be simultaneously sustained. This reflected his preference to multiply options rather than foreclose them.

In contrast to the revisionist view, Nehru displayed a willingness to communicate with adversaries and search for acceptable compromises. When the difficulties of an overall plebiscite in Kashmir became apparent he toyed with various options, including partition with or without a plebiscite, a limited plebiscite, and elections to a constituent assembly. Nehru's subsequent failure to manage relations with Sheikh Abdullah considerably weakened his hand. The relationship fractured owing both to Nehru's unwillingness to contemplate the idea of independence and to Abdullah's refusal to consider viable alternatives with equanimity. Thereafter, Nehru was ready to move in the direction of a plebiscite followed by partition. But this was less of a definite decision than a working assumption based on the hope that the situation in the valley would improve. The US–Pakistan alliance ensured that the assumption would not be tested.

All along, Nehru's policies on Kashmir were shot through with domestic concerns. These did not arise, as is routinely claimed, from an abstract or ideological commitment to secularism but reflected his practical concern for the position of Muslims in India. The bloodbath during Partition, the massacres in Hyderabad, the riots during the refugee crisis had all underscored the fragility of inter-communal relations in India. In consequence, he was wary of making any move that might result in further churning. Nevertheless, when the events of 1963–4 demonstrated the ferment in Kashmir and its cascading effects on Muslims in India, Nehru undertook a course correction. Would he have managed finally to settle the problem? Domestic constraints, for one thing, would have been difficult to overcome, not least because of Nehru's circumscribed political standing after the defeat against China. It seems fair to say that he would have tried hard.

On China, too, Nehru started out with the view that a deal could be struck in the fulness of time. Until early 1960 he was open to compromise on Aksai Chin, which presumably was the core Chinese interest. He was unwilling, however, to treat the entire boundary as negotiable. This position stemmed from longstanding apprehensions about Chinese irredentism. Beijing's handling of the issue buttressed these concerns and convinced Delhi that the Chinese were not trustworthy. Furthermore, Nehru's willingness to accommodate China's interests in Aksai Chin suggests that a solution such as a long-term lease of territory could have been worked out. Here, Beijing's unyielding insistence that it had controlled the area for the last two centuries queered the pitch. In retrospect this might not seem much of a concession. But given the pressures on Nehru from parliamentary and public opinion it might well have been the only feasible arrangement.

Similarly, the revisionist charge of recklessness seems widely off-beam. If anything, Nehru was rather circumspect in his handling of crises. The possibility of escalation was always a cause for concern to him. To minimize it he sought to pick his way through crises one step at a time, ensuring that the calibration was right, probing the will of the adversary before moving on to the next step. The method accorded with Nehru's temperament and his instinctive caution in any exercise of power.

Such an approach relied heavily on the ability to understand the sources of urgency of a crisis as well as to evaluate the interests of all concerned and the options available to them. In the crises with Junagadh, Hyderabad, and Pakistan, it seemed to work. Nehru was undoubtedly perspicacious in his grasp of fundamentals amidst the tension and drama of a crisis. Assessing interests, not just of adversaries but also of external powers, seemed to come naturally to the realist in Nehru. And the method succeeded to varying degrees in each of these crises. For the most part Nehru managed at once to secure India's key interests and avoid full-scale hostilities. Importantly, his handling of these crises indicated the ambit of acceptable behaviour, and so instilled a degree of caution in the Pakistani official mind. It is no coincidence that after the crisis of 1951 Pakistan desisted from using force to settle the Kashmir dispute. The subsequent decision to attack

Kashmir in 1965 is beyond the scope of this book. Suffice it to note that following Delhi's inept handling of the Rann of Kutch crisis in the spring of 1965, Pakistan concluded that the Indians had lost resolve.[7]

The experience of successive encounters gave Nehru increasing confidence in this method. At the height of the China crisis it contributed to the unwarranted confidence that India could control the escalatory process. But the approach demanded a degree of nimbleness, an ability continually to feel the pulse of a situation, which was lacking in the later stages of the crisis. Nehru was correct in his initial calculation of the interests of all parties and of the risks attached to certain courses of action; but he failed to keep up with the evolving situation. The absence of a functional and effective mechanism to collate and analyse the available intelligence contributed in no small measure to this failure.

Compounding these problems was the unsound relationship between political and military leaders. The central problem of civil–military relations throughout this crisis was not, as is frequently claimed, the civilians' meddling in military matters and their pushing the military to undertake impossible tasks;[8] rather it was their unwillingness to scrutinize the design and implementation of military plans. Military commanders at lower levels did vigorously dispute the top brass's schemes. But differences between military professionals pointed to the need for greater civilian involvement in operational matters, not less. Indeed, had Nehru and Krishna Menon taken a more active interest, they would have realized early on that in implementing the forward policy the military had not catered for adequate reserves in the rear areas. Nehru was aware of the dicta that war was a continuation of politics and that it was too serious a business to be left to the generals,[9] but lost sight of their import.

[7] Sumit Ganguly, *Conflict Unending: India-Pakistan Tensions since 1947* (New Delhi: Oxford University Press, 2001), 35–43. Also see Jahan Dad Khan, *Pakistan Leadership Challenges* (Karachi: Oxford University Press, 1999), 51.

[8] Dalvi, *Himalayan Blunder*, 397–446; Kundu, *Militarism in India*, 100–21; Stephen Cohen, *The Indian Army: Its Contribution to the Development of a Nation* (New Delhi: Oxford University Press, 1990), 176.

[9] Talk by Nehru on 3 November 1962, cited in Palit, *War in High Himalaya*, 278.

In a deeper sense, Nehru's strategic vision was flawed in its purblind-ness to ideological factors in international politics. His belief that Khrushchev would not want India shoved towards the West by Chinese actions was correct; not so the assumption that the USSR would or could restrain the PRC. Nehru interpreted the support for India as motivated by the Soviet Union's own interests and concerns in relation to China. If Nehru overestimated the role the Soviet Union would play, it was because he underestimated the importance of ideology in international relations. Contrary to received wisdom, the problem with Nehru's China policy was not his idealism but his realism.

The crises examined in this book also show that arguments about the disjunction between Nehru's articulation of "pacific standards of international conduct" and his "failures in practice" are overstated.[10] It is evident that as far as possible Nehru refrained from adopting steps that could lead to war. A key axiom of his style of crisis management was to try and avoid the actual use of force. To be sure, stronger meas-ures were often contemplated; but Nehru tended to resist the tempta-tion to employ them.

Then again, it could be argued that the use of coercive strategies itself aggravated tensions with Pakistan and China: the former signed up to the Cold War alliances; the latter resorted to *force majeure*. It would, however, be misleading to view either outcome as the result of promiscuous threat-making rather than the product of a deeper con-flict. Given the circumstances attending Partition and the multitude of disputes, it is not clear that India–Pakistan relations, especially in the early years, could have been anything but fraught. As for Pakistan's entry into Western alliances, India's use of coercion only imparted mo-mentum to a process that was driven by multiple considerations, including Pakistan's claim to Kashmir. Similarly, short of acquiesc-ing in a *fait accompli* or in China's demands—both of which were non-options in the context of Indian domestic politics of the time—deterrence was the only course open to Delhi. Then too India's forward policy was just one of the factors in China's decision to go to war.

As we look back at the events covered in this book, what is striking is not the occurrence of these crises, nor the use of threats or limited

---

[10] For example, Maxwell, "Jawaharlal Nehru."

force. Rather, it is the fact that very few of them turned into hot wars.
During each of the crises with Pakistan, this was a distinct possibility. It is to Nehru's credit that he swerved from the wars which were
pregnant with internecine consequences and which seemed imminent at various points. That he managed to do so without conceding
India's core interests was Jawaharlal Nehru's major achievement in strategic affairs.

Arguments about Nehru's handling of foreign policy resonate well
beyond the precincts of academia. Indeed, they have played a central
role in constructing India's self-understanding. On the one hand, the
much overdrawn portrait of Nehru as a naïve idealist is frequently
evoked to explain why India has been unable to pull its weight in world
politics. Unless India overcomes its squeamishness and ineptness in
the exercise of power, the argument goes, it cannot become a player to
reckon with on the global stage. As an erstwhile foreign minister,
Jaswant Singh, puts it, "that very same [Nehru's] legacy . . . continues
to bedevil India to the present day."[11] Self-proclaimed Nehruvians,
on the other hand, have whittled down Nehru's distinctive strategic approach to an anaemic notion of "strategic autonomy"—an
idea that is pressed into service to justify often contradictory policies
and choices.

    By contrast, the underpinnings of Nehru's approach excavated in
this study suggest that the intellectual and practical understanding
worked out by Nehru might be of considerable importance to contemporary India. To be sure, the international context in which India
has to pursue its interests and aims is radically different from that of
the period covered in this book. Moreover, India's own reservoirs of
economic and military power have been greatly enhanced over the
last forty years. Yet, the key foreign policy challenges now confronting
India are not entirely dissimilar to those faced by Nehru.

    Much like the early years after Independence, India's relations with
Pakistan in the last decade have been punctuated by periodic crises that
threaten to boil over. Pakistan's patronage of militant anti-India outfits

---

[11] Singh, *Defending India*, 267.

and the possession of nuclear weapons by both sides have given a dangerous edge to these encounters. Thus, during the Kargil conflict in 1999 and the crisis following the terrorist attack on the Indian Parliament in 2001, India and Pakistan seemed balanced on the brink of ruinous war. The experience of these crises led to a reassessment of India's options *vis-à-vis* Pakistan. Heretofore, India had relied primarily on the threat of retaliation in Punjab to deter Pakistani adventurism in Kashmir—a strategy laid down by Nehru in 1949. During the Kargil conflict the Indian army was duly mobilized in the plains as well as in Kashmir. But the presence of nuclear weapons rendered this strategy unacceptably risky. Similarly, in the crisis of 2001–2 India held out the threat of war only to realize that its coercive leverage was rather limited. Thereafter, India adopted a new doctrine termed "Cold Start" which would enable it to impose substantial costs on Pakistan without having to wait for a full, time-consuming military buildup. This shift was premised on the dubious assumption that the time taken for large-scale mobilization enabled external powers to intervene, so diluting the potency of India's threat.[12]

India's handling of the crisis of 2001–2 and its aftermath indicates a deeper problem, one that is not doctrinal but intellectual and political: the assumption that successful coercion depends solely on the ability to impose military costs on the adversary. However, the experience of the Nehru years demonstrates that military moves must be coupled with robust diplomacy; that channels of communication and diplomatic options should be kept open; that threats must be balanced with inducements; that force should be used sparingly, if at all; that the opponent's ability to impose costs in turn should not be overlooked; that influencing external powers might be as important as directly pressurizing the adversary; that domestic pressures and international opinion must be assessed and moulded; that events cannot fully be controlled nor can unfortunate and unhelpful incidents always be avoided. Crisis management, in short, entails much more than the mere management of violence.

[12] Walter C. Ladwig III, "A *Cold Start* for Hot Wars? The Indian Army's New Limited War Doctrine," *International Security* 32: 3 (Winter 2007–8): 158–90.

The most important and relevant aspect of Nehru's strategic approach is his grasp of the nature and the limits of power. It is perhaps not surprising that as India's military and economic strength has increased, Indians have come to set much store by "hard" power. As India prepares to join the club of great powers, it is essential that its policy-makers and citizens reacquaint themselves with Nehru's subtle understanding of power. The exercise of power, Nehru realized, has both immediate and long-term consequences. During a crisis it will be aimed at preventing the adversary from acting in ways that are inimical to our interests at stake. Yet it is important to remember that every strategic choice feeds into the adversary's set of assumptions and anticipations about our behaviour, and so influences the relationship in the long run. A well-thought-out strategy will seek to create long-term conditions that will preclude the outbreak of crises. Military power is thus most effective when it is latent. In time, the sting might be drawn from the underlying antagonism, so paving the way for an eventual normalization of the relationship.

Nehru's brand of liberal realism also sensitized him to the fact that moral and political legitimacy was as important as economic and military resources. His commitment to norms of international behaviour stemmed not from an airy idealism but from a shrewd understanding that power should never be divorced from legitimacy. The latter is valuable in itself; yet it is equally important in backstopping an efficacious exercise of power. Even a cursory acquaintance with the current plight of the world's sole superpower, the United States, bears out this point.

Finally, Nehru understood the multidimensional character of power. The use of military power certainly enables us to constrain the options of our adversaries. But power is also exercised when we devote our efforts to creating or reinforcing political norms and practices that limit the opponents' freedom of manoeuvre. This process of setting and cementing norms requires a close and acute sense of the sources of legitimacy in international politics, and a willingness to work through and strengthen international institutions. Great powers have usually faltered when they have lost sight of the importance of norms and legitimacy in the exercise of power. At a time when India was much weaker and poorer, Nehru realized that preserving India's interests and fulfilling its international ambitions would require a dexterous amalgam of material and ideational resources. As a rising India navigates its way through a fraught world order, it would be an irony and a pity if it neglects his fundamental insight.

Bibliography

A. Unpublished Primary Sources

1. Manuscript Sources

Nehru Memorial Museum and Library, New Delhi

Subimal Dutt Papers
P.N. Haksar Papers
Mirza Ismail Papers
T.N. Kaul Papers
T.T. Krishnamachari Papers
K.P.S. Menon Papers
D.P. Mishra Papers
K.M. Munshi Papers
R.K. Nehru Papers
Vijayalakshmi Pandit Papers
Apa Pant Papers
C. Rajagopalachari Papers
K.S. Thimayya Papers

National Archives of India, New Delhi

K.M. Cariappa Papers

Asia, Pacific, and Africa Collection, British Library, London

Ali Ahmedshah Papers
George Cunningham Papers
Amar Devi Gupta Papers

Louis Mountbatten Papers
Francis Mudie Papers
Richard Powell Papers
Permanent Under-Secretaries' Papers

Imperial War Museum, London

B.L. Montgomery Papers

Liddell Hart Centre for Military Archives, London

Hastings Ismay Papers
Basil Liddell Hart Papers

National Army Museum, London

Roy Bucher Papers
Rob Lockhart Papers

School of Oriental and African Studies, London

Frank Moraes Papers

University of Southampton Library, Southampton

Louis Mountbatten Papers

Bodleian Library, Oxford

Paul Gore-Booth Papers
Harold Macmillan Papers
Walter Monckton Papers

Centre of South Asian Studies, Cambridge

Malcolm Darling Papers
P.C. Garrett Papers

John F. Kennedy Presidential Library, Boston

National Security Council Files
Robert Komer Papers

2. Official Records

Asia, Pacific, and Africa Collection, British Library, London

IOR L/PS: Records of the Political and Secret Department of the India Office
IOR L/WS: Records of the War Staff
IOR L/PO: Private [India] Office Papers

The National Archives, London

CAB 21: Records of the Cabinet Office
DO 35: Records of the Dominion Office and Commonwealth Relations Office
DO 196: Records of the Commonwealth Relations Office and Commonwealth Office
FO 371: Records of the Foreign Office
PREM 8: Records of the Prime Minister's Office

US National Archives and Records Administration, Maryland

Record Group 59: Records of the Department of State

National Archives of Australia, Canberra

Series A1838: Records of the Department of External Affairs

3. Oral Testimony

Oral History Transcripts, Nehru Memorial Museum and Library, New Delhi

J.N. Chaudhuri
B.M. Kaul
S.S. Khera
T.T. Krishnamachari
Dalai Lama
Kingsley Martin and Dorothy Woodman
K.P.S. Menon
R.K. Nehru
H.C. Sarin
Dharma Vira

Interviews

Romesh Bhandari, New Delhi, 9 May 2005
Mira Sinha Bhattacharjea, New Delhi, 12 May 2005
A.K. Damodaran, New Delhi, 12 May 2005
Kuldip Nayar, New Delhi, 13 May 2005
Major General D.K. Palit, London, 27 June 2005
K. Subrahmanyam, New Delhi, 11 May 2005

B. PUBLISHED PRIMARY SOURCES

1. Documents

Alam, Jawaid, ed. *Jammu & Kashmir 1949–64: Select Correspondence between Jawaharlal Nehru and Karan Singh.* New Delhi: Penguin Viking, 2006
Cold War International History Project. "New East-Bloc Documents on the Sino–Indian Conflict, 1959 & 1962." *Cold War International History Project Bulletin* 8/9 (Winter 1996): 258–69
——. "Memorandum of Conversation of N.S. Khrushchev with Mao Zedong, Beijing, 2 October 1962." *Cold War International History Project Bulletin* 12/13 (Fall/Winter 2001): 262–70
Das, Durga, ed. *Sardar Patel's Correspondence 1945–50.* 10 vols. Ahmedabad: Navjivan, 1971–4
Fursenko, Aleksandr, ed. *Prezidium TsK KPSS 1954–1964: Chernovye Protokolnye Zapisi Zasedani, Stenogrammy, Postanovleniia.* Moscow: Rosspen, 2003
Gandhi, Gopalkrishna, ed. *Gandhi is Gone. Who Will Guide Us Now? Sevagram, March 1948.* Delhi: Permanent Black, 2007
Gopal, Sarvepalli, ed. *Selected Works of Jawaharlal Nehru,* 1st series. 15 vols. New Delhi: Orient Longman, 1972–82
Gopal, Sarvepalli, Ravinder Kumar, H.Y. Sharada Prasad, A.K. Damodaran, and Mushirul Hasan, eds. *Selected Works of Jawaharlal Nehru,* 2nd series. 37 vols. New Delhi: Jawaharlal Nehru Memorial Fund, 1984–. In the process of publication
Lakhanpal, P.L., ed. *Essential Documents and Notes on Kashmir Dispute.* New Delhi: International Books, 1965
Mansergh, Nicholas, E.V.R Lumby, and Penderel Moon, eds. *Constitutional Relations between Britain and India: The Transfer of*

Power 1942–7. 12 vols. London: Her Majesty's Stationery Office, 1970–83

Mehra, Parshotam, ed. *The North-Eastern Frontier: A Documentary Study of the Internecine Rivalry between India, Tibet and China.* 2 vols. New Delhi: Oxford University Press, 1979–80

Nanda, B.R., ed. *Selected Works of Govind Ballabh Pant.* 18 vols. New Delhi: Oxford University Press, 1994–2003

Nehru, Jawaharlal. *India's Foreign Policy: Selected Speeches.* New Delhi, Government of India, 1961

Parthasarathi, G., ed. *Letters to Chief Ministers 1947–1964.* 5 vols. New Delhi: Jawaharlal Nehru Memorial Fund, 1985–9

Patel, Manibehn and G.M. Nandurkar, eds. *Sardar's Letters—Mostly Unknown.* 2 vols. Ahmedabad: Sardar Vallabhbhai Patel Smarak Bhavan, 1978

US Department of State, *Foreign Relations of the United States 1948.* Vol. 5. Pittsburg: US Government Printing Office, 1978

———. *Foreign Relations of the United States 1950.* Vol. 5. Pittsburg: US Government Printing Office, 1978

———. *Foreign Relations of the United States 1951.* Vol. 6. Pittsburg: US Government Printing Office, 1978.

———. *Foreign Relations of the United States 1958–1960.* Vol. 19. Pittsburg: US Government Printing Office, 1996

———. *Foreign Relations of the United States 1961–1963.* Vols. 19 and 22. Pittsburg: US Government Printing Office, 1996

Zaidi, Z.H., ed. *Jinnah Papers,* 1st series. 9 vols. Islamabad: Quaid-i-Azam Papers Project, Culture Division, Government of Pakistan, 1993–. In the process of publication

2. Official Publications

Notes, Memoranda and Letters Exchanged between the Governments of India and China. 8 vols. New Delhi: Ministry of External Affairs, 1959–66

Prime Minister on Sino-Indian Relations: Parliament. 2 vols. New Delhi: Ministry of External Affairs, Government of India, 1963

Report of the Officials of the Government of India and the People's Republic of China on the Boundary Question. New Delhi: Ministry of External Affairs, 1961

The Sino-Indian Boundary Question. Beijing: Foreign Language Press, Ministry of Foreign Affairs, 1962

Yearbook of the United Nations, 1947–48. New York: United Nations, 1949

White Paper on the Jammu and Kashmir Dispute. Islamabad: Ministry of Foreign Affairs, Government of Pakistan, 1977

Recurrent Exodus of Minorities from East Pakistan and Disturbances in India: A Report to the Indian Commission of Jurists by its Committee of Enquiry. New Delhi: Indian Commission of Jurists, 1965

3. Newspapers and Periodicals

The Daily Telegraph (London)
The Dawn (Karachi)
The Economist (London)
The Hindu (Madras)
The Hindustan Times (New Delhi)
The Indian Express (Bombay)
The Indian News Chronicle (New Delhi)
The Manchester Guardian
The New York Herald Tribune
The New York Times
The Pakistan Times (Karachi)
The Statesman (Calcutta)
The Sunday Times (London)
The New Republic (Washington, D. C.)
The Times (London)
The Times of India (Bombay)
Vigil (New Delhi)

4. Memoirs, Autobiographies, and Diaries

Abdullah, Sheikh. *Flames of Chinar.* New Delhi: Viking, 1993

Ali, Chaudhri Muhammad. *The Emergence of Pakistan.* Columbia University Press: New York, 1967

Banerjee, P.K. *My Peking Memoirs of the Chinese Invasion of India.* New Delhi: Clarion Books, 1990

Brezhnev, Alexei. *Kitai.* Moskva: Mezhdunarodnye Otnosheniye, 1998

Campbell-Johnson, Alan. *Mission with Mountbatten*. London: Robert Hale, 1951

Chopra, P.N. and Prabha Chopra, eds. *Inside Story of Sardar Patel: The Diary of Maniben Patel, 1936–50*. New Delhi: Vision Books, 2001

Cohen, Maurice. *Thunder over Kashmir*. Hyderabad: Orient Longman, 1955; reprint 1994

Dalvi, J.P. *Himalayan Blunder*. Bombay: Thacker, 1969

Dutt, Subimal. *With Nehru in the Foreign Office*. Columbia, Mo.: South Asia Books, 1977

Gundevia, Y.D. *Outside the Archives*. New Delhi: Sangam Books, 1984

Jung, Ali Yavar. *Hyderabad in Retrospect*. Bombay: Times of India Publications, 1949

Kapitsa, Mikhail. *Na raznykh parallelyakh*. Moskva: Kniga i biznes, 1996

Kaul, B.M. *The Untold Story*. New Delhi: Allied Publishers, 1967

Kaul, T.N. *Diplomacy in Peace and War*. New Delhi: Vikas Publishing House, 1979

———. *A Diplomat's Diary*. Delhi: Macmillan, 2000

Khan, Akbar. *Raiders in Kashmir*. Karachi: Pak Publishers, 1970

Khan, Ayub. *Friends not Masters: A Political Autobiography*. London: Oxford University Press, 1967

Khan, Muhammad Zafrullah. *The Forgotten Years: Memoirs of Sir Muhammad Zafrullah Khan*. Edited by A.H. Batalvi. Lahore: Vanguard Books, 1991

Khan, Sardar M. Ibrahim. *The Kashmir Saga*. Mirpur: Verinag, 1965

Khan, Shaukat Hyat. *The Nation that Lost Its Soul*. Lahore: Jang Publishers, 1995

Khrushchev, Nikita. *Khrushchev Remembers: The Last Testament*. Translated and edited by Strobe Talbott. London: Andre Deutsch, 1974

Mahajan, M.C. *Looking Back*. London: Asia Publishing House, 1963

Mehta, Jagat S. *Negotiating for India: Resolving Problems through Diplomacy*. New Delhi: Manohar, 2006

Mehta, K.L. *In Different Worlds: From Haveli to Head Hunters of Tuensang*. New Delhi: Lancer, 1985

Menon, V.P. *The Story of the Integration of Indian States.* London: Longmans Green, 1956

Mullik, B.N. *My Years with Nehru: The Chinese Betrayal.* New Delhi: Allied Publishers, 1971

———. *My Years with Nehru: Kashmir.* New Delhi: Allied Publishers, 1971

Nehru, Jawaharlal. *An Autobiography with Musings on Recent Events in India.* London: John Lane, 1936. Reprint, New Delhi: Penguin, 2004

———. *The Discovery of India.* 1946. Reprint, New Delhi: Penguin, 2004

Palit, D.K. *War in High Himalaya: Indian Army in Crisis, 1962.* London: Hurst, 1991

Prasad, Niranjan. *The Fall of Towang.* New Delhi: Palit and Palit, 1981

Rustomji, Nari. *Enchanted Frontiers: Sikkim, Bhutan and India's North-Eastern Borderlands.* Calcutta: Oxford University Press, 1973

Singh, Karan. *Autobiography.* Rev. edn. New Delhi: Oxford University Press, 1994

Singh, K. Natwar. *My China Diary, 1956–88.* New Delhi: Rupa & Co., 2009

Thorat, S.P.P. *From Reveille to Retreat.* New Delhi: Allied Publishers, 1986

Verma, S.D. *To Serve with Honour: My Memoirs.* Kasauli: Published by General S.D. Verma, 1988

C. Secondary Sources

1. Books

Ahmed, Ziauddin, ed. *Liaquat Ali Khan: Leader and Statesman.* Karachi: The Oriental Academy, 1971

Akbar, M.J. *Nehru: The Making of India.* London: Penguin, 1989

Ali, Syed Mahmud. *Cold War in the High Himalayas: The USA, China, and South Asia in the 1950s.* New York: St Martin's Press, 1999

Bamzai, Sandeep. *The Bonfire of Kashmiriyat.* New Delhi: Rupa, 2006

Basu, Aparna. *Mridula Sarabhai: Rebel with a Cause.* New Delhi: Oxford University Press, 1996

Bazaz, Prem Nath. *Kashmir in the Crucible*. Bombay: Pearl Publications, 1969

Behera, Navnita Chadha. *State, Identity and Violence: Jammu, Kashmir and Ladakh*. New Delhi: Manohar, 2000

Benichou Lucien. *From Autocracy to Integration: Political Developments in Hyderabad State 1938–1948*. New Delhi: Orient Longman, 2000

Bhattacharjea, Ajit. *Sheikh Mohammad Abdullah: Tragic Hero of Kashmir*. New Delhi: Roli Books, 2008

Brands, H.W. *What America Owes the World: The Struggle for the Soul of Foreign Policy*. New York: Cambridge University Press, 1998

Brecher, Michael. *India and World Politics: Krishna Menon's View of the World*. London: Oxford University Press, 1968

Brown, Judith. *Nehru: A Political Life*. New Delhi: Oxford University Press, 2004

Burke, S.M. and Lawrence Ziring. *Pakistan's Foreign Policy: A Historical Analysis*. Karachi: Oxford University Press, 1990

Carr, E.H. *The Twenty Years' Crisis, 1919–1939: An Introduction to the Study of International Relations*. London: Macmillan, 1939

Chatterji, Joya. *Bengal Divided: Hindu Communalism and Partition, 1932–1947*. Cambridge: Cambridge University Press, 1994

———. *The Spoils of Partition: Bengal and India, 1947–1967*. Cambridge: Cambridge University Press, 2007

Cohen, Stephen. *The Indian Army: Its Contribution to the Development of a Nation*. New Delhi: Oxford University Press, 1990

Conboy, Kenneth and James Morrison. *The CIA's Secret War in Tibet*. Lawrence: University Press of Kansas, 2002

Copland, Ian. *The Princes of India in the Endgame of Empire*. Cambridge: Cambridge University Press, 1999

Crocker, Walter. *Nehru: A Contemporary's Estimate*. London: George Allen and Unwin, 1966

Damodaran, A.K. *Jawaharlal Nehru: A Communicator and Democratic Leader*. New Delhi: Radiant Publishers, 1997

Darwin, John. *Britain and Decolonisation: The Retreat from Empire in the Post-War World*. Basingstoke: Palgrave Macmillan, 1988

Dasgupta, C. *War and Diplomacy in Kashmir 1947–48*. New Delhi: Sage, 2002

Deshpande, Anirudh. *British Military Policy in India, 1900–1945: Colonial Constraints and Declining Power*. New Delhi: Manohar, 2005

Donaldson, Robert H. *Soviet Policy toward India: Ideology and Strategy*. Cambridge, Mass.: Harvard University Press, 1974

Fisher, Margaret, Leo Rose, and Robert Huttenback. *Himalayan Battleground: Sino–Indian Rivalry in Ladakh*. New York: Praeger, 1963

Freedman, Lawrence. *Kennedy's Wars: Berlin, Cuba, Laos, and Vietnam*. Oxford: Oxford University Press, 2000

———. *Deterrence*. Cambridge: Polity, 2004

Ganguly, Sumit. *Conflict Unending: India–Pakistan Tensions since 1947*. New Delhi: Oxford University Press, 2001

Garver, John. *Protracted Contest: Sino-Indian Rivalry in the Twentieth Century*. Seattle: University of Washington Press, 2001

Gat, Azar. *A History of Military Thought: From the Enlightenment to the Cold War*. Oxford: Oxford University Press, 2001

Gerth, H.H. and C. Wright Mills. *From Max Weber: Essays in Sociology*. New edn. London: Routledge, 1991

Gittings, John. *Survey of the Sino-Soviet Dispute: A Commentary and Extracts from the Recent Polemics, 1963–1967*. London: Oxford University Press, 1968

Gopal, Sarvepalli. *Jawaharlal Nehru: A Biography*. 3 vols. London: Jonathan Cape, 1975–84

———. *Radhakrishnan: A Biography*. New Delhi: Oxford University Press, 1989

Guha, Ramachandra. *India After Gandhi: The History of the World's Largest Democracy*. London: Macmillan, 2007

Gupta, Karunakar. *The Hidden History of the Sino–Indian Frontier*. Calcutta: Minerva Associates, 1974

———. *Sino-Indian Relations 1948–52: Role of K.M. Panikkar*. Calcutta: Minerva, 1987

Gupta, Sisir. *Kashmir: A Study in India–Pakistan Relations*. London: Asia Publishing House, 1966

Hodson, H.V. *The Great Divide: Britain–India–Pakistan*. London: Hutchinson, 1969

Hoffmann, Steven. *India and the China Crisis*. Berkeley: University of California Press, 1990

Howard, Michael. *War and the Liberal Conscience*. London: Temple Smith, 1978

Huttenback, Robert A. *Kashmir and the British Raj, 1847–1947*. Karachi: Oxford University Press, 2004

Jalal, Ayesha. *The Sole Spokesman: Jinnah, the Muslim League and the Demand for Pakistan*. Cambridge: Cambridge University Press, 1985

———. *The State of Martial Rule: The Origins of Pakistan's Political Economy of Defence*. Cambridge: Cambridge University Press, 1990

Jeffrey, R., ed. *People, Princes and Paramount Power: Society and Politics in the Indian Princely States*. New Delhi: Oxford University Press, 1978

Jha, Prem Shankar. *The Origins of a Dispute: Kashmir 1947*. New Delhi: Oxford University Press, 2003

Johri, Sitaram. *Where India, China and Burma Meet*. Calcutta: Thacker Spink, 1962

Kavic, Lorne. *India's Quest for Security: Defence Policies 1947–1965*. Berkeley: University of California Press, 1967

Khan, Jahan Dad. *Pakistan Leadership Challenges*. Karachi: Oxford University Press, 1999

Khanduri, C.B. *Thimayya: An Amazing Life*. New Delhi: Knowledge World, 2006

Khera, S.S. *India's Defence Problem*. Bombay: Orient Longman, 1968

Khilnani, Sunil. *The Idea of India*. London: Hamish Hamilton, 1997; reprint Harmondsworth: Penguin, 2003

Knaus, Kenneth. *Orphans of the Cold War: America and the Tibetan Struggle for Survival*. New York: Public Affairs, 1999

Korbel, Josef. *Danger in Kashmir* Rev. ed., Princeton: Princeton University Press, 1966

Kundu, Apurba. *Militarism in India: The Army and Civil Society in Consensus*. London: I.B. Tauris, 1998

Lall, Arthur. *The Emergence of Modern India*. New York: Columbia University Press, 1981

Lall, John. *Aksai Chin and Sino–Indian Conflict*. New Delhi: Allied Publishers, 1989

Lamb, Alastair. *The China–India Border: The Origins of the Disputed Boundaries*. London: Oxford University Press, 1964

———. *The McMahon Line*. 2 vols. London: Routledge and Kegan Paul, 1966

———. *The Sino–Indian Boundary in Ladakh*. Columbia: University of South Carolina Press, 1975

———. *Kashmir: A Disputed Legacy, 1846–1990*. Karachi: Oxford University Press, 1992

———. *Incomplete Partition: The Genesis of the Kashmir Dispute, 1947–48*. Hertingfordbury: Roxford Books, 1997

———. *Birth of a Tragedy: Kashmir 1947*. Karachi: Oxford University Press, 2001

Mankekar, D.R. *The Guilty Men of 1962*. Bombay: Tulsi Shah, 1968

Maxwell, Neville. *India's China War*. London: Jonathan Cape, 1970

———. *China's "Aggression" of 1962 and the Unresolved Border Dispute*. Oxford: Court Place Books, 1999

MacFarquhar, Roderick. *The Origins of the Cultural Revolution 2: The Great Leap Forward, 1958–1960*. Oxford: Oxford University Press, 1983

———. *The Origins of the Cultural Revolution 3: The Coming of the Cataclysm, 1961–1966*. Oxford: Oxford University Press, 1997

McMahon, Robert. *Cold War on the Periphery: The United States, India and Pakistan*. New York: Columbia University Press, 1994

Mehra, Parshotam. *The McMahon Line and After*. New Delhi: Macmillan, 1974

———. *Negotiating with the Chinese, 1846–1947*. New Delhi: Reliance Publishing House, 1989

———. *An "Agreed" Frontier: Ladakh and India's Northernmost Borders, 1846–1947*. New Delhi: Oxford University Press, 1992

———. *Essays in Frontier History: India, China and the Disputed Border*. New Delhi: Oxford University Press, 2007

Michel, A.A. *The Indus Rivers: A Study of the Effects of Partition*. New Haven: Yale University Press, 1967

Morgan, Patrick. *Deterrence Now*. Cambridge: Cambridge University Press, 2003

Moore, R.J. *Escape from Empire: The Attlee Government and the Indian Problem*. Oxford: Clarendon Press, 1983

————. *Making the New Commonwealth.* Oxford: Clarendon Press, 1987

Munshi, K.M. *Somanatha: The Shrine Eternal.* Bombay: Bharatiya Vidya Bhavan, 1965

Niebuhr, Reinhold. *Moral Man and Immoral Society: A Study in Ethics and Politics.* New York: Charles Scribner's Sons, 1932

Pernau, Margrit. *The Passing of Patrimonialism: Politics and Political Culture in Hyderabad 1911–1948.* New Delhi, Manohar, 2001

Prasad, S.N. and Dharam Pal. *History of Operations in Jammu and Kashmir (1947–48).* New Delhi: Ministry of Defence, 2005

Prasad, S.N. *Operation Polo: Police Action Against Hyderabad 1948.* New Delhi: Ministry of Defence, 1972

Praval, K.C. *Red Eagles: A History of the Fourth Division of India.* New Delhi: Vision Books, 1982

Rai, Mridu. *Hindu Rulers, Muslim Subjects: Islam, Rights, and the History of Kashmir.* Delhi: Permanent Black, 2004

Rao, G. Narayana. *The India–China Border: A Reappraisal.* New York: Asia Publishing House, 1968

Robinson, Ronald and John Gallagher. *Africa and the Victorians: The Official Mind of Imperialism.* London: Macmillan, 1961

Saraf, Muhammad. *Kashmiris Fight for Freedom.* 2 vols. Lahore: Ferozsons, 1977

Sarila, Narendra Singh. *The Shadow of the Great Game: The Untold Story of India's Partition.* London: Constable, 2006

Schelling, Thomas C. *The Strategy of Conflict.* Cambridge, Mass.: Harvard University Press, 1960. New edn, Cambridge, Mass.: Harvard University Press, 1980

————. *Arms and Influence.* New Haven: Yale University Press, 1966

Schofield, Victoria. *Kashmir in Conflict: India, Pakistan and the Unending War.* London: I.B. Tauris, 2003

Singh, Anita Inder. *The Limits of British Influence: South Asia and the Anglo–American Relationship, 1947–56.* New York: St. Martin's Press, 1993

Sinha, P.B. and A.A. Athale. *History of the Conflict with China, 1962.* New Delhi: Ministry of Defence, 1992

Srinivasan, Vasanthi. *Gandhi's Conscience Keeper: C. Rajagopalachari and Indian Politics.* Ranikhet: Permanent Black, 2009

Swami, Praveen. *India, Pakistan and the Secret Jihad: The Covert War in Kashmir, 1947–2004*. London: Routledge, 2007

Taseer, Bilqees. *The Kashmir of Sheikh Muhammad Abdullah*. Lahore: Ferozsons, 1986

Tharoor, Shashi. *Reasons of State: Political Development and India's Foreign Policy under Indira Gandhi, 1966–1977*. New Delhi: Vikas Publishing House, 1982

————. *Nehru: The Invention of India*. New Delhi: Penguin, 2003

Whitehead, Andrew. *A Mission in Kashmir*. New Delhi: Viking, 2007

Whiting, Allen. *The Chinese Calculus of Deterrence: India and Indochina*. Ann Arbor: Center for Chinese Studies, University of Michigan, 1975. Reprint, Ann Arbor: Center for Chinese Studies, University of Michigan, 2001

Woodman, Dorothy. *Himalayan Frontiers: A Political Review of British, Chinese, Indian and Russian Rivalries*. New York: Praeger, 1969

Wolpert, Stanley. *Nehru: A Tryst with Destiny*. New York: Oxford University Press, 1996

Zachariah, Benjamin. *Nehru*. London: Routledge, 2004

Zaheer, Hasan. *The Times and Trial of the Rawalpindi Conspiracy*. Karachi: Oxford University Press, 1998

Zeigler, Philip. *Mountbatten: The Official Biography*. Glasgow: William Collins, 1985

Zubrzycki, John. *The Last Nizam: The Rise and Fall of India's Greatest Princely State*. London: Pan Macmillan, 2006

Zutshi, Chitralekha. *Languages of Belonging: Islam, Regional Identity, and the Making of Kashmir*. Delhi: Permanent Black, 2004

2. Articles and Book Chapters

Chen, Jian. "The Tibetan Rebellion of 1959 and China's Changing Relations with India and the Soviet Union." *Journal of Cold War Studies* 8, no. 3 (Summer 2006): 54–101

Freedman, Lawrence. "On the Tiger's Back: Development of the Concept of Escalation." In *The Logic of Nuclear Terror*, ed. Roman Kolkowicz, 109–52. Boston: Allen and Unwin, 1987

John Garver. "Review Essay: India, China, the United States, Tibet, and the Origins of the 1962 War." *India Review* 3, no. 2 (April 2004): 171–82

————. "China's Decision for War with India in 1962." In *New Directions in the Study of China's Foreign Policy*, eds. Alastair Iain Johnston and Robert S. Ross, 86–130. Stanford: Stanford University Press

Guha, Ramachandra. "The Challenge of Contemporary History." *Economic & Political Weekly* (28 June 2008): 192–200

————. "Opening a Window in Kashmir." *World Policy Journal* (Fall 2004): 79–94

Hoffmann, Steven. "Rethinking the Linkage between Tibet and the China–India Border Conflict: A Realist Approach." *Journal of Cold War Studies* 8, no. 3 (Summer 2006): 165–94

Ilahi, Shereen. "The Radcliffe Boundary Commission and the Fate of Kashmir." *India Review* 2, no. 1 (January 2003): 77–102

Khilnani, Sunil. "Nehru's Judgement." In *Political Judgement*, eds Raymond Geuss and Richard Bourke (forthcoming, 2009)

Ladwig, Walter C. III. "A *Cold Start* for Hot Wars? The Indian Army's New Limited War Doctrine." *International Security* 32: 3(Winter 2007–08): 158–90

Hsiao-Ting, Lin. "Boundary, Sovereignty, and Imagination: Reconsidering the Frontier Disputes between British India and Republican China, 1914–47." *Journal of Imperial and Commonwealth History* 32, no. 3 (September 2004): 25–47

Maxwell, Neville. "Jawaharlal Nehru: Of Pride and Principle." *Foreign Affairs* 52, no. 3 (April 1974): 633–43

Mehta, Jagat S. "India–China Relations: Review and Prognosis." In *Indian and Chinese Foreign Policies in Comparative Perspective*, ed. Surjit Mansingh, 457–83. New Delhi: Radiant Publishers, 1998

Menon, K.P.S. "India and the Soviet Union." In *Indian Foreign Policy: the Nehru Years*, ed. B.R. Nanda, 131–49. New Delhi: Vikas, 1976

Niu, Jun. "1962: The Eve of the Left Turn in China's Foreign Policy." *Cold War International History Project Working Paper* 48 (October 2005)

Noorani, A.G. "Of a Massacre Untold." *Frontline* 22, no. 5 (3 March 2001)

————. "Our Secrets in Others Trunks." *Frontline* 22, no. 14 (2 July 2005)

————. "History as Prison." *Frontline* 22, no. 19 (10 September 2005)

————. "Kashmir: Bridge, Not a Battle Ground." *Frontline* 23, no. 6 (30 December 2006)

————. "The Legacy of 1953," *Frontline* 25, no. 17 (16 August 2008)

————. "Brought to Heel," *Frontline* 25, no. 18 (30 August 2008)

Prozumenshchikov, Mikhail. "The Sino-Indian Conflict, the Cuban Missile Crisis, and the Sino-Soviet Split, October 1962: New Evidence from the Russian Archives." *Cold War International History Project Bulletin* 8/9 (Winter 1996–7): 251–7

Raghavan, Srinath. "The Sino-Indian Boundary Dispute, 1948–60: A Reassessment." *Economic and Political Weekly* 41, no. 36 (9–15 September 2006): 3882–92

————. "A Bad Knock: The War with China, 1962." In Daniel Marston and Chandar Sundaram (eds). *A Military History of India and South Asia* (Westport, CT: Praeger, 2006): 157–74

————. "Civil–Military Relations in India: The China Crisis and After." *Journal of Strategic Studies* 32, no. 1 (February 2009), 149–75

Sherman, Taylor C. "The Integration of the Princely State of Hyderabad and the Making of the Postcolonial State in India, 1948–1956." *Indian Economic and Social History Review* 44, no. 4 (2007): 489–516.

Subrahmanyam, K. "Nehru and the India–China Conflict of 1962." In *Indian Foreign Policy: The Nehru Years*, ed. B.R. Nanda, 102–30. New Delhi: Vikas, 1976

Westad, Odd Arne. "Introduction." In *Brothers in Arms: The Rise and Fall of the Sino–Soviet Alliance, 1945–1963*, ed. Odd Arne Westad, 1–46. Stanford, CA: Stanford University Press, 1998

3. Unpublished Secondary Sources

Kennedy, Andrew Bingham. "Dreams Undeferred: Mao, Nehru and the Strategic Choices of Rising Powers," PhD Thesis, Harvard University, 2007

Peers, Douglas. "Stocktaking the New Military History of India." Paper presented at Workshop on New Military History of South Asia, Wolfson College, Cambridge, April 1997

Radchenko, Sergey. "The China Puzzle: Soviet Policy Towards the People's Republic of China, 1962–1967." PhD Thesis, London School of Economics and Political Science, 2005

Reid, William Alan. "Sir Owen Dixon's Mediation of the Kashmir Dispute." BA Honours thesis, Deakin University, 2000

Roosa, John. "Quandary of the *Qaum*: Indian Nationalism in a Muslim State, Hyderabad 1850–1948." PhD Thesis, University of Wisconsin-Madison, 1998

Index